M000283021

DÉCADENCE MANDCHOUE

THE CHINA MEMOIRS OF SIR EDMUND TRELAWNY BACKHOUSE

EDITED AND INTRODUCED BY
DEREK SANDHAUS

EARNSHAW BOOKS
HONG KONG
2011

Décadence Mandchoue

Edmund Trelawny Backhouse (1943)

Edited by Derek Sandhaus

ISBN-13: 978-988-19445-1-1

© 2011 Earnshaw Books

Cover portrait of Edmund Backhouse (MS. Eng. misc. d. 1226, fol. ii), image of Edmund Backhouse on his deathbed (MS. Eng. misc. d. 1225, fol. 237), and three images of the original *Décadence Mandchoue* manuscript (in order of appearance, MS. Eng. misc. d. 1224, fols. 32 and 400; MS. Eng. misc. d. 1226, p. 326) courtesy of the Bodleian Libraries, University of Oxford. Image of Edmund Backhouse in the early nineteen-forties courtesy of Tom Cohen.

This book has been reset in 10pt Book Antiqua. Spellings and punctuations are left as in the original edition.

HISTORY / Asia / China

EB037

All rights reserved. No part of this book may be reproduced in material form, by any means, whether graphic, electronic, mechanical or other, including photocopying or information storage, in whole or in part. May not be used to prepare other publications without written permission from the publisher except in the case of brief quotations embodied in critical articles or reviews. For information contact info@earnshawbooks.com

Published by Earnshaw Books Ltd. (Hong Kong)

Edmund Backhouse in his mid-forties

TABLE OF CONTENTS

INTRODUCTION
BY THE EDITOR

IN 1939, a mysterious old man moved to the Foreign Legation Quarter of Japanese-occupied Peking. Dressed in an ankle-length robe with a long white beard and a brimless cap adorned with a large red gemstone, he could easily have been mistaken for an aging Chinese gentleman. He spoke the northern dialect beautifully and addressed the local servants with a familiarity that must have seemed shocking to the foreign residents of the Legation Quarter meeting him for the first time.

But the man was not Chinese, he was an Englishman, once one of the most famous foreigners in all of China. After years of quiet scholarship on the western edge of the city, he had abandoned his home and possessions, believing that the Japanese occupiers had left him no choice but to seek refuge elsewhere. As in 1900, when the Boxer and Manchu soldiery laid siege to the Legation Quarter demanding foreign blood, the threat of violence had driven him to rejoin his compatriots.

Soon after the start of the Pacific War a couple of years later, another Legation Quarter resident, a Swiss physician named Reinhard Hoeppli, passed the man in his rickshaw. Hoeppli's Manchu rickshaw puller, upon noticing the man, informed Hoeppli that they were in the presence of greatness. The man they had passed, the rickshawman said, was rumored to have once been the lover of the late ruler of all China: the Empress Dowager Tz'u Hsi. His name was Edmund Backhouse.

Sir Edmund Trelawny Backhouse,[1] a British baronet of well-established Quaker ancestry, was born in Richmond, Yorkshire in 1873 and educated at St. George's School, Ascot; Winchester College and later Oxford University. He failed to complete his undergraduate studies, but he was a voracious learner with a rare gift for languages. By the time he arrived in Peking in 1898, he professed fluency in French, Latin, Russian, Greek and Japanese. Less than a year later, he was working as an interpreter and informant for *The Times* and the British Foreign Service. "No one in Peking," wrote Dr. G.E. Morrison of *The Times*,

---

1   Sir Edmund introduced himself in both English and Chinese as "Bacchus" (Pa K'o-ssu 巴依思), though his siblings' descendants assure us that the surname is actually pronounced as it appears.

"approaches him in the ease with which he can translate Chinese." In 1903 the Chinese government appointed him professor of law and literature at the Imperial Capital University (later known as Peking University). A year later, we find him as an agent of the British Foreign Office, gaining fluency in Mongolian and Manchu.

The crowning moment in Backhouse's career came in 1910 when, together with another *Times* correspondent, J.O.P. Bland, he published *China under the Empress Dowager*. This book provided readers with the first comprehensive look at the last great ruler in Chinese imperial history as she presided over a tottering Ch'ing Dynasty. Written in an accessible and entertaining style, the book contains an incredible depth of knowledge, owing largely to the book's central text, "The Diary of His Excellency Ching Shan," supposedly discovered by Backhouse during the looting that followed the Boxer Rebellion in 1900. An international bestseller, the book was declared a masterpiece and when the Ch'ing Dynasty collapsed a year later, its reputation, and Backhouse's too, seemed unshakeable.

This was just the beginning of the story. Sir Edmund co-authored another book with Bland, *Annals & Memoirs of the Court of Peking* (1914), also highly regarded for its scholarship, and donated a large collection of valuable printed Chinese books, together with a few scrolls and manuscripts, to the Bodleian Library at Oxford between 1913 and 1922. In 1918, working with Sir Sydney Barton, he completed a revised version of a Chinese-English colloquial dictionary by Sir Walter Hillier, a respected diplomat and sinologist. It was on Hillier's personal recommendation that Backhouse was also appointed chair of the Chinese department at King's College, London, but he was unable to fill the position on account of ill health.

Backhouse's contemporaries described him as eccentric, soft-spoken, polite and exceedingly humble. He was a charming and engaging conversationalist, yet he was also a recluse. For almost all of his 45-odd years in Peking, he lived far away from the protective bubble of the Foreign Legation Quarter. Abandoning the dapper style of his earlier years, he adopted Chinese dress and customs. He went out of his way to avoid contact with Westerners in the city, sending servants ahead to places he intended to visit to make sure there were no foreigners present. He even went so far as to cover his face when passing foreigners in a rickshaw. Yet despite these quirks, almost all who met Backhouse found him hospitable and entertaining.

After his death in January 1944,[2] Backhouse seemed destined to pass quietly into respectable obscurity. He may have done just that if not for British historian Hugh Trevor-Roper.

In 1976, Trevor-Roper published *A Hidden Life: The Enigma of Sir Edmund Backhouse* (later republished and more commonly known as *Hermit*

---

2   Backhouse's official cause of death was listed as "softening of the brain," but was preceded by months of gradual failing health that, according to his physician, included "high blood pressure, dizziness, prostatic hyperplasia with urinary troubles." Shortly before his death Backhouse fell and, given his physicians' description of facial asymmetry and difficulty speaking, one would guess he died of complications from a stroke.

f Peking),[3] which painted a very different and somewhat sinister portrait of Backhouse. The book charged that Sir Edmund perpetrated systematic perjury, fraud and deception. The authenticity of the Ching Shan diary in *China under the Empress Dowager* had already been questioned during Backhouse's lifetime,[4] but few had suspected him of being the forger. Trevor-Roper not only accused Backhouse of deliberately playing a role in the diary's fabrication, but also uncovered evidence indicating a pattern of fraud and deceit in other realms. He showed that Backhouse repeatedly lured people into bogus business ventures, ranging from the sale of nonexistent imperial jewelry all the way to covert international arms transactions using fictitious weapons shipped on imaginary boats. Backhouse was able to get away with it, says Trevor-Roper, because the foreign community was ill-informed about China and inclined to believe the treachery of the Orientals as the primary cause of any wrongdoing.

The most shocking revelation in Trevor-Roper's book was that Backhouse had, in his final year, authored two outrageous and obscene autobiographical manuscripts, *The Dead Past* and *Décadence Mandchoue*. In these, his "memoirs," Backhouse chronicled his youth in England and Europe (*The Dead Past*), and his life in China during the twilight years of the Manchu Ch'ing Dynasty (*Décadence Mandchoue*). He claimed not only to have met many of the most notable literary and political figures of his era, but also to have slept with them. In often highly graphic detail, Sir Edmund recounted his sexual escapades with personages including Oscar Wilde, Aubrey Beardsley, Paul Verlaine and Prime Minister Salisbury.[5] The love affairs to which he confessed were almost exclusively homosexual, with one notable exception: China's longtime despot, the Empress Dowager Tz'u Hsi, who died in 1908.

Before passing judgment, Trevor-Roper added one last charge to his list of Backhouse's offenses: treasonous sympathy for the enemy. In his final years, he says, Backhouse showed great admiration for the Axis powers, and took a visible delight in their victories over the Allies. His fascist fixation was no product of senility, says Trevor-Roper, as his writings were filled with a longing for the days of European despotism and showed a profound respect for iron-fisted leaders of the Napoleonic mold. In his country's darkest hour, Trevor-Roper says, Backhouse turned coat.

---

3   Trevor-Roper, Hugh. *Hermit of Peking*. London: Eland, 1993.

4   The diary was first considered a hoax by former Backhouse colleague Dr. G.E. Morrison (on Mar. 21, 1911, he notes in his diary: "Backhouse whom I went to see in the evening . . . blushed badly when he spoke of Ching Shan's diary.") and later by Shanghai-based journalist William Lewisohn. The first persuasive refutation of the diary's veracity was put forward by one of its early authenticators, J.J.L. Duyvendak ("Ching-Shan's Diary a Mystification." *T'oung Pao*, 1937 [2nd Ser., Vol. 33, Livr. 3/4], pp. 268-294). The diary has more recently been discredited in "The Ching-shan Diary: A Clue to Its Forgery" (*East Asian History*, June 1991 (No. 1), pp. 98-124) by Lo Hui-min, who convincingly shows major discrepancies between the actual life of Ching Shan and the story presented in his "diary." Despite overwhelming evidence of the diary's forgery, it has remained influential as a source of information and its questionable claims have been repeated countless times by Eastern and Western scholars.

5   "[W]hen a young man is privileged to have sexual intercourse with a Prime Minister, any proposal regarding the modus operandi must emanate from the latter," Backhouse writes in *The Dead Past*.

Backhouse was, in Trevor-Roper's estimation, "both socially and intellectually, a snob," yet undeservedly so, in that he was neither high-class nor sophisticated enough to put himself on the same plane as those with whom he claimed association. Backhouse's shallowness, born of the "insolent deviation" of 1890s aestheticism, stuck with him throughout his life and devolved into his later fascist leanings.

His vanity, says Trevor-Roper, also caused him to invent wild self-aggrandizing fantasies, which he increasingly confused with reality. So convinced was Backhouse of his own imaginings, Trevor-Roper says, that he could recount them without a moment's hesitation down to the minutest of details. His rich imagination in tandem with abundant natural charm provided an irresistible talent for deception and manipulation, often to the great detriment of those who trusted him.

Trevor-Roper concludes that Backhouse was fundamentally unable to distinguish between fact and fiction, and that whatever historical value Backhouse's writings might once have had, they were completely overshadowed by their author's chronic unreliability.

Given his dubious track record, says Trevor-Roper, we should assume that "The Diary of His Excellency Ching Shan" in *China under the Empress Dowager* was a willful forgery perpetrated by Backhouse himself, while the sensational memoirs were merely "a pornographic novelette."

"No verve in the writing can redeem their pathological obscenity," Trevor-Roper says. They should be considered, he added, nothing more than the salacious imaginings of a closeted homosexual, the "last explosion of repressed and distorted sexuality."

The charges stuck. With the publication of *Hermit of Peking*, Sir Edmund Backhouse and his contributions to Chinese scholarship were relegated to the dustbin. He became nothing more than a historical curiosity, the punch line to a dirty joke. To the extent that he was remembered at all, it was as a pathetic homosexual fantasist and a con artist.

Yet there is still the matter of Dr. Reinhard Hoeppli and his gossipy rickshawman.

Previously employed by Peiping Union Medical College, Dr. Hoeppli acted as the honorary Swiss Consul to Peking in charge of overseeing Allied interests during the Japanese occupation. He befriended Backhouse, who became his patient, and they spent many a day discussing Backhouse's earlier years. Astounded by what he heard, Hoeppli convinced Sir Edmund to write down his life story, going so far as to pay the destitute and sickly old man a fee for his work. What came out of this commission were the two manuscripts, *The Dead Past* and *Décadence Mandchoue*. Hoeppli edited them and added his own postscript.

Hoeppli did not wish the manuscripts to be published in his own lifetime. Six months after his death in 1973, the original manuscripts were given to Hugh Trevor-Roper by Hoeppli's friend and former colleague, Dr. Rudolf Geigy, in a clandestine handoff at Basel Airport. At first Trevor-Roper considered preparing the works for publication, but later, after uncovering many of Backhouse's deceptions, decided instead to write a biography of Backhouse. While his publishers urged him to include passages from the memoirs in *Hermit of Peking*, Trevor-Roper declined, believing that they would damage the integrity of the project and perhaps invite the scorn of the Backhouse family. He instead left the memoirs to Backhouse's beloved Bodleian Library at Oxford University. Hoeppli had also prepared copies of the final manuscript to be left to the British Museum in London, Bibliothèque Nationale in Paris and Harvard University in Cambridge, Massachusetts. They were largely ignored for decades.

Hoeppli was once described by a friend as "a dignified, portly man, his manners an old-fashioned kind of formal courtesy [and] a sophisticated intellectual,"[6] yet Trevor-Roper's assessment was far less complimentary. He accused Hoeppli of being naïve in placing credibility on Backhouse's writings, though he still considered Hoeppli to be a sufficiently reliable source to borrow generously from his postscript when describing Backhouse's later life in *Hermit of Peking*. Trevor-Roper even included the story of Hoeppli's Manchu rickshawman recognizing Backhouse as the late Empress Dowager's lover.

This story is an inconvenient anomaly for Hugh Trevor-Roper. The rickshawman is the only non-foreign commentator in *Hermit of Peking* and he backs up Backhouse's extraordinary claim without any prompting. Having mentioned it, Trevor-Roper never again refers to it or attempts to explain it. But in my mind this inconsistency justified reopening the case of Sir Edmund Backhouse, and a review of Trevor-Roper's outright condemnation and dismissal.

I began by ordering the full 1,393-page original manuscript of *Décadence Mandchoue* from the Bodleian Library. Backhouse's handwritten manuscript was difficult to decipher (a sample is to be found in the appendix) and the second and third chapters were absent. On page 328, I arrived with relief at the first page of Dr. Hoeppli's complete typewritten transcription. Aside from Backhouse's margin notes, the remaining 600-odd pages, including Hoeppli's postscript, were perfectly legible. A second batch of papers, numbering 476 pages, contained an edited "final" version of *Décadence Mandchoue* prepared after the author's death.

I first read Hoeppli's postscript. Much of the information contained within was familiar from *Hermit of Peking*, but Hoeppli did not come across as the credulous, unwitting accomplice that Trevor-Roper had made him out to be.

In the appendix to the 1993 edition of *Hermit of Peking*, Trevor-Roper responded to Hoeppli's defenders by reminding them that Hoeppli had "repeatedly and publicly declared the essential veracity of Backhouse's 'memoirs.' " If Hoeppli was really aware of Backhouse's deceptions, Trevor-Roper says, "why did he never record his doubts?"

But he did. In his postscript, Hoeppli says he believes the Backhouse memoirs are "not purely imaginary but are fundamentally based

---

6   Morrison, Alastair. "Defending Dr. Hoeppli," *The New York Review of Books*, Sept. 14, 1977 (Vol. 24, No. 14).

on facts," but qualifies this by adding, "How far these facts have been distorted by a confused memory and to what extent purely imaginary happenings have been added can only be judged by a future critical examination which will have to make use of all the available documents." Later, he recalls that, when questioning Backhouse about part of *The Dead Past*, he was able "more or less to ascertain that [a] meeting [with Rimbaud] could not have taken place." Hoeppli repeatedly makes reference to Backhouse's wild imagination, and notes that the author seemed unable to separate things in his mind from events he had actually experienced. In short, while Hoeppli believed the memoirs to contain more truth than fiction, he cautioned readers to be skeptical.

The Hoeppli postscript (also included in this edition) was the source of several of Hugh Trevor-Roper's supposed revelations in *Hermit of Peking*. It includes the first mention of an undeniable parallel between *Décadence Mandchoue* and Victor Segalen's novel *René Leys*, a book about a foreign lover of the Empress Dowager published in 1922. The postscript also mentions Backhouse's alleged involvement in an attempt to steal the Empress's pearl jacket in the 1910s. As to the Ching Shan diary, Hoeppli says he is convinced it is a forgery, and agrees that it is "only natural to suspect Sir Edmund," but he does not himself support such a conclusion.

Most striking perhaps is the portrait that Hoeppli paints of Backhouse's character and personality. It differs in a number of significant ways from the Trevor-Roper view, and deserves consideration if for no other reason than Hoeppli had the advantage of actually knowing Backhouse. He says that Backhouse was not a snob at all; he treated those of the upper classes "haughtily" and displayed a "tendency to become rapidly intimate with members of the lower classes." Hoeppli does not deny that the ultra-sensitive and often moody Backhouse was a thoroughly flawed individual, but he says the fundamental kindness of the man allowed people to look past his shortcomings. Sir Edmund's "good-heartedness," Hoeppli adds, "was the chief secret of his charm."

In the postscript, Backhouse also does not appear to be the unrepentant "spiritual fascist" described in *Hermit of Peking*. Hoeppli says Backhouse was the most anti-British Briton he ever met,[7] but he also notes that "he did not like to hear other people attacking them." He suggests Backhouse's pro-Axis stance, with praise for Japanese civility and talk of "mighty Gross-Deutschland," might have been the result of a fear of reprisals from the Japanese occupiers. This interpretation is reasonable in light of what we know of Backhouse. By the time Japan had occupied Peking and the Nazis were rampaging across Europe, Backhouse was old, his health was failing and he only avoided internment as an enemy national because the Japanese afforded him special

---

7   Missionary and Chinese linguist Paul Serruys notes, in a letter to David Helliwell (Dec. 1, 1986), that when speaking with Backhouse at the Catholic Hospital of the Sisters, Sir Edmund made a "constant attack on the British Government's *perfidity*, personified in the man W. Churchill whom he had known as a schoolboy in England. They had once had a boxing fight in which Churchill knocked him down saying: someday I'll be prime minister!" It seemed, in Serruys' estimation, "like the ramblings of an old man."

consideration.[8] Backhouse was, both by his own and others' accounts, a coward. He had a history of running away or feigning illness in the face of threatening situations.

There is a cryptic passage in *Décadence Mandchoue* in which Backhouse seems to be wishing misfortune upon the Axis powers:

> Peradventure, the reference [fortune misfortune fortune] is to current events and to good emerging out of evil: *Sê Weng Shih Ma* 塞翁失馬, *Wei Ch'ang Fei Fu* 未嘗非福, as the adage has it: The old gentleman outside the Pass (Mongolia) lost a horse, but it turned out to be a blessing in disguise. (The new owner of the animal had a bad fall and broke his thigh in consequence.)

In another section, the author decries the Italian Fascists for destroying some of Italy's natural beauty, and at one point he refers to a Boxer chief as a "Gauleiter" (regional Nazi leader). Backhouse certainly had no love for the rabidly nationalistic Boxers, and it is unlikely that a linguist who so carefully chose his words would make the comparison by accident. Backhouse does make one off-hand anti-Semitic remark, alleging that the King of England had secret Jewish ancestry and delighted in the company of chubby Jewesses. "Alas!" he declares, "for the empire governed by such." This view, while rather offensive, was hardly uncommon for someone of his era. In any event, it seems unlikely that Backhouse, who spent almost all of his last 45 years thousands of miles away from home and in almost complete isolation from his compatriots, cared very much one way or the other about European politics.

This discussion of Hoeppli's reliability and Backhouse's political leanings suggests Trevor-Roper may have ignored or downplayed certain inconvenient evidence. But the real issue at hand is what value *Décadence Mandchoue* has, and whether the story it conveys has some basis in reality. Is it possible that Backhouse was, as he claimed, a regular fixture at the late Ch'ing court and the Empress Dowager's lover?

The story begins with Backhouse in the ironically named "Hall of Chaste Pleasures," a luxurious gay bordello in the heart of Peking. There, he meets Duke Lan and his favorite male prostitute, Cassia Flower. He watches the couple perform various sexual acts and then joins in the proceedings himself. In this first chapter, with its incessantly explicit sexual descriptions, it immediately becomes apparent that it is highly unlikely Backhouse was, as Trevor-Roper has it, a *repressed* homosexual. At the brothel, he seems very familiar with, for lack of a better expression, the ins and outs, and takes an obvious delight in recounting them.

It is curious why Trevor-Roper even thought that Backhouse was repressed in the first place. In his Oxford days he ran with a crowd of openly homosexual writers and poets, but Trevor-Roper says Sir Edmund's relationships, as described in *The Dead Past*, with the likes of

---

8   Officially the exemption was granted because of old age and failing health, but Hoeppli notes Backhouse's claim that in the 1920s the Japanese Government had forced him to do translation work. The exact nature of this relationship remains mysterious.

Aubrey Beardsley and Oscar Wilde could not possibly have been real. Yet Trevor-Roper does admit that Dr. G.E. Morrison reported hearing that Backhouse was involved in the Wilde scandal. Also, in his 1993 afterword, Trevor-Roper adds that Backhouse was mentioned in a letter from the literary editor of Beardsley's journal, *The Yellow Book*.

Regardless, it seems, of the evidence, Trevor-Roper wants us to believe that this outrageously persuasive man, this embodiment of charm, could not have talked the most prominent of England's homosexual community into bed. And why? Because "no one seems to have made any explicit accusations against him." As if they would.

What is more likely is that Backhouse, as he himself claims repeatedly, was always sexually active. In the "naughty nineties" it is fair to assume he emulated his peers and heroes, like Wilde, who represented the possibility of a new and previously unthinkable openly homosexual lifestyle. Then in 1895, Wilde was jailed for sexual deviance. Backhouse, as Trevor-Roper agrees, was involved in raising funds for Wilde's defense, and the case may have been one reason for the resentment he developed against the British. We can only speculate as to how this episode affected him, but we do know that three years later he was living in Peking outside of the Foreign Legation Quarter, and spent most of the rest of his life avoiding Westerners.

In the Peking depicted in "Décadence Mandchoue," around the turn of the twentieth century, Backhouse would have found a community that was far more hospitable to his tastes. As historian Wu Cuncun notes in *Homoerotic Sensibilities in Late Imperial China*:

> By the end of the reign of the [Ch'ien Lung] emperor (1735-96) [Peking] boasted several districts catering for male-love and boy-actors were idealized as objects of sublime beauty, receiving clients in nightclubs or brothels . . . In late imperial China male-love became so popular as to cause the overshadowing of female brothels by male homosexual brothels in the capital city . . . People who enjoyed homosexual relations existed in every class, from the male favourites of the imperial court to cases of homoerotic vogue among the laboring classes, and the literati were the most prominent and active class of supporters. Not only was homoerotic behavior not condemned, feminized boys were considered fascinatingly romantic.[9]

This toleration of open homosexuality in as traditional a society as China's is almost inconceivable to someone from a Western background, all the more so given the social and institutionalized persecution experienced by Chinese homosexuals in the past hundred years. It would be a mistake to view homosexuality in imperial China, which developed in almost complete isolation from its Western analogue, as two offshoots of the same subculture.

---

9   Wu Cuncun. *Homoerotic Sensibilities in Late Imperial China*. London: RoutledgeCurzon, 2004.

Homosexuality, specifically male homosexuality, has an intimate relationship with Chinese classical culture. References to homosexual love date back to ancient times and are featured prominently in several popular works of classic literature including *Ch'in Ping Mei* (*The Plum in the Golden Vase*) and *Hung Lou Meng* (*Dream of the Red Chamber*), arguably the most influential Chinese novel ever written.

One reason that male same-sex relationships were allowed to flourish in Chinese society was that, unlike in the West, there existed no religious stigma against homosexuality. So long as homosexuality was expressed within the prescribed Confucian cultural limits, there was little cause for moral indignation. Moreover, for much of the Ch'ing Dynasty it seems unlikely that social delineations were made between same-sex and heterosexual love, or that their practitioners viewed themselves as representative of distinct categories. Early sexologist and gay rights advocate Magnus Hirschfeld picked up on this while visiting China in the early twentieth century, noting:

> Homosexual men are almost all of them married. But they never take concubines and later on frequently separate from the women assigned to them by their parents. Among them there were relatively few of a pronounced feminine type— most of them showed only slight feminine characteristics or seemed to be entirely virile.[10]

Indeed, Backhouse's Cassia Flower explains that he, too, would like to have a family one day despite having no sexual interest in women. In a later passage of "Décadence Mandchoue," the Empress Dowager gives her sanction to homosexual relations, but reminds her subjects, "don't forget your conjugal duties."

Laws were occasionally passed that placed restrictions on homosexual expressions of affection, but these laws were generally aimed at curbing homosexual rape and limiting the excesses of imperial officials inclined to spend too much time in pleasure houses. They almost never cast the practice of homosexuality as immoral, or even abnormal, behavior. The increase in the number of decrees against officials cavorting with male prostitutes and song-boys in the final centuries of imperial rule indicated not an increase in homophobia, but the elevated importance of homosexuality in Peking's nightlife. In any case, laws targeting homosexual acts were rarely enforced.

The preference for gay relationships and the celebration of male beauty reached its apex in the late Ming and Ch'ing dynasties, and specifically within the city of Peking. Part of the reason for this was logistical, for Peking in the days of emperors was a city dominated by men. Scholars, all of them male, who passed the national imperial exams flocked to the city from around the country, hoping for work and advancement, but often languished unemployed. If they received a government appointment,

---

10 Hirschfeld, Magnus. *Curious Sex Customs in the Far East* (also published as *Men and Women*). New York: Grosset & Dunlap, 1935.

they would send for their wives, but this could sometimes be many years in the making, if ever. So large groups of young, literate men gathered and waited in Peking, bored and sexually frustrated. As a missionary study from 1921 notes:

> The population of Peking is 811,556. Of these, 515,535 (63.5 percent) are males and 296,021 (36.5 percent) are females. In some police districts, 77 percent of the population are males. These figures are almost enough to tell the story of the social life and problems of Peking, especially since a very large proportion (61.7 percent) of the men are less than 35 years old.

On the subject of homosexuality, it adds:

> Legalized houses of sodomy used principally by the decadent Manchu nobility were conducted in Peking prior to the Revolution in 1911, but since then have been abolished.[11]

The more significant factor in this sexual awakening, however, was cultural. Attitudes towards sexuality, influenced by the neo-Confucian philosophies of Wang Yang-ming and his followers, began liberalizing among the scholarly class in the late Ming Dynasty. The heralding of same-sex relationships in literature continued to gain prevalence in the Ch'ing Dynasty. By the 1670s, writer Mei Keng was declaring openly of the famous song-boy Purple Clouds:

> The leading beauty in the land, no question,
> A woman is no longer number one.

This rise in homoerotic writing among the Chinese literati also coincided with an important artistic innovation in the capital: the rise of Peking opera in the eighteenth and nineteenth centuries. Sexual relationships between scholars and song-boys, as Mei Keng's statement indicates, were nothing new, but found their fullest expression with the *Tan* actors of Peking opera. *Tan* actors, who played female roles and were usually no older than twenty, became the focal point of Peking's homosexual community. They were the objects of desire onstage and often the purveyors of exclusive sexual favors to the elite offstage. By the mid-nineteenth century, these song boys were so popular that writer Huang Ch'un-tsai noted:

> A banquet in the capital is a flop if there are no boy-actors present, and prostitutes are detested. A literatus who patronizes [female] brothels becomes a general object of contempt.[12]

---

11   Gamble, Sidney and Burgess, John Steward. *Peking: A Social Survey.* New York: George H. Doran Co., 1921.

12   Huang Ch'un-tsai (trans. by Wu Cuncun), *Ch'inhu Tunmo* (Vol. 2), in *Pichi Hsiaoshuo Takuan* (Vol. 13). Yangzhou: Jiangsu Guanling guji keyingshe, 1995.

In the daytime, the Peking elite would attend performances at the popular opera houses, and in the evenings they would set off for the nearby restaurants and brothels. The male brothels at the time, *Ssu Yu* (private apartments) or *Hsiang Kung Hsia Ch'u* (resorts of catamites), were initially just the shared apartments of *Tan* actors overseen by their master-trainers, but evolved into what were essentially high-class male bordellos. One anonymous source from the era describes these establishments as follows:

> The houses of boy-actors match those of the residences of the highest dignitaries. The salons are furnished in the most splendid manner, with large brocade partitions and curtains of gauze silk, large dining tables with matching tea-tables overlaid with rare jade. They boast bronzes of great antiquity, mirror stands, and chiming clocks, the likes of which are not seen in many of the most influential families. As for the bedrooms, the amount of green jade and white pearl reminds one of the boudoir, or a heavenly mirage, such that an immortal who ventured there might even find himself bewitched. Seeing the [actors] standing there ready to greet you in dulcet tones, who knows how many visitors have had to cover their mouths in case they gasp.[13]

There can be little doubt that The Hall of Chaste Pleasures, as described in the first chapter of "Décadence Mandchoue," is one such establishment. Not only does Backhouse refer to the venue using more or less appropriate terminology, he also gets the details right. A formal invitation is required for admission and payment is given after services are rendered, both significant ways in which actors' apartments differed from female Chinese brothels. The location, Shih T'ou Hut'ung, was in the heart of a popular red-light district little more than five minutes' walk from the city's most popular opera theaters. Even the costs given for the services provided are consistent with known earning estimates of popular male actors from the era.

All this does not mean that Backhouse was at The Hall of Chaste Pleasures in 1898 with Duke Lan and Cassia Flower, or even that such a place actually existed. He could have referenced works written around the time known as *Hua P'u* ("flower guides," flower being a euphemism for prostitute), which described and ranked the quality of song-boys and their brothels. These guides avoid the explicit sexual detail provided by Backhouse and, as Wu Cuncun and Mark Stevenson note, "Most [flower guides] were published and circulated privately, but more literary examples also found outlets in the flourishing Beijing book trade."[14] It is therefore unlikely that Backhouse would have been able to find the more

---

13 Anonymous (trans. by Wu Cuncun). 燕京雜記 *Yenking Tsa Chi* in 北京歷史風土叢書 *Peking Li Shih Feng T'u Ts'ung Shu*. Taipei: Ch'inhsueh Shushe (reprint), 1969.

14 Wu Cuncun and Stevenson, Mark. "Speaking of Flowers: Theatre, Public Culture, and Homoerotic Writing in Nineteenth-Century Beijing," *Asian Theatre Journal*, Spring 2010 (Vol. 27, No. 1), pp. 100-129.

factual, privately circulated descriptions without at least knowing someone within this community.

Given what we know about Backhouse in the 1890s a simpler explanation presents itself: that he actually associated with Peking's homoerotic elite. Trevor-Roper's biography has precious little to say about
Backhouse's Oxford years (ending 1895), but does include a few bits of
information. Backhouse was a regular fixture among the homosexual
cliques of Oxford and Cambridge. He was also obsessed with the theater,
once renting out an entire row of seats for his friends and lavishing expensive gifts upon the leading ladies of the day like Ellen Terry. He spent
so much money in this period, Trevor-Roper tells us, that he accumu-
lated a debt of £22,000.

Based on our understanding of Backhouse and Peking in that period,
the two seem to have been made for each other. Peking's homoerotic
culture was radically different from that of London's but in ways that
perfectly accentuated Sir Edmund's unique tastes. It combined the two
things we know he actively sought: the company of sophisticated homosexual writers and the theater. Moreover, it was an environment in
which ostentatious spending, Backhouse's predilection in England, was
common. If Backhouse lavished gifts upon the leading "ladies" of the
Peking opera stage, there is evidence that indicates he would have been
amply rewarded in a venue similar to the Hall of Chaste Pleasures.

Within such a context Backhouse would have been able to meet cour-
tesans and partake in what he called "*nuits d'amour.*" It is reasonable to
assume, as Backhouse says, that high-ranking court nobles would sometimes bring with them their eunuchs who were, by default, restricted to
homosexual intercourse. It is equally plausible that some of the palace
eunuchs of the Empress Dowager would find themselves at such establishments from time to time. Backhouse, fluent in Chinese, Manchu
and Mongolian (the official court languages), would surely have been
popular or at least something of a novelty in such a place. Just as he
charmed his way into the confidence of many high-ranking Western officials through his professed knowledge of the Manchu elite, he could
just as easily have done the same with Chinese officials. If he did, and
the opportunity was certainly there, then Hugh Trevor-Roper's claim
that Backhouse was neither well informed nor politically connected is
thrown into doubt.

We can get all this merely by following the trail Backhouse leaves
behind on the first two pages of the first chapter of "Décadence Mandchoue." So what else might have been overlooked in this supposedly
worthless manuscript?

At the beginning of Chapter Two of *Décadence Mandchoue* it is late
summer 1900, the Summer Palace is in the care of Russian and later Italian and British troops. Backhouse claims to have rescued huge quantities
of documents from the Summer Palace at the time of the Boxer Rebellion
to prevent their destruction in the looting that followed the arrival of

foreign relief forces. Is it true? Backhouse says that he, with the aid of several trusted Manchus, endeavored to extract items of value from the Palace. As Trevor-Roper notes, Backhouse was indeed at this time arrested by Russian troops for lifting items from the Palace, which means he was at least where he claimed he was.

Backhouse then says that, upon the return of the court, he personally arranged to have the treasures returned to the Forbidden City.

Trevor-Roper's 1993 afterword states that evidence had emerged of a British Army major, Noel du Boulay, who did in fact make such a delivery of treasures to the palace. The inventory, meticulously itemized by dynasty, was prepared, according to du Boulay, "with the assistance of Mr. Backhouse." Backhouse's embellishment, extracting du Boulay's men from the story and taking sole credit for the transfer, is enough for Trevor-Roper to dismiss this incident altogether. Yet this is an extraordinary revelation, for it suggests that Backhouse was working for the British detachment in some capacity as a liaison with the Chinese/Manchu community, and would have probably assisted in the delivery of these items to the Forbidden City.

And could he have met and possibly bedded the Empress Dowager? This story, while more far-fetched, is still within the bounds of possibility.

Following her return to Peking in 1902, having barely escaped execution for ordering the deaths of all foreigners during the Boxer Rebellion, the Empress Dowager was eager to mend fences. She more actively engaged the foreign community, organizing social gatherings with diplomatic wives and sitting for an American painter. Backhouse had acted as interpreter at meetings between the Manchu community and the British Legation, through which he could have attracted her attention. It is also possible that she had heard about Backhouse from his alleged romps with the Manchu aristocracy. She was curious and interested in the exotic, and may well have expressed the desire to meet this strange foreigner who understood Manchu customs and spoke their languages so well.

It seems less likely that this gay man could have had a four-year love affair with the "Old Buddha." His descriptions of these acts in "Décadence Mandchoue," in contrast to his homosexual dalliances, are not as detailed or as convincing. At one point *he* claims to have been penetrated by *her*, although it is plausible that the Empress Dowager had an enlarged clitoris as he claims.[15]

Moreover, the idea of a Chinese Empress freely indulging her sexual appetite (as in the histories of Empress Wu Tse-t'ien) is very believable, and it is entirely possible the Old Buddha was curious to try a Western man. Tz'u Hsi may have indeed had other foreign lovers; Backhouse mentions a Frenchman named Wallon and a German, Rab (or Raab), as possibly having graced her bedchamber. The Empress would have been a difficult woman to refuse. It is admittedly the least believable element

---

15   Known as "clitoromegaly" in medical terminology.

of the story, and its author seems to have been capable of presenting such a rumor in a superficially credible manner. Whether Backhouse did indeed have sexual relations with her is now impossible to prove one way or the other, so it must be left to speculation.

While the tantalizing possibility of a relationship with Tz'u Hsi is sensationally fascinating, it is the homosexual relationships in *Décadence Mandchoue* that provide the missing pieces to the Backhouse puzzle. They supply an explanation for why he harbored anti-Western sentiments and chose to live far away from the Legation Quarter. They explain why he made every effort to present the outward appearance of a recluse and went to such pains to avoid being seen by his compatriots. They also explain why he lived most of his adult life in the company of other men, promised to shower so many of them with jewels, and why he had such unconventional and unusually familiar relationships with his local "servants."

They could also explain why he might have felt the need to fabricate the sources of his information, like the infamous "Diary of His Excellency Ching Shan." He could hardly have accurately attributed information obtained from eunuchs and noblemen in bordellos and bathhouses. The information that he garnered from these sources, however, might well have been, as Hoeppli says, "fundamentally based on facts," or, at the very least, well-informed gossip. He had to present the information to his contemporaries in such a way that they could accept it, while also protecting himself from scandal. At the end of his life, though, he clearly wanted to come clean on some level.

This is not to say that all of what Backhouse writes in *Décadence Mandchoue* should be accepted uncritically as fact. I would not try to justify the many instances of dishonesty found both in his life and writings. No doubt some of Backhouse's supposed deceptions can, as was believed at the time, be attributable to the unscrupulous maneuverings of Chinese officials. Peking was in a state of constant political upheaval in the 1910s and 1920s. An arms deal one agreed upon with an official one day might be cancelled when the balance of power shifted, and it shifted constantly. This could explain many inconsistencies in his stories, but not all of them.

There are a number of scenes in *Décadence Mandchoue* that seem to conflict with official reports, such as the manner in which Tz'u Hsi and Emperor Kuang Hsü meet their ends (Chapter Seventeen). In 2008, the latter was definitively proved to have been murdered, but there is a disconnect with the method given (albeit secondhand) in "Décadence Mandchoue." Also, as Hugh Trevor-Roper correctly notes, Backhouse's private audience with Junglu (Chapter Three) and his final conversation with Chief Eunuch Li Lien-ying about another alleged diary (Chapter Nineteen) are particularly hard to believe, as Backhouse gave several conflicting accounts of the documents' whereabouts in his later life. The séance at the White Cloud Temple (Chapter Fifteen), supernatural elements aside, also contains a number of outright factual errors that would be difficult, if not impossible, to explain away. But there may be other justifications for Backhouse's actions of which we do not know, and we should not put aside his claims as easily as Trevor-Roper does in *Hermit of Peking*.

It is tempting to accuse Hugh Trevor-Roper of getting the facts wrong and being sloppy in his scholarship. His own legacy as a historian was later tainted by his role in the "Hitler Diaries" scandal,[16] which raised questions about his judgment. But the research he presents in *Hermit of Peking* is on the whole solid. Few would now dispute that Backhouse took liberties with the truth, and Trevor-Roper was the first person to really shed light on Backhouse's hidden life. It is highly unlikely that many more significant discoveries bearing on the issue will come to light. All we have is a mountain of informed speculation and the word of Backhouse as corroborated by a lone rickshawman.

Trevor-Roper's main error in his research was omission; he makes no mention of having made any effort to consult Backhouse's Chinese and Manchu contemporaries. It would have been next to impossible for Trevor-Roper to conduct interviews in Peking during the Cultural Revolution years in which he wrote *Hermit of Peking*, but he could have spoken with former Peking residents who had left China around the time of the communist takeover in 1949. They would have been in a unique position to confirm or refute Backhouse's claims, but the opportunity has now been lost.

Trevor-Roper writes in *Hermit* that he initially presented *Décadence Mandchoue* to two scholars, a professor of English and a professor of history. Both read the manuscript and believed it to be a significant and singularly groundbreaking work, but Trevor-Roper later concluded they had been hoodwinked, because they did not understand who Backhouse really was. There is no indication that he consulted these scholars, or other relevant historians, for a follow-up. Yet the significance of the book's historical claims warrant at least a second opinion.

From Backhouse's near-perfect recall of classical allusions in several languages without access to reference materials, it is clear that his memory must have been close to photographic. We can also say that he knew Peking and its people better than just about any of his foreign contemporaries, and his descriptions and accounts of incidents have relevance in that context alone.

In retrospect, Trevor-Roper's assessment of Backhouse appears in many ways to be mean-spirited and narrow-minded. As historian Robert Aldrich writes, Trevor-Roper's "manifest discomfort at even reading the more salacious passages of Backhouse rendered his judgement questionable."[17] Trevor-Roper seems incapable of looking past Backhouse's sexual "deviance" and anti-British leanings, and his biography amounts to a systematic condemnation of the man. There is an apparent

---

16   In 1983, Trevor-Roper independently verified the authenticity of the "discovered" diary of Adolph Hitler, which was shortly thereafter proved to be fraudulent.

17   Aldrich, Robert. *Colonialism and Homosexuality*. London: Routledge, 2004.

unwillingness to accept that Sir Edmund could have ever been telling the truth about anything.

Backhouse was, however, a far more complex individual than that. We cannot always take him at his word, but we would be equally foolish to reject everything he ever wrote without proper historical analysis. What his work, *Décadence Mandchoue* in particular, demands is careful analysis of each individual claim on the basis of the best available evidence.

There is much to be learned from these memoirs, even if some of the detail is imaginary. Backhouse's worth as a historical source can perhaps be compared to Marco Polo's. He may, like Polo, have overstated his personal importance or placed himself in situations where he was not present when creating his historical record of China. But such a chronicle still has worth in contextualizing late imperial China and examining as enigmatic a personality as Tz'u Hsi. *Décadence Mandchoue* is, by any measure, a remarkable book.

Backhouse's intentions in writing *Décadence Mandchoue* and *The Dead Past* seem less to shock and self-aggrandize than to recollect and inform readers of the two fondest periods of his life in England and China, when he could for a time love and be loved by other men without fear or shame. But his writing is indeed outrageous. His willingness to challenge his readers' boundaries, particularly in the realm of sexuality, is relentless in a way reminiscent of Burroughs' *Naked Lunch*, published almost two decades later in 1959. In many sections of the book, Backhouse seems to positively revel in the orgiastic proceedings he describes. Chapter Ten, for instance, is an aside from the central narrative describing the similarities between Asian and European practices of bestiality, and seems written almost entirely to push even the most tolerant of readers outside of their comfort zone. His attitude is unflinching throughout; this is the story he wants to tell and he will not compromise in its telling.

Yet this is not a purely sexual book, and it has literary merit beyond shock value. This, his final work, is a eulogy for the Ch'ing Dynasty; an erotic love letter to a bygone era. Even if it were completely fabricated, and I do not personally believe it was, it would still be an engaging and often hilarious historical fiction by a well-informed linguistic genius. As Italian diplomat Daniele Varè once said, "Sir Edmund Backhouse appears worthy to be classed with the famous translator of Ossian's poems,"[18] so gracefully does he move from one language to another.

As with everything else about Backhouse, assessing his literary worth from an exclusively Western perspective only gives half of the story. It is likely that in writing a work that showcases his command of the Chinese language, Backhouse was consciously imitating not only Western

---

18   Varè's comment (*The Last of the Empresses*. London: John Murray, 1936.) refers to James Macpherson (1736-96), best known for his English "translations" of the Gaelic poet Ossian. The Ossian works were popular in the 18th century, and their authenticity has long been challenged. Today the consensus is that the works were most likely based on a variety of real sources, though, in combining them into a single narrative, Macpherson changed names and greatly embellished the works with his own flourishes.

but also Chinese literary traditions. Some of the "flower guides" circulated among Peking's homoerotic literati around the time of this story, for example, provide a telling model for this kind of narrative. These flower guides were often, like "Décadence Mandchoue," loosely organized around their authors' conquests. In commenting on the beauty of various boy-actor lovers, they were intended to display the authors' refined taste and elevated social standing. It is hard to imagine that the obvious parallel between this writing style, popular when Backhouse moved to Peking, and the author's own sometimes self-congratulatory Peking memoir was accidental.

Novelist and translator Wang Xiaoge has also written of Backhouse's place within the Chinese literary tradition in the introduction to her Chinese-language edition of "Décadence Mandchoue." She believes that behind the book's salacious exterior lies a subtle meditation on the Chinese concept of *Shuli*, the sorrow wrought by life's impermanence. In this way, writes Wang, it can be viewed as analogous to the erotic classic *Chin P'ing Mei*:

> *Chin P'ing Mei* is best known as a piece of pornographic literature, but has been considered by distinguished writers like Yüan Hungtao and Lu Hsün to be "an authentic record of the social landscape with significant value despite its lewd phrases." Thus is it possible to look beyond the veil of eroticism and discern the sorrow that lies beneath. I see sorrow as the essence of *Ch'in P'ing Mei* and also the primary virtue of this book. There is a profound sadness buried within its abrasive words ... [Backhouse's] ability to apprehend and convey complex Chinese literary themes so elegantly in another tongue is a noteworthy achievement.

It is with great pleasure that we can finally bring to light the memoirs that Backhouse had so much hoped to see published. I have aimed, as best I can, to present a defense of his work that Hugh Trevor-Roper never afforded him; to show that a different conclusion can be drawn from the same basic set of facts. But Backhouse, that inimitable persuader, defends his work in the pages of *Décadence Mandchoue* better than anyone else could:

> Memory and imagination; the first counts as nothing without the second which is verily the ode of the agnostic to immortality and gilds old age with the after-glow of youth. These dear phantoms of the past, if they cannot restore happiness to one who moveth in what is certainly not an ampler ether, a diviner air, at least make life easier to be borne. "*Ich habe gelebt und geliebt*": is there more to say?

NOTES ON THE EDITION

When *Décadence Mandchoue* was written in 1943, its graphically sexual content made its publication impossible. Almost 70 years later, though the subject matter is no longer so much of an issue, the work still presents a publisher with significant obstacles.

Sir Edmund Backhouse was a brilliant linguist and a gifted writer, but like most writers he was in need of a good editor. With his most famous works, *China under the Empress Dowager* and *Annals & Memoirs of the Court of Peking*, he had the assistance of his co-author, *Times* correspondent J.O.P. Bland. Their collaboration produced fluid, readable text that rarely strayed into the esoteric. With *Décadence Mandchoue*, the man who took on the task of editing Backhouse's prose was Dr. Reinhard Hoeppli, neither a native-English speaker nor a writer by trade, and the results were mixed. Hoeppli's laissez-faire editorial approach has left us with valuable insights into Backhouse's thinking but also with a work that is in some ways challenging for the average contemporary reader.

Backhouse arrived in Peking in 1898 and returned to England only for short visits in the years that followed. He lived until 1944 and wrote these memoirs in 1943, but his style is firmly rooted in the late nineteenth century. He wrote like the erudite Victorian-era scholar that he was, and was heavily influenced by the gilded style of his heroes, Oscar Wilde and Paul Verlaine. The tone is conversational and sprinkled with classical allusions, historical references and frequent amusing asides. His writing is also flavored with a liberal use of many languages, most often Chinese, French and Latin.

Sir Edmund's prose – Chinese passages aside – would have presented no difficulties for his Oxford peers of the 1890s, but the literary and linguistic expectations placed upon his readers may be demanding by today's standards. To help the reader along, we have heavily annotated this edition. Sections and phrases written in other languages, so far as the author did not himself translate them, have been rendered in English. Many of the historical references and allusions to classical texts and ancient mythology have also been identified and explained.

In all, there are about a thousand footnotes throughout the work explaining various references. There could have easily been many more, but we believe the current number should suffice for most readers. The author originally inserted several footnotes of his own, all of which are indicated here by the name **Backhouse** in boldface.

Hoeppli's editing approach to the manuscript was, with very few exceptions, to simply transcribe Backhouse's handwritten original. In some instances he decided to delete or modify sections he deemed too anti-British or libelous to certain figures, all of whom have long since passed away. A few of these deletions were so heavily crossed out in the original manuscripts that they are no longer legible, but where possible we have reinserted the author's original language, and this edition should comprise a volume as complete and as true to Backhouse's original intent as is feasible.

In a few instances we have made small corrections to the text, but only with obvious errors in English spelling or clearly incorrect punctuation. We have also made a number of minor changes to the punctuation to ensure that it is internally consistent and more easily read. Also in the interests of consistency, every footnote uses, to the extent possible, spelling and punctuation that keeps with the author's style. All corrections were checked against all three versions of the original manuscript before any change was made. We have made no corrections to errors in other languages or quotations, not to show the author's shortcomings, but to demonstrate his undeniable gift for languages and near-perfect recall. That this was written by memory without the aid of reference materials, as Hoeppli explains, makes it all the more remarkable.

Several stylistic alterations have also been made to the text for ease of reading. In many instances when two or more characters are conversing, Backhouse often chose not to begin a new paragraph to indicate a shift in speaker. This decision led to many overly long and unnecessarily confusing paragraphs, so we have added additional paragraph breaks. We have also decided, in keeping with the early drafts of the work, to italicize Romanized words written in foreign languages as opposed to the single quotation marks employed by Hoeppli in later edits. In making these changes, none of the author's words were modified.

What we have decided to change, after much deliberation, is the numbering of the chapters. Very early in the editing process, it became clear that the chapters may have been labeled incorrectly. A close examination of the manuscript indicates that the hand that numbered the chapters was not Backhouse's, but in lieu of any external corroboration we were forced to follow clues within the text. For example, the author often invites readers to recall previously mentioned episodes, many of which occur in later chapters according to the original structure. The author also left behind hints in the form of dates provided near the beginning of most chapters. Although it is possible that he did not intend a strictly linear narrative, the reordering according to the textual references results in the chapters progressing in a more or less chronological order. The two exceptions are Chapter Seventeen: Her Last Autumn Picnic and Chapter Nineteen: A Retrospect of Diviner Hours, both of which provide references to the chapters that directly precede them despite occurring chronologically out of sequence. Also of note is Chapter Five: Eunuch Diversions, which contains reference to a character who does not appear until later in the story (Chan Pao-ch'en) but otherwise appears to be in the correct position.

One final note should be made on the Romanization of Chinese words. The standard in modern China is the Pinyin system created in the 1950s, but at the time in which this book was written, the standards were Wade-Giles and, for place names, the Chinese Postal Map system. Despite a few personal flourishes, Backhouse used both of these Romanization systems, so we have opted to use them throughout the text and footnotes for internal consistency. Thus the Empress Dowager's name is T'zu Hsi and not Cixi, and the story is set in Peking, not Beijing.

ACKNOWLEDGMENTS

RESURRECTING and preparing *Décadence Mandchoue* for publication was a long, challenging and ultimately rewarding undertaking. This manuscript, to a much greater degree than is typical, required the assistance and support of a number of generous people from diverse backgrounds. Each of them deserves recognition for their unique contributions and I must apologize in advance to anyone whose name I have neglected to include on this list.

For their invaluable guidance from the very earliest stages of this project, I would like to thank Frances Wood, head of the Chinese Department of the British Library, and David Helliwell, curator of the Chinese collection at Oxford's Bodleian Library. Without your feedback and support in the initial stages, this book might still only be available in your respective archives.

A number of additional distinguished scholars helped tremendously in guiding my research and filling in some of the missing pieces in the Backhouse puzzle. Jeremiah Jenne, PhD candidate studying Ch'ing history at UC Davis and prolific history blogger at *Jottings from the Granite Studio*, was kind enough to guide me through some of the manuscript's more complex historical issues. T.H. Barrett, Professor of East Asian History, School of Oriental and African Studies at the University of London, was an invaluable resource in forming an academic rationale for publication as well as steering me toward other academics who could comment on the manuscript's many facets. Vincent Goosaert, Adjunct Professor of Religious and Cultural Studies at the Chinese University of Hong Kong, helped shed some light on the work's more obscure religious aspects and debunk the séance at the White Cloud Temple. Robert Aldrich, Professor of European History, University of Sydney, deserves thanks for his earlier study on Backhouse's place in the history of homosexual literature as well as for his further most helpful comments on this project. For his considered opinion on the likelihood of a meeting between Backhouse and Sun Yat-sen, I would also like to thank John Y. Wong, Professor of Modern History at the University of Sydney.

Of critical importance were the contributions of our gifted team of translators, and I would like to acknowledge the valuable work of Paul Hansen and Brendan O'Kane (Chinese), Christine Leang and Sylvie Chapuis (French), the Reverend Dr. William Craig (Latin) and Catherine Mathes (Italian). I would also like to thank Fifi Kao and Wang Xiaoge for their additional assistance with Chinese characters and quotations.

Tom Cohen, a relation of Backhouse colleague J.O.P. Bland, was kind enough to provide me with the excellent photograph of Backhouse in full Chinese dress found in the Appendix.

I also owe a significant debt to my colleagues at Earnshaw Books: co-editors Andrew Chubb, Alice Polk and Audrey Murray, designer Frank Zheng and his talented wife for her work on the cover. Gareth Powell provided me with inspiration and sage wisdom throughout. My cell door is always open to you. Finally, I would like to thank Graham Earnshaw, who set this project in motion and gave it (and me) his full support. It would not have been possible without him.

Derek Sandhaus
Shanghai
January 2011

DÉCADENCE MANDCHOUE

To Kuei Hua, My Own Cassia Flower

Fain were I to see thine adorable name at the inception of these pages; for thou art of them "the only begetter" and they owe to thee the pythian inspiration, written as they are from first to last in deathless love of thee; though much is alien from thy precious environment and from our blessed association sundered alas! too soon; yet is nothing herein separable from my sempiternal devotion toward thy darling self; thou who art the climax and the crown of my waking and dreaming imaginings, thou that even today, when the light of the windows is darkened and the clouds return after the rain, still stirrest immortal longings in me; scarce other than in days of our vanity, two score and three years ago. "Gilding old age with the afterglow of youth."

Stands the dark gate of Death; then a light; then thy face!
O! heart of my heart! to enclose thee again! –
By Buddha's dear grace!

30. VI. 43.

FOREWORD TO THE READER

I, Sir Edmund Trelawny Backhouse, a Baronet of the United Kingdom, do hereby positively affirm on my honour and on that of my respectable family which has played a not negligible part in English public life that the studies which I have endeavoured to write for Dr. Hoeppli contain nothing but the truth, the whole truth and the absolute truth. Nothing has been added to embellish the facts, but dates, owing to the loss of my records, cannot always be accurately given, although the year or month of an official's degradation is verifiable by record; that is an event may have occurred before or later than that recorded. My intercourse with Tz'u Hsi started in 1902 and continued till her death. I had kept an unusually close record of my secret association with the empress and with others, possessing notes and messages written to me by Her Majesty, but had the misfortune to lose all these manuscripts and papers thereto relating, largely through the cowardice of my domestics and the treachery of people in whom I trusted; so that my large collection of books and documents was lost *in toto*; that is excepting for a few dictionaries and handbooks of a linguistic nature which, however, contain no notes on the (secret not to say erotic) matters whereof I have written.

Naturally, my name as compiler cannot be revealed during my life, owing to the nature of the topics under discussion. But I can only affirm my *bona-fides* solemnly and seriously *urbi et orbi*[1] without the shadow of a shade of reservation. As Shylock says: "Would I lay perjury on my soul? No, not for Venice." There may be *omissions* in my narratives, as memory sometimes fails; and when I was doubtful, I left a blank; but I can assure any unprejudiced persons that *no romance nor embroidery* finds a place therein for, as the great Sage[2] says, I am a *transmitter* not a literary creator, and could not be if I tried, any more than was the case regarding the journal of Ching-shan which I once had the honour to translate exactly as I discovered it without the addition of a syllable of extraneous matter. I may add that calumny and misrepresentation move me very little but that to one who flatters himself in being a scholar (at any rate, a student), such an action, i.e. of fiction supplanting facts, would assuredly be despicable and indicative of no sense of honour whatsoever, rendering me unworthy of decent people's society!

E. Backhouse

7. III. 1943.

---

1   "To the city and to the world", signifying that a papal document is addressed not only to the City of Rome but to the entire Catholic world.

2   Confucius; K'ung Fu Tzu 孔夫子, K'ung Tzu 孔子 (Master K'ung).

The measureless waste of waters encompasseth them, but the merciful Raft of AVALOKITESVARA ever waiteth Ready to rescue the drowning, even in the midst of the sea.

Sanskrit proverb.

Every sin, except the sin against itself, Love shall forgive:
All lives, save loveless lives, True Love shall pardon.

Oscar Wilde.

CHAPTER I

PEKING INTERLUDE
OR
CASSIA FLOWER

He, if such there be, who peruses the following pages may deem that they are from the pen of a depraved, peradventure even if a talented, man; yet it is the simple truth that what is recounted hereafter and in subsequent papers from my pen, emanates not from unholy lust nor *décadence raffinée*[1] so much as from instinctive curiosity and the spirit of Shakspere's[2] sonnets. I have known men who in the accepted sense of the adjective were called, ay and were, depraved, e.g., Wilde, Robbie Ross, Huysmans, Verlaine; but in morality religion has the last word; and religion is inspired by sentiment and not by intelligence. It speaks to the senses and thus brings us down to a common level; whereas intelligence engages in disputation and argument. He, who would judge his neighbour, should first ask pardon for himself. These are simple, but everlasting, verities.

"Les choses de l'amour sont de profonds secrets."
"Qui de nous est assez pur pour jeter la première pierre?"[3]

> "We shall know if hell be not heaven;
> We shall see if tares be not grain;
> And the joys of thee seventy times seven
> Our Lady of Pain."[4]

On an April afternoon of 1899, my *charrette chinoise*[5] (in those halcyon days rickshas were unknown) deposited me armed with a note of introduction from Prince Ch'ing, himself homosexual in the *forme active et passive* of the word, at the gate of the Shu Ch'un T'ang 淑春堂, Hall of

---

1 Refined decadence.
2 Due to a lack of uniformity in Elizabethan English, records of the spelling of Shakspere's (Shakespeare's) name vary from source to source.
3 "Matters of love are profound secrets." "Who among us is pure enough to cast the first stone?" Both from Anatole France (*Les poèmes dorés* and a eulogistic appraisal of Dumas in *La Vie Littéraire*, respectively).
4 **Backhouse:** Swinburne, but "Lady" should be changed into the male gender for me, though both exist in my dual nature, *par l'effet de ma complexion*, as Anatole France has it ["owing to my disposition" a misquotation of *"par l'effet de sa complexion"* from *Les sept femmes de la Barbe-Bleue*].
5 "Chinese chariot", probably a Peking mule cart.

Chaste (!) Joys, in Shih T'ou Hut'ung 石頭胡同 (Stone Lane) where were many brothels and more than one *Ssu Fang* 私方, Secret Establishment, or *Hsiang Ku*[6] *Hsia Ch'u* 像姑下處, Resort of Catamites.[7] This type of bawdyhouse was, at that time, tacitly recognized by the authorities and naturally had to pay very heavy taxes as well as irregular impositions which were freely levied by the Pu Chün T'ung Ling 步軍統領 or Pei Yamen[8] 北衙門, the then head office of the Gendarmerie of which Junglu 榮祿 had formerly so long been chief, the local Banner captain, the *Tu Ch'a Yüan* 都察院 or censorate and the nearest sub-section or *T'ing Erh* 廳兒. The managing director of the establishment was a charming Manchu named Tsai Mu 載穆 who, in fact, was a yellow girdle, an imperial clansman, a distant cousin of Emperor Kuang Hsü 光緒, and therefore not without a definite *piston*,[9] who told me that he had to disburse *mensuellement*[10] nearly ¥1,000 in presents, squeezes and "legitimate" taxes. He was about 35, extremely handsome and had, I believe, been himself in his day a fashionable catamite. "As Prince Kung 恭 used to say," remarked Tsai Mu, "pederasty is very nice but very costly." (I remember that Li Hungchang's 李鴻章 eldest son, Li Ching-shu 李經述, who only survived his father a short time, is recorded as having said with his latest breath, "My chiefest pleasure in life has been to enjoy passive copulation *a tergo*."[11] When in London, in 1921, I recollect reading a *graffito* in a cultivated hand on the wall of a lavatory (*für Manner*)[12] at Piccadilly Circus: "Have you ever been *possédé* (had) by a man? Do so! It's great!")

"Well," said Mr. Tsai Mu, "you are a devil (*Kuei Tzu* 鬼子)[13] and therefore to us here a novelty (*Hsin Hsien* 新鮮). You are young and goodlooking (!). I shall let you see everything. You foreigners are said to be very *Yin* 淫 (lustful), in fact men say that your males have a duplicate sexual equipment; but your eyes may be opened by certain new spectacles, especially as there is nothing "faked" in this house. Duke Lan[14] 載 is coming here this evening by appointment. I shall tell him that you are here by special recommendation of old Prince Ch'ing 慶, and, as he is my relative and very good-natured, you can just amuse yourself by watching everything he does from the inception to the conclusion. I shall only charge you Taels 50[15] and you can stay the night and indulge in gambols

---

6   **Backhouse:** Vulgarly at that time was called *Hsiang Kung* 相公, Young gentleman. [This term came to denote actors who played female roles onstage and worked in wine shops and male brothels offstage. *Hsiang Kung* was used interchangeably with *Hsiang Ku* (woman-like; effeminate) and was probably the origin of the latter term.]

7   Male prostitutes, a term derived from the Greek "Ganymede", a mythological Trojan prince seduced by Zeus.

8   "The Infantry Command" or "Northern Office".

9   Connection.

10   Monthly.

11   From behind.

12   For men.

13   Foreigner.

14   **Backhouse:** The Boxer leader, banished to Turkestan in 1901; one of the most xenophobe princes, brother of Prince Tuan 端.

15   A unit for weighing silver (generally about 30-40g, depending on region and era) used as currency in China. The following chapter gives an exchange rate of approximately Taels 6.25 to £1.

with any of our "*Lung Yang Chün*" 龍陽君 (name of a historical catamite)[16] you may prefer, adding a small present say Taels 20 for the favoured one and the attendant. You shall see all the "expectants", fourteen in all; Cassia Flower 桂花 is retained by Duke Tsai Lan 載瀾 for this evening; but he is very intelligent and not shy. You might like him best; he will bathe in perfumed water after Duke Lan has had enough gratification."

Then Mr. Tsai explained to me the tariff: simple or unipartite copulation with the pathic[17] costs Taels 30; reciprocal copulation costs Taels 45; *P'in Hsiao* 品簫 (flute savouring, in allusion to the shape of a Chinese flute which resembles the male organ) or *fellatio* is Taels 10 extra if limited to the pathic; Taels 15 if practiced by the latter on the client *irrumatio* or *coitio per buccam*[18] is Taels 30 inclusive of *Feuilles de Rose*,[19] or what we call "Cinnamon Leaves", *Kuei Yeh* 桂葉, if applied by the client to the pathic's anal, pubic and perineal region but if the client requires this labial business on his *verge*, posterior, etcetera, he must disburse Taels 45. If the client's passions are dull and he needs aphrodisiac stimulation, *Vyenki*[20] are available. To be chastised by the selected pathic, charges vary according to the severity of the whipping. Usually, added Mr. Tsai Mu with a meaning grin, twelve strokes make the client call "Halt": he must pay a minimum of Taels 12 for a normal flagellation and Tael 1 for the *Vyenki* which, of course, breaks under use. If he is unsated after twelve strokes, he must pay Tael 1 per *Hieb*.[21] But if the client desires to retaliate on the buttocks of the pathic, he must pay an extra Taels 45 as a personal compensation for the catamite's broken skin and a nominal fee to the establishment of Taels 5 plus Tael 1 for each extra *Vyenki* as aforesaid. The catamite's *pudenda* (*Ch'iao Tzu* 巧子 or penis, "cunning tool"), testicles (*Tan Tzu* 蛋子), anal region, fundament and perineum are all delicately perfumed and, as goes without saying, kept most scrupulously clean: the pubic and anal hair is clean shaven like the face. Naturally, if the client desires intimate labial contact on his person, he will wish to perform appropriate ablution on his secret parts. An exquisite scent from Java (or Borneo) is available for Taels 5 a bottle; so that the practical and aesthetic side of what might appear gross and physical (even filthy) be not neglected. However, you shall have everything for a fixed tariff of Taels 50, plus a fee for the "pleasuring" to him whom you deem worthy of your regard. But, if you come back to us, as I hope you may, I shall have to charge you at the same rate as Duke Lan who will probably disburse at least double that figure exclusive of gratuities which are naturally lavish, as he is a "unicorn claw" (imperial kinsman). The pathics are trained by

---

16 A favoured official and lover of the King of Wei, whose name became synonymous with male prostitutes.

17 The passive partner in homosexual intercourse.

18 "To give suck" or "sexual intercourse by mouth".

19 "Rose leaves", from the homoerotic 1893 novel *Teleny*, believed to be the work of Oscar Wilde.

20 **Backhouse:** This is a Russian word, *Vyenik*, plural *Vyenki* [Венки], or rod, is employed after the bath both in Russia and Finland – I forget the Finnish name – the buttocks and adjacent parts of the bather being severely whipped by the bath functionary till blood comes. It is supposed to be a skin stimulant but I suspect it to be a form of Masochism and to have aphrodisiac motives.

21 Blow.

practice *not* to have an erection and are absolutely forbidden to *lancer un pet*;[22] unless, of course, the client desires to be possessed *a tergo* by them. If they ejaculate during the *coitus per buccam*, the client will usually add a moderate *solatium*[23] in recognition of their virility. Their *fondements*[24] are all very elastic (anal dilators of various sizes were in regular use) and the most largely developed clients find no difficulty in achieving full penetration and enhancing the *jouissance*.[25] Practice renders them all quite impassive to any discomfort, when – as we say – *I Ken Chi Pa Wang Li Ch'o* 一根肌巴往裡戳 – (quotation from *Hung Lou Meng*[26] 紅樓夢 i.e. the penis pricketh its forcible way inside. "You probably know," went on Tsai, "that for bilateral copulation, our slang phrase is: 'Turning the bun (so that top and bottom may be roasted) *T'ieh Shao Ping* 貼燒餅'." (There is a famous chapter in the *Dream of the Red Chamber* where the hero Pao Yü 寶玉 and his school-friend Ch'in Chung 秦鍾 are caught in the act of reciprocal copulation by another class-mate, who shouts out to the other boys: "they are busy at it, turning the bun.")

We were sitting in a charmingly furnished room tastefully hung with practical scrolls and somewhat suggestive pictures. One pair of antithetical scrolls by the late Prince Kung[27] was as follows: "To the bird the air, to the fish the water: each enjoys its natural element: To the male his function, to the female hers; who shall speak of violation of propriety?" There were albums of *Ch'un Kung*[28] 春宮 or indecent pictures on the table; one of exquisite indecency portrayed three males in suggestive postures, the central one being active agent and pathic in simultaneous ecstasy; another painting showed a fair youth after copulation wiping his *membrum virile*[29] with a silken serviette, while the Charmides[30] reclines languidly on a yellow rug in an intertwined five clawed dragon pattern. Another scroll was inscribed: "Wine and flowers provide us a perpetual spring: Moonlight and lamplight are not necessary to illume our nocturnal joys." Another *Tui Lien*[31] 對聯 ran: "He who standeth outside the door is alien from our cult: he who is initiated into our mysteries is the true esoteric."

Next Tsai Mu summoned two of the catamites, both beautiful boys about 18 or 19, one called Peony 牡丹 and the other Chrysanthemum 菊花. They had the surprise of their lives on seeing a European, although being in Chinese dress, I was not conspicuously alien-looking, had not Tsai introduced me as a foreign devil. (In those days, and in fact now also, the term *Kuei Tzü* 鬼子 was universal and connoted no offence being in fact

---

22   Break wind.
23   Compensation.
24   Anuses.
25   Sexual climax.
26   *Dream of the Red Chamber*, an 18th century work by Ts'ao Hsueh-ch'in widely considered to be one of the greatest classical Chinese novels.
27   Prince Kung (1833-98) was a high-ranking statesman who served under his brother, Emperor Hsien Feng, and the Empress Dowager Tz'u Hsi. He is best known for negotiating the treaties that opened much of China to the Allied Powers following the Second Opium War (1856-60).
28   Spring Palace pictures.
29   Male member; penis.
30   The handsome subject of Plato's *Charmides*, who was also the philosopher's uncle.
31   A matched couplet usually hung on walls or columns.

complimentary). They were certainly free from shyness, made most lewd gestures and sidled up, expectant and apparently amorous. At a word from Tsai Mu, they exhibited their persons behind and before and told me to caress their respective *chybres*[32] and anal regions. Both lads were exquisitely dressed and well groomed, exhaling an admirable perfume.

I am not proud of the fact but owe it to candour to admit that I was sensitive to the exotic attraction and erotically disposed. What would not Verlaine or Wilde have given to have my opportunities: I could imagine "Oscar" saying: "You beautiful boy: we are made for each other; you are green and yellow wine to me"; or Verlaine quoting his line: "*J'aime ton trou-fignon de mes lèvres caressé.*"[33] However, the moment was not opportune and other boys came in, all of them powdered and rouged but still beautiful, despite the rouge which I thought a disfigurement. There was one catamite, however, of whom Tsai had spoken as he *qui fut pour le duc Lan comme la prunelle des yeux*,[34] whose lovely face was innocent of cosmetics; eyes of a rare lustre and an angelic smile like a cherub of Murillo, delicate tapering fingers and a slender, well knit frame, a mouth that Saint Simon's Duc de Bourgogne – "*la plus belle bouche du monde*"[35] – might not have disdained, teeth whiter than ivory, clearly defined eyebrows and a straight shapely nose with short upper lip and a delicate chin. This was Cassia Flower, Kuei Hua 桂花, and after seeing him, I had no eyes for the others. We made friends at once, and he said: "What a nuisance I am retained by Duke Lan for this evening. I can see that you and I have affinity, and you are so much younger than he. We could have such fun together."

"Never mind," put in Tsai Mu: "after His Highness leaves, this gentleman will be at your disposition for the whole night."

"The night is short, but dreams are many," (or, as the English poet says: "Gather ye rosebuds while ye may.")[36]

"Oh! that's good news," said Cassia Flower. "I must not tire myself out and then I shall be fresh for our 'happy union'."

At this moment, Tsai Lan was announced: he was a typical Aisin Gioro[37] in appearance, with high forehead and strongly marked cheekbones. I did not then know the evil notoriety that would soon gather round his name.

The Manchu princes are nothing if not polite and Tsai Lan (especially after learning that I was a friend of old Prince Ch'ing) bowed courteously to me, while Tsai Mu explained my presence and asked His Highness' permission to allow me to *assister à la séance*[38] of the "Clouds and Rain" (sexual intercourse). "He is, as you see, a foreigner and wants to *Chan Yang* 瞻仰 (gaze respectfully) at the various developments."

---

32 Penises.
33 I love your anus caressed by my lips.
34 Whose sight was the apple of Duke Lan's eye.
35 The most beautiful mouth in the world.
36 **Backhouse:** Robert Herrick 1591-1674.
37 **Backhouse:** *Aisin*: Manchu for gold, *Gioro*: the clan name.
38 Watch the show.

Tsai Lan made no more objection than (I suppose) we should, if a monkey were chained up in a prostitute's chamber during her reception of a guest. "Has the foreign devil the same tastes? Is he a sleeve cutter (active, because the Emperor T'ang Ming Huang 唐明皇 cut off his sleeve rather than awake the slumbering catamite by his side) or does he enjoy *Lung Yang Chün* 龍陽君 (passive, as I have already mentioned)?"

"If he joins you here," (said Tsai Lan *finement*),[39] "he will be a foreign rabbit," *T'u Tzu* 兔子 being a *sobriquet* of pathics! (This was a pretty compliment to me!) Some delicately scented tea was brought in, after which Lan, Cassia Flower, the attendant and I (curious and amused) went to Cassia Flower's boudoir, small but richly furnished, and containing many souvenirs from his admirers, jade ornaments, gold watches, rings, brooches, jewelry and so forth. Tsai Lan bade me be seated *Sui Pien* 隨便 (at your ease) and sent the attendant out for some Chinese aphrodisiac which he named: at that time Yohembine was not known in China. The two removed all their clothes, stark naked except for the socks, and I noticed that Tsai Lan, though slightly too stout, had a comely figure. He was in a clearly defined state of sexual excitement and began fondling Cassia Flower whose lascivious gestures, albeit minus an erection, were no whit behind those of the imperial prince. As the servant came back with the potion and looked lustfully at the naked pair, I was reminded of a painting in the "Cabinet Secret" of the Museo Borbone at Naples; where sodomy is being performed upon a recumbent woman and the *échanson*[40] who has brought the love potion looks erotically back at the antics of his young lord.

I observed several *Vyenki*, of which Tsai Mu had spoken, on the dressing table; evidently Cassia knew his client's tastes: they were *poignée de menus brins de bouleau*[41] and reminded me – *infandum renovare dolorem*[42] – of the rods with which the present prime minister of England and I (*aetatis nostrae anno decimo et undecimo*)[43] had been remorselessly flogged respectively by the Sadistic whiskered tyrant, Dr. Sneyd-Kynnersley, who lacerated (with his birchen sceptre stained with infant gore) us unhappy pupils, a *Plagosus Orbilius*,[44] like Horace's old pedagogue. I wondered with what Tsai Lan would start the ball rolling: he began by squatting on the floor and telling Cassia to present his back toward him. The prince *nozzled*[45] the pathic's anal region and put his finger inside the fundament; then he *renifla*[46] the anal orifice for a very long time and put his index finger well inside what Cassia called his *Yin Men* 陰門 or vulva!! Cassia obediently turned to face Lan who inserted the former's penis in his mouth, retaining it for some moments, but no ejaculation

---

39 Finely.
40 Cupbearer.
41 A handful of small birch rods.
42 **Backhouse:** Dido in Virgil's *Aeneid* ["To revive unspeakable suffering" (II.3)].
43 In the 10th or 11th year of our age.
44 "Flogger" Orbilius (*Epistles* II.I.70-1).
45 Nosed.
46 Sniffed.

followed neither was there the least erection. He kissed the whole pubic region with gusto; then embraced Cassia all over his fragrant body not once but many times, no sign of desquamation[47] being apparent on his (Lan's) membrum. Then he knelt in ungainly fashion over the *K'ang*[48] 炕 and bade Cassia chastise his buttocks with the *Vyenki*. Cassia obeyed *con amore,*[49] as if he were not indulging in a maiden effort, and applied (I think) fifteen strokes (Taels 15 according to tariff) drawing a small quantity of blood. Lan started groaning after the first lashes but continued to exclaim: "*Hai Tei Shih Chin* 還得使勁 – harder, harder"; like the flagellants under Henri III's leadership in the 16th century, till the buttock was quite raw. (As the Sage says, speaking of a very different subject: "*Lo Tsai Ch'i Chung* 樂在其中, pleasure exists therein." *Chacun son goût:*[50] as Sophocles writes: "There are many wonders, but nothing is more wonderful than man: *Polla ta deina kòuden anthropou deinoteron pelei.*")[51] Cassia kept looking in my direction and seemed greatly amused by the diversion. Lan consummated his pastime by *pedicando:*[52] it seemed to me an endless process (certainly over ten minutes) but all things come to an end and after an apparently ample ejaculation which flowed back over Cassia's posterior, he got up from the strategical (or should it be tactical) position which he was occupying, with a *Hao Lei* 好累 "very tiring", *Pu Suan Pu Fei Shih* 不算不費事, "quite a business", breathing so stertorously that I feared for him a *coup de sang*.[53]

Tsai Lan and Cassia (after dressing themselves) had several cups of tea and liqueurs which I did not identify. Lan kissed the latter many times, imprinting a voluptuous last *baiser*[54] on posterior and on penis, and handed to him a solatium of Taels 150, over and above the brothel's fees of Taels 100 plus Taels 30 for the service.[55] He made me a courtly bow, half genuflexion, which I returned, with a "I hope you were interested" and walked back to the reception room, where he and Tsai Mu chatted as friends and kinsmen. Cassia Flower said he was going to have a bath of "purification" and would see me immediately afterwards; so I waited in the courtyard chatting with several of the other boys who at the moment were still disengaged. (I don't know what the explanation may be, but the catamites said that *des écoulements visqueux mensuels ou bimensuels*[56] from their fundaments were their MENSES!![57] and that, when these

---

47 Shedding of skin.
48 A traditional stove in northern China used for sitting and sleeping.
49 Lovingly.
50 To each his own.
51 **Backhouse:** *Antigone.*
52 Anal intercourse.
53 Stroke.
54 Kiss.
55 This may seem an excessive amount at a time when many Peking families had an annual income of about Taels 100, but one source from the era (in 燕京雜記 *Yenking Tsa Chi*) claims that the best-known catamites in Peking could generate Taels 100,000 annually. A projection of Cassia Flower's revenues based upon this chapter would amount to at least Taels 65,700 annually, most of which would presumably be turned over to the establishment's proprietor, Tsai Mu.
56 Viscous monthly or bimonthly flow.
57 Menstruation.

occurred, they did not receive clients.) I thought how that *étrangement poétique*[58] Monarch, Henri III, would have revelled in the environment and felt as if I were living with Schomburg, Maugiron and Saint Luc, when the terrible Bussy d'Amboise, that scourge of the Mignons, served the Duc d'Anjou in intrigues against the latter's royal brother.

After an interval, Cassia, fragrant with perfumes, emerged: he gave to me an aromatic scent and a balsamic anodyne[59] wherewith to anoint myself, offering the use of his dressing room for ablution and purification. At my request, he commanded a few delectable dishes from the Hui Feng T'ang 惠豐堂, one of the oldest of Peking restaurants. My preparations completed, we sat chatting in the open courtyard till supper was ready. I asked Cassia which feature in the love congress most appealed to his heaven kissing *essor*.[60] "First", said he, "*pedicatio ascendante*[61] to which I am to be initiated this night; second, 'cinnamon leaves' (*feuilles de rose*) by the long application of my lips *au fondement et aux parties adjacentes de mon amant*,[62] because a perfect affinity is thus established, exalting both giver and receiver to heaven. The perfection of line gives to me a rapture like that derived from a work of art; the labial contact excites my inmost being: my lips are never sated of caresses. When I am the recipient, the gratification is more sensual but less aesthetic. Uncleanness forsooth! as if the fairest portion of the male body could be unclean. You must curb your *Yang* 陽 proclivities for to-night and let your *Yin* 陰 element[63] be in the ascendant; so that we two can achieve an ideal union. And their four lips became one burning kiss," said Cassia, suiting action to the word; "because I know that in your brimming veins run longings like mine own, but to-night you must let me begin, continue and end each act in our love comedy." We had a delightful meal together, not without (*à l'avenant*) wines and liqueurs. Then the attendant withdrew and Cassia, whose amorous exaltation was manifest, said: "Let us undress and revel in the contemplation of each other's nudity." He took control of the business from the inception; and one would have said that I was the pathic and he the "incubus", as H. H. Pope Alexander Borgia would have called, and did call, the relationship, in a Papal Bull *orbi et urbi*, allowing to the clergy and (I think) to the lay brothers homosexual commerce during a space of three months in each year. I made no objection and did exactly what Cassia required, even as a *fantoche*[64] or a Robot at his call.

In those dead days fires of erotic ardour, whereof not a flicker nor vestige remain, *salvo il ricordo dei felici tempi*,[65] blazed within me like a great white flame; but they were as nothing beside Cassia's ebullient lubricity. His *verge*, most fair and most admirable, must have been several

---

58 Strangely poetic.
59 Painkiller.
60 "Taking flight; blossoming; expansion; boom", probably meaning erection in this instance.
61 Ascending anal sex; on top.
62 To my lover's anus and adjoining parts.
63 *Yang* and *Yin* are opposing forces in Taoist philosophy, the former traditionally representing the masculine and the latter representing the feminine.
64 Puppet.
65 I hold onto to the memory of happy times.

nches longer and thicker than the recognized super-normal measure of
eight inches. We fondled each other in lewd dalliance for a season and
kissed each other's secret parts to our hearts' content. Then Cassia suggested, or rather commanded, a course of *soixante neuf* and we indulged
in mutual simultaneous *fellatio*, *Ni Wo P'in Hsiao* 你我品簫 (or *Liang Hsia
T'ung Kan* 兩下同幹, joint operations). This diversion was most pleasing
but was not allowed to consummate itself; for Cassia then presented to
me his posterior for my lustful caresses, and my labial reactions were no
more elegant than those of the Manchu prince earlier in the day. I perpetrated *Kuei Yeh* 桂葉, "cinnamon leaves", upon his beautiful anal orifice
fragrant as meadow daisies and inserted my tongue inside his *Kang Men*
肛門 (or "vulva", as he called it)! Then he bade me titillate the anus with
inserted index finger and after a few minutes the whole region was wet
with a discharge of viscous, white mucus, quite inodorous, which Cassia
called *Yin Shui* 陰水, "sensual waters", which I erroneously presumed
to have been prostatic fluid but which, he said, gave to him a sensation
most pleasureful, without peer or parallel. Then he fondled my anal region in a similar orgy of lust, for his will was law; although the *feuilles de
rose* manoeuvre was not unfamiliar to one who had sojourned in Paris
and Saint Petersburg, to say nothing of other European store-houses
of salacious devices. This done, Cassia bade me kneel over the settee:
he took a new *poignée de brindilles de bouleau, la discipline ou les verges*[66]
to which I have referred, and chastised me *sans miséricorde*[67] across the
buttocks. I think he dealt to me eighteen or nineteen running strokes: it
was *exceedingly* painful but I was determined to clench my teeth and to
submit without flinching, awaiting his good pleasure since the *sadismus*
was to him such a source of poignant gratification. My back was greatly
lacerated and, as I have an unusually thin skin, bled freely, splinters from
the twigs having broken off into the flesh. Cassia graciously removed
these and applied some salve; but I am free to confess that for some days
thereafter I sought the juxtaposition of several cushions before sitting
down. Meantime, Cassia's orgasm became more and more developed, a
sight for Hermes or the great god Pan: I feared a spontaneous ejaculation
to interfere with his pleasuring but by the grace of God none came. Next
he held out to me a new *discipline*, knelt in most gracious posture on the
sofa and bade me *lui donner la fessée*; "*frappez fort*",[68] quoth he. Naturally
I complied with his sovereign wish and chastised him *à bras raccourci*.[69]
After a dozen strokes I wished to stop, but he would not allow it and he
submitted gamely to another half dozen strokes without a murmur or
the least signs of flinching or distress. My force was perhaps inferior to
his: at any rate, his buttocks were less bruised than mine, but he assured
me that he should receive no clients during the next day or two, letting
"Peony" 牡丹 who was his understudy act for him, "unless, of course,

---

66   Handful of small birch rods, obedience or flogging.
67   Without pity.
68   Give him a spanking; "hit hard".
69   With all of my strength.

Duke Lan comes and insists upon my ministering to him, which I hardly expect".

Then Cassia, whose orgasm surpassed my wildest imaginings, ordered me to recline face downwards upon the couch and in the gentlest, most effortless fashion proceeded to the *pedicatio*. Thanks to his timeous salve which lubricated and had analgesic properties, there was no difficulty about penetration, which was comparatively speaking *sans secousse ou douleur*;[70] so that his very long, nay colossal (elephantine is the best epithet at my disposition), penis suffered little delay in entering my rectum up to the hilt. I had no sensation other than pleasurable, while he uttered a series of joyful exclamations, "this is heaven", "what joy is this", "how comforting", "the nicest experience of my life" and so forth. Then he exclaimed: "*Pa Ch'iao Tzu Ko I Ko* 把巧子攔一攔, leave my *verge* for the moment in motionless inactivity;" he certainly succeeded in protracting the enjoyment in a way that an Arab (who specializes, according to Sir Richard Burton, in slow copulation) could not have surpassed. Then he resumed his forcible action and after something like a quarter of an hour ejaculated in an abounding overflow like a salmon river in spate. Relieved and sighing with content, he lay back on the couch. "Now it is your turn: you must *Kan I Hsia Erh* 幹一下兒 (have one) with me." He prepared himself for my onset and, rather clumsily I fear, I perpetrated *la réplique*[71] which he sought. It seemed to delight him and assuredly rejoiced me.

Cassia assured me, and I do not doubt it, that it was his initial effort in the "active voice", even as one who draws a maiden sword; for heretofore he had had perhaps a century (*I Pai Tso Yu* 一百左右) of experiences of *la forme passive*. His wonderful nimbleness and easy, alert grace in the active posture, as to the manner born, certainly belied his words. "Young Harry, with his beaver on", ready for the battle. *Chia Ch'ing Chiu Shu*[72] 駕輕就熟; "Light is the equipage and the road is familiar", saith the proverb. It is a fact that the sexual act, passive even more than active, afforded to me a ravishing pleasure: the intromission of Cassia's highly militant organ instead of being a prod or a goad, connoted an exquisite, entrancing gratification, *une sensation des plus exquises*;[73] like the first night in heaven. Peradventure, I am what is vulgarly called *Ta Yen'rh* 大眼兒, or *Ta P'i Ku* 大屁股, possessing a large fundament (or a posterior on a generous scale), *Nalgudo* as the Spanish say: of large posterior, or *fessu* (the gibe which is jocular but good natured, implying that one is a pathic); yet it is exact to say that my personal acquaintance with passivity had never been, though frequent, quite so perfect as it now became by frequent blissful contacts with Cassia's super-abundant carnality.

"Some are born eunuchs: some are made eunuchs of men"; and I suppose that I was semi-femininely constructed (as the Empress Dowager once told me) with the *Yin* 陰 element more predominant than the *Yang*

---

70   Without a shudder or pain.
71   The reply.
72   One well versed in something.
73   A most exquisite sensation.

陽; although I am no *Erh Yi Tzu* 二疑子 (or hermaphrodite). On this occasion, as Saint Paul says, "I was caught up to the third heaven, whether in the body or out of the body I cannot tell, God knoweth."[74]

Cassia was a perfect Confucianist, in that he adopted the give and take principle: *Chi So Pu Yü Wu Shih Yü Jen* 己所不欲勿施於人: do not to others what you would not for yourself, *Shu* 恕, or forbearance being the true philosophy of life. As I have said, he loved to initiate each manoeuvre but was fain to allow (nay, rather to compel) the opposite side (when he had a congenial partner to deal with) to retaliate in kind after he had wrought his will. As I have narrated, he bade me kneel to *passer par les verges*[75] in most severe chastisement but insisted on my taking a reluctant reprisal on his adorable buttocks, *le mele*, the apples as Italians denominate them; and indeed they were beauteous as that rosy fruit in the garden of the daughters of Hesperus, "beyond the red sand drift where is the palace of Zeus."[76] As a catamite, he was ordinarily relegated to the lower place, *Chu Jen Hsia Feng* 居人下風, and was glad to assume with me the room of the giver, instead of the receiver! I imagine that his other clients refused for themselves the passive pleasuring, regarding it as beneath their dignity.

However, "all these perfections come to an end," as the Psalmist says, "but thy commandment is exceeding broad." I could not lose him yet; dear night, delay: like Joshua's moon in Ajalon.[77]

Before sleeping the sleep of the just (or should it not be the sleep of the carnally minded) Cassia and I performed ablutions in scented medicated waters and cleansed *nos fondements et nos parties sexuelles*[78] from taint of impurity; then we lay down to rest.

Tired out, but we were young and: "*La giovanezza si ricupera presto dagle conseguenze di sua volupta*"[79] we passed, bosom to bosom, the most golden of nights.

When sated, as Homer says, of love and bed with returning dawn which came alas! too soon for us, announcing the end of our golden sodality, we re-enacted the joys of the evening before with the exception of reciprocal flagellation which Cassia preferred to postpone to a more convenient season, as in fact we were both too much bruised for repetition at the moment; *la gamme réciproque, les feuilles de rose* (cinnamon leaves) *mutuellement appliquées* on proctodaeum *et les parties adjacentes*, the lewd dalliance, *le commerce sexuel*, the ineffable lock, *ce bonheur indescriptible et sans fin, les manoeuvres labiales de part et d'autre, tout en se livrant à la jouissance inouïe avec frénésie*.[80] Cassia interpolated our rejoicings with

---

74 **Backhouse:** *Epistl. Cor.* II. 12.
75 Receive a flogging.
76 Euripides.
77 **Backhouse:** Vide *Josue* X. XII. 13, "Move not, O moon, toward the valley of Ajalon."
78 Anuses and sexual parts.
79 **Backhouse:** D'Annunzio, *Il Trionfo della Morte* ['Youth recovers quickly from the consequences of its sensual pleasure". The correct quotation is " . . . *profondi sonni ristoratori che nella giovinezza seguono una notte di voluttà*'].
80 The reciprocal game, the rose leaves mutually applied on the anus and the adjacent parts . . . the sexual habits . . . This unlimited and inexpressible happiness, the labial manoeuvres of both partners, while giving in to incredible pleasure with frenzy.

apposite and epigrammatic comments, his high ardour remained unabated: his thick set voluminous sexuality, pledge of undying love, was *inassouvie*[81] even as Messalina's "vulva" of old; while I (albeit somewhat less richly endowed) was scarcely less libidinous, equally *en proie à ces passions communément (au dire des Pères) dites ignobles et déshonorantes* but I was verily *tout feu d'un embrasement de convoitise*,[82] *Wei So Yü Wei* 爲所欲爲, fulfilling the measure of my desire, which Paul flays in his first epistle to the Romans: "men with men working that which is unseemly and receiving in themselves *la récompense de leur égarement qui leur fut due*."[83]

Michel Ange, that lover of ideal male beauty, he who wrote a century of sonnets to his beloved "lord", in speaking of the human form divine said that the lines of the posterior were the most alluring portion of the frame. Socrates, as Plato tells us, one day caught a glimpse of Charmides' secret parts (the folds of the robe worn by the Athenian youth having opened accidentally and disclosed the hidden wonder within) and almost fainted from emotion. Could the Hellene, the most perfect of men, and that Master spirit that was Buonarotti, have seen Cassia's goodly, delectable body, I can imagine that they too, even they, in the diviner air ("the purer air which Plato trod") in which they moved and had their being, would have been conscious of an adoration which should cause them to hush and bless themselves with silence, even as frail mortals such as I, *moi qui parle*.[84]

I do not know whether I am of the type known in the gay quarters of Paris as *renifleurs*,[85] who, they say, *nascuntur, non fiunt*:[86] but, as candour is the order of the day, I confess that the nozzling of Cassia's secret parts, behind and before, in particular the former, gave to me the most unmixed pleasure. "Tis true, tis pity: pity tis, tis true!" And certainly Cassia's sensations were identical with mine, for (*je me fais fort de dire*)[87] he was madly in love with me, few claims though I might appear to possess for this signal honour; at any rate as I today recall my wasted youth, even if not wholly lacking a certain personal charm.

Naturally, I presented Cassia, beside the brothel fees, with a rich present which he was genuinely most loth to accept.

The Psalmist says that the Most High created man to be a "little lower than the angels." Well! if it be so, it does not say much for the angels' morals.

In what my *rapports* with Cassia consisted has now been unblushingly revealed to the reader, for better or worse. I am fain to confess that I often found myself thereafter in the "Hall of Chaste Joys" and was

---

81 Unsatisfied.
82 Part of those passions usually qualified (by the Fathers) as atrocious and dishonourable ... burning with a compulsive fire.
83 The deserved fruits of their deviation.
84 I who speak.
85 Sniffers.
86 "Are born, not made"; possibly a play on the early Christian writer Tertullian's *"Fiunt, non nascuntur Christiani"*, Christians are made, not born (*Apologeticum* XVIII.4) or the popular aphorism *"Poeta nascitur, non fit"*, a poet is born, not made.
87 I can ascertain.

ever happy in Cassia Flower's delicious vicinity (sweet as new buds in spring). My servants certainly thought me a depraved rake, for, of course, they learned where I was repairing and had the impudence to demand a commission! I think they deemed me a *relaps*, a "dog returning to his own vomit again".

Je me flatte[88] that I was decidedly popular at the "Hall of Chaste Pleasures", partly, perhaps, due to the "novelty" (as Mr. Tsai Mu had remarked) of a foreign devil who had assimilated Chinese or Manchu proclivities – in a different sense from Horace's "*Graecia capta ferum victorem cepit et inde*"[89] . . . . for China was not annexed by the European "devils" nor were the latter conquerors, but I was in some ways *plus royaliste que le roi*[90] and perhaps am still. I became acquainted with, I think, all the pleasing fraternity of catamites (except, as regards Cassia, where the relations were scarcely *platonique pas précisément*)[91] in a strictly platonic sense. They all told me that they were specially enjoined to control any tendency to an orgasm when being "pleasured" by clients. As Cassia artlessly remarked (he reminded me of Chin Sheng-t'an's 金聖歎 famous hero, the fair Pao Yü 寶玉):[92] "it is often rather difficult and," added he, "impossible if there is affinity so strong as between you and me!" It seemed that the clients were all men of high place or rank; no doubt the monthly receipts ran into many thousand Taels; several imperial princes were regular visitors. Prince Tuan 端, the Boxer leader, was a welcome guest of the establishment despite his truculent manners and *crapulerie outrée*;[93] Duke Lan told me, if I met his elder brother there, not to be discomposed because of his anti-foreign leanings, and in fact the Duke mentioned meeting me (in equivocal circumstances) apparently to most of his relatives so that I fear the reputation of my country (of which I was an unworthy type) must have suffered, *I Lo Ch'ien Chang* 一落千場, 10,000 feet at one drop; "what a falling off was there!" However, the imperial clan was so "steeped", as Oscar Wilde would have said, in association *vis à vis mares* (males) (as Suetonius remarks of Galba) that it was a case of Mencius' saying: "Soldiers who run (like the brave British) 50 paces have no cause to mock those who run 100 paces", each and all being "tarred with the same brush", "the black crow alighting on the black hog's back", *Lao Kua Lo Tsai Chu Shen Shang* 老鴰落在豬身上.

Cassia was as beautiful as Praxiteles, Apollo at Olympia, perfect as Charmides in Socrates' sight. He was in his twentieth year and sexually most passionate and as impetuous as *la foudre du ciel*.[94] He told me that

---

88 I flatter myself.
89 **Backhouse:** *Ars Poetica* ["Captive Greece took captive her fierce conqueror and thence (introduced her arts into rude Latium)", which is actually from *Epistles* II.1].
90 More of a royalist than the king.
91 Not precisely platonic.
92 Backhouse seems to be confused here. Chin Sheng-t'an (1608-61) was a scholar living around the time of the fall of the Ming Dynasty who, with many others declined to serve the Ch'ing. Proud, eccentric and learned, he wrote critical works on the many Chinese classics and was executed during the Shun Chih period. Chia Pao Yü is a character in *Dream of the Red Chamber*, written well after Chin's death.
93 Outrageous misdeeds.
94 Lightning from the sky.

he liked Lan personally but had no amorous feelings in his regard. I should think Lan was madly enamoured of Cassia; but, as I have said, he never displayed any jealousy (*Ch'ih Ts'u* 吃醋 eat vinegar) toward me. Cassia was prone to what in Paris used to be called (and perhaps is still, except that there are now no English there) "English Vice", that is, he delighted in bizarre *parerga* or side-shows. To me Masochismus and Sadismus are alike of equally attractive meaning, the idea of *fouaillées*[95] as a diversion presenting unparalleled zest; it is passing strange that one who needed no sexual stimulation should have wished thus to quicken passions which were already in the stage of *Se Yü K'ang Chin* 色慾亢進, i.e. at the apex and culmination of desire, very far from dormant (like a certain peerage which is in abeyance, but to which I have a claim).

It was pleasing to observe the perfect harmony that seemed to exist in our little community (not that I have right to use the pronoun our): when I recalled my school days at Winchester, where the prevailing morals would have been most displeasing to Lot of Sodom or to the young angels who graciously called upon him,[96] I remember how there was almost perennial friction between the reigning catamites and the "Autumn fans" (*Ch'iu Shan* 秋扇, who had outlasted their attractions). I do not recall any bloodshed resulting from rivalry (except in one instance, for the British "ruling" classes are in no sense a fighting race, being degenerate like the Manchus to the backbone) but there was unceasing *mesquinerie*[97] and wanton suggestion, at which the Briton (who often runs away in battle) is past master and adept, for the tongue (quicker than a team of four horses, as Confucius says) with him, is mightier than the sword.

Cassia, who probably hyperbolized slightly, one day quoted to me Po Chü-yi's 白居易 lovely lines from the "Ode of Perpetual Wrong" *Ch'ang Hen Ko* 長恨歌, where T'ang Ming Huang 唐明皇 and his adored concubine, Yang Kuei Fei 楊貴妃, say to one another "*T'ien Shang Yüan Tso Pi I Niao, Ti Shang Yüan Tso Lien Li Chih* 天上願作比翼鳥地上願作連理枝[98] – Above in the air we would fain be as the twin birds of inseparable wing; on earth we would fain be as the two-forked branch;" but I would gladly believe that he was genuinely attached to one whose qualities were hitherto out of his ken (I do not mean to imply that there was anything outstanding in me, but only something unfamiliar). He told to me a curious story of the great empress which I can unhesitatingly believe from my own knowledge – but that is another story and has nothing to do with this story, though it shall be told in its own place and time. The chief eunuch, who was intimate with Tsai Mu, the owner of the "Resort", called at the time of the *coup d'état* in September 1898; when one would

---

95 Flagellations.
96 **Backhouse:** Voir *Genèse*, XIX, Versets 1-23, "things written for our learning" as Henry VIII's heretic archbishop of Canterbury puts it.
97 Pettiness.
98 Should read "*Tsai T'ian Yüan Tso Pi I Niao, Tsai Ti Yüan Wei Lian Li Chih* 在天願作比翼鳥在地願爲連理枝".

have thought that Tz'u Hsi 慈禧 had other preoccupations than amorous oyance, to command Cassia's presence in the Chung Hai 中海, where the Old Buddha was then staying, having probably heard of the beautiful boy from Duke Lan. Naturally he obeyed the order, feeling rather anxious at what might there befall (for visits to the empress were only to be paid, as I was later to learn, in fear and trembling). The empress gave to him rich wines and dainty refreshments, as she did on another occasion to the ill-starred Yin Liu[99] 陰劉. Liu exhibited his personal attractions to the empress and is said to have caressed her. But he did not leave the palace alive. However that may be (and it is undoubtedly so), Cassia seems to have pleased the erotic old lady; was it perchance a great desire begot in strong despair, a great despair cast out by strong desire?[100] Where was Junglu 榮祿 at the time, I wonder.

When brought into the presence of Tz'u Hsi and expected to exhibit the fullness of his perfect charms, he was overpowered (he said) by the august proximity, and the necessary incentive founded on desire and built up on passion was wanting in order to display the abounding plenitude of his most active and Brobdingnagian[101] sexuality, "strong as iron, firmer than lacquer" (Wang Wei's 王維 poems). She made him undress before her and bade him touch her sacred person in amorous dalliance. But Li Lien-ying[102] 李蓮英 told me three years later that the Old Buddha had revelled in the libidinous spectacle, even though Cassia's fear of that august despot dame prevented the complete revelation of his goodly virility, as a consummation devoutly to be wished by Her Majesty. She was fain, said Li (and in fact Cassia had told me the same thing), to handle his large, shapely *membrum virile* and *Hodensack*[103] as a toy of great price, a jewel *qui n'avait point son semblable*[104] (I recount the fact, without criticising the deed which later I, even I, was to rival). After completion, she ordered Li Lien-ying (who was not far off) to shower upon him lavish gifts (affluent fortune indeed emptied wide her horn) as well as a large sum of money; thus he escaped unscathed. "So far," added he, "she has not sent for me again: she frightened me despite her wonderful charm and grace." Later I was myself to see her as she was, alike in her magnificent anger and in her alluring attraction that passeth the wit of man, like Shakspere's Cleopatra "I have imperial longings in me".

It is not strictly germane to the present essay and may be referred to in another excursion on *moeurs mandchoues*,[105] but there is no doubt that the T'ung Chih 同治 emperor used to visit incognito the brothels of the gay

---

99 **Backhouse:** Liu of the "uncertain" sex, the beautiful pastry cook, fair but *infelix* [barren], one of those called *Erh I Tzu* 二疑子, hermaphrodite or twofold doubts; Swinburne's "Two loves at either blossom of the breast, and both are fire upon the amorous air" (in reference to the Louvre painting). Some say that his nickname *Yin* 陰 was due to his enormous penis, just as the suppositious father of the First Emperor was known as *Ta Yin Jen* 大陰人, "large-tooled".

100 **Backhouse:** Swinburne.

101 "Gigantic", from the land of the giants, Brobdingnag, in Jonathan Swift's *Gulliver's Travels*.

102 Chief Eunuch under Empress Dowager Tz'u Hsi from 1869 to 1908.

103 Scrotum.

104 Without equal.

105 Manchu mores.

quarter, under the pseudonym of Wild Dalliance Seeker (Yeh Yeh Yu Jen 野冶遊人) and there contracted the syphilis of which he died. That Tz'u Hsi followed (without knowing it) the example set 1,850 years before of the empress Messalina who, as Juvenal tells us, in his fourth satira, disguised with false hair of a different hue from her own, nightly visited the Suburra and received a sequence of clients, till, still unsated of lust and "with swelling vulva, she must needs wend her way back to Claudius' imperial couch reeking with the odour of the stews", that the Old Buddha, I say, made erotic excursions outside the palace, I have the best reason for knowing, although there was no difficulty in arranging rendezvous, like that of Cassia, in the "Profound Seclusion of the Forbidden City" or at Wan Shou Shan[106] 萬壽山. But a woman's whims are as changing as the tides.

Cassia told me that the Manchus, mostly prominent men or scions of a decadent nobility, did not resent a European having relations with him, not only because I was personally sympathetic and (if I may say so) a gentleman, but also owing to the Manchus in these respects being devoid of race prejudice. (It is curious that Chinese, with rare exceptions, were not welcome at the Hall of Chaste Pleasures). Had the brothel been exclusively a Chinese, not Manchu, concern, he doubted if a European, however well introduced, could be allowed to set foot in the precincts, the Chinese (whom he rudely called *Mantzu*[107] 蠻子 as was the custom of the time) regarding the white race as malodorous and unclean and would consider sexual contact as a defilement rendering further *commerce charnel* with his own compatriots (did they know) *dérogeant*.[108] The same prejudice against *den Geruch der Europäer*[109] prevails in Japan; and I have heard say (in fact, read in a *Fachzeitung* article by a Japanese physician) that the presence of men of Aryan race in a room where Japanese are assembled pollutes the atmosphere, so that the Europeans' departure is the signal for opening windows and purifying the air befouled by their alien environment and effluvium.

In the autumn of 1899, Mr. Tsai Mu, with whom I had established a pleasant amity, granted to me permission, as an unusual favour, to take Cassia home with me (*Ch'u T'iao Tzu*[110] 出條子), on the understanding that he should return next morning, thus obtaining an *exeat*[111] and a salutary change. Everyone who saw him was attracted by his charm, for he had a face made for the luring and the love of man. My servants, although quite alien to any pederastic instincts, called him Living God, *Huo Shen* 活神, and he was indeed an Amour, a Cupid, as beautiful as the morning star or as Hadrian's Greek favourite, the giton Antinous. Naturally, I had to pay to the Hall of Chaste Pleasures the prescribed Taels 100 fee and was at pains to make sure that Duke Lan was not expected that evening; for I did not wish to raise a storm of jealousy over the "fair

---

106 "Longevity Hill", part of the Summer Palace.
107 "Barbarians", a contemptuous term applied to southerners by northerners since ancient times.
108 Sexual commerce . . . a defilement.
109 "The Smell of Europeans", title of a 1903 article by Japanese anatomist Adachi Buntaro.
110 A summons for prostitutes.
111 "Let him leave", used in English public schools and universities for permission for absence.

who caused his care".[112] I made use, however, of Duke Lan's name with the local *T'ing Erh* 廳兒 or police station, he being one of the three highest officials of the Banner Gendarmerie; because I found that the presence of a celebrated mignon[113] in my house might have the same effect, as I have already hinted, that Lot's comely celestial visitants had upon the citizens of Sodom. "Bring them out hither that we may know them," saith *l'Ecriture* (*Genèse* XIX). After a golden night in Cassia's adorable companionship (after 44 years why can I not restrain my pen in writing of him?), I escorted him back to his daily vocation in my Peking cart, he sitting with curtains drawn inside and I on the space in front of the shafts; thus screening him from the squint of lust or glare of malice, the former, owing to the fatal star of his beauty making it so hard to save a moth from the fire in view of his fame as the leading *luron*[114] of the day, the latter to avoid the possibility of some attack on the cart with an idea of kidnapping him by rivals or enemies of Tsai Mu, whose unparalleled success caused jealousy, especially as imperial clansmen were not legitimately entitled to engage in enterprises of a dubious nature, and the censors were always glad of a chance to impeach members of the ruling house, so as to win notoriety. We arrived safely at our destination and Cassia seemed thoroughly to have enjoyed his *randonnée*:[115] "The plum and the cherry blossom need no advertisement; a path is trod toward them by the steps of their admirers."

I met Duke Lan again on several occasions and there was nothing but cordiality on his part; while Tsai Mu and I became good friends, especially as I was a fairly profitable client. Cassia assured me that he was well treated by his patron and allowed to retain all private fees, so that he had saved some Taels 6,000 and looked forward to marrying a year or two later. Tsai Mu was a poet and literate, while Cassia was distinctly well read; in fact all the boys whom I saw impressed me as being, apart from their morality which is not a criterion (other than relatively so), of a superior type.

Cassia assured me that women did not appeal sexually to his sentiments which were definitely limited to his own sex. "All the same, I should like to marry and to have an heir who would sacrifice to my manes[116] after death; but there would be no pleasure for me in the act of sex, merely[117] the desire to perpetuate my name to another generation", concluded Cassia.

It has been suggested to me – and I would gladly believe it if it connoted dear Cassia's happiness – that, as Tsai Mu was intimately associated with the Manchu Boxer leaders (in fact, the Grand Councillor Ch'i Hsiu 啓秀 who was decapitated in January 1901 by the Empress'

112 **Backhouse:** Dryden, "Alexander's Feast".
113 Favourite.
114 Entertainer.
115 Long walk.
116 Soul after death.
117 **Backhouse:** As St. Paul says, "*je me permets d'interpoler à ce point*" [I take the liberty to interpret at this point] for Cassia never heard of Saul of Tarsus "But if thou takest a wife, thou hast not sinned" and "for fear of fornication, let every man have his own wife" – *Cor* I. VII, 2nd 28.

order on the demand of the Powers, was *lui aussi*, a welcome *habitué*[118] of the Hall of Pleasures and a very courtly gentleman, anti-foreign or not, for after all he only did his imperial mistress' bidding), Ying Nien 英年 and Prince Chuang 莊 (each of them had to commit self-slaughter), Prince Tuan 端 and Duke Lan 瀾 besides others who were only deuter-agonists or *Hsiao Chüeh Erh*[119] 校爵兒, he would be assured of full protection during the noon-tide of Boxer madness from VI to VIII moons (June to August 1900); but, after the fall of the city, he may have left with Tuan and the rest to seek "fresh woods and pastures new" in Shensi 陝西, like James II at St. Germain by Le Roi Soleil's[120] grace. Cassia, being Tsai Mu's *Fidus Achates* and *le disciple bien aimé*,[121] may have accompanied his patron thither and ultimately have shared Duke Lan's "banishment" to Uramtsi in Turkestan, where he would have wanted for nothing and while participating in Lan's exile, felt less dreary, perhaps, than Ovid of old by Augustus' order on the inhospitable Euxine shore, "So mote it be, *Plût à Dieu*".[122] I have reason to believe that Lan still lives, an old man, in his remote retreat. When I watched him at his indecent diversions with dear little Cassia, I did not think him as shameless as he might appear to the reader of the episode touching his manoeuvres: it was not so much a conscious indecency as a desire to oblige that induced him to tolerate my presence, a sort of laudable *Mien Tzu*[123] 面子 toward his relation and my friend, old "Fu T'ing" 輔廷 (his courtesy name), Prince Ch'ing 慶. And I doubt if my proximity affected him in the least: it had no affinity with the filthily minded visitor in Paris, who loveth to divert himself as a *voyeur qui clame*[124] indecent spectacles artificially devised for his vulgar benefit.

I would fain add that, albeit I have employed very vulgar *T'u Hua*[125] 土話 regarding *les organes sexuels*, I am not unaware of the literary and elegant equivalents, but am quoting His Highness Duke Tsai Lan's decidedly homely vernacular. Hence, I hope that a Chinese literate will not think too badly of my morals nor of my want of *Wen Ya*[126] 文雅, especially where the very indecent passage from *Hung Lou Meng* 紅樓夢 is quoted. I am familiar with phrases such as *Yin-ching (king)* 陰莖, *Yin-ken* 陰根, *Yang-wu* 陽物, *Yü-king (ching)* 玉莖, *Yü-ken* 玉根, *Yü-heng* 玉緪, the long and straight rope of jade, with multitudinous other designations of the *membrum virile*, especially *Yü-keng* 御緪, the imperial cord, used by eunuchs and palace concubines of the Son of Heaven's imperial "tool".

Next year was the Keng Tzu 庚子, 26th year of Kuang Hsü 光緒, with the Boxer *émeute*[127] and the siege of the Legations. Much of the gay quarter

---

118 As well . . . regular.
119 Secondary actors.
120 The Sun King, Louis XIV.
121 "Faithful Achates" and "beloved disciple". Achates was the loyal companion of Aeneas in his journeys. He is given the epithet *"fidus"* only once (Virgil, *Aeneid* VI.156-9).
122 God's will.
123 Face; respect.
124 Voyeur who claims.
125 Local dialect; colloquial language.
126 Refinement.
127 Riot.

was burnt in June 1900, the fire having spread from a foreign drugstore which the Boxers had pillaged and burnt. I know not what happened to Tsai Mu and the rest: the house passed into other hands and became a female brothel and I never saw Cassia Flower again; although during the foreign occupation catamites were in large demand by the allied troops. He is gone with *les neiges d'antan*[128] but I hope that, long emancipated from his cabined existence as a catamite at the mercy of clients' whims, he is alive and perhaps occasionally thinks of the once young foreign devil who was so deeply attached to him. *Vanitas Vanitatum:*[129] if, as Homer makes Helen say, "it is not all a dream! (*ei pot eien ge*)".[130] When souls turn bodies and unite in the ineffable, the whole, rapture of the embodied soul; it may all be a mirage, an illusion of the senses: a vexing of soul and a vain desire, but still 'tis something to have lived for, something whereof the goodly memory shall survive, even in the dust of death: "Till the day breaks and the shadows flee away."

---

128 The snows of yesteryear (François Villon, *Ballade des dames du temps jadis*).
129 Vanity of vanities (*Ecclesiastes* I.2).
130 **Backhouse:** Ει ποτ εην γε [*Iliad* III.180].

CHAPTER II

THE BEGINNING OF A TIME

AFTER the departure of the Manchu Court on August 15, 1900, the Summer Palace was for a time in the charge of the Russian troops. By a conciliatory-like gesture worthy of Muscovy which greatly gratified the Empress, they were soon withdrawn from Peking and the Palace was then taken over by British and Italian detachments. Looting was still rearing its ugly head to disgrace the counterfeit Caucasian civilisation.[1] With the aid of trusty Manchus I caused the removal of bronzes, jades, porcelain, ivories, paintings, calligraphy, cloisonné, lacquer, tapestries, carpets (some 600 pieces in all) and about 25,000 volumes to a place of safety, not my own house, as I did not wish my name to appear, knowing as I do the inveterate, calumnious suspicions of my unctuous, hypocritical compatriots. Before removal from the Palace, this property was valued by curio experts at Taels 500,000; but it was really only a tentative estimate. It included one enormous block of jade most beautifully carved and dating from 1420 which was as dear to the empress as *la prunelle de ses yeux*,[2] whose return seemed to her a veritable gift of the gods by my most humble medium.

On the Court's return early in January 1902, I got into touch with the Chief Eunuch with the object of returning personally Her Majesty's property intact. Through the all-powerful Li Lien-ying 李蓮英, the eunuch aforesaid, Her Majesty graciously accorded to me the promise of an audience, when I was to deliver the collection at the entrance to the palace in the Forbidden City, the Ning Shou Kung 寧壽宮, or Palace of Peaceful Old Age, which had been the Ch'ien Lung 乾隆 retreat after abdication in 1796 till his death three years later. Today anyone can enter those once forbidden precincts, for the old order changeth, yielding place to new; but at that time, apart from receptions given by the Old Buddha to the diplomatic ladies as a sort of adroit feeler to gain their good graces (as she succeeded in doing), few Manchus or Chinese,

---

1   Backhouse's outrage is perhaps slightly disingenuous here, as a Feb. 1903 letter to *The Times* correspondent G.E. Morrison has him declaring: "I wish another chance of procuring furs such as we had after the siege could occur!"

2   The apple of her eye.

except women of the Household, eunuchs and favourites such as Junglu 榮祿, had set foot inside.

I was to attend, then, on a May morning just after Her Majesty's return from a visit to the Eastern Tombs; where twenty-two years later her hallowed remains, hearsed in death, were torn from their cerements and her sacred body, stark naked, covered with horrid black spots, hair dishevelled, her tiny features fully recognizable was exposed in front of the sacrificial hill to the gaze of the *profanum vulgus*.[3]

Special orders had been given to the Banner troops (in those days the police force was highly rudimentary and quite ineffective), through Grand Secretary Junglu himself, to allow to the long, long procession of porters and bearers right of way. It wound its serpentine trail into the Eastern gate of the Forbidden City, where it was met by Li Lien-ying himself who ticked off each package, I having already submitted an approximate *inventaire ou dénombrement (par écrit et par article) des biens;*[4] and none knew better than he (except Her Majesty herself) exactly of what the original collection consisted. Unhappily a few pieces (not many) had been stolen by the Russians or their Chinese interpreters. Naturally this unusual convoy attracted a good deal of attention; but the gendarmerie had forbidden press comment, although the Japanese owned *Shun T'ien Shih Pao*[5] 順天時報 did publish next day a short report as a *fait divers*[6] inaccurately adding that the properties had been brought down by imperial command from the Jehol palaces. Her Majesty had providentially made good choice of a day, as the foreign community was holding the spring races; and, so far as I know, not even the inquisitive and perfidious correspondent of the London *Times*[7] had wind of the matter, nor associated me, whom he regarded as his enemy, with part or lot in the transaction.

I followed in the wake of the procession not unprovided with an order on a "money-shop" outside the Cheng Yang Men 正陽門 (Ch'ien Men 前門) for Taels 500, say £80, as a peace offering to the Chief Eunuch. He most graciously came out to meet me at the gate which was the scene of most admired disorder, some 200 porters jostling each other and a large court staff attending the order of their chief as to the bestowal of the stuff. A contractor had arranged the coolie hire for Taels 200 which Her Majesty graciously reimbursed to me, besides adding a generous donation of her own to the men. With Li Lien-ying and myself at the head, we marched together from the main gate to the entrance of the Dowager's palace, perhaps 300 yards' distance. I had the Chief Eunuch's permission to leave my Peking cart inside the forbidden entrance, not knowing that before my departure Her Majesty was to confer upon me the brevet

---

3   Unholy crowd (Horace, *Odes* III.1).

4   Inventory or enumeration (in writing and articles) of properties.

5   *Shuntian Times*, a local newspaper.

6   News in brief.

7   G.E. Morrison (1862-1920), famous Australian travel writer and journalist, who used Backhouse as an unpaid translator and informant during the period discussed in this book. He later had a falling out with Backhouse when the latter began writing with Morrison's rival at *The Times*, J.O.P. Bland. Morrison later became one of the first to accuse Backhouse of being a fraud.

of a Board President, or *Shang Shu* 尚書, the First Button of official rank (jewelled, not coral), a hereditary II class nobility, the coveted twin-eyed peacock's feather, a set of court spring and autumn robes which were decidedly on the small side for my inches, and a sable robe with yellow riding jacket, the coveted privilege (of which I never availed myself) of riding on horseback across the Forbidden City (*Ch'ao Chung Ch'i Ma* 朝中騎馬), a special gold tablet, three inches by two, with the ideographs "*Huang T'ai Hou T'ê En*" 皇太后特恩 (by Her Majesty the Empress Dowager's special favour) which would gain my admittance at any hour at the gate of all the palaces (Forbidden City, Winter and Summer Palaces) when Her Majesty might happen to be in residence, besides a gold *Ju Yi*[8] 如意, weighing 28 ounces and a fine collection of books now in a European library,[9] a painting by Her Majesty's own hand and a manuscript history of the Yehonala clan; finally, she graciously accorded to my heir the highly coveted rank of a V Class metropolitan official, which is quite distinct from the V Button of official rank, the latter being no particular favour.

Before announcing our arrival to Her Majesty the Chief Eunuch led me into his private quarters, while his coadjutor was busy with the opening up of the cases. Favourite of the Empress Dowager and perhaps the best hated man in the empire, Li Lien-ying impressed me not unfavourably; his features were quite unhandsome and, like the generality of eunuchs, flabby and wrinkled: to me it seemed quite a good face, perhaps belying his reputation. He spoke with the falsetto tones of the *castrato*, talking in the colloquial with an accent that was not wholly pure Pekingese. In answer to my query, he told me that he was 53. He was quite simply dressed in a spring robe of unlined "*Mo Pen*" 幕本, black satin and a light riding jacket of very dark purple. He had no official rank which the dynastic House Law denied to eunuchs, unlike the Ming 明 and previous dynasties.

Speaking of the Boxers, he frankly confessed that he had believed in their magical powers and thought that the failure of the enterprise was due to their having allowed sordid love of gain to interfere with the "hallowed" (!) purpose of their mission (presumably the massacre of foreign devils). Some good had come out of the movement and of the very uncomfortable exile of the empress and himself in Shensi 陝西, in that foreign "barbarian" states had at last recognized Her Majesty's regency and were showing toward her proper respect.

"She is looking forward to receiving her lost property back from you," he said, "and I can assure you that you will find her most magnanimous and grateful. You are like the nenuphar emerging from the slime (*Ni Chung Lien*[10] 泥中蓮), one honest man among so many looting and murderous Europeans and Americans, rare as the morning star which

---

8   The "As you wish" sceptre, a symbol of the Buddha.
9   The Bodleian at Oxford, to which Backhouse did indeed make a significant donation.
10 The image of the lotus (nenuphar) emerging from the mud is usually symbolic of the Buddha living unsullied in the impure world.

quivers, a point, on the bright verge of dawn. By the way, your foreign officials seem singularly dense in regard to etiquette. Can you believe me that at the audience to the Diplomatic Corps none of the Ministers (except the Japanese and Russian) left the customary fees to the palace inmates? Their lapse of manners might be explained away on the ground that it was an official audience; but what is one to say of the omission of the foreign women, when invited to *déjeuner*[11] here, to leave the regular fees? Ten nations were represented, and the sum of Taels 1,000 per country would have been the least to which I was entitled. None gave a single "red cash" (again except the Japanese and Russians) and one or two of the women actually had the effrontery to go off with several pieces of crockery! I asked one of them if I should send a vase she stole to the Legation for her. Mencius says: 'How shall I argue with a beast?' and really no comment on such unspeakable behaviour is called for. When the *Ta Kung Chu* 大公主 (Crown Princess specially so created, daughter of Prince Kung 恭) called on the Legations, she left Taels 5,000 for the various Chinese staffs, in order to shame your vulgar and discourteous women."

Li told me that Her Majesty was most interested in Queen Victoria's late gillie, John Brown; and asked me whether he was "cut off from the family" like himself. When I informed him that, to the best of my belief, he was a normal male, the chief eunuch expressed astonishment and asked why Parliament did not intervene in the interest of the Royal Blood. I did not deem it expedient to tell him how the late Queen had been reviled in the streets of Edinburgh as Mrs. John Brown. Truly, we live in a whispering gallery and Edward VII's private and decidedly undomestic life seemed to be as familiar to the Court of Peking as the gossip, mostly apocryphal, regarding Yehonala was to the foreign community in China. Li enjoyed his opium pipe and regaled me with delectable tea, while putting to me innumerable questions respecting the siege and the misdoings of the European and American contingents.

By this time, most of the cases had been unpacked and their contents were suggestive of an open-air exhibition; so Li said the time had come to intimate to Her Majesty that we were awaiting Her good pleasure. He went in with a pair of jade bowls to show to Her Majesty some tangible proof of her retrieved property and emerged almost at once with a broad smile: "The Old Ancestress is much inspirited by this news and will see you at once. Do not be uneasy but follow me; you will find Her the very incarnation of benevolence, the true Goddess of Mercy, reborn into the world of men, and not disdaining this mundane dust."

Passing the Huang Chi Tien 皇極殿, or Hall of Imperial Heaven's Supremacy where Ch'ien Lung had once received his ministers after abdication and which, six years from now, had to be the place of Lying in State for the empress' catafalque pending her sepulture one year later, we entered the second court and were before the door of the Yang Hsing Tien 養性殿, Reception Chamber. Li hurried ahead and kneeling before

---

11   Lunch.

the Old Buddha announced that the "foreign servant" *Wai Ch'en* 外臣 was without. I heard a falsetto voice: "Bring him in at once", and I was in the presence of the Empress. Genuflecting on one knee, I prepared to prostrate myself thrice in accord with etiquette, but she stopped me: "You are excused ceremony. Come forward and let me thank you for your honesty."

"Your servant from a far land (*Yüan Ch'en* 遠臣) presents his humble duty and thanks for your Majesty's bounty. Honesty is the best policy, *Kung Tao Wei Shang Ts'ê* 公道爲上策, but it is a bad reason for being honest."

This rather trite sally of mine greatly amused the Empress and her attendants; she laughed loudly, saying: "Virtue is its own reward, but I am going to try and make it pay in a material sense."

"*Lao Fo Yeh Ti En* 老佛爺的恩, by the grace of the Old Buddha", said Li and I simultaneously.

A very goodlooking *échanson*,[12] who was replenishing the Empress' tea cup and relighting her cigarette, said rather familiarly: "Why, that's the young looking 'devil' to whom Your Majesty spoke the other day, after your burning incense at the God of War's shrine. You remember? I was standing by in the temple court."

"Of course," said the Old Buddha, "I thought I knew your face. You recollect that I waved to the Spanish Minister's wife who was standing next to you on the top of the wall and asked after her daughter. You called back: 'By Your Majesty's favour, she is quite well'. And then I stood there with my opera glass and waved my handkerchief at you all. By the way, Junglu said that it was beneath my dignity to stand there so long after a religious ceremony like that of sacrifice to Kuan Ti[13] 關帝. Tell me, what would your Queen Victoria have done in my place?"

"She would perhaps have bowed to any diplomats or their families, but she would not have been as gracious as Your Majesty in acknowledging our homage. To us all it seemed to confer upon Your Majesty an additional dignity, and your servant is especially honoured that Your Majesty should remember him among so many foreign vassals of Your Majesty all intent upon gazing at the 'Benevolent Countenance'." At this point, the three Pekingese all started vociferous barking, and Her Majesty scolded them in a jocular way. How shall I describe Her Majesty? Many abler pens than mine have (from the feminine side) written about her appearance, however inaccurate their presentment of her character; pictures are familiar to the public in scores, and the external features of her physiognomy. She was wearing that day an unlined robe of flaming scarlet with a design of phoenixes, the symbol of empresshood, alternating with cranes, the symbol of long life; this dress was covered with *bouillonnés de tulle*[14] of the same shade printed with tufts of *Lan Hua* 蘭花

---

12   Cupbearer.
13   The God of War.
14   Gossamer overskirt.

or orchids. She wore over it a deep bronze-coloured jacket in the *Shou*[15] 壽 character design and had a pearl necklace of very fine orient. Among her many rings was a lovely ruby and emerald one which, I should think, hailed from the Rue de la Paix.[16] Little thought I that I should one day behold her desiccated, naked corpse in the blistering July sun: *Expende Hannibalem*[17] and "Imperial Caesar dead and turned to clay". Another very large black pearl had an aluminum setting which contrasted happily with a diamond of unusual pinkish hue which she wore on her third finger. In conformity with fashion, her nails were allowed to grow: two were encased in gold protectors and cannot have been under three inches long, probably more. She wore a profusion of jade bracelets, all of rare beauty, and graciously presented me with two "for your wife from me". On my explaining that I was still unmarried, she asked me (as I expected she would do) the reason.

"I had hoped to marry, Your Majesty, but the match was broken off."

"You are not the only person," said the Empress pensively, "whose happiness has been shortened by that fate which never lets us be, lord above lords and god behind the gods." (Was she thinking of her own betrothal to Junglu?) "But you are young and when you do marry, give to your bride these bracelets and say to her that the Empress Dowager liked you because you were unlike other foreigners she had seen."

"Your Majesty's bounty is lofty as heaven, and earth is not deep enough for me to conceal my unworthiness, *Feng Shang Tzu T'ien Kan K'uei Wu Ti* 奉賞自天感愧無地."

The Old Buddha laughed: "I see you have all our hackneyed compliments and shibboleths by heart. But I suppose your English language is equally provided?"

I thought of the official: "I have the honour to be, Sir, your most obedient servant" and similar hollow formulae, and replied: "We have plenty of sonorous platitudes in English and other European tongues, Your Majesty, but your servant's gratitude is as immutable as the hills and wholly unfeigned."

The Empress whose face was heavily powdered but not, of course, rouged owing to widows eschewing red cosmetics, was seated on a low chair of red lacquer; she told me that she was of the same height (I think 4 feet 11) as Queen Victoria whom she greatly admired. She looked many inches taller than her actual stature, because her beautiful hair was dressed in the then Manchu fashion on parallel silk covered frames heavily padded with thick paper and with leather foundation, several inches high. She was wearing the so-called "flowerpot shaped shoes" which were mounted on a sort of wooden tapering rest rising at least four inches from the ground. As she seldom walked, I presume that they were less uncomfortable than they looked.

---

15 Longevity.
16 An extremely posh street in Paris, home to many upscale jewellers in this era.
17 Weigh (the dust of) Hannibal (Juvenal, *Satires* X.147).

At first sight, the Old Buddha gave to one the impression of a dear, good-natured, elderly lady who wished to look juvenile, kind-hearted to a fault, fond of gossip, perhaps a little *médisante*,[18] very anxious to win others' good opinion and inclined to be touchy. But, as one listened to her conversation, now and then the expression of her eyes completely changed as she alluded to some person or some incident which had caused umbrage, those eyes which could fascinate and terrify, that Medusa-like stare which had almost petrified a Tung Fu-hsiang[19] 董福祥 when he attended unbidden in the room where I now was, to demand the execution of Junglu for high treason, or the horde of Boxers who had burst in one July morning and disturbed the Empress Dowager as she was painting flowers on silk in a design after the bamboo ideograph, *Chu* 竹. It was the basilisk glance before which China's greatest men had quailed, even her nearest and dearest Junglu himself. She exhibited this phase of her complicated temperament when she upbraided the rudeness and want of tact of the foreign women at her reception. One of them, said she, an Austrian, told me that she was wearing a medal given to her by Franz Josef himself for her part in the defence of the Legations against "Your Majesty's troops". Another, an American, had asked as a souvenir the bowl which Her Majesty was using. When the Empress graciously ordered it to be wrapt in a cover of imperial apricot silk and given to her, this lady had the effrontery to say: "Is not a pair of bowls more usual?"

The Empress then remarked: "Would you not like the whole set?" which apparently, much to the chief eunuch's delight, acted as an effective snub.

Even more angry was she when she told me of her present to the foreign children of gold roubles and 20 Mark pieces with some Carolus 5 dollar coins; all those, except those given to Japanese and Russian children, were returned next day through the Foreign Office, as the Ministers thought it "beneath their dignity" to accept presents from the Empress. Speaking with an "off with his head" expression: "How dare they insult me and refuse my gifts? Would they have acted so to the empress of Russia at Tsarskoe Selo or to Queen Victoria?"

I tried to make some excuse, such as that the diplomatic corps did not wish the children to be spoiled by over-indulgence, but could see that Her Majesty thought the slight was wilful and intended as a covert reminder of the Boxer year.

Then the Empress asked me what foreign nations thought about her personality. "I know that they say I am a Cantonese slave girl by birth; Cantonese indeed!" laughed the Old Buddha in a voice indicative of temper which seemed greatly to frighten the attendant eunuch, familiar with the vagaries of his great mistress.

---

18 Slanderous.
19 Muslim general in command of the Kansu soldiers during the Boxer uprising (1900). His story is recounted in Ch'ing-shan's infamous diary in Bland and Backhouse's *China under the Empress Dowager*.

I replied: "European nations regard Your Majesty as a unique person-age, *Ch'ien Ku I Jen* 千古一人, a feminine Yao 堯, and Shun 舜 (*Nü Chung Chih Yao Shun* 女中之堯舜) or as we might say a feminine Augustus or Charles the Great, a model of empresshood and motherhood, queenly as a woman and womanly as a queen."

The Old Buddha seemed gratified: "I am afraid that *vous brodez un peu,*[20] do you not?"

"No, Madame, they do indeed admire your strong personality: apart from the Sage himself and perhaps Li Hung-chang[21] 李鴻章, it is of Your Majesty that they think when China comes upon the *tapis.*"[22]

"I see," said Her Majesty, "but what do they think of my share in the Boxer movement?"

This rather embarrassing question found me at a loss for an appro-priate and more or less truthful reply. But before I had had time to com-pose the answer, she said: "I know: it was my guilt. I am to blame, *Lai Wo; Wo Ti Tsui* 賴我, 我的罪. But you foreigners brought it upon your-selves by demanding my abdication and now, as you see, the Powers feel that I am indispensable, so in a way I was justified in opposing them as I did.

"During the attack on your Legations, I sent water-melons, ice and cakes for the besieged. What did the foreigners say?"

"Some of them, including myself, were very grateful to Your Majesty; but many imagined that the sweet-meats were poisoned and feared to partake of them."

"How suspicious," said Her Majesty, "and how typical of foreign be-haviour towards China. Perhaps they judged us, and in particular my-self, by what they would have done in similar circumstances."

"I think," ventured I, "that the western mind is sadly stereotyped and inflexible and that, once an idea gets into the head of a European, he or she is unable to eradicate it. People thought that Your Majesty favoured the Boxers and could not realize that your only motive was kindness of heart and conveyed no political connotation."

"They told me," continued the Old Buddha, "that one of the besieged 'devils' went mad and was found roaming the streets and asking for mercy."

"Yes, Your Majesty, it was a Norwegian missionary who became de-mented and everyone was grateful to Your Majesty for ordering Junglu to send him back unhurt."

"It was like a nightmare," said the Empress, "for me to live through these two months, cooped up here in the Forbidden City like a frog at the bottom of a well and hearing different reports every day. You foreigners had a gun which made a most exasperating noise and kept me awake during my siesta."

---

20 You embellishing slightly.
21 Li Hung-chang (1823-1901), Chinese statesman and diplomat best known for negotiating the high-ly unfavourable (for China) terms of surrender that concluded the First Sino-Japanese War.
22 Literally "carpet", i.e. is discussed.

"It was a makeshift, Your Majesty, and would have been useless as a weapon."

"Now tell me about the Summer Palace during the foreign occupation. I heard that an Italian officer had slept in my bedroom and caused a ribald inscription to be inscribed on the wall. What was it?"

I replied with some hesitation: "My homage to Your Imperial Majesty and apologies for occupying your bed. Alas! that I must occupy it alone without your company."

The Old Buddha did not seem displeased. "Well, well," she observed, "boys will be boys. Let me hope he is at home now and contented with his wife or sweetheart. But he would hardly have dared to scribble such an inscription in his own Queen's bedchamber. However, the foreign troops behaved better than when they burnt down the Yüan Ming Yüan[23] 圓明園, which was an act of senseless vengeance and broke the emperor's heart. Fan Kuo-liang 范國良 (Mgr Favier)[24] told me that you British were to blame and that the act was quite contrary to the wishes of the French Commander in Chief.

"I have a letter from the Emperor of Russia which Li Lien-ying will bring. Please translate it for me; I cannot trust the versions that Prince Ch'ing 慶 brings to me. By the way, do you know him?"

"Yes, Your Majesty, His Highness has always been kind in receiving me."

"Did you ever hear him give a definite opinion on any subject? I never did, though I have known him over 40 years. He is like the rat which does not know whether to leave his hole or to return to it: 'Shu Shou Liang Tuan' 鼠頭兩端."

"As the English poet says, Your Majesty," replied I, "letting 'I dare not' wait open 'I would', like the poor cat i' the adage."[25]

"Yes," said Her Majesty, "the ideas of mankind are alike, despite geographical frontiers."

Li Lien-ying now came in with the letter which ran:

Tsarskoe Selo, March 1902.

Good Friend and Deeply Honoured Aunt,

I was happy to learn of your return to your Capital and sympathised with you during your absence from Peking. As you know, I have always been your friend and it was by my initiative that the concert of Europe decided to recognize Your Majesty's Regency *de jure* as well as *de facto*. Our empires share a common frontier, and I trust that the relations already happily

---

23 Better known as the "Old Summer Palace", destroyed in 1860 by British and French soldiers during the Second Opium War (1856-60).

24 Bishop Alphonse Favier (1837-1905), Catholic missionary who spent forty years in Peking, oversaw the construction of the Northern Cathedral (Pei T'ang) and famously organised its defence during the Boxer siege.

25 "Like the poor cat i' the adage" (Shakspere, *Macbeth* I.7). The adage referred to is "The cat loves fish but she's loth to wet her paws".

existing will for ever continue. I have commanded my army to withdraw from Manchuria immediately and am only retaining enough guards to protect the railway against the bandits who are the curse of the region.

Your niece, the Empress Alexandra Feodorovna, joins with me in offering devoted homage at the feet of Your Imperial Majesty. May heaven bless Your Majesty's August person with all happiness!

Your good friend and devoted nephew,
Nicolas.

"You have met the Emperor?"

"Yes, Your Majesty, he received me six years ago just after his coronation. He is charming but, I should think, entirely under his wife's influence. He does not like my compatriots whom he calls Jews, probably referring to the great influence this race enjoys in England."

"The Empress is beautiful, Li Hung-chang told me: as you know, we sent him to Moscow for their coronation."

"Yes, Madam, and as arrogant as the Sun goddess, or, as we say, Lucifer. She believes in soothsayers and omens."

"Well," said Her Majesty, "it is time for me to have my midday meal and siesta. Li Lien-ying will act as host at your lunch and I hope that good digestion may wait on appetite. Pray do not stint yourself."

She then left me and, while I was awaiting Li's return, I noticed that the Old Buddha's reception room was a museum rather than a boudoir. There were numerous clocks, all chiming at different times, "mountains of longevity" in different kinds of jade, mirrors galore, Ming 明 cupboards, Buddhas of all shapes and sizes, cloisonné altar pieces, lacquer tables, jade gongs, silken rugs, a large collection of porcelain, gold plate, old coins, ivories, blackwood furniture: the congestion was such that it was necessary to walk with great circumspection to avoid collision. At night (there being then no electric current available in the palace) locomotion must have been hazardous to any one in a hurry. The Japanese aesthetic sense denudes a room of superfluous ornament; I recall that when the present emperor (then crown prince) of Japan visited the Duke of Atholl (Bardic) in 1921, the latter told me that the majordomo of the former had paid a visit of inspection at the Duke's place and had requested the removal of nine-tenths of the furniture prepared for the Crown Prince!

Li, to whom the Old Buddha had been giving some orders, now appeared to escort me to a side apartment; there was a long buffet loaded à la Russe with Zakuski,[26] wines, liqueurs and bottles of Narzan, the Caucasus table water. The wines were mostly Crimean and included magnums of sparkling white wine and a sort of Bourgogne, to say nothing of aperitifs, fine champagne, whiskey and every imaginable liqueur.

---

26   In the Russian style with appetisers.

There were a dozen or more different sorts of *hors d'oeuvre* which, so Li informed me, had been prepared by a Russian chef; the whole environment reminded me of banquets in Petersburg, the most elaborate, I suppose, in the world. For a party consisting of two persons the preparations seemed somewhat overdone, but I appreciated Her Majesty's generous hospitality.

Dickens would have been in his element to describe in detail the menu which followed; it is quite beyond my ineffectual pen. With the Russian dishes after a long sojourn in Muscovy I was naturally familiar; among the Chinese *plats*, apart from the regulation *Yen Ts'ai* 燕菜, *salangane*[27] nest soup, sharks' fins, duck, etc., there were unwonted dishes (of which Li faithfully told me the nomenclature) that I had heard of as palace culinary dainties but had never seen. He indicated several favourites of the Old Ancestress, adding that Her Majesty was a very small eater and suffered from night-hunger, so that some special dish had often to be prepared for Her Majesty long before *le premier blanchissement du jour*.[28] She slept badly and liked to have women of the Bed-chamber in attendance until she had actually fallen asleep after her opium pipe nightcap! He went on to say that the Old Buddha had bidden him see that I did not "starve" – the fact being that there was enough food for a dozen people – and that she was "pleased" with my replies to her questions.

"Give him," had said Her Majesty, "Taels 5,000 to compensate him for the expenses of storing my collection: I could not bear him to be out of pocket."

Li handed to me a draft on his own private *Lu Fang*[29] 爐房 for this sum, as well as Taels 1,000 for my servants and an additional Taels 200 as largess for the two attendants who had accompanied me to the Palace. "Her Majesty has various other honours in store for you after she has had her siesta. High desert, says she, merits high rewards, *Kung Mao Mao Shang* 功懋懋賞; but she orders me to bestow upon you now this gold tablet (of which I have already spoken) which will give you admission at any hour without let or hindrance to any of the Palaces.

"We shall shortly be leaving for the Lake Palace, and if you care to inspect the Forbidden City at your leisure, you can conveniently do so after the Court's departure."

I told Li how I admired Her Majesty's large ideas.

"Yes," said he, "she is the incarnation of generosity but she cannot endure 'small men' taking advantage of her kindness and 'squeezing' her in a 'hole in the corner' way. She knows the prices of every commodity and will not brook the *fournisseurs*[30] taking an inordinate commission. For example, supposing that one of her favourite eunuchs (such as "little Ts'ui" whom you saw just now (not to be confounded with Ts'ui Te-lung 崔德隆) and who runs beside her chair during her progresses) were to say

---

27 A type of swallow with an edible nest, popular in Chinese cuisine.
28 The break of dawn.
29 Bank (literally "silversmith's shop", the predecessor to the bank in China).
30 Suppliers.

to her: "Old Ancestress, these eggs will cost Your Majesty six taels", she would willingly accept the charge which, of course, is twenty times too dear; but if he were to inform Her Majesty that the market price was 20 tael cents apiece (when they actually cost at present, as you know, about 1 tael cent) her wrath would be terrible to witness. It is over 35 years since I 'left the world' (suffered castration) and I know Her Majesty's whims better even than my predecessor An Te-hai 安德海, who met with such a sad fate at the hands of the Eastern Empress and Prince Kung." (N.B. Any one interested can read an account of this episode in *China under the Empress Dowager*, a work that is to me fraught with the memory, as Milton says, of an "immortal hate" apart from "study of revenge" which is not permissible, for I was associated therein with a detestable personality, *la lie du peuple*.)[31] "In dealing with Her Majesty, you must always remember that she is a woman with a woman's caprice and mutability." (I thought of Disraeli's *mot*[32] with regard to Queen Victoria: "She is a woman first and a queen next; hence, always flatter and extol her.")

I asked Li about the Boxers. "Personally," said he, "I still believe that their magic arts made them invulnerable to bullets, but unfortunately the righteous movement degenerated into a blood-lust and rapine.[33] It has been ever so throughout our history; enterprises of great pith and moment have their currents turned away and terminate in a fiasco, like the tiger's head tapering into a serpent's tail. Still, the events of the Keng Tzu 庚子 year (1900) did undoubtedly consolidate Her Majesty's position *vis-à-vis* the world and she is recognized everywhere today as the rightful sovereign of China. So out of evil came good."

Said I: "You heard of the murder of the Briton, Huberty James, early in the siege of the Legations?" (June 22, 1900) "Yes indeed: I witnessed his execution outside the eastern gate of the Imperial City. Junglu tried to save him, but the Old Ancestress heard that he was connected with the Imperial University which she hates, as Weng T'ung-ho[34] 翁同龢 and the Reform Party had affinities therewith; so she gave orders that Hsiao 蕭 (James) be decapitated on the spot. It was heart-rending to hear his appeals for mercy.

"With the exception of Junglu who was consistent from beginning to end and, I suppose, the Emperor" (here he spoke with a certain contempt) "we all believed in the Boxers, even Prince Ch'ing 慶, although he never expressed any definite opinion. So you see we really all deserved decapitation at the hands of you foreigners, myself included! In fact, I believe that it was owing to my Russian friends' intervention that my name was not included in the list of the proscribed."

Then he spoke very frankly about his intimate relations with the Russian Legation, at the time the most prominent of all the Missions and

---

31 "The lowest of scum", referring to his co-author J.O.P. Bland.

32 Remark.

33 Plunder.

34 Tutor to the Kuang Hsü Emperor and later Grand Council member, who famously recommended the reformer K'ang Yu-wei to the Emperor as an advisor and was relieved of office following the latter's unsuccessful attempt at a massive government overhaul in 1898.

with M. Pokotiloff of the Russo-Asiatic Bank who was later Minister to China. It was generally known that the Chief Eunuch received an annual subvention of Roubles 50,000 through Admiral Alexeieff, the Viceroy of the Kuantung 關東 Peninsula, apart from larger sums that had been conveyed to him for signal services such as his good offices in regard to the Cassini Convention and other amicable arrangements which practically made a present of Manchuria to Muscovy. He was equally responsible with Li Hung-chang, although behind the scenes, for what would have involved the loss of the three provinces, had not the Russo-Japanese war metamorphosed the whole situation.

Li told me, as I already knew, that he went almost every Sunday to the White Cloud Taoist Temple by invitation of the Abbot Kao 高, where to meet Lessar and Pokotiloff on "matters of mutual interest". Speaking of the discourtesy of most European diplomats – a subject on which he was distinctly sore, so that I presume he had been snubbed by Their Excellencies the Foreign Ministers who failed to acknowledge his powerful position, even if it were behind the scenes – he asked me if there were training colleges in Europe for diplomats aspiring to the "career".

"If not," said he, "there should be schools for manners and deportment, since they are regularly rude and ill-behaved." (Presumably with the exception of the Russians!) He added that he had kept a journal ever since he entered the Palace which he would gladly lend to me, in which he recorded every event in the Old Buddha's life of which he had cognizance. (It may not be without interest to mention here that this journal came into my possession after Li's death in 1911 and that it is a human document of extraordinary interest. *Tout comprendre, c'est tout pardonner*:[35] and although Li's devotion to the Old Buddha sometimes leads him into hyperbole and he is never able to admit the possibility of her being in the wrong, nevertheless it is *convaincant*[36] and rings true. It would repay translation but in these days an unexpurgated Pepys[37] could find no readers. At a rough guess, I should judge that it would run into fifteen volumes in a European language, a veritable L'Estoile[38] twice over, and the Manchu Dynasty is today one with Nineveh and Tyre. Perhaps, some day, the author may publish some salient extracts, unless he comes meantime to a place where they tell no stories; it is more revealing than Ching Shan's 景善 journal which was mainly hearsay; whereas Li Lien-ying is writing of events *quorum pars magna fuit*.[39]

"By the way," said I, "did Your Honour know Ching Shan, the former Vice President of the Board of Civil Appointments who was also connected with the Imperial Household, though not on the roster of the three senior Banners?"

---

35   To understand all is to forgive all.
36   Convincing.
37   Samuel Pepys (1633-1703), a famous English diarist.
38   Pierre de L'Estoile (1564-1611), chronicler of Henri III's reign.
39   In which he himself acted so conspicuous a part (Virgil, *Aeneid* II.5).

"Oh yes, quite well; *à la verité beaucoup trop même*:[40] he was a *raseur*[41] of the first order and was for ever coming to my house, being *gourmand*[42] of news. I found him insupportable and used sometimes to let him *trouver visage de boise*.[43] He was fond of expatiating about his endless family squabbles: in fact, he ended badly (*il finit mal*); as his eldest boy pushed him down a well on the day the city fell."

"Was he really deaf?" I asked.

"No; he feigned deafness when asked embarrassing questions and used to say that it was an asset to hear badly." (So said Napoléon: "*Une surdité bien organisée n'empêche jamais rien*.")[44]

"I forgot to tell you," went on Li, "that my brother wished to be remembered. He says that you interceded for him when a British officer had him flogged, in order to make him disclose the whereabouts of his supposed treasure."

"Yes, Your Honour, it was much against my wish: I was acting as interpreter under orders from the British Commander in Chief who was, in fact, anxious to know whether you were in Peking and used this pretext to perform a domiciliary search. The Captain, a man named Berger, was supercilious and arrogant; he was a typical product of the British army, one of those Britons swift of foot like Achilles, *Pódas okùs Achillus*,[45] as their recent displays in battle (1940-43) have shown to an admiring world, and always knew better than the man on the spot. I might as well have argued with a wolf: the man was incapable of pity, void and empty of any dram of mercy. I remember that poor Mr. Li received fifteen strikes with the *Chiu Wei Pien* 九尾鞭, nine tailed whip, and that he hardly rallied from the humiliation and shocking pain. However, I saved his treasure for him; as your sister-in-law took me aside and told me the silver was concealed under a large heap of coal. So I distracted the attention of this officer, who went away leaving unlooted the premises (a *rara avis in terris*);[46] and finally I frightened him by the prestige of your great name. He was a coward and a cad, as well as a monocled idiot, a typical product of Whitehall, an amateur army."

Speaking of Russian open-handedness, I told Li a story which amused him, of the Emperor Nicholas II during his tour of the Orient in 1891, when Tsarevich. On his visit to Canton a grand banquet was offered under orders from the Throne by the Viceroy; no less a personage than the *maître d'hôtel*[47] at this function told me that, at the time, he had conceived a very low opinion of the House of Romanoff, because H.I.H. omitted to recognize the service of the large staff of waiters. It was only much later that he ascertained that the Tsarevich had handed a princely *pourboire*[48]

---

40   If truth be told too much.
41   Bore.
42   Eager.
43   "See a wooden face", i.e. closed the door on him.
44   A well-organized deafness accomplishes nothing.
45   Πόδας ταχύς ἄγγελος (Homer, *Iliad* XIII.482).
46   A rare bird on the earth (Juvenal, *Satires* VI.165).
47   Butler.
48   Tip.

to his interpreters for distribution, apparently Roubles 2,500, but that the temptation had proven too strong for the venal *truchement* (interpreter) who appropriated the whole sum. As the Chinese are always quick to return thanks to the actual donor for gratuities received, Nicholas must have wondered at the head waiter's omission to acknowledge his generosity and, I suppose, left China with an impression of oriental ingratitude no less clearly defined than the Cantonese head waiter's reflection on his, the Tsarevich's, supposed niggardliness. I remembered how Count Leo Tolstoi, when giving to me a letter of introduction to His Imperial Majesty, had warned me to be punctilious in handing to the Ethiopian *heiduque*[49] (incidentally the tallest man I have ever seen) who ushered visitors into the *cabinet de travail*[50] of His Majesty a *storublyovka*[51] or 100 rouble note, apparently the minimum fee; as I imagine that Russian aristocrats were expected to disburse much more.

A propos de bottes,[52] Li asked to correct (as in fact he had already done) his remark made to me on entering the Palace that the Russian diplomats had failed to come up to his expectations regarding eunuchs' fees. It seemed that, as I should have expected, they had paid the regulation honoraria of, I suppose, Taels 1,000 on each occasion. I imagine that a trifling item of this nature might easily be omitted from Li's voluminous intake ledger. Incidentally I wondered if he would expect me to pay Taels 500 on future occasions: if so, *mes moyens ne me permettraient guère cette dépense*.[53] It is only fair to the Chief Eunuch to say here that he graciously declined to accept from me any payments thereafter, although we exchanged fairly costly presents for some years thereafter at New Year and at the two other great festivals of the Dragon and of the Full Moon. Whenever he called upon me – and he did so very frequently – he invariably presented my attendants with Taels 50; so he was an extremely popular visitor. I do not consider he was a bad man: his devotion to his Imperial Mistress was whole-hearted; he was not ungenerous and had a saving sense of humour. He had a certain charm of manner which I have perhaps failed to convey. It seems to me that his influence with the Old Buddha, an influence which became after Junglu's death unchallenged and unassailable, was less sinister than that of a Rasputin on the Tsaritsa or of her Italian astrologer on Catherine de Médicis.[54] Li detested nearly all foreigners, though he was good enough to make an exception in my case; and I believe that Mgr Favier, that prince of good fellows, brilliant musician and sinologue, and he were good friends. His journals of which I have spoken disclose *une naïve personnalité* which attracts: for example, he says: "None would say of me that I ever presumed on my positions! I am not like the eunuch of the 'First Emperor' Ch'in Shih Huang 秦始皇 and his successor,

---

49   Anti-Ottoman outlaw or mercenary in Hungary, later slang for "thief" or "robber".
50   Office.
51   Стоⲣⲩблёвка.
52   Regarding the tip.
53   My means would not allow this expenditure.
54   Cosimo Ruggieri (d. 1615), the lesser known fortune-telling contemporary of Nostradamus in Médicis' court.

who marked out for destruction those courtiers who failed to comply with his bidding in disclosing that the painting of a stag depicted a horse – *Chih Lu Wei Ma* 指鹿爲馬." (It is in allusion to this that the Japanese expression *Baka, Ma-lu* 馬鹿 in Chinese, for "fool" originates).

"What is Your Honour's personal opinion of Junglu?"

"He is my friend; although we often failed (and still fail) to see eye to eye with one another: during the Boxer days we were, as you know, 'like fire and water' *vis-à-vis* the situation. But I always knew that I was in the presence of a great Manchu whose only motive was certainly (forgive me!) not any pro-foreign feeling, for he detests the foreign devil (and more now than ever), but a loyal wish to safeguard and, if possible, to enhance the dignity of the Old Ancestress. Well, the result has justified both him and us: we travelled by different roads but had the same goal (*Shu T'u T'ung Kuei* 殊途同歸): you foreign devils (here he laughed immediately) are still in the land of the living (and as far as you personally are concerned, I am glad of it): the Boxers succeeded in their campaign to this extent that the foreign Powers have had to recognize willy-nilly that the Old Buddha is indispensable and that Tsai T'ien 載湉 (he impudently called Kuang Hsü 光緒 by his tabooed personal name which even the Empress never, except once in my hearing, used) is perfectly useless, more so than a god of the nearest shrine, who at least possesses real dignity, whereas Kuang Hsü has none, 'a little fool who does not know chalk from cheese'."

At last, at long last, for Li was an excellent trencherman and *avait son pompon*[55] before the last liqueur, the banquet, like everything else in this world of *fantômes*,[56] came to an end.

Li's hands trembled and I could perceive that the opium craving was heavy on him. "You can see that I have a strong *Shih Hao* 嗜好", a common euphemism meaning Relish and Fancy. "You must excuse me 'waiting upon you' any longer, unless you will come and join me at the opium pipe?"

"Alas, Your Honour, I am not fortunate enough to be a votary of those delights (*Mei Na Mo Ta Fu Ch'i* 沒那麼大福氣). Pray do not let me detain you: I am deeply grateful to have heard your winged words and to meet one whose name is a household word."

So Li left me, adding that the Old Buddha would send for me after her siesta. "In the meantime, smoke and drink here: pray do not stand upon ceremony."

As I sat waiting for the imperial summons, I wondered, while enjoying admirable Russian cigarettes, of whom Tz'u Hsi reminded me. At last it came to my mind that it was Baroness Burdett-Coutts, famous in the latter part of the nineteenth century as a philanthropist, a sort of Lady Bountiful. She was homely of appearance; but, despite the great gulf fixed between the empress and the baroness, there were definite *traits de ressemblance* in the voices and gestures of the two women. As

55 Had his pom-pom.
56 Ghosts.

a child, I had often been invited to Christmas parties for juveniles at her house off Piccadilly and recalled vividly the falsetto accents and the manner half imperious, half appealing, of that typically Victorian personage. Others, such as Lady Susan Townley, wife of a Chargé d'Affaires in China and later Minister to Den Haag, who had several meetings with Her Majesty, were impressed by the same resemblance; and she was no bad judge.

As I sat there, wondering if it were not a dream, the youthful Ganymede Ts'ui 崔 entered to summon me to the presence; he was bedizened like a woman, shameless, and supercilious, a *giton*[57] who would have been in his element among the mignons at the Court of Henri III or a character in Petronius' great novel of the Roman *décadence*. His manners were alluring, even fawning, and recalled to me the classical phrase: "Rats of the Altar" in relation to eunuchs, and that other phrase: "Be on your guard against eunuchs and women." The notorious murderer of the Emperor by Her Majesty's order Ts'ui Tê-lung 崔德隆 was his uncle; young Ts'ui still lives, I believe the former also.

Entering Her Majesty's presence, I knelt to thank her for her bounty.

"The chief eunuch says that you appeared to enjoy the collation. I suppose that you do not take opium? At your age, it would be a mistake, although for old people like myself a small quantity is a boon. My brother, Duke Kwei 桂, is a slave to his craving. Tell me, are not you ashamed of the opium hulks in Shanghai which belong to your Jewish traders?"

"They are indeed an eyesore, Your Majesty, and discredit my nation's fair fame."

Then Her Majesty was graciously pleased to confer upon me the honours which I have already recorded. "I am bankrupt in thanks, Your Majesty: were I to be born a hundred times and serve Your Majesty for eternity, I could not repay one ten-thousandth part of the gratitude that I owe to the heaven-sent bounty of Your Majesty."

"Next time we send for you, you may come in a sedan chair, wearing your robes and red button; you will have to engage more retainers to be in keeping with your new dignity. Tell me: you must be lonely without female society. Have you no hankering for dalliance? Yet, after all, 'tis only, as the Buddha says, a mirage and a sensual delusion, like the morning dew or the evening glow."

Although Her Majesty asked me this question out of ephemeral curiosity, I recalled that Catherine de Médicis once put the same enquiry to the young Comte de Montgoméry, he who later caused the (perhaps accidental) death in a tourney of Henri II, and that he had taken it as a declaration of love from a young queen who knew herself dispossessed by the King's favourite, Diane de Poitiers. Naturally, I had just then no such illusions; although at the moment the expression of Tz'u Hsi's face reminded me of a portrait of Catherine in late life in the Louvre. The Empress then graciously allowed me to sit down and went on: "Tell me

---

57 Pathic.

about Queen Victoria: was she in love with her Jewish Prime-Minister (Disraeli)?"

"No, Madame; she was faithful to her husband's memory." (I wondered if I had not made a slip of the tongue.)

"Why then did she not abdicate and spend her last days in retreat?"

"Immeasurable power, unsated to resign, Your Majesty: besides, she mistrusted her eldest son who was debauched." - "Like the Emperor T'ung Chih 同治" - ejaculated Tz'u Hsi - "Ay and unfilial." - (Like the Emperor Kuang Hsü 光緒 interrupted she.) "Well," asked Her Majesty, "was the Prime-Minister in love with her?"

"He used language to her in his memorials which were suggestive of love, but he was a man who indulged in vivid hyperbole. He called her his goddess and fairy queen but he revelled in flattery, as did the queen herself from her subjects."

"Why did not Victoria disinherit her unfilial son?"

"Madame, the Constitution denied to her the right. In order to deprive him of the right of succession, a bill of attainder would require to be passed by the Three Estates of the Realm, even then the Throne would have devolved by primogeniture on his eldest son or grandson."

"So much power," said Her Majesty, "and yet so little. Have you had a prime-minister in your family?"

"Not one of my surname, but two on the distaff side, one in Napoléon's day (Chia Ch'ing 嘉慶) and one during the early part of Your Majesty's regency."[58]

"Will there be a revolution in England?"

"Never again, Your Majesty; not until water runs uphill and the sun stands still on his course; they tried the experiment once, in fact twice: and it was not a success."

"As we say, till the Yellow River's waters become clear," said the Old Buddha. "Yet your dynasty is foreign, is it not?"

"Yes, Your Majesty, even now German is the language of Court."

"So is it with our dynasty; Manchu used to be the Court language, and all our customs differ from the Man Tzu 蠻子 (derogatory word for Chinese). Outsiders see clearer than the actors themselves, as the proverb says. Do you anticipate a revolution?"

"Not under the benevolent rule of Your Majesty."

"Well, the people love me in the north, but the south fears and hates me. I shall not live forever; but it will last my time and what is it all this panoply of power, this dream of wealth, but a phantasy like some bright exhalation in the evening?" (I thought of Le Bien Aimé's: "Cela durera bien autant que moi . . . Cela sera pour mon successeur qui aura à s'en charger.")[59]

58 Backhouse often falsely claimed politically powerful familial ties as he does here, most notably substituting the unrelated statesman Charles James Fox for a real ancestor, the Quaker merchant Charles Fox.

59 Louis XV (Le Bien Aime): "It will last as long as I am alive . . . My successor will have to deal with it."

At this point the eunuch brought in three bowls of chopped liver for the Pekingese; two of them started fighting and the Empress separated them with considerable adroitness. Then Her Majesty who passed from one subject to another with lightning-like rapidity, standing and speaking with vehemence, said: "You have heard, I imagine, of the Pearl Concubine?"

"Yes, Your Majesty, she was undutiful and Your . . . "

"Put her to death," said the Old Buddha. "Yes; but you do not know all the facts. I will tell you."

Her face took on an entirely new expression and she seemed transfigured; pent up rage had gained the mastery; she looked like an avenging goddess, a Hera venting her hatred toward the Trojans, "*Tantaene animis coelestibus irae?*"[60] Thus may she have appeared to her sister empress when she learned of her beloved favourite's death at the former's hands, or to Prince Tuan 端 when she denounced his overweening ambition as worthy of the dog's name he bore. (His prenomen was partly composed of the radical for *Ch'üan*, 犬, dog.) As I think of Tz'u Hsi at that moment, I can say with Dante "*Nel pensiero rinuova la paura*",[61] my fear renews itself at the thought, so that a little more had been death. After forty years the scene is indelibly recorded on the tablets of my memory; like a corroding acid burned into my quivering brain. Not Mme. Bernhardt as Cléopâtre or Théodora, nor Mrs. Siddons as Lady Macbeth could have surpassed Her Majesty in her tragic grace, her passionate gestures, the pose of her lovely hands, *la voix d'or*[62] which covered the whole gamut of emotion, the unforgettable remembrance of past mockery and insult from the transgressing concubine, the poignant emotion which was not to be borne and literally rendered her beside herself. If this was acting, the world did not contain *sa pareille* as a *tragédienne*;[63] but it was certainly no play staged for my benefit, no theatrical presentation for the sake of subsequent publicity in order to gain the sympathy of the world for a cruelly maligned woman. As Her Majesty's voice became louder, several more eunuchs (two were already in attendance) entered the audience chamber: they knew the story only too well and seemed glued to the ground in terror.

Li Lien-ying approached his mistress but scarce gathered voice to speak, shaking in every limb, numb and green with fear: "Old Ancestress, do not make yourself unhappy by remembering past events."

But she ignored his admonition, as if she were living over again those tragic moments, not indeed from any remorse but as if, *nondum satiata*,[64] with unglutted vengeance she would fain kill the concubine a second time.

Even thus I recall the divine Sarah in Fédora: "*Tue-le, Tue-le*",[65] of the lover who had proven faithless, or in La Tosca: "Why can I not kill him

---

60   Can heav'nly minds such high resentment show? (Virgil, *Aeneid* I.11.)
61   Misquotation of "*Che nel pensier rinnova la paura*" (Dante, *Inferno* I.6).
62   The golden voice.
63   An equal as an actress.
64   Unsatisfied.
65   Kill him, kill him.

(her beloved's perjured assassin) a second time? *Que ne pourrais-je le tuer une fois de plus?*"

Aristotle says that tragedy is the purgation of the passions by pity and terror: in my case there were no passions to purge but there was a surfeit of those twin emotions. Knowing Her Majesty's temperament, I asked myself whether in her rage and fury she would forget that I was her guest and suddenly become anti-foreign again with dire consequences for me. This thought may seem ridiculous; but it occurred to me that the empress might be in a sort of psycho-neurotic hysteria: today I feel ashamed of my poltroonery, although at the time I should have been glad if the floor had opened and received me in some subterranean depth. I felt much as a rabbit probably does when fascinated by the cobra.

This is what Her Majesty said: "On the 20-21 VII Moon, when you foreigners were bombarding the city and shells were falling in the proximity of the Palace, I and a few ministers with the eunuchs were busy preparing to leave Peking. Junglu was not there; had he been with me, perhaps . . . . . " The Empress did not complete the sentence. (Perhaps she meant that the Grand Secretary might have induced her to spare the Pearl Concubine's life).

"The dawn was just breaking; the four carts, in which we were to travel, disguised as country folk, were waiting on the road leading to the gate of Divine Prowess. So I sent for the Emperor and my daughter-in-law, the Empress, to join us. I never intended to take the Pearl Concubine with me nor wished even to see her, for I knew her influence over the Emperor and her abominable rudeness and defiance where I was concerned. Unexpectedly, she came with the Emperor: we were standing by the postern, the entrance to the 'Commune' of the palace, where there is a deep well. When you visit the Forbidden City again, for I have granted permission for you to enter where you will, you can see for yourself.

"I asked the rebellious girl: 'What are you here for, without my orders?'

"She replied most insolently: 'Because the Emperor must not leave Peking, whatever you may do. He can conduct negotiations with the foreign devils who trust him but don't trust you.'

" 'Unfilial wretch, do you know that you are speaking to the Empress Dowager?'

" 'You, you are not the Empress Dowager: you were the unfaithful concubine of His Majesty Hsien Feng 咸豐, but now your crimes deserve death; you are the mistress of Junglu!'

"I heard her to the end and bade Li and another eunuch take her up and throw her into the well, as a warning to monsterhearted birds which peck out their parent's eyes. I waited to leave in the carts until her shrieks had ceased and the servants had placed a great stone slab over the well."

Then, after a pause: "You are a foreigner. Tell me: Was I right or wrong? Dynastic house law decrees death for any concubine who insults the imperial ancestors."

"She brought her fate upon herself," said I. "Your Majesty could no other." What else could I say? I am no *vox clamantis in deserto*,[66] no leader of hopes that others hold forlorn. The attendant eunuchs looked greatly relieved at my reply: Li Lien-ying told me later that he had half feared some remonstrance on my part, which, as he said, would have been bad for me and worse for him!

Gradually, to my relief, the Old Buddha regained her composure; again I was reminded of the benevolent manner of the prim Victorian grande dame I have mentioned. "Now," said she, "you know the facts and can correct any false rumours about my supposed inhumanity. Your audience is at an end; but I shall send for you again, if not here, then to the Lake Palace or to Wan Shou Shan 萬壽山. Be circumspect in all things regarding your health and remember Confucius' saying: 'Time does not wait for us.' Go in peace." Then she dismissed me with a gracious gesture, while I genuflected for the last time.

Li Lien-ying politely escorted me through the Hall of Imperial Supremacy where, six years later, come November, I was to attend wearing the robes of mourning, a white sheep skin turned outward, an official cap without button or tassel, white shoes, hair unkempt and untrimmed as was *de rigueur* during Court mourning, to do homage before the huge catafalque wherein were encoffined Her Majesty's sacred remains, while Lamas chanted monotonous dirges for the repose of her august soul. We passed the outer gate together and he called my attention to the geomantic wall-screen of nine dragons design which the Ch'ien Lung Emperor regarded with superstitious awe. My cart was awaiting me; my new promotion had secured to me the right to mount my carriage at the palace door.

"I shall call upon you," said Li, "do not forget next time you attend, that you are to ride in a chair." (Li Lien-ying duly kept his promise and I saw him frequently during subsequent years.)

"Pray escort me no further. Restrain your steps."

"I obey your injunction," and I drove away, listening to the voluble congratulations of my attendants who had gained considerable face and a rich largess.

---

66   Voice crying in the wilderness (*Isaiah* XL.3).

CHAPTER III

HIS EXCELLENCY JUNGLU

VERY early on the day set for Edward VII's abortive coronation and the sudden access of perityphlitis,[1] quite the hottest of my 45 years in Peking, I was agreeably surprised to receive Junglu's 榮祿 visiting card (in unostentatiously small ideographs which I contrasted with that of the British Envoy with the three characters of his name as large as small tea-cups) and to be informed that a Manchu official wished to see me with a message from the Grand Secretary, the most important man in the empire, the Old Buddha's devoted adorer, the father-in-law of the future Regent and grandfather of the present emperor of "Manchoukuo".[2]

A very tall, handsome Manchu in official dress with a marked aquiline nose and a clear, healthy complexion, wearing the Third Button, was ushered in and, after our exchanging the orthodox salutation of bended knees, said: "The Grand Councillor has just come back from Audience and invites you to attend immediately at his house for an important conversation. Will you come? He will give orders at the gate that you shall be admitted without delay to his study."

Would I not! Would I come and discuss 18ᵉ Brumaire with Mgr the unfrocked Bishop of Autun or the First Consul's career with Charles James Fox?[3] Rather elated and decidedly bewildered at an honour for which I was scarcely ripe, I replied: "Pray convey my humble homage to His Excellency and say that I shall honour myself by gazing on the Northern Star 北斗 and on Mount T'ai 泰山, whilst hearkening to his conversation to which the yak-tailed whisk[4] shall give emphasis and harmony."

---

1 Appendicitis.
2 滿洲國, the puppet government of Manchuria established by the Japanese in 1932. The last Ch'ing Emperor, P'u Yi, was instilled as its nominal leader.
3 Charles de Talleyrand-Périgord (1754-1838), Bishop of Autun prior to his excommunication from the Catholic church, and Charles James Fox (1749-1806) were among the leading statesmen of their day. As previously noted, Backhouse often falsely claimed to be a relation of Charles James Fox.
4 **Backhouse:** The ancients employed this instrument at social gatherings and the phrase *Chu T'an* 塵談 has remained as a conventional symbol. [Perhaps Backhouse was thinking of *Ch'ing T'an* 清談, a form of witty, philosophical chat which developed from the end of the Han Dynasty. Its adepts frequently carried a horse-tail fly whisk.]

Junglu's handsome deputy, Mr. Ch'i Shan 耆善, left me to inform his patron; while I, not unmindful of the Chinese saying: "Before visiting a home, be sure to enquire what subjects are to be avoided in conversation", thought that in this case a more pressing matter was to ascertain from a competent authority what fees were expected at the gate, so I hurried to ask a friend who was secretary to H.E. Ch'ü Hung-chi 瞿鴻璣, native of Hunan 湖南 (president of the Foreign Office and later Grand Secretary and Grand Councillor until dismissed in 1907 for associating with newspaper correspondents) and, as a Manchu, had intimate knowledge of this all-important technique, what sum he would suggest as appropriate in the circumstances. He told me that the receipts at Junglu's gate from visitors, clients and office-seekers were at least Taels 2,500 *per mensem*,[5] at that time £400 (probably, I should think, much more), that there was a regular tariff according to which viceroys or governors would pay Taels 500 and lower provincial officials in proportion. In my case, I had been specially summoned and in those conditions Taels 100 would be adequate. After duly providing myself with the sycee[6] which was wrapt in an elegant package and euphemistically inscribed, I handed it to my *Koshihhu* 戈什護 (Manchu word for mounted attendant) and set off for Tung Ch'ang Hut'ung 東廠胡同 the street of the Eastern Court, which was at no great distance from my home opposite to the Imperial City Wall. The name referred to an important institution under the Mings in control of eunuchs which was a sort of star-chamber trying political offenders, infamous for tortures and illegal executions, acquiring a specially evil notoriety under the chief eunuch Wei Chung-hsien 魏忠賢, the Lord of 9,000 Years in the third decade of the sixteenth century. The house to which I was bound had been Wei's private residence, for the "Court" proper was situated within the precincts of the Imperial City, at that time included in the Palace area.

On arrival at the entrance, I was reminded of the saying: "Grand Secretary Junglu's mansion is like a market". The narrow lane was literally packed with mule-drawn vehicles (in those days rickshaws were scarce and would not have been *convenable*),[7] scores of retainers and their ponies, blue and white buttoned officials hoping for an audience, two sedan-chairs in a favoured position inside the gate, to say nothing of multitudinous pedlars and vendors of eatables and cold summer drinks, beggars galore and a score or more of tatterdemalion Banner troops, while a squad of Junglu's personal bodyguard, truculent and suspicious, armed to the teeth, barred the entry.

The *Koshihhu* handed in my card together with the all-important accompaniment of "gate-money"; the venerable moustached gate-keeper in official dress and wearing an honorary blue button came out to meet me. "The Grand Secretary is expecting him," said he to the corporal.

---

5   Monthly.
6   An ingot, usually silver or gold and often boat-shaped with an engraved pattern, that came in various weights and was used as a form of currency.
7   Suitable.

"*Hung Jen-rh,*" 紅人兒 replied the latter, "a favoured guest," *Shang To Ta Lien* 賞多大臉 "what an honour for him!"

"He understands etiquette," remarked the warden of the gate. "Of all the foreign ministers who came here to return the Grand Secretary's call, only two paid the fees,[8] the Japanese and Russian envoys. When His Excellency called on the Legations after the guests' return, he left Taels 2,000 to be divided among the respective Chinese staffs. He was insulted by the ministers and called a Boxer leader by the French representative: only the Japanese and Russian thanked him for saving the Legations." Turning to me, "His Excellency is expecting you, but the Grand Secretary Wang Wen-shao 王文韶 is with him just now and remaining to lunch; so you will please wait a while in the inner study."

He then escorted me through a labyrinth of courts, remarking that there were over thirty callers distributed in the various rooms who had been waiting since early morning for a word with Junglu, and finally led me into a picturesque court at the back of the mansion with a moon door and two magnificent acacias. The wall was decorated with paintings depicting scenes from the novel *Dream of Wealth* (mistranslated *Dream of Red Chamber*); an aviary adorned one corner with talking mynahs and macaws; there was a pond full of gold-fish with water-lilies not yet out and an enormous vine not improbably dating from the days of the omnipotent eunuch Wei Chung-hsien. The study into which the gate-keeper ushered me faced south and, though in those days electric fans were unknown in Peking, was deliciously cool with long blocks of ice in two cloisonné ice-chests and a punkah[9] of the old style manipulated by an unseen hand.

"Please rest here, and luncheon will be served," said the gate-keeper as he left me. "You are a happy man, since His Excellency very rarely receives visitors in this room: only his son-in-law Prince Ch'un 醇 and the Chief Eunuch, Li Lien-ying 李蓮英."

It did not require much imaginative faculty to picture "the secrets of the inner chamber" – to quote from the *Odes*. Doubtless, it was here that the all-powerful catamite who ruled the empire for six years and induced his master, the T'ien Ch'i 天啓 Emperor, to erect shrines in his honour as a divine sage received the emperor on his frequent clandestine visits to his favourite, when the pair indulged in homosexual *délices*[10] in the intervals of planning the ruin of the brave men who had dared to impeach the *improbus cinaedus*[11] usurping the highest place. It may well have been here that he concealed himself when the demise of his master and the accession of the virtuous Ch'ung Chen 崇禎, brother of T'ien Ch'i 天啓, connoted his own inevitable ruin. His suicide saved him in

---

8   **Backhouse:** It is almost axiomatic to say that Europeans are unpopular in China. Sometimes, I think that their contempt for Chinese etiquette is a prime cause. As Chinese custom demands the return of an equal sum to the donors of a *pourboire* [tip] from the recipients, Junglu not only gave to my attendant Taels 5 for "food-money" but also sent Taels 100 for my household staff.

9   Stationary fan operated by a lever.

10   Delights.

11   **Backhouse:** Catullus ["Shameless Sodomites" (57)].

the nick of time from the death penalty, but his faction was relentlessly proscribed. During the troubles of 1900, the house was still the property of Huai T'a-pu, a Boxer sympathiser and a kinsman of Tz'u Hsi 慈禧, but a friend of Junglu so that, when the latter's mansion in Mao'rh Hut'ung 帽兒胡同 was burnt, Huai received him as his guest. After the flight of the Court, Huai killed himself and Junglu bought the property, only a small corner in the N.E. being retained by the brother Fo Ssu 佛四 who opened a restaurant there under the name "My still remaining garden" Yü Yüan 餘園.

Junglu's study contained an autograph scroll of the Empress: "Saviour of the Dynasty", and another from the Emperor: "Shield and Buckler of the State." He had lately celebrated his 67th birthday and a jade sceptre with a gold service of plate were presents from the Old Buddha. There was a "Mount Sumeru"[12] in jade, two magnificent Yung Cheng 雍正 yellow bowls, a Lang Yao 郎窯 vase, several Shang 商 bronzes.[13] The books were mainly historical and included a fine Ming 明 edition of the Tso Chuan 左傳 annotated by Junglu. I did not think then that this work would pass to me by purchase after his death and it is now in the Bodleian.[14] Junglu was not regarded as a great scholar, but his calligraphy was greatly prized. The furniture was in keeping with the room, mostly Ming Tzu T'an[15] 明紫檀; the western wall was hung with Chi'en Lung 乾隆 tapestry woven under direction of the Jesuit fathers in imitation of a Gobelin design: "The emperor goes a-hunting".

The good-looking attendant, in whom Junglu evidently inspired the devotion and fascination which all who came in contact with his magnetic personality could not but feel in spite of themselves, was determined that I should admire another imperial gift, a clock from the interior of which, on pressing a button, a doll in the court-dress of Versailles wearing a perruque[16] emerged brush in hand and wrote on a slip of cardboard in exquisite minute ideographs the inscription: "Sung Wen Hua Tien Ta Hsüeh Shih Shou Jo Pu Lao Sung 頌文華殿大學士壽若不老松: May the life of the Grand Secretary of the Western Throne Hall be as long as the pine tree of immortality".

My attention was also called to a fine Kashgar carpet which had been offered to Junglu by the Mahomedan community of Peking in gratitude for the protection which he had extended to their religion during the Boxer émeute.[17] It is, of course, known that the Muslims were scarcely less anathema to the fanatics than the Christians themselves; although among the Boxer generals Tung Fu-hsiang 董福祥, the intrepid leader of the attacks on the Legations, was a devout worshipper at the Mosque

---

12　**Backhouse:** Buddhist Paradise.
13　Yung Cheng period: 1723-35. The Lang Kiln was renowned for a glaze called "Lang Kiln Red", produced during the reign of the Kang Hsi (1662-1722) Emperor. The Shang Dynasty reigned from the middle of the second millennium BC until 1122 BC.
14　An annotation of the Confucian classic Spring and Autumn Annals, which Backhouse did indeed leave to the Bodleian.
15　Ming-era furniture made of red sandalwood.
16　Powdered wig.
17　Uprising.

inside the Chang Yi Gate 彰義門. The attendant informed me that a fine full-length mirror with a wonderfully carved blackwood stand, also presented by the Old Buddha, had been one of the articles of "tribute" brought to Peking by Lord Macartney in 1793. As a mirror does not appear on the official list of the presents despatched by George III to the Emperor of China, I surmise that this object was procured in Canton by Lord Macartney or his colleague Sir Geo. Staunton to replace a painting of the dissolute Prince of Wales (later George IV) which had disappeared on the journey from Calcutta (no great loss, most people would say).

A sumptuous luncheon was now brought in, bird's nest soup, sharks' fins in scrambled eggs, whiting stewed in a wonderful *sauce piquante au gingembre*,[18] "*P'a Lan*"[19] 扒爛 duckling, bamboo shoots, a delectable *macédoine*,[20] with Moët Chandon nicely chilled though not extra sec and an anisette type of liqueur from the Caucasus whose name I forgot (Anisovka, perhaps), a case of which had been presented (so the servants said) to the Grand Secretary by S.E. M. Lessar, the Russian Minister. With a temperature (as I later learned) of 115 in the shade, it was not possible to do justice to these manifold delicacies. I wondered if H.E.'s regular menu was as elaborate as this, or whether a special *déjeuner* had been ordered in honour of Grand Secretary Wang Wen-shao. I was fortunate in gaining the approval of the two waiters and the attendant aforesaid by presenting each of them with Taels 5 *pourboire*: "He has big ideas" *T'a Ta Fang* 他大方, said they.

Somewhat elated at this undeserved, if insincere, praise, I cannot help recalling (*parvis componere magna*)[21] an occasion in 1790 when Philippe Egalité, in enforced residence in England, "Prinny" (the infamous George, Prince of Wales), "Sherry" (Sheridan) and Charles James Fox repaired to Brooks' Club and gambled all night at faro in the baywindowed room on the first floor. Orléans won some £5,000 and made a largess of £300 to the staff, what would be called in China "*Ling Ch'ien*" 零錢 or "*Ti Tzu Ch'ien*" 底子錢. Fox writes to his brother, Lord Holland, reporting the hall-porter's comment: "Your prince friend, Sir, is bawdy and as full of pox as an egg of meat, but he knows how to behave hisself (sic) though he is only Mossoo froggy!" (At that time an insulting sobriquet for Frenchmen: like Goddams in France for Britons).

Visits to Grand Secretaries are expensive, but I consoled myself with the reflexion that I was gaining face for my servants, as His Excellency would surely send to them the counterpart of what I had given; and, of course, he did.

At this moment I heard a shout: "The Grand Secretary is coming," but before going, as in duty bound, to meet him, I wish to take the reader (if indeed I have any) into my confidence and disclose a secret which

---

18 Spicy ginger sauce.
19 Braised.
20 Fruit salad.
21 Comparing small with great (Virgil, *Eclogue* I.24).

perhaps he has already divined. When I write about Junglu, my admiration knows no bounds; I had already idealized him partly from Ching Shan's 景善 diary[22] and partly knowing that but for him every alien in North China would have been massacred. I have been fortunate in knowing fascinating men and women, such as Cardinal Newman, Lord Rosebery, Mme. Sarah Bernhardt, Dame Ellen Terry, Barrès, Verlaine, Beardsley, Huysmans, Count Tolstoi, whose patronage, or friendship, was verily worth more than rubies, ay than all the manuscripts in the Vatican; but not one of them exercised on me to the same degree the quality that we call charm, which I found in Junglu. His single hearted loyalty to his great mistress, not to speak of a love that he sought not to dissemble, far more sincere than that of an Essex for the misnamed "Virgin" queen or of a Fersen for Marie Antoinette, his stand like *Athanasius contra mundum*[23] against the imperial princes and the other counsellors of the Throne, when a despot's word, despite her real affection, might have at any moment meant death, make him to me a character of peerless chivalry. Whatever records leap to light, he never shall be shamed: he is the perfect knight, the paragon of faithfulness and disinterested service. It is a fascinating thought to imagine the course of events, had he lived another ten years. To begin with, he would have prevented the Regent from dismissing Yüan Shih-k'ai 袁世凱 in 1909 and the two men would have cooperated. It is quite possible that there would have been no revolution in 1911 and he would have remained leader of the Grand Council with Yüan as his right-hand man, the Old Buddha *toujours en vie*.[24]

As Junglu entered the compound, I made the Manchu salutation which he returned with the exquisite grace of the grand seigneur. "*Shou Teng*" 受等, I have kept you waiting, he said: "you know that Grand Secretary Wang came unexpectedly and he is so deaf that his visits are always prolonged. I hope you enjoyed your luncheon."

"Humble thanks to your Excellency for summoning me here and for the bestowal of such lavish hospitality."

"The reason I sent for you," said Junglu, "was partly because the Old Buddha told me her approval of what you said to Her Majesty, namely that she was the model of motherhood and empresshood and that foreign nations regarded her as a unique personality, *Ch'ien Ku I Jen* 千古一人, partly because I wished you to know certain matters concerning the Boxer rebellion for future publication. But it is hot outside, let us come in." I noticed that Junglu had difficulty in mounting the few steps leading to the study and was supported by two retainers. He was wearing horn rimmed glasses which he removed on entry, and I was able to study him minutely, while the servant presented his *Narguilé*[25] which he started to smoke with evident zest. He was dressed in a grass-cloth

---

22 The diary in *China under the Empress Dowager* that Backhouse was later accused of fabricating.
23 "Athanasius against the world", an expression coined by historians to describe the stance of Athanasius (293-373), Bishop of Alexandria, against the Arian heresy, supported by the imperial government and, it seemed, the whole world.
24 Still alive.
25 Water pipe.

gown with a short riding jacket of pale blue silk; he was of spare, almost emaciated, frame about 5.8 in height; his complexion was remarkably fresh for a man of 67 – and I understood why for so many years his so-briquet has been "Girl-faced" general.

In earlier life he had been famous for horsemanship and ponies were brought to him to tame whom none else could master. Since the Court's return in January 1902, he had given up riding but, while at Hsianfu 西安府, he had made many excursions on horseback. He had a sensitive mouth largely concealed by a heavy moustache, a chin which indicated even to the casual observer great firmness and decision, a straight nose and high cheek bones, strongly marked eyebrows and a lofty forehead. As is well known, the Chinese regard large ears as a sign of greatness; if this is so, Junglu failed to attain this ideal, as his ears were small and shapely. He had the most luminous and expressive eyes that I have ever seen; it seemed at first that their colour was grey; but, as he became animated in conversation and especially when he felt keenly about a subject, their tint changed to a much darker hue. When he smiled, his whole face, and particularly his eyes, were lit up in sympathy; like many Manchus, he had a delicate sense of humour and his laughter was ebullient. There was something *je ne sais quoi*[26] noble and harmonious in his every movement; his gestures were full of dignity but without a trace of arrogance. I noticed his delightful courtesy to the servants. He had the rare quality that Saint-Simon's beloved Duc de Bourgogne, of whom France and the world were not worthy, possessed, of making a visitor feel, be he ever so humble, that he was the one person Junglu was yearning to see. He had a *belle prestance*[27] (as Saint-Simon calls it) that Le Roi Soleil[28] could not have surpassed; one had only to approach him to feel absolutely at home and as if one had known him all one's life. In this respect he resembled Charles James Fox who inspired such love in his contemporaries – while his great rival, Pitt, was cold and unapproachable. Junglu was said to smoke opium; I am not competent to express an opinion, but noticed that his pupils were dilated, which is, I presume, an indication to the contrary.

I should not have noticed signs of failing health, except for the difficulty in ascending steps; but Junglu told me that he suffered from what he called "a belt of pain" which never left him night or day, as well as from excruciating migraines. There was a marked puffiness round the eyes, but his vigour did not seem impaired. He died in the following April, having suffered greatly during his last weeks: his disease is said to have been poliomyelitis (so a foreign physician told me) which, I believe, causes intense agony.

"Pray make yourself perfectly at home," said Junglu; "by the way, Master Wang Wen-shao wished to be remembered; he told me that you were loyal to the ruling dynasty and that you were remarkable for intelligence."

---

26 Indefinable.
27 Great bearing.
28 Louis XIV.

"The first remark is true," said I, "but the second is above my desert."

"You must allow me to judge for myself: I can see already that there exists an affinity between us. Wang spoke of old Ching Shan's diary which he told me you found and which he has read. He speaks of me, does he not?"

"Many times, Your Excellency: he seems to praise you in spite of himself."

"That is the highest praise of all," said Junglu, "being from an enemy."

"Should Your Excellency consider Ching Shan's deafness serious enough to prevent his grasping a conversation?"

"No; his deafness was largely put on, because the old man did not know whether to praise or to blame the Boxers; so he wished to be on the safe side, or rather, as we say, to 'bestride the wall'."

"Should Your Excellency consider his information reliable?"

"Yes; he was an inveterate gossip and liked to be in the know. Old Wang Wen-shao supplied him with much news and in fact lent him his own journal to copy more than once."

"He mentions Tung Fu-hsiang attending on Your Excellency with the request to lend your 5 inch Krupp guns."

"Yes: I pretended not to hear what he said. In fact, there was a plot against my life, but a former pupil of mine warned me in time."

"Now," went on the Grand Secretary, "you may ask me any questions you choose. I am not afraid of your putting to me the absurd query of the French Minister, when I called on him: 'Why did Your Excellency believe in the Boxers?' My answer was: 'I believed that they would end in destroying the Dynasty'." Junglu laughed rather bitterly (as I thought) at this tactless question of M. Pichon and mentioned that none of the Ministers, except the Japanese and Russian, had been in the least courteous, insulting him even in his own house on their return calls.

After some hesitation, I put the following question: "Can Your Excellency tell me why H.M. the Empress Dowager suddenly decided to sanction the Boxer movement after strongly condemning it?"

"I can," said Junglu: "when the Old Buddha came into Peking from the Summer Palace on the 13. VI Moon (July 9), she told me that she meant to put a stop to the whole agitation, as being dangerous for the Dynasty. But a day or two later I received a message from Liu K'un-yi 劉坤一, Viceroy of Nanking, that an official British newspaper of Shanghai, bearing the British arms, had published an article demanding H.M.'s abdication, if necessary by force. Naturally, I had to inform the Empress; and she said at once, 'If this can be borne, everything can be borne' (as you know a quotation from the *Lun Yü* 論語 of the Sage),[29] 'I shall exterminate these people before breakfast', *Mieh Tz'u Chao Shih* 滅此朝食" (a quotation from the *Tso Chuan* 左傳 implying that the task does not involve much difficulty, still used in Japan). "Now, let me ask you: what would your late queen have said, if such a suggestion as to her

---

29   The *Lun Yu* or *Analects* by China's most influential thinker, Confucius (551-479 BC).

₁8

abdication had been made by a Chinese journal in London known to be in touch with our Legation?"

"She would have been rightly indignant, but, as a constitutional sovereign, she could only react by demanding retraction from the Legation and possible suppression of the journal."

"Quite so; but the Empress is not a constitutional monarch, and you must not forget that her position is ill-defined. You have read our history; therefore, you know that there is a House law of the Dynasty which debars any member of the Yehonala clan from being empress. It is true that this law was ignored forty years ago, but apart from that fact, there is a great prejudice in China against the rule of an empress or empress dowager. You know that the Great Empress Wu Tse-t'ien 武則天 of the T'ang 唐 Dynasty is regarded as a usurper by history, while the Empress Lü's 呂 misdeeds are a byword and a scandal. The tendency has always been to uphold an emperor against an empress dowager. There is no subject, not even the reform movement of K'ang Yu-wei 康有爲 four years ago, that causes such displeasure to Her Majesty as the suggestion that her position has only force to back it and that the emperor has been improperly deprived of his sacred rights. Her Majesty felt that at the worst foreigners might be massacred but that the resultant chaos would still require the continuance of the Regency. Happily, the Legations were not taken, but it is a fact, is it not, that the allied powers agreed that without the Empress chaos would continue?"

Junglu, who had been speaking with considerable vehemence, paused at this point to offer a "prise" to me: his snuff bottle was a thing of beauty in Lang Yao 郎窯: the snuff was very highly scented and not ungrateful. With the conventional, *Pu Hui Ching* 不回敬, "I do not return the compliment", I handed the bottle back and noticed the rare delicacy of the Grand Secretary's hands which were small and shapely. As I was admiring the large cabochon emerald on his ring finger, he told me it was a birthday present, with other jewels, from Nicholas II who always remembered his *fête*.

"The emperor of Russia wrote to Her Majesty every year for her birthday addressing her as Aunt according to the translation. Was that diplomatically correct?"

"Yes," I answered, "he addressed Queen Victoria in the same way, although actually the latter was his wife's grandmother."

Junglu added that the large pearl in his skull cap which he now removed, disclosing a massive head and slightly grizzled hair, had been a gift from Alexeieff, the viceroy of Kuantung, and that he had sent in return a large sceptre or *Ju Yi* 如意 in white jade.

"To resume my questions in regard to the events of the Boxer year, if I am not importunate, can Your Excellency tell me what Her Majesty thought of the assassination of Freiherr von Ketteler on the 24th VI Moon?"[30]

---

30 Baron Clemens August Freiherr von Ketteler, German Minister to China, was murdered in Peking en route to the Tsung Li Ya Men (Foreign Office) on June 20, 1900, effectively starting the war known as "the Boxer Rebellion".

"She blamed me for it, rather unjustly. Ketteler (K'olintê) had written to ask for an interview at the Tsung Li Ya Men 總理衛門: the Empress was told of this note and instructed me to communicate with him and to propose instead a conference at the German Legation. Although I was not on the Tsung Li Ya Men, she appointed me specially to act as plenipotentiary with a view to arranging for the diplomatic corps and the whole foreign community to leave Peking under my escort. Owing to the foreign sentries refusing admittance into the Legation Street, my a.d.c.[31] was unable to deliver the letter that I had sent by the Empress' direction. As you know, v. Ketteler insisted on going to the Ya Men next day and Her Majesty was angry that En Hai 恩海 should have shot him dead, because Prince Tuan 端, unbeknown to her, had ordered him to fire at any passing foreigner. She reproached me for lack of finesse and asked me if I regarded Prince Tuan as the de facto ruler of China! She did not deplore the murder so much as the fact that it had been ordered without her authority. I have known the Empress for over fifty years, intimately in her girlhood, when both her family and mine were in straitened circumstances and I used to accompany her on her marketing. Who could have foretold her high destiny and the share I should have in her career?" (Junglu spoke half wistfully, half contentedly, an old man before the "puppet show of memory". Naturally, I did not ask him the question; but it is generally known that she had been betrothed to him when the fateful order to admit her to the palace was received from the widow of Tao Kuang 道光 in 1854.)

Persons unacquainted with conditions in Peking (Lao Pei Ching 老北京, as men now say) might wonder at the freedom between the sexes as evinced by Junglu's reminiscence of the Empress' girlhood, how he accompanied her regularly during marketing expeditions and even joined her on rides and excursions to the fairs. There would be nothing surprising therein; since it has long been a saying all over China: "In Peking there are three wonderful things: the horses do not kick; the dogs bark not; maidens of sweet sixteen run all over the town." (The domestic animals, being accustomed to the busy *va et vient*[32] of the streets, take it as a matter of course. *Pei Ching Ch'eng San Tsung Pao, Ma Pu T'i, Kou Pu Yao, Erh Pa Ku Niang Man Chieh P'ao* 北京城三宗寶馬不踢狗不咬二八姑娘滿街跑). Other Chinese cities are or were more populous than Peking; but the Manchu domination brought to the capital a great emancipation from the time-honoured rule of the Mings which confined women to the perennial monotony of the home, where intrigue was the order of the day.

Junglu told me that the then designated officially as "Morally Admirable Concubine" (Yi Fei[33] 懿妃) was accorded permission by Hsien Feng 咸豐 in 1856 after giving birth to an heir to the Throne, to revisit her

---

31   Aide-de-camp; personal assistant.
32   Coming and goings.
33   Yehonala, the low-ranking concubine of Emperor Hsien Feng who would go on to become the Empress Dowager Tz'u Hsi.

mother's home; he was among the old acquaintances, male and female, invited to meet her.[34] It was a winter's day and she had to return to the Forbidden City before sundown in the yellow chair to which her new prestige entitled her. He vividly recalled her eagerness to see once more the old familiar faces and how she revelled in talking of buried days. It was a pathetic occasion, one may guess, for an old lover who had to tell her of his own recent marriage. She overwhelmed the party with questions, asking how her younger brothers were advancing with their schooling, how old servants were faring, and had a word for everyone. One cannot help recalling the well known scene in the *Hung Lou Meng* 紅樓夢 (mistranslated as *Dream of Red Chamber*) – *Vision of Wealth* – when the Imperial consort Yüan Fei 元妃 revisits her home for the last time.

"I consider," said Junglu, "that the foreign powers erred in exacting decapitation, enforced suicide and exile for the Boxer 'leaders' (like the "sanctions" of the defunct and hypocritical S.D.N.[35] thirty odd years later) when in the nature of the case one personage, who was the fount and origin of the campaign (*T'ou Teng Chüeh Sê* 頭等角色 or protagonist) was not only not named, but even regarded as indispensable to the existence of China. That personage is *innomable*[36] (Mr. Lloyd George had no such hesitancy, when he proclaimed his "Hang the Kaiser" slogan, surely the most insensate of watchwords). Your governments also omitted many *deuteragonistes*, or *Hsiao Chüeh Erh*[37] 小角兒, such as my friend the Chief Eunuch, who acted, in acclaiming the Boxers, as an efficient counterpoise to my influence with the Old Buddha and had readier access to her at all hours than I who was living outside the Palace."

"What of Yü-hsien 毓賢," I asked, "and the famous extermination?"

"Yes," said the Grand Secretary, "I half expected that question; you mean the Old Buddha's rescript to Yü-hsien's memorial asking for orders relative to foreigners in Shansi 山西: 'Let not chicken nor dog remain'. I will now narrate the conversation which the Empress had with Governor Yü-hsien in T'aiyüan 太原, on the day of her arrival, some time in the intercalary VIII Moon (September). I was present and can record it word for word:

"Empress Dowager. 'You executed all the Shansi foreigners, Yühsien, including many children. Do you know that the world blames me for what it calls this fiendish massacre?'

"Yü-hsien. 'I acted in obedience to Your Majesty's Imperial rescript and in fact executed over thirty foreign devils in a courtyard of this very *Yamen*[38] 衙門 where Your Majesty is graciously sojourning today. Also in another Shansi town a pregnant foreign woman who was near her

---

34 **Backhouse:** This passage was erased from *The Empress Dowager* (Edition Vetchiana) by my enemy Mr. J. O. P. Bland whose ownership of the copyright gives him no right to alter my manuscript. He thinks himself a greater stylist than I; but this (if true, which is uncertain) does not justify his omission of salient episodes or of altering my translations in ignorance of the original text.

35 Société des Nations (League of Nations).

36 Unnamable.

37 Characters of secondary importance.

38 Government office.

delivery was slain after an iron bar had been forced into her pudenda' (let us trust, abridging her agony).

"Empress Dowager: 'What bestial savagery hateful to gods and men! I never meant my rescript to be taken literally as to women and children. You took too much upon yourself.'

"Yü: 'The imperial orders are like perspiration which cannot be recalled (a quotation from the *Yi Ching* 易經). Your slave took Your Majesty's orders to mean what they said.'

"Empress Dowager: 'One must always take attendant circumstances into account. It is going to be serious for you. The price of coffins is rising daily; be advised in time.'

"But Yü-hsien failed to take the hint and, as you know, paid the penalty with his head. I always was against his transfer to Shansi: Li Lien-ying arranged it for the sum of Taels 250,000 paid up by the Ssu Heng banking firm here" (the then great Shansi bankers, "The Four All-pervading").

"If it is not too indiscreet, what should Your Excellency estimate the amount of the annual perquisites of the palace eunuchs?"

"I should think much more than Taels 500,000 net, apart from special fees. When the late Li Hung-chang 李鴻章 was viceroy of Chihli 直隸 his revenues were at least double that figure gross; but you must not forget that he had heavy commitments *vis-à-vis* the Palace, including not only the eunuch horde but those in the highest place of all" (meaning Tz'u Hsi).

"Regarding the 'extermination' rescript, Yü-hsien's original memorial, following the normal custom, should have been returned to him with the 'Vermilion Rescript' thereon by the channel of the governmental couriers. You may not know that every provincial memorial is returned to the sender with formal acknowledgment 'Noted' of receipt or with an appended detailed rescript. But in this case Li Lien-ying, unbeknown to me and my colleagues on the Grand Council, privily obtained the Old Buddha's autographed personal rescript and sent it to Yü-hsien's son-in-law, a man named Chi Shou-ch'ing 濟 卿 一 ."

"Excuse me, Your Excellency, old Ching Shan names him in his journal: the two men were intimate friends."

"Quite so," proceeded Junglu: "He lived in the north of the city and his main purpose in life was to '*T'an Feng*' 探風, see how the wind was blowing, on behalf of his father-in-law with whom he was in regular communication through the good offices of the great Shansi banking firm, Ssu Heng 四恆. It was thus that Her Majesty's order was delivered at T'aiyüan to Yü-hsien: as it was not sent by the usual means of the government post, (you remember Mencius' aphorism that virtue travels swifter than the official couriers themselves? – *Ch'uan Tê Chih Tao Su Yü Chih Yu* 傳德之道速於置郵) Yü-hsien would have been justified in treating it as *non avenu*[39] and in again asking for instructions. As, however, his own bloodthirsty lusts tended toward wholesale extermination, he acted

---

39 Void.

on the 'instructions' thus conveyed to him through his son-in-law. It was wholly irregular, but of course Her Majesty (with all respect) could not fairly reproach him.

"None living knows Her Majesty as I do: to those she favours she will concede everything, more than in reason and beyond what the occasion demands. But she never forgets a slight and, if you understand this, you will comprehend the tragedies of the past forty years, the deaths of A-lu-tê 阿魯德, the wife of T'ung Chih 同治, of her colleague the 'Eastern Empress Dowager', of the Pearl Concubine who had wantonly defied her."

At this point Junglu stopped to warn me (as was hardly necessary) against repeating this conversation during his life or until 10,000 years had elapsed (i.e. after the death of the Empress). "You saw," said he, "the decree which I drafted for H.M. at Hsi-an 西安 nearly a year and a half ago, which announced a policy of gradual reform. I quoted therein from the Yi Ching classic: 'Change after change may occur, but in the end stability shall ensue'. I suppose that the structure of the earth with its primeval convulsions and its existing permanence, despite the recent eruption of the Mont Pelé volcano in Saint Pierre,[40] proves the truth of this saying. You will probably see great changes in China, 'The ocean being transformed into an orchard', as we say in speaking of cataclysmic change."

"Does Your Excellency mean that you foresee possible dynastic mutations in China?"

"As you know, China is unlike Japan, in that she has changed the dynasty more than twenty times in her history. In this respect, she resembles your country which, like us, at the moment is ruled by a foreign race; although personally I would not admit that we Manchus are really alien, whatever the reformers may say. You recall the Sage's remark that dynasties come and go, and that if some day the Chou 周 Dynasty (under which he lived) should fall, 'his words would not require to be changed'. You will forgive my saying that in my opinion our Dynasty will outlast the British Empire which is centrifugal and devoid of cohesion. Come a shock, and it will topple over. Kublai Khan once told his chief adviser, Bayan, that the Chinese people were like grains of sand and therefore easily governed by playing one section against another. But Great Britain lacks homogeneity of race that China at least possesses."

In a further reference to my experience in Russia, the Grand Secretary said: " 'Fullness is well, but that which is full to the brim is in danger of overflowing', says the Canon: even so is it with a dynasty which, sooner or later, exhausts the Mandate of Heaven. The House of Romanoff and the Ch'ing 清 Dynasty have each lasted nearly 300 years. The Empress Dowager has prolonged the life of the latter, when everything pointed to its fall forty odd years ago. Is the present Tsar strong enough to hand over his prestige unimpaired?"

"What is Your Excellency's opinion regarding foreigners?"

---

40   This had occurred in the previous spring, causing 20,000 deaths.

"I could not say, with the late Li Hung-chang, that I disliked them all equally. The Japanese and Russians are to me most sympathetic, but you will excuse me say," ("there are always exceptions, you know" said Junglu with a courteous smile) "that you British seem to me to be arrogant and ignorant, where China is concerned. For instance, your Minister asked me why I did not stop the Boxers, and I replied that I spent several months in attempting (at least) to do nothing else. The troubles of the besieged, I added, were as nothing compared to mine. 'I see,' replied the Minister, 'I should not have thought it'; a remark that I interpreted to mean: 'I do not believe you'. No Russian nor Japanese diplomat would have spoken with such lack of courtesy."

"May I ask a rather delicate question? Does Your Excellency believe that the Empress wished the diplomats to arrive safely at the coast, supposing that you had undertaken to escort them there?"

Junglu: "I cannot answer you directly; but the reply must be clear to you from what I have said already. In any case, if I had been entrusted with this duty, I should have taken a division of my picked troops from the Wu Wei 武衛 Army (military garrison) of which I am Commander in Chief and should have ensured their safe arrival, as far as Chinese forces were concerned. But," and here he sardonically laughed, "for all I know, the foreign forces in Tientsin might have come out and joined battle with me; in which case I could not be responsible for the outcome."

"Could the Old Buddha have quashed the movement?"

"Yes; at any moment: unfortunately she halted between two opinions and wavered between her own instinct that the Boxers were perfectly useless and credence in the reports of their powers which were brought in to her daily."

"Will Your Excellency speak of the execution of Hsü Ching-ch'eng 許景澄 and Yüan Ch'ang 袁昶? Ching Shan expatiates on the incident in his journal. What were the real facts?"

"They were put to death, I am sorry to say, for carrying out my order to change the telegraphic code number for 'Slay' into that for 'Protect'. The Old Buddha was in a towering rage one morning and issued a secret decree that all foreigners in the interior, whether they fled or whether they remained, were to be put to death. Knowing as I do the moods of Her Majesty I felt certain that she would regret her order, when it was too late; so I took upon myself the heavy responsibility of altering the 'silken words' of the Throne, for which I deserved death ten thousand times over.

"After the issue on the 4. VII Moon (July 29) of the Vermilion Decree commanding the execution of Hsü and Yüan for disloyal conduct, I was grieved beyond words and knelt to implore Her Majesty to display her great attributes of the Merciful Goddess, Avalokitesvara, and pardon to them their lives. I said: 'It is entirely the guilty act of me, Your slave. Those two men's memorials condemning members of the Imperial Family and ridiculing the Boxers were really and truly drafted by me, Your slave. The unauthorized alteration of the code number was also previously arranged with me, solely in the interest of the State and to protect unimpaired Your Majesty's dignity. So I venture to entreat Your Majesty to order Your slave's execution in order to appease the Empire. Then, although I die, I shall be, as it were, reborn and each of my rebirths shall humbly recall Your Majesty's bounty.'

"The Empress answered: 'You are talking nonsense in asking to die in their stead. What I detest about these two traitors is the fact that, as Prince Tuan and others are for ever repeating to me, both of them have actually dared to put forward the wanton suggestion that I ought to abdicate and abandon state affairs. But, since you have interceded for them, I will open the net at one corner and give to them a chance of life. I give you three days' grace to write to the foreigners and to demand the immediate withdrawal of the troops. I appoint you to be Peace Plenipotentiary. If the foreigners give in to our demands, you may take those two men with you to Tientsin and negotiate the matter. A successful consummation will be for you a high desert. But in no possible circumstances will I abdicate and thus increase the existing dire confusion.' I knelt to thank Her Majesty and applied for three days' leave to enable me to get in touch with the foreign Ministers. I wrote to invite them to attend at the Tsung Li Yamen 總理衙門 and discuss the procedure; but they were distrustful of untoward events and their 'suspicion bred devils' in their hearts, so that they failed to comply.

"And so, early on the 7. VII Moon (August 1) when my leave expired, I attended to report the failure of my mission. Her Majesty was enraged and nothing would move her. During those three days, Hsü and Yüan had been temporarily detained at the North Yamen (of the Gendarmerie) and were not sent to the Board of Punishments. At 11 a.m. on this day they were bound and conveyed to the execution ground. I heard that Hsü was already completely unconscious (he had been given opium to render him so), but Yüan was firm and calm. The street was completely blocked by Boxer bands who insulted and mocked the two men as traitors. The supervising officials were Hsü T'ung's 徐桐 son (since decapitated by request of the Diplomatic Corps), Duke Lan 瀾 and Ying Nien 英年. Yüan calmly answered: 'Who's the traitor? Certainly not we. It is you (pointing to Duke Lan), members of the reigning house, who deserve decapitation for your crimes. Happily, you rebellious ministers and traitorous children (as Confucius says) shall not enjoy length of days.' When Lan heard that, his wrath became uncontrollable: he rose and made as if to strike Yüan. But the Boxers struck wildly at them with a thousand swords until they were dead, and their corpses were duly decapitated."

Junglu during this vivid narration seemed very greatly affected: he next handed to me a decree dated 16. VII Moon (August 10), which has never (I think) been published. It ran: "The present hostilities caused by the foreign bandits were not the desire of the Throne. Everyone recognizes that right is on our side, while those others are in the wrong, for these fellows have fired their heavy artillery and killed innocent people. Is it not natural that we should resist their attacks? Whoever heard of such a state of things that acts of outrageous violence should be perpetrated beneath the very 'chariot wheels' of the Throne (i.e. in the imperial capital)! Not only so, but the foreigners have interfered with our internal affairs and have amazed us all by uttering words that none should venture to suggest (i.e. the abdication of Tz'u Hsi). We had previously notified in earnest language the Rulers and Presidents of the world regarding the lawless acts of the foreign soldiery and are now in receipt of a reply from the Tsar of Russia which is most courteously and reasonably worded. Does not this show that the conduct of those people moves gods and men to abhorrence and leaves to them no foothold in the inhabited world? We repeat our previous decree that Junglu shall confer with the envoys and make them withdraw all the troops, while reverting to the *status quo ante*,[41] so as to display the impartiality and absence of prejudice that animate our Dynasty."

Junglu laughed heartily, while I perused this document. "The idea was mine," said he, "but the wording is not exactly conciliatory and differs from my original draft. It is a fact that Nicholas II conveyed his sympathy and willingness to bring about peace; but we had no replies to our messages to Queen Victoria, the German Emperor and the U. S. President. Two further decrees were issued, one on the 18. VII Moon (August 12) and the other on the 20. (August 14) prior to the Throne's departure. The first runs: 'The present unfortunate hostilities between China and the world were far from being the Throne's original desire, the cause being that those fellows imposed upon us excessive pressure and forced us to put our backs to the wall in taking one chance in a thousand. If only the foreign bandits will retire immediately to Tientsin, we will at once appoint Grand Secretary Junglu as our Peace Plenipotentiary to arrange with them for a definitive procedure. That peace may once more be assured and eternal tranquility ensue is our earnest hope!' "

"Regarding the second decree," remarked Junglu, "it was drafted entirely by the Empress: it refers to me in far too eulogistic terms, so that I hesitate slightly in allowing you to see it. It runs: 'We have recently received a mandate from Her Majesty *Tz'u Hsi Tuan Yu K'ang Yi Chao Yü Chung Ch'eng Shou Kung Ch'in Hsien Ch'ung Hsi* 慈禧端佑康頤昭豫莊誠壽恭欽獻崇熙 the Empress Dowager as follows:

> The Grand Secretary of the T'i Jen Ko 體仁閣 (Hall of Embodied Benevolence), Grand Councillor and Commander in Chief of the Wu Wei Armies, Junglu, is a loyal statesman, sage and experienced, honest and no flatterer, respected throughout the country. We hereby appoint him Peace Plenipotentiary with absolute powers. This statesman who receives his appointment at a time of dire crisis has now the opportunity to display most gratitude for our high bounty. He shoulders a heavy

41   Prior state (before war).

burden but we are convinced that he will not disgrace his mission. It is incumbent upon him to obtain the entire withdrawal of foreign troops and to achieve a speedy and ordinary peace, in order to conform with our desire to accomplish the best results in face of circumstance and to let bygones be bygones.

"Finally," said Junglu, "before terminating what to me has been a very agreeable chat, let me show you the decree issued by the Empress on the eve of her departure from the capital. You will understand that Her Majesty had to put the best face on a difficult situation and give to her subjects an explanation of her hurried departure. 'In consequence of the present crisis and the dangers attending the State, I do hereby, in reverent accord with the traditions of our glorious ancestors who proceeded on autumnal and winter tours of the country, leave Peking with the Emperor on a journey of inspection. With exception of the princes and ministers in attendance, all our officials, civil and military, are here enjoined to remain in the capital and to discharge their respective duties as usual. Let each and all exert himself as his conscience directs him and not disappoint our high expectation.' "

Junglu concluded the conversation by saying with considerable emphasis: "Your foreign intelligence department (except in the case of Japan and Russia) is sadly to seek. In the list of Boxer leaders, the Diplomatic Corps omitted the names of Yi Ku 貽穀, Fen Ch'ê 芬車 and Kuei Ch'un 桂春 who were the authors of the deaths of thousands of Christians and of an equal number of harmless citizens whom they allowed to be proscribed for private grudges. There were *canaille*[42] like a certain seller of water-melons who rose to a high place in the Boxer hierarchy and used to bawl: 'Secondary devil' at me, when he saw my chair. He had murdered many respectable people, and for that reason, not from any personal spite, I ordered his decapitation after the Court's return. Equally in the case of the murderers of the foreigner Hsiao 蕭 (James), not one escaped from the net, but the British Minister gave to me no thanks and seemed to hold me responsible for his unfortunate death. Perhaps you heard of the execution of Yang Li-shan 楊立山 (usually known as Li-shan, Yang being his original surname) with the aged Hsü Yung-yi 徐用儀 and Lien Yuan 聯元 on the 16. VII Moon. It shows the class of men from which the Boxers came, far inferior to a Marat or Robespierre. The 'patriots' surrounded the three men at the place of execution, cursing Li-shan as a friend of the foreigner Fan Kuo-liang 范國良 (Mgr. Favier). Li-shan with perfect calmness answered: 'You are just the dregs of the rabble. What do you know about state affairs? Yes; I did have some acquaintance with Fan but that does not make me a Christian convert. For example, you are lewd fellows of the baser sort, with a robber father and a harlot dam. Perhaps, when your mother (*Atsiye*, said the Grand Secretary using the Manchu word for mother) was taken ill with birth pangs, having no home to go to, she was fain to betake herself to the nearest street trough

---

42 Scum.

and there to be delivered of her babe. Does this make you, though born in a horse trough, a horse or a mule?' Then the Boxers stabbed him till he died!"

The Grand Secretary had already hinted – and I did not wish to outstay my welcome – that it was time to take leave, and thanking Junglu for his exceeding kindness I was about to depart; but he stopped me to present a poem by Grand Secretary Liu Lun 劉綸 written for the Ch'ien Lung Emperor and bound in jade covers. It is now in a European library.[43] "Come again," said Junglu, "in the autumn, and I will gladly resume this conversation."

Bowing most graciously he escorted me to the door of the study and Mr. Ch'i 耆 walked with me to the gate. After contact with such a personality the world seemed suddenly to have become dispiriting and devoid of zest. Although he sent his card to wish me a New Year greeting, I never saw him again. When the Empress who was staying at Paotingfu 保定府 learned of his death in the following April, she was greatly moved and is said never fully to have regained her former cheerfulness. What were the exact relations between them? I had no certain knowledge then, but he was surely in love with her.

---

43   The Bodleian Library at Oxford.

CHAPTER IV

SUMMER PALACE NOCTURNE:
THE PASTIMES OF MESSALINA

ON August 8, 1904, Li Ch'iu 立秋 or Beginning of Autumn, I was sojourning at Pa Ta Ch'u 八大處 in the Pi Mo Yen 碧默巖 when a note arrived from Li Lien-ying 李蓮英: "Decree from the Benevolent Mother: *Kung Feng Tz'u Chih: Cho Pa K'o-ssu Chin Wan Lai Yüan Yu Yao Shih Ch'in Tz'u* 恭奉慈旨著巴恪思今晚來園有要事欽此 – Pa K'o-ssu[1] is hereby commanded to attend at the Summer Palace this evening on important business. From the Empress." Li wrote: "Better to come in a *P'a Shan Hu*[2] 爬山虎 (a sort of mountain palanquin), "so as to attract less attention: leave the chair a li[3] or so from the Yi Ho Yüan Men[4] 頤和園門. Will have you met. Her Imperial Majesty will present your servants with Taels 250 as a special grace. Secret." I felt a second Königsmark commanded to Herrenhausen by Sophia Dorothea, or Potemkin; except that (as to the latter) I was going to Her instead of Her coming to her favorite at his Tauride Palace.[5] Guessing what the "important business" might be, I asked myself: was I sexually adequate for Her Majesty's overflowing carnality? Alas! I doubted it and wondered if I should develop the necessary timely orgasm to meet her unsated lust which would assuredly not have failed me, had another type of love been in question. I was thirty-two and she sixty-nine. What would she think of me, if, like le Capitaine Morhange in Pierre Benoist's great novel, *L'Atlantide*,[6] I failed toward my Antinea and was killed by Saint-Avit at the former's order?

My servants were naturally delighted and recommended a stiff dose of *Ma Ch'ien Tzu*[7] 馬前子; but I thought I would liefer[8] depend on Li

---

1   Pa K'o-ssu 巴恪思, a Chinese transliteration of "Backhouse".
2   Mountain-climbing tiger.
3   A Chinese distance measurement, approximately 645 meters in the late Ch'ing Dynasty.
4   The Summer Palace gate.
5   Philip Christoph von Königsmark (1665-94) was a Swedish count and the lover of Sophia Dorothea, wife of King George I. Königsmark was discovered and killed by the king, while Dorothea was divorced and imprisoned for the remainder of her life. Grigori Potemkin (1739-91) was a Russian prince and the longtime lover of Catherine the Great.
6   The author's last name is correctly written "Benoit".
7   A blended herbal remedy which is said to relieve arthritis and cure the bone injuries of martial arts practitioners.
8   Gladly.

Lien-ying and obtain some *Mei Yao*[9] 媚藥 aphrodisiac from him which would provoke sufficient stimulation to prevent my presenting to the Old Buddha a *telum imbelle et sine ictu*, a tool unwarlike and devoid of thrust,[10] like the faltering sword of Priam, slain by Pyrrhus at the fall of Troy.

There was heavy rain at forenoon, but the sun emerged and we managed to make our way along the water-logged country bypaths, some eight or nine miles distance, to the Wan Shou Temple's[11] 萬壽寺 imperial road, Yü Lu 御路, where two eunuchs met me and escorted me thence on foot. The chair bearers were told to attend at this trysting place the following morning and were given there and then an extra largess of Taels 50 from the Old Buddha, the fountain of munificence. I was wearing a grasscloth gown and had only a small satchel of toilet requisites. The eunuchs said that the Old Ancestress intended to take me for a short boating excursion on the K'un Ming Lake 昆明湖 after supper. As we entered the main gate and passed by the Jen Shou Tian 仁壽殿 or Hall of Audience, the name "The good are longlived" being in reference to Confucius' saying[12] and conveying a compliment to the Empress Dowager, I felt very self conscious, as if I were the cynosure of every eye. Of course, the eunuchs and palace women guessed the purport of my evening visit: in fact, I heard one Manchu girl of great beauty say: "There goes the foreign Junglu: *Chê Chiu Shih Yang Junglu Pa* 這就是洋榮祿吧."

Li Lien-ying was coming to meet me, wreathed in smiles, but on hearing this gibe, he changed countenance: "Insolent slave, how dare you! If the foreign marquis, *Wai Kuo Hou Yeh* 外國侯爺, (did I mention that the Empress had accorded to me the second hereditary rank, as well as ennobling my ancestors for three generations?) tells the Old Ancestress of your insult, she will have you flogged to death this very evening. Keep silent, *Shao Shuo Hua* 少說話, in future." The wretched girl knelt to implore pardon: naturally, I did not inform the Empress, there being no subject so calculated to incense her fury as her relations with Junglu, and I am not naturally malicious.

I asked Li what he would counsel regarding the aphrodisiac: he assured me that there was ample provision in the Palace for such an emergency. Laughing, he said: "We have a *Mei Yao* which will make you as erect as the man in the *Liao Chai* 聊齋: after quaffing the potion, *Ting Tsu Erh San*[13] 鼎足而三, his tool extended itself into a third leg, until he became a tripod!"

Li then gave me some valuable suggestions as to *modus operandi*, while we walked toward the small apartment which adjoined the Phoenix Bed

---

9   Spring medicine.

10   Virgil, *Aeneid* II.544.

11   The private temple of the Ch'ing imperial clan, located on the water route from the Forbidden City to the Summer Palace.

12   The Master said, "The wise find pleasure in water; the virtuous find pleasure in hills. The wise are active; the virtuous are tranquil. The wise are joyful; the virtuous are long-lived" (*The Chinese Classics, vol. I, Confucian Analects*, 論語, trans. by James Legge).

13   "Three-legged Ting", an ancient cooking vessel.

Chamber. "The Old Ancestress will require the most intimate contact: you must perfume your whole person for the occasion. She has never seen a naked European of decent birth and will want to inspect you closely behind and before. (Did she imagine that knight and clown are different under their skins? A tool or an anus is unconnected with social rank.) Custom ordains that you should remain on your knees and I have prepared stuffed cushions for the purpose."

"Excuse me, Your Honour, but I do not perceive how genuflexion can fail to impede my freedom of movement: in any case, sexual excitement will be difficult of attainment, even with your potion; and I suppose that the Old Buddha would desire an adequate measure of response on my part."

"Of course," said Li, "a flaccid unmilitant member is not at all what the Empress welcomes. You must be guided by circumstances and the Old Buddha will certainly make allowance for any difficulties you might have before obtaining the desired orgasm."

By this time, Li had shown me into my temporary bed-room and a fair young eunuch named Lien Yung 連榮, from Hochienfu 河間府 came forward to meet me, bringing with him a new unlined satin gown *Tan Mo Pen* 單模本 to replace my grasscloth *Hsia Pu Shan'rh*[14] 夏布衫兒 which was distinctly chilly after the heavy rain and not at all suited for a jaunt on the lake.

"I'll go and announce your arrival to the Old Ancestress," said Li; "she has ordered the evening meal for you *al fresco* if you prefer it." In a minute he returned with a "Follow me: she will see you now for a moment."

So we passed into the boudoir which adjoined her bed-chamber; she was playing chess with a maid of honour and smiled most graciously: "You are always punctual. Have a good meal and I will take you for a short excursion on the lake after I have had a whiff or two of opium. I need not command you to be *sans gêne*:[15] you are always welcome here." I knelt to thank Her Majesty who presented me to the lady in waiting as the "foreign marquis" in whom she reposed absolute trust. Then I left the Presence and in due course Li Lien-ying joined me at a moderately elaborate dinner, the cuisine being perfect but on a more reasonable scale than the banquets with which she and he had regaled me in town.

Li talked sex during the meal: "The Old Buddha," said he, "loves to rub her person (*crede experto*)[16] against her *vis-à-vis*: you will probably find that she will *Ts'eng* 蹭 (*frictionner*) your anus (*Yen'rh* 眼兒) with her clitoris (*Yin T'i* 陰蒂, in Japanese *Inkaku*, or *Yin Ho* 陰核) which is abnormally large." (In other words, Tz'u Hsi 慈禧 was a *tribade*[17] like Mrs. Asquith – now Lady Oxford – Mme Bernhardt, and the English actresses

---

14 Gown of summery material.
15 At ease.
16 Believe one who has experienced (Virgil, *Aeneid* XI.283).
17 This term can often mean lesbian, but in this instance it would seem to mean someone who enjoys tribadism, rubbing the vulva and clitoris against another object.

Mrs. Bernard Beere, Miss Marion Terry and the *danseuse*,[18] Mrs. Asquith's homosexual intimate, Miss Maude Allen. She had, like those ladies, what I can only call, a definite erection (*en miniature*) at her disposition.)

Chacun son goût,[19] and I am making no criticism; it exhilarates me however, to note the interest that great persons in the Manchu régime, from the Old Buddha downwards, took in the posterior and anal region as well as in the more obvious *parties sexuelles*. Octave Mirbeau (whom I once slightly knew in the "naughty nineties") writes in his *Souvenirs d'une femme de chambre* how one of that young woman's mistresses says to her on entering service: "*J'exige la plus absolue propreté des parties secrètes.*"[20] Li Lien-ying reminded me of that artless dame, when he kept on repeating *ad nauseam*: "The Old Ancestress is most particular; be sure to perfume your entire body, especially the hinder parts and above all the fundament. I have prepared for you an exotic sandal-wood scent and you shall have your entire pubic and perineal region in the aroma of Mientien 緬甸 (Birmanie).[21] The Old Buddha affects violet perfume, from (*si je ne me trompe pas*)[22] Roger et Gallet, but the sandal-wood fragrance of her *vis-à-vis* excites her wildest passion." It was true: the Empress' scent of fresh violets which assailed the nostril brought to me a curious souvenir of Sarah the immortal who had admitted me for a brief season to the number of her intimates (or ever she discarded me like a fan in autumn) in the days after her opening of the Théâtre de la Renaissance in 1893, when Oncle Sarcey was delivering heavy conferences from the stage as a sort of *lever de rideau*[23] prior to Mme. Bernhardt's divine interpretation of *Phèdre*.

I asked Li when I was to take the potion. "After you return from the lake outing, the Old Ancestress will require to rest awhile for her opium night-cap. If you will quaff it quite slowly – the flavour is most agreeable – you will gradually find a pleasing *fraîcheur*[24] (as Louis XVI once said, not knowing that he would one day *facere experimentum*,[25] when he saw, as a new model, for the first time in 1790 the guillotine and suggested certain improvements, remarking that decapitation connoted no pain but *une légère fraîcheur*)[26] steal over your lower limbs and the sexual instinct will only be excited after about one hour's interval. You will – and I speak from experience, although alas! I lack the necessary instrument of passion and am only left with *le foyer érotique qu'est mon trou fignon, Yen'rh Tso Yu So Lai Ti Chin'rh*[27] 眼兒左右所來的勁兒, still I can assure you that you may rest easy as to the desired erection, especially as the drug protracts the pleasure in delaying consummation, which is

---

18 Ballerina.
19 To each his own.
20 I demand absolute cleanliness of secret parts (*Diary of a Chambermaid*).
21 Burma, now Myanmar.
22 If I am not mistaken.
23 Raising of the curtain.
24 Coolness.
25 Have a trial.
26 A slight coolness.
27 The erotic centre that is my anus.

Shun Lao Tsu Tsung Ti Hsin Ssu 順老祖宗的心思, exactly what Her Majesty desires. You will have to repeat the dose during the night, as the Old Buddha will certainly order your attendance before dawn, when she has to go to the Throne Hall for morning audience of the Council and one or two high provincial functionaries who have arrived in the metropolis and are attending here to salute Their Majesties. After the Council, she will rest for some hours; but you must be prepared for the *bouquet qui terminera pour le moment ce feu d'artifice*[28] in the afternoon before you leave us."

"I can assure Your Honour that Europeans of decent birth are no less nice in their personal cleanliness than Manchus themselves; it may well be that the white race exudes a particular odour of its own, due to dietary causes or the action of the skin; but I trust that I shall be found worthy of this unique honour of being the Old Buddha's temporary *Amour*; albeit only a *comparse* unworthy of the name of *Cupidon*.[29] But I doubt my capacity for so many acts of sex in sequence."

"*Chê Hua Shuo Yüan La*[30] 這話說遠啦, you are too modest," said Li; "but there is one matter I must needs mention. Do you perspire freely in this weather? I ask because the Old Buddha cannot abide the odour of perspiration: you must by all manner of means free yourself from the slightest *soupçon*."[31]

"*Vous prêchez un converti*,"[32] said I, "but in this autumnal humidity I can only hope for the best and shall obey your injunctions *à la lettre*."[33]

"One word more: don't allow my young eunuch catamite to fascinate you: I know your exotic tastes and if you and he indulge in love-caress, you will be like sweet bells jangled, out of tune and harsh, for the Old Buddha's phoenix couch: and she will blame me."

At this moment, the palace launch came puffing up, as if weary of the effort, to the landing place. The Old Buddha had bidden her niece, daughter-in-law, the young Yohonala, wife of Kuang Hsü 光緒 to join our party which consisted only of the two empresses, Li and myself with two young Manchu attendants. The young empress was unprepossessing but personally charming. On my being presented and offering to kneel in homage, she said: "You are excused. I am glad you have come to keep the Old Buddha company: you amuse Her Majesty with your gaiety and jokes." The empress was wearing a cream-coloured gown of *Hu Chou*[34] 湖縐, *diaprée*[35] with swallowtail butterflies: her hair was dressed in the then prevailing *La Chih*[36] 拉翅 fashion. Her hare-lip imparted to her face a disagreeable impression despite a pleasant smile. When the Old Buddha

---

28   Bouquet which will end in fireworks.
29   Minor player . . . Cupid.
30   This strays from the point.
31   Suspicion.
32   You preach to the converted.
33   To the letter.
34   A variety of silk produced in Huchow.
35   Mottled.
36   A head ornament popular among the Manchu and other palace women during the late Ch'ing period.

appeared on the terrace, supported by Li Lien-ying and her favourite attendant Ts'ui 崔, the young empress knelt to receive her and I naturally did likewise.

"What do you think of my foreign favourite, *Yang Hung Jen'rh* 洋紅人兒? Isn't he amusing and, I think, handsome? *Pu Shih Wei Mei Shao* 不失爲美少, quite a good-looking young fellow!"

"Oh! yes, Old Buddha: he has just said to me that there's an autumnal feeling in the air." (As a matter of fact, Li Ch'iu 立秋 fell that year in the evening, but the coolness that I had noticed was due to proximity of the lake.)

"Well," said the Old Buddha, "rise both of you from your knees and join me on the launch:" addressing Ts'ui: "go and call those two girls, Ts'ui Huan 翠環 and Yü Huan 玉環, and we'll start at once."

The two young ladies duly appeared and seemed not unfavourably disposed to me, clad as I was in the decidedly picturesque robes graciously provided by Li. "*To Ta Tsao Hua* 多大造化, you are a fortunate mortal," said one of them to me. As a fact, I was not so sure about the *Tsao Hua* 造化 or felicity: because there were grave doubts in my mind, love potion or no, whether I would induce myself into the required sexual plenitude: and then the curtain would fall on a fiasco (*cela ferait four*) and my nation's reputation for virility would be shaken for good and all. And if I succeeded, what a wreck I should be after three ejaculations or more!

The Old Buddha sate on a lacquer chair in the bows; cushions were prepared for the rest of the party, the young empress sitting at her mother-in-law's knees and the three of us to her right and left. It was delightful on the water and we made a tour of the lake while the Empress Dowager addressed herself mainly to me: "Tell me, was Queen Victoria in love with her attendant Po Leng (Brown)? I have seen a photograph of him carrying her in his arms across a stream near her 'Summer Resort' (Balmoral) and he looks very handsome and very amorous."

"Madame, the late Queen made herself most ridiculous by the attention she paid to him. In fact, the people of her Scottish capital resented her affection for a Scot of such low class and actually mocked the queen as she drove through the streets of Edinburgh by shouting 'Mrs. Brown!' at her carriage procession."

"Did not Victoria have the rebels punished for their treason? I should like to see the people of Peking mocking me, because of you, Lien-ying: they would not repeat the insult."

"In these matters, Your Majesty, royalty in Great Britain is quite helpless. In Germany or Russia, there would be charges of *Majestätsbeleidigung*[37] but in England only in case of an actual *Attentat*,[38] in which case the offender is liable to flogging from the 'nine-tailed cat'."

"Your 'Limited' Monarchy is indeed limited: if these are the blessings of a constitution, I am sorry for our Dynasty if China obtain what

37   Insulting the monarch, a criminal offense in most parts of Europe since the Medieval period.
38   Attack.

Yi K'uang 奕劻 (the personal name of Prince Ch'ing 慶 whose courtesy name was Fu T'ing 輔廷) and the rest of them are always urging me to promulgate. But how stupid of Victoria to allow such a snap-shot to be taken of her in amorous dalliance with a coolie!"

"The photo was snapped by the then Princess of Wales, now queen, who is very mischievous and wished to get 'even' with her mother-in-law who ill-treated her for thirty odd years till even King Christian IX of Denmark protested at the unbearable cruelties inflicted on his dear daughter by the Queen of England."

"Do you hear that, *Huang Hou* 皇后," (to my interest the Old Buddha called her daughter-in-law by her title of empress and not by her name). "Have I ever maltreated you?"

"Never, Old Buddha, you have been kinder to me than my own mother."

"Tell me, K'o-ssu," said the Old Buddha, "how did Victoria ill-treat her daughter-in-law? Surely not by beating or torturing her, as too many *Man Tzu* 蠻子 (Chinese) women do. We Manchus always treat the younger generation well."

"No, Madame: in a moral, not a physical sense. Victoria always belittled poor Alix and mocked her little country, being pro-German and hating everything Danish ever since the Prusso-Danish war early in Your Majesty's Regency."

"If Victoria had asked you to 'dine and sleep', I suppose you would have gone? You dared not decline?"

"She would not have accorded me such an honour, Madame, as my age and rank were not adequate, although my grandfather and great uncle were intimately associated with the prince consort Albert, but she might have received me in Scotland for a short audience, as I was intimate of her life-long friend Sir John Clark, Baronet of Tillypronie (near Balmoral)."

"Was the Queen salaciously minded?"

"It is said that during her husband's life time, she was with difficulty *assouvie*[39] of her lust: the prince consort had to perform carnal commerce five, six, or even seven times a night, *I Yeh Chih Ch'i Ch'i Chih To* 一夜至七起之多. But since his death at 42, due to *Fang Shih Kuo Tu* 房事過度, over much lechery, which caused his weakened system to succumb to typhoid fever, I suppose that she has remained chaste, despite gossip to the contrary."

"I don't believe it," said the Empress: "like your Virgin Queen, I suppose, who had – how many – lovers; over twenty, they tell me!"

"The prince himself," said I, "was hot-blooded: Your Majesty may not know what is a court secret of which my family has sure and certain cognizance, that he was legitimized after birth by the Grand Duke of Saxe-Coburg but was the product of a liaison between the Grand Duchess and a Jewish violinist: hence his artistic tastes and the marked *Yu T'ai*

---

39   Satisfied.

猶太 (Jewish) traits of our present King who is never so happy as when reposing with a bevy of fat Jewesses from Baghdad. Alas! for the empire governed by such."

"You are talking treason," said the Empress Dowager, gallantly retrieving the name of her brother sovereign. "You know our adage: *T'u Ssu Hu Pei* 兔死狐悲 – when the hare dies, the fox weeps," an allusion to the fellow-sympathy between peers in weal and in woe.

"When Prinz Heinrich v. Preussen was here in the spring of the 24 Kuang Hsü (April 1898) he told me that neither the emperor nor he were friendly to his mother the Empress Friedrich. Why was that?"

"Because, Madame, the Kaiserin Witwe, though a brilliantly talented woman, had no tact and was despotic like Queen Victoria."

"Was she like me?"

"No, Your Majesty, because you win universal devotion and she was never popular except in the land of her birth, England."

"I am told that the Tsar is filial to his mother but that his wife is most wilful and disobedient."

"Yes, Your Majesty, she encourages Nicolai to defy the empress dowager."

"Do you hear that, empress," said the Old Buddha: "What about our family ménage here?"

The young empress answered: "Here we have a dutiful daughter-in-law, at least I think so, but an emperor who is not exactly . . . . "

"Filial," put in the Old Buddha: "no, certainly *not* filial!!"

"Tell me," turning to me, "about the empress Friedrich's second morganatic marriage."

"I have heard from Germans, Madame, that she was married to a Graf v. Seckendorf, but do not know for certain."

"Is it true," asked the Old Buddha, "that the late President of the French Republic, M. Félix Faure, died of an apoplectic stroke after a too hearty function while engaged in amorous dalliance with a well-known demimondaine?"[40]

"I have heard so, but the details were kept officially secret; and I was not in Paris at the time," (February 1899, Kuang Hsü 25. I Moon). "The death was given out as from a *coup de sang*."[41]

Changing the subject, *more suo*,[42] the Empress asked if I had read of her recent order that the revolutionary Shen Chin 申蓋 be flogged to death in the Palace precincts. "This is an auspicious year for me and, were it not for the war between Japan and Russia, I should have sanctioned special celebration for the 70th anniversary of my birth next X Moon. I was also the more reluctant to impose the death penalty on Shen Chin, but he was a second K'ang Yu-wei 康有爲 and I had no alternative. You foreigners think me cruel but know nothing of the provocation which compels drastic punishment. Is flogging still used in England?"

---

40 Promiscuous woman; prostitute.
41 Stroke.
42 In her usual manner.

"Yes, Madame; in schools and colleges it is the habitual punishment and is sanctioned in the law courts for certain offences, such as robbery under arms for which the nine-tailed whip is applied."

"Were you ever flogged as a boy?"

"Yes, Your Majesty, during my school days, aged ten to sixteen."

"When I was a girl, I remember old people saying that when your King sent a tribute mission to the Ch'ien Lung 乾隆 Emperor in 1793, the soldiers of the ambassador's escort were cruelly flogged across the bared shoulders, in some cases, till they died."

"It is so, Your Majesty, a diary kept by a member of Macartney's staff records the fact."

"Is it true that homosexuality between males is punishable with flogging?"

"Not exactly, Your Majesty, but there is an old ordinance which permits 'incorrigible rogues and vagabonds' to receive twenty-four strokes on the naked posterior, so that notorious pederasts might render themselves liable to this humiliating chastisement."

"Well, well," said the Empress Dowager, "*Shui Pieh Shuo Shui* 誰別說誰, neither of our nations has the right to criticise the other; but I think you English are hypocritical in your catchwords about humanity."

The Western Hills were almost unbelievably green after the rain and the sun set in a bank of blood-red cloud, symbolizing perchance the unsated craving of the most passionate of women like a Marie Antoinette for her Fersen. The palace and its spacious precincts were illumined in the gathering dusk with a thousand delicately shaded electric lights, here, there and everywhere: 'twas a veritable fairyland, the 'Peach Fountain' T'ao Yüan 桃源 of T'ao Yüan-ming 陶淵明, *Yu I Tung T'ien* 又一洞天, a new heaven and a new earth.[43]

"We will go round the lake once more," said the Empress Dowager who was wearing a deep purple satin cloak with a Wan Tzu Pu Tao T'ou[44] 萬字不到頭 pattern, perpetual longevity renewed again and again. Li Lien-ying handed to her the "Russian gold" cigarettes which she affected. She bade the empress and the rest of us be at our ease and smoke as fancy willed, forgetful of her presence.

"They tell me," said she to me, "that you *Wan'rh Piao* 玩兒票 sometimes – engage in amateur theatricals – with the young princes and that you rather excel in women's parts."

"Your Majesty is most gracious: before coming to China I had some foreign theatrical training under M. Got of 'La Comédie Française' and later under Mme. Bernhardt, so the technique, which is the same in China or abroad, is fairly familiar. I took Yang Kuei-fei 楊貴妃 (Ch'ü Kuei Fei 去貴妃) in 'The Hall of Immortality' and in Ma Wei P'o 馬嵬坡 with Prince

---

43 The Peach Blossom "Fountain" (Spring) is an account of a rustic utopia discovered accidently by a fisherman during the Ch'in Dynasty and never found again. "*Tung T'ien*" is a traditional Taoist term, usually means a cave which is spiritually blessed.

44 "A Myriad of Characters with No End" is a traditional, auspicious pattern employed in fabric and other designs.

Kung 恭 as Ming Huang 明皇, also in T'ien Ho P'ei 天河配 the heroine's part."[45]

"You never met the late Sixth Prince, Liu Yeh 六爺, his grandfather, I suppose?"

"No, Your Majesty, he died, as you know, in 24. IV. of Kuang Hsü (May 1898) shortly after my arrival from Tokyo."

"He hated your countrymen but would have liked your lively wit and *insouciance*.[46] His grandson, P'u Wei 溥偉, takes after him in his *penchant* for his own sex: the boy is absolutely in the hands of his pet eunuch who keeps him away from his wife, so that the pair cannot even enjoy natural intercourse."

"Yes, Your Majesty, the eunuch is mad with jealousy. There is a bath house outside the Hou Men[47] 後門 where Prince Kung and he often visit, it being conveniently close to Kung Wang Fu[48] 恭王府. Your foreign servant frequently amuses himself there, playing chess with members of the imperial clan or talking scandal."

"More scandal than chess, I suppose," said the Old Buddha: "*Ch'iao Tzu Lun, Yen'rh Chuan* 巧子論, 眼兒傳, gossip about tools, expatiations concerning the anus."

"What is the *Tzu Hao* 字號, sign of the house?"

"Hsin Ching 新淨, Your Majesty, the renovation of cleanliness."

"Do you know it, Lien-ying?"

"Oh yes! Old Ancestress."

"After our return to town, you must arrange for me to go there in disguise: it would amuse me to see all you dissolute young men diverting yourselves 'after the tea, and subsequent to the wine', *Ch'a Yü Chiu Hou* 茶餘酒後."

"I often see the dispossessed *Ta A Ko*[49] 大阿哥, P'u Ch'un 溥儁 there."

"Tell him from me to behave himself: I expect *un peu de tenue*[50] from that naughty boy who might have been emperor today but for your foreign devils. Ask him if he remembers the whipping on his posterior which I ordered for him owing to his insolence during the Boxer troubles."

"Well," went on the Old Buddha, "it is getting chilly: let us go back to the landing stage."

There were many female attendants and eunuchs awaiting our return, including the young "eunuch" who was detached for my service and to whom I was irresistibly attracted, *vu mon penchant assez fort*,[51] as Saint-Simon says of the Duc de Bourgogne, toward the sex which I

---

45 Yang Kuei-fei (d. 756) was the infamous concubine of Ming Huang (712-56), who was strangled in the town of Ma Wei P'o at the demand of the soldiery when the court was fleeing during the Rebellion of An Lu-shan. The romance of Ming Huang and Yang Kuei-fei has been a popular subject in Chinese art and literature.

46 Indifference.

47 Rear gate.

48 Prince Kung's Residence.

49 Eldest son of the emperor.

50 A little behavior.

51 Knowing which side I was leaning.

dishonour! Her Majesty graciously leant on my arm as we disembarked. "Now go," said she, "and do what Lien-ying told you. But don't be *T'ao Ch'i* 淘氣, (mischievous, said to children) with your little 'eunuch', or I shall smack your buttocks (*Ta Ni Ti P'i Ku* 打你的屁股)," holding up a warning finger.

The young empress bade me a cheery good-bye with a "Now don't tire yourself out and keep the Old Buddha (who is lonely) pleasant company."

"Aren't you jealous of me," asked the Old Buddha: "he is my personal property for the time being!" Addressing my eunuch myrmidon: "Take the *Hou Yeh* 侯爺 (honouring me with my title of nobility) to his room." To me she said: "I shall send for you after about two hours, so be ready and don't fail me."

Thus we parted, while the attendants murmured audible compliments such as: "Heaven sends him unique fortune:" "Affinities are made by God:" "The phoenix alights amidst a flock of geese." (This phrase is not so rude as it sounds: "*Feng Huang Lo Tsai Ch'ün Chih Chung* 鳳凰落在群鵝之中". It suggests the descent of a goddess to the home of a mortal.)

My small bedroom was furnished with three hundred candle power lights. There was a comfortable settee and adequate appointments. The 'eunuch' obligingly offered to assist me at my ablution and I, nothing loth, started to fondle him, tactics which he partially returned, adding, however: "This is not the time, *Chê Pu Shih Shih Hou* 這不是時候: *Kei Tsan Men T'ien Shih* 給咱們添事, you will get us both into trouble. I should like to enter into *Mi Mi Ti Kuan Hsi* 秘密的關係, secret relations, with you, as there is evident *Yüan* or affinity. I could come to your temple some days hence, after you are rested. We can amuse ourselves there. Ask the *Tu Tsung Kuan* 都總管 (chief eunuch) to give me leave. I shall only ask Taels 150 fee plus expenses, but you must let me copulate with you as well as vice versa."

"How can that be?" said I: "if you have left the family" (*Ch'u Chia* 出家 became eunuch).

"But I have only partially been emasculated," said he, exhibiting to my astonished eyes a well developed shapely penis in substantial erection and a scrotum with only one testicle which he bade me feel, the other having been emasculated at the time of his entry into palace service. He began washing me all over with the sandal-wood scent, imprinted his lips on my glans penis and anal region; then he "*K'ei Yen'rh*" 扣眼兒 inserted his finger in my fundament (*K'ei* is not a recognized character, probably a corruption for *K'ou* 扣; the term *K'ei Yen'rh* is a somewhat vulgar expression equivalent to possession of a person up the Arschloch. If the fore finger of the right hand is placed between thumb and left forefinger held in conjunction, a lewd suggestion is conveyed, just as when emperor Caligula Gaius Caesar made this obscene gesture to the tribune Chareas who later avenged himself for the implied disparagement by assassinating his sovereign). I kissed the eunuch's fundament which was nicely scented with cinnamon and was putting my finger inside the anal cavity, when Li arrived with the *Mei Yao* or potion.

"Now you two must behave yourselves," said Li: "he shall come and see you one day soon. For the moment, a truce to any privy relations. Sit down and take the medicine slowly." It was a deep crimson fluid, very pungent and aromatic. After I had drained the cup (*bu le calice jusqu'à la lie*), Li said: "You must walk up and down the chamber, until you feel your lower limbs becoming cold. Then lie down and await events." Even so did the gaoler in Socrates' prison on the Areopagus bid Athena's wisest son to move about the cell after taking the *ciguë* or hemlock, until the chill rigor, harbinger of death, ensued. Not that I felt nervous of any sinister developments, but the parallel crossed my mind. Owing to the eunuch's attractions, I was already in a state of robust erection which augmented as the drug took effect. Both Li and the attendant then left me and it was not long before the aphrodisiac engendered a plenitude of carnality such as I have never experienced before nor since; not even in my naughty school days when I was the desired of many. I was literally aflame with lust and exclaimed with Romeo "Oh wise apothecary" in honour of the inventor of so blessed a drug.

Li returned and again anointed my secret parts, anus, perineum, pubic region with the undiluted sandal-wood scent: he put a light cloak which reached as far as the thighs round me and summoned me to the Presence. Her Majesty's bedchamber was blazing with a score of lights; the spacious apartment was lined with a series of mirrors which reminded me of the Galerie des Glaces at Versailles. They all reflected my homely features red with passion and a-hungered for the encounter. Li accompanied me to the phoenix couch, and the Empress exclaimed: "My bed is cold: come and soothe my loneliness."

Li said: "Kneel down on the cushion and let the Old Buddha caress you behind and before."

"Nonsense," said the Empress, "how in the world can he do what he wants to do, *Wei So Yü Wei* 爲所欲爲, in a kneeling posture! Let him disclose his bounteous nudity; for I wish to feast my eyes on his personal charms, *Yüan Pao Yen Fu* 願飽眼福." Li then took leave of the Majesty and left us together. She was clad in a light robe of *Hu Chou* 湖縐 open at the front and unveiling her pudenda. Several electric fans, as well as large blocks of ice in lovely cloisonné chests, cooled the room: I had no fear of offending Her Majesty by the perspiration which she held in such abhorrence, for I was as one in a desert drought, burning with desire – what for? the woman of sixty-nine who awaited me, or was she only the symbol, the substitute, for other persons nearer to my heart?

"You must forget that I am empress: regard me as Yang Kuei Fei 楊貴妃 and yourself as T'ang Ming Huang 唐明皇, that poetic Son of Heaven."

"How could I dare, Old Buddha? To me Your Majesty is Avalokitesvara, the Goddess of Mercy, ever young, ever fair; what the Catholics call

'Stella Maris', the star of hope which emergeth from the sea and symbolizeth peace and harmony, even as the Blessed Virgin of their faith."

"You foolish boy: you are thirty-three (am I right?) and I am sixty-nine: how old would you think me, if you did not know, and were guessing my age?"

"Between thirty and thirty-five, Your gracious Majesty; nothing can wither your infinite variety."

"Flatterer! now exhibit to me your genitals, for I know I shall love them." I had by this time an enormous orgasm and the Old Buddha fondled my *verge* and glans penis, kissing many times the urethral orifice or *meatus* (*Ma Yen* 馬眼) which was saturated in the exotic perfume. Then she played with my voluminous scrotum, and I thought of Juvenal's decidedly uncomplimentary 4th Satire on Women, "*Sic volo sic jubeo*",[52] where the slave's genitals are discussed. She fondled my abundant pubic hair, saying: "But I thought you foreigners always shaved the *Chi Pa Mao* 肌巴毛 (hair adjoining the prick)?"

"No, Your Majesty, it is not now the custom; but the ancient Greeks and Roman Patricians were particular to allow no hair to grow round and on penis or fundament."

"But I have seen foreign paintings of nude men and women without a trace of hair."

"Yes, Your Majesty, because it is not considered decent to portray the secret hair upon the canvas."

Next the Empress took my penis into her mouth and continued titillation with her tongue. God was very good, and I had no ejaculation, as the potency of the drug retarded the flow of sperm. She bade me contemplate her august Person and I admired the abundant wealth of pubic hair, while at her command I took in my hands her abnormally large clitoris, pressed toward it my lips and performed a low but steady friction which increased its size. She graciously unveiled the mysteries of her swelling vulva, even as that of Messalina,[53] and I marvelled at the perennial youth which its abundance seemed to indicate. She allowed me to fondle her breasts which were those of a young married woman; her skin was exquisitely scented with the violet to which I have made allusion; her whole body, small and shapely, was redolent with *la joie de vivre*; her shapely buttocks pearly and large were presented to my admiring contemplation: I felt for her a real libidinous passion such as no woman has ever inspired in my pervert homosexual mind before nor since. And I, God forgive me, had wondered if I could retrieve the necessary orgasm in her adorable proximity! Was it the love potion, or was it the charm in presence of which I must need hush and bless myself with silence? For the moment, in the ardour of my compelling erection, I felt: "*Vivit sub pectore vulnus* (*Enéide*, IV. 67),[54] this wound (of love) will abide

---

52 So I wish, so I command (Juvenal, *Satires* VI.223).
53 Valeria Messalina (d. 48 AD) was a Roman Empress, who exercised great influence on her husband, Claudius.
54 The wound lives beneath the skin (*Aeneid*).

me for ever." Then Her Majesty bade me place my scented fingers inside her vulva and apply my lips to its ample surface. As I expected, she next told me to kneel over the couch in the full glare of the garish light and the reflection of the mirrors which presented the counterfeit resemblance of my buttocks which she graciously likened to a peach; she minutely inspected the fundament until she bade me open up with my two fore-fingers and caressed it with her long-nailed index, inserting it (to my discomfort) inside the anus. Then she drew closer and brought her erect clitoris into juxtaposition of my *trou fignon*[55] which she poetically com-pared to a rose-bud. She worked the member (which Marie Antoinette so loved in the princesse de Lamballe) backward and forward inside my anus; until, after perhaps five minutes or more, the gratifying titillation caused her to exclaim: "*Shu Fu* 舒服", "*Hao Shou* 好受", Agreeable, pleas-ing sensation. I cannot explain why, but a definite discharge of a sticky fluid wetted me in and around the anal cavity.

"*Ta Yen'rh* 大眼兒," said she: "Large anus: I'll warrant that it has seen service."

"Yes, Your Majesty, I'll not deny it and plead guilty to the impeach-ment."

"How many times?"

"Innumerable as the hairs of the head," replied I unblushingly.

"We are all as nature makes us," said the Empress: "what are we but puppets! *So Hao Pu T'ung*[56] 所好不同 *De gustibus nil disputandum*."[57]

She then administered to me across the buttocks half a dozen sound slaps with the handle of her ivory fan. My sexual energy remaining una-bated, she said in the vulgar tongue: "*Hsien Tsai Ni K'o I Ts'ao Wo* 現在你可以奮我, *K'o Shih Lin Tsou Shen Tzu Shih Hou*, 可是臨走身子時候, *Ni Yen Yü I Sheng* 你言語一聲. *Wo Yüan Ni Pa Ch'iao Tzu Pa Ch'u Lai* 我願你把巧子拔出來, *Wang Wo Tsui I Ko Wo Hao Pa Ching Yen Liao* 往我嘴一攔我好把精咽了, *Tê I Yang Shen* 得以養神. – You are now permitted to have me, but just before you are coming, let me know. I want you to take your tool out and put it in my mouth, so that I may swallow the semen and thus enjoy a tonic." (Oscar Wilde used to say that the male sperm, if swallowed, was beneficial to the system and he should know!)

Naturally I obeyed and the act was, thanks to the potion, abnormally slow: it gave to me intense pleasure and, I think, to the Empress equally. Her consummation practically synchronized with mine, but I did her bidding and was just able to ejaculate in her mouth. "*Suan Pu Chi Ti* 酸不積的," said she, "it has a sourish taste."

"I am sorry, Your Majesty."

"Don't apologize: I like it and enjoy the tart flavour."

It was now about midnight, and she called for Li who apparently had been waiting, more or less within earshot, and doubtless feeling a certain responsibility regarding the success or failure of our enterprise.

55   Anus.
56   Our preferences differ.
57   There can be no disputation about matters of taste.

"*Hao T'ung K'uai* 好痛快, most pleasant," said she: "take the marquis away now but bring him back about 4 a.m. I hereby confer upon him an advancement of one grade, from Class III to Class II in the *Hou* 侯 rank, and the Triple Peacock Feather in commemoration of our union. Now leave me and have a short repose."

Li was enthusiastic: "*Tso Lien* 作臉, you have done us credit; I never saw the Old Ancestress better satisfied."

"It is largely thanks to you and your potion. I suppose that I shall have to trouble you again, *Ch'ung Fan Kao Ming* 重煩高明, for the next dose."

"First lie down for a couple of hours and I will see that your servant calls you in good time for Act II."

I felt very weary and the reaction had begun: it was impossible to close my eyes and I lay dry and listless under the electric fan. As I lay there, naked as when I emerged from the womb of my mother, flaccid and limp, I marvelled that I should have found favour in the sight of the *Chiu Yu Chih Tsun* 九有至尊, *Chiang Shan Chih Chu*[58] 江山之主, the sovereign of a mighty empire. What a wreck I shall be after two more ejaculations, thought I: how am I ever going to get back to the temple without falling by the way! Will the Empress often require my presence hereafter? I cannot refuse but doubt my own strength to comply.

Well: after an interval Li returned with the tonic philter, bidding me take a double dose. It took longer to act on this occasion, but the orgasm slowly but surely returned and I felt the former ardour revive. By the time the Empress commanded me, I was erect as ever and ready, if need be, to do and die. We went through identical evolutions, except that this time she bade me ejaculate during the sexual congress. I timed it well and the wished for consummation synchronized *de part et d'autre*.[59] In the interval, she asked me about the discoveries at Pompei and was interested in my description of the *Cabinet Secret* in the Museo Borbone at Naples, where the salacious goat is being possessed by a no less lustful human, the Roman soldier at Pompei with his abundant erection imprinted on the lava for perennial ages, the picture on the wall of the husband copulating from behind with his mistress while the slave approaches with the philter, interested and libidinous.

So all went merry as a marriage bell, until Li arrived to announce the hour for Her Majesty's *Ch'ing Shui Yin* 清水癮 or morning opium pipe, prior to her going to audience of the Grand Council. The morning was quite chilly and she had put on a warmer wrap, while I was still in a state of nudity as to my lower limbs. She graciously gave me tea and then dismissed me until the afternoon, "just before you go!" So I returned to my court after performing ablutions and actually achieved a short sleep.

At about 7 I heard the chair bearer cry: "The Old Ancestress has returned," and in due course my eunuch arrived with a collation which

---

58   "Most honored among the Nine States; ruler of rivers and mountains", Nine States refers to the
      geographical divisions of China under the mythical Yu the Great.
59   On both sides.

included birds' nest soup, a comforting cordial, for I was on the verge of exhaustion.

As the morning advanced, I took a short walk by the lake side and incidentally met Kuang Hsü who was in a cane palace chair and scrutinized me (as I knelt on his passage) in no friendly guise, without however asking me to explain my presence in the Forbidden Precincts.

Li and I partook of an abundant luncheon in my room, as it was too hot to sit outside. He brought to me a third dose of the philtre at about one o'clock: thanks to its ultra-potency I again achieved an ample orgasm and was able to satisfy my Messalina, *nondum satiate*.[60] Once more I accomplished successful coitus, after she had kissed, and applied her lips to, my private parts and anus not once but a hundred times, while I retaliated in full measure to her pleasure and mine own. She bade me an affectionate farewell, kissing my face and hands and saying that I had greatly cheered her with my genial sexuality and naive charm. "Don't let people know," said she; but secrets are not well kept in China and I am afraid the matter was soon noised abroad with appropriate additions. Her Majesty bade Li hand to me Taels 500 for my servants and bearers. I offered Li a similar sum for his kind offices but he would accept nothing, while promising to send the young eunuch to my temple at no distant date for a fee of Taels 200 *tout compris*.[61]

I was so weak that I had to be supported in the short but painfully hot walk to my mountain chair and on reaching the temple just about sundown happened to meet the abbot who remarked: "What a wreck you look!" And my appearance belied not my weariness and lack of vitality.

My household naturally was all agog and deemed that they were no less honoured than their master by the Old Buddha's unparalleled favours. In fact, I think that my majordomo really believed that *he* had copulated with Her Majesty!

News certainly travels fast in China, for next day, as I was taking the air on the temple terrace, the rustics watched me, one of whom said: "Do you see that devil?"

"Oh yes: what about him?"

"Do you notice anything unusual?"

"No: he is quite a good looking devil."

"Well: *T'a Ts'ao Kuo Lao Fo Yeh*: 他𢎠過老佛爺 *T'a Tao La T'ou'rh La* 他到啦頭兒啦, He has had the Empress Dowager and thus attained the summit of anyone's ambition."

"What an honour!" said the other: "what a condescension! *Shang To Ta Lien* 賞多大臉."

P.S. As at the end of my life, I recall those garish days, the phantom and the delusion of power, those Gods dethroned and empires of the past, I bow before the Buddha's precept: "Learn happiness by abolishing desire."

---

60   Not yet satisfied.
61   All inclusive.

CHAPTER V

EUNUCH DIVERSIONS

JUST one week after my passage of love with Messalina, the fair eunuch, Lien 連, whose style or *Tzu* 字 was Tzu-yen 子延, arrived at my temple in a smart Peking cart attended by several porters all holding small yellow flags with the legend "*Huang Ch'ai* 皇差", "Imperial business", attached to their burdens. There were six cases of Pommery et Greno, four cases of Anisovka, the Anise Caucasian liqueur which the Old Buddha greatly savoured, two dozen bottles of assorted perfumes from Paris, a pair of Yung Cheng 雍正 covered bowls[1] in that almost unobtainable yellow glaze, as well as sundries, cigars, cigarettes galore and (strange to say) six pieces of *Louis d'or* dated from the reign of Le Grand Monarque (1702)[2] which, I imagine, had been presented to the K'ang Hsi 康熙 Emperor by Jesuit fathers. Truly the grace of Her Majesty was boundless as the ocean!

Li Lien-ying 李蓮英 sent a polite note: "The Old Ancestress *Ch'uan Chih Chia Chiang* 傳旨嘉獎 extends toward you her praise and satisfaction and hopes you are not tired. She bids you be circumspect in your diversions and not to overdo your strength, presuming on young virility (*Hsüeh Ch'i Fang Kang* 血氣方剛 – Confucius).[3] *Ch'in Tzu* 欽此. I am sending you a small gift most suitable for your proclivities, *I T'ou Su Hao* 以投素好. *Ying Ch'ai Shih Mang* 應差事忙, I am preoccupied by throning duties or would have come in person to salute you, *Fou Tsê Ting Ch'u Tai Tuan* 否則定趨台端, *So Hsing Hsiang Wu Pu Yao* 所幸相晤不遙, but we shall soon meet. *Ying K'ou* 英叩."

As Mme. de Sévigné writes of Lauzun's amazing episode with La Grande Mademoiselle, *je vous le donne en dix*[4] as to the "appropriate" present of the Chief Eunuch. It consisted of two dozen *condoms* of the

---

1   From the Yung Cheng Emperor's reign (1723-35).
2   "Louis' gold". Refers to the gold coins used in France from 1640 during the reign of Louis XIII until the French Revolution. *Le Grand Monarque* refers to Backhouse's beloved "Sun King" Louis XIV.
3   Full of vim and vigour (*Analects of Confucius*).
4   "I bet you'll never guess" (literally "I'll give you ten chances"). This obscure aside refers to "*La Grande Mademoiselle*" Anne Marie Louise d'Orléans (1627-93) and her romance with Antoine Nompar de Caumont, Duc de Lauzun (1632-1723). The source is the letters of Marie de Rabutin-Chantal, Marquise de Sévigné (1626-96).

latest *chic* from Paris and four brand new *martinets*[5] of the type employed in the Palace for chastising the buttocks of mischievous eunuchs. What a compliment to my *penchant ignoble*.[6]

I wrote in reply: "*Feng En Tzu Shang Wu Ti Chien Jung* 奉恩自上無地見容: *Kung Meng Ch'in Wen Chih Tz'u Kan K'uei Hsi Ssu* 恭蒙親溫之詞感愧奚似. *Yang Ch'eng Yin Pi Chien Ch'ü Shang Tang Hsiao Ch'ih Ch'ü Ta Pao Tz'u En Yü Wan I Yeh* 仰承蔭庇賤軀尚佳當效馳驅答報慈恩於萬一也. The earth containeth no place for me after such favour from on High. My gratitude and my shame are beyond compare and I reverently receive Your Majesty's gracious enquiry. Thanks to Your Majesty's overshadowing protection, my humble person is moderately well, so that I may still bestir myself in Your Majesty's service, thus repaying Your bountiful kindness in a ten-thousandth portion. Your slave from afar prostrates himself nine times in the dust. *Yüan Ch'en Chiu K'ou* 遠臣九叩."

To Li I wrote: "I am touched by your generous gift which exactly suits my exotic tastes! Looking forward to the next meeting . . . . . " I wrote on my card to Li: "*Ching Shih Yin Wu Pai Liang* 敬使銀五百兩 – Herewith Taels 500 out of respect for your messengers" and obtained the silver ingots therefore from my major-domo, who was verily *T'ung Ch'ou* 銅臭, full of the stench of copper, *il roulait sur l'or*.[7]

Lien was comely as the dawn, just twenty-four; he was less beautiful than my dear Cassia – "could I forget that name and that name's woe" (woe, I mean as the food of love); – he was, as I have already indicated, only nominally a *castrato*: his voice was not falsetto; his face lacked the flabbiness of a eunuch; his eyes were luminous: lust and passion radiated from them like twin candles shedding their beams in a naughty world; *sa bouche était on ne peut plus libidineuse*,[8] sensual and superlatively so; he walked like a conqueror on foreign soil, taking hold of me as if already in possession.

"I have brought you some more *Mei Yao* 媚藥, love philter, from the *Tu Tsung Kuan* 都總管, the Chief Eunuch, but have a notion that you won't require it, nor I either," added he with a salacious wink!

After my previous experiments with the potion, I felt that only a similar emergency would induce me to repeat the dose (did I mention that Li had kindly given to me a phial of the aphrodisiac against future use?); in any case, I was quite certain that nature would take its course in my intercourse with Lien, that of a wild horse gambolling on the Mongol plateau. Lien, being young and not an aristocrat by birth, had none of the gracious manner toward servants that was instinct in my Manchu friends: he treated them *de haut en bas*[9] and I could see that my major-domo deemed him an intruder who would sap his master's vitality. Lien was a devout Buddhist and, it being, if I remember right, the I Day of VII

---

5 Whips.
6 Wicked proclivities.
7 He rolled in gold.
8 His mouth could not be more libidinous.
9 Haughtily.

Moon, offered up incense at the main altar of the temple. He was dressed like the glass of fashion and the mould of form, heavily perfumed, as usual, with his cinnamon scent, truly a sight for *sair een* (sore eyes), *en me faisant mille coquetteries*,[10] ogling me after a manner which my table attendant (who was proud as Lucifer) evidently resented.

Well; the reader (knowing my amoral dispositions) can easily anticipate events: we had a moderately sumptuous repast washed down with the Old Buddha's *vin de Champagne* whose arrival was opportune, since I had brought none to the hills and in fact usually eschew it in the hot weather. Dinner over, we did not delay our lewd dalliance, the details of which are a hackneyed tale, *crambe repetita*.[11] Lien reminded me of my undertaking to let him repay my sallies in kind and it was a case with him of "out-heroding Herod" (*Hamlet*). His tool was long, voluminous and substantial; but his scrotum had been partially enucleated and I could only feel a sort of testicle within an apology for a *Hodensack*.[12] It in no wise impaired his sexual activity, however, and the ejaculation of thick, healthy semen left nothing to be desired. To my surprise, after I had completed for the moment my amorous advances in his direction including the labial erotic acts and the multitudinous kisses on his penis and anal region, Lien insisted upon copulating with me *inter crura*,[13] which is usually unacceptable to homosexualists owing to the *"P'ao K'ung* 跑空*"*, ejaculation in the void, which is supposed to be prejudicial to health. Tzu Yen 子延 may have of set purpose selected this usually deemed in professional circles less rapturous and more banal method of sexual communion, because it enabled me to insert the fore-finger inside his anal cavity during the slow act of *coitus*, thus enhancing the divine *jouissance*[14] connoted by the supreme moment of passion, when souls turn bodies and unite in the ineffable rapture of love freely bestowed, with ecstasy received. Who shall say that I have lived in vain? A mirage, it may be, but a joy forever in retrospect. (I recalled at school that this method was not unpopular but it gave no pleasurable reaction to the passive factor as regards the delectable titillation of the *proctodaeum*[15] with its concomitant soothing *proctorrhea* or discharge of mucus). Lien, however, reverted to the time-honoured path at his second effort; we indulged in sensual embraces for a very great while, and then he announced his intention of chastising my *mele* (apples, as Italian speech puts it) with the apposite newly received *discipline*. I reminded him of the "give and take" principle and assured him that he must allow me to do even so unto his buttocks before I could submit to his chastisement. He reluctantly consented and, after inflicting upon me very severe pain which reminded me of school-days floggings (and caused my table servant to exclaim: "*Ta Jen Ti P'i Ku K'uai Ch'eng Tieh Ti* 大人的屁股快成鐵的,

10 Sucking up to me.
11 Literally "warmed over cabbage".
12 Scrotum.
13 Between the legs.
14 Sexual climax.
15 Part of the anal canal.

your lordship's buttocks will soon be like iron"), graciously bent over the couch, while I dealt a dozen running but mild strokes on his admirable *fesses*.[16] He bore the punishment with an ill grace, groaning and exclaiming: "*Shih En* 施恩: *Chu Shou* 住手, spare me: stay your hand."

Truly the reaction to pain differs for each and all *à un haut degré*,[17] or perhaps one should rather say the readiness to endure. At school, I recall how Winston Churchill, when being flogged as very frequently occurred, would vociferate and flinch in coward poltroonery almost before he was hit; while other boys (including myself) bore the chastisement without a groan or the least sign of flinching, despite the almost unsupportable physical pain. But I suspect that this enforced self-control only enlisted a stronger reaction to the system, for I used to cool my wounded posterior after punishment (we were sent to our dormitories to reflect on our misdeeds when birching was over) cherishing thoughts that lay too deep for tears, including the most murderous of designs on my sadistic pedagogue. Graf von Kessler, my schoolfellow, a protégé and disciple of Bismark, the son of an Irish mother, describes in his memoirs the brutality of these floggings at Dr. Kynnersley's school: had they been ventilated in the press, there would surely have ensued a public scandal. Our unfortunate buttocks after chastisement became raw as a beef-steak, with lacerations and bleeding weals; but the inspectors of schools passed us by and we suffered in silence by the world forgot. It was public justice (the revenge of Até Ἄτη, the Greek revengeful power, goddess behind the gods) that the dominie died of heart failure in the act of flogging a small boy some years later, and we lads all arranged that the birch-rod he had used in his ultimate effort should be placed in Orbilius the pedagogue's coffin as a symbol of his Neronian persecution and lust of cruelty.[18]

But I am meandering, as Dickens would say; at any rate, for better or worse, Lien bore his pains without dignity and with a resentful sense of grievance, although in fact I struck him very lightly, much as if I had been wielding a lily rather than *les verges*.[19] He soon rallied however from his sulky humours and we passed a seductive night; the dawn came too soon and found me saying: "I cannot lose him yet: dear night! delay." We parted the best of friends after repeated reciprocal gestures, including, on his part, two successive acts of *pedicatio* (this time in the normal course) which caused me to marvel at his undaunted virility, far beyond what I could compass. *Fellatio, irrumatio*, titillation, *feuille de roses*, fig leaves, labial acts of every sort and shape, *nihil a nobis alienum fuit*.[20] He was more lustful, if less attractive, than Cassia, but I thoroughly revelled in his vitality and fullness, and am fain to think that his sexual reactions

---

16   Buttocks.
17   To a high degree.
18   Orbilius "the Flogger" was a teacher of the Roman poet Horace (65-8 BC); "*Neronian*" refers to the Roman Emperor Nero (37-68 AD), an early persecutor of the Christians infamous for his bloodlust.
19   Rods.
20   "Nothing was strange to us", nor indeed should it be to the reader, who can find more detailed explanations of these acts in the first chapter.

to myself were equally compelling. He left me for the Summer Palace after the morning carousal and seemed well pleased with the Taels 200 fee: truly such manoeuvres as these predilections entail connote much money, as a similar payment would have kept a female prostitute for at least 15 days. "Where the heart lies, let the pocket follow suit." We often encountered each other thereafter; but I do not know whether I ought to include him among my eunuch souvenirs for he was only eunuch in name, *de jure* but hardly *de facto*.[21]

Less than a month later, about the 6th September, 1904, I returned to town, wondering what strange adventures were still in store for me. The Empress Dowager was remaining over at the Yi Ho Yüan[22] 頤和園 for her approaching seventieth anniversary, and I expected, as was the fact, she would send for me again. My next meeting with Her Majesty differed only in detail from the last and, thanks to the philter and, to be frank, my own genuine, if not sexual passion, at least strong sense of the magnetism that emanated from her, I was able to do twice, or thrice, in successive bouts, what was expected of me and incidentally to wonder at Her Majesty's vocabulary of *argot* (quite worthy of Paname[23] itself) dealing with the private parts, male and female, and the hinder equipment.

She called me her "tame" foreign devil "*Shu Shih Kuei Tzu*[24] 熟識鬼子" now and thus made of me an object of natural jealousy: it is obvious that she could not allow her passions (as she might have wished) to run riot among the many good looking Manchus of her court, so that in a sense I was *Lan Yü Ch'ung Shu* 濫竽充數, the stop-gap of the orchestra, famed in history for his musical performance, until the prince summoned him to play a solo, when it was found that he was an impostor who could not play the mandoline at all! That was hardly my case, as my sexual activity toward her was adequate, if not superabundant; in fact, Her Majesty paid to me the dubious compliment that I was "*Yin Ti Li Hai* 淫的利害, awfully salacious."

Naturally, I did not make the obvious *réplique*: "And you, Madame, *Wu Ko Jen Kan Pu Kuo Nin Na* 五個人幹不過您吶, five males in succession could not satisfy your needs and desires." It always took me a week or more to recover from my debauches with Messalina: the truth being, as the *soi-disant*[25] "poet of empire", Kipling, says in another connexion, I was "too weak to sin to the height of my desire", *Li Yü Hsin Wei* 力與心違, the spirit is willing but the flesh says nay.

Although it is hardly germane to the present essay, I may as well mention here that on my second visit to the Summer Palace the Emperor sent for me and honoured me with a short conversation in this my first and last audience. I had, naturally, to obtain Her Majesty's approval

---

21 In principle, but hardly in actuality.
22 Summer Palace.
23 A slang name for the city of Paris, supposedly derived around the turn of the century due to the popularity of Panama hats.
24 A foreigner whom one knows well.
25 So-called.

before repairing to his *bureau de travail*:[26] except that the Emperor had no *travail*, no *bureau*.

She said laughingly: "Now don't talk scandal and don't let the Emperor 'handle' you, *Wan'rh Ni*[27] 玩兒你, or I shall make it hot for you both!" This was the first suggestion I had heard that he, Tsai T'ien 載湉, was homosexually minded; be that as it may, he gave me no indication of carnal desires in his short talk.

"You are the foreign devil (sic) Her Majesty so much affects? Are you afraid of her?"

"Yes, Your Majesty; Her sacred presence inspires the awe which would fill my inmost being, were the goddess of Mercy (*P'u Sa*[28] 菩薩) to revisit this mundane dust."

"I suppose you have 'talked' with empresses in other lands, your own for instance? Are they all like her?"

"No, Your Majesty, I have only had the honour of meeting the Tsaritsa and the Empress Dowager of Russia, as well as for a moment or two our British Queen Alexandra."

"Why do you not come to the Empress Dowager's court receptions?"

"I am not a member of the Corps Diplomatique, officially at least; besides, Her Majesty prefers to receive me in private."

"In private," said Kuang Hsü 光緒 and *Leng Hsiao* 冷笑, laughed sardonically: "Yes, I quite understand (*Wo Chen Hen Ming Pai* .... 我朕很明白) that she likes that best: more intimate, is it not?" (*Keng Wei Mi Mi Yu Chia Wu I* 更爲秘密有加無已).

I thought we were treading on rather thin ice, and was distinctly relieved when the Emperor began speaking of his manifold personal grievances; e.g. how one of the Legation "ladies" (?) had squeezed his imperial hand at the Empress Dowager's reception and how Her Majesty rebuked him for *his* want of *tenue*.[29] "*My* want of *tenue*, if you please," said the Emperor. "Your females have no manners and no dignity; but I rather like your small children."

During this brief colloquy I was humbly kneeling on the bare brick floor *sans même un coussinet quelconque*[30] and did not feel sorry when His Majesty's personal eunuch (he who afterwards gave his life for his master) entered to say that the "Old Buddha required my immediate presence, *Jang T'an Ti Wai K'o Jen Li K'o Hui Ch'ü* 讓您的外國人立刻回去."

"All's well," said Kuang Hsü, "you are excused; go back to the Empress Dowager without delay, or she will blame me and things will be worse than ever, *Shih Ch'ing Keng Tsao* 事情更糟."

What the Emperor's tastes in love may have been, I have no means of saying; except that his appearance after death disclosed a normal sexual

---

26 "Study" (literally "occupational office"). The author's comments that follow refer to the fact that the Emperor, having been stripped of power by the Empress Dowager in 1898 no longer had a real occupation or duty to perform.

27 Toy with you.

28 "Bodhisattva", in this case the Avalokitesvara Bodhisattva.

29 Dignity; bearing.

30 Without even a small cushion.

apparatus as capable, did he choose, as a Louis XVIII, of *un commerce charnel*;[31] but I have no hesitation in adding my opinion to the general impression that he possessed an exceedingly violent and (at the same time) irritating temper. Sulkiness exuded from his eyes and mouth; choleric at times, he would be silent for days together; he was of the type most repellent to one of the Old Buddha's *complexion*.

"Well," said the Old Buddha (as I entered), "you see I have come to your rescue, or the Emperor" (she always called except on one occasion in my hearing, and spoke of, him as *Huang Shang* 皇上 and not by his personal name) "might have kept you kneeling there indefinitely. Now, I'll wager that he asked you what you thought of me?"

"Yes, Your Majesty, it is exact; and I told him that you were the queen of earthly queens, a goddess come down from heaven to this world of man."

"Foolish, foolish boy," said the Empress Dowager who was evidently pleased by my reply; "don't you know that he hates me, has attempted my life (in 1898) and will remember against you your devotion to me!"

"As long as I have you to protect me, my Goddess of Mercy, he can think to do what he chooses in my direction." Her Majesty then slapped me playfully (this time) on the cheek and not on *l'ignoble partie*[32] of the last occasion.

She broke into vulgar colloquial: "*Chi Pa Wei'rh* 肌巴味兒, *Fang T'a Ti P'i* 放他的屁 (literal: *Son chybre sent mauvais, il ne vaut pas la peine de lâcher un pet*).[33] Prick stench (a fig for him), let him emit gas *ad libitum*[34] from his fundament." So we say: *Chen Chiao Ko Fang P'i Ti Shih* 眞扣個放屁的事, like Wang Fu Jen 王夫人 in *Hung Lou Meng*[35] 紅樓夢: "a petty matter like wind from the intestine".

It happened that Prince Kung 恭 (P'u Wei 溥偉) was paying his respects at the Summer Palace that morning; this gentleman was commonly known as *Ta Ch'iao Tzu* 大巧子, large tooled, and the sobriquet was entirely appropriate. He and I had acted together in amateur theatricals and were quite intimate, so that when he saw me by the lake side, he hailed me: "Why! it's old man Pa (Lao Pa 老巴); come and see me this evening in town. What are you up to here?" asked Prince Kung rather pointedly.

Summoned by the Empress to bid her goodbye, she asked me once more if I really burned in my heart toward her, or whether I was merely rhapsodizing for her benefit. "Madame," said I, "you must have felt my soul in a kiss, even as I did (Thank the Lord Buddha for the signal honour) your own exalted soul, poor mortal as I am. It is for me in Your Majesty's sacred environment, even as flesh holds flesh and as soul the soul." I reminded the Old Buddha of Semele, mother of Bacchus, who

---

31 Sexual commerce.
32 The ignoble part.
33 **Backhouse:** Note 肌巴 is used in 紅樓夢 [*Dream of the Red Chamber*] *I Ken Chi Pa Wang Li Ch'o* 一根肌巴往裡擂. Someone's tool pricks right inside.
34 At will.
35 *Dream of the Red Chamber.*

was consumed to white ashes when Zeus revealed himself to her in his divine panoply.

"Your Zeus should have had the sense to remain incognito," said the Empress, "as I do, in theory and at least with you, when I become your equal and cease to be your sovereign, exactly like the moon in the legend, who loved a mortal. Do you have sensual reactions when you think of me?"

"Ay, indeed, Old Buddha: *mea rigida* (Ciceronian and golden Latin term for *erectio penis*) forces for itself a hole in my apparel" (*la plénitude de l'orgasme fait un trou à mon vêtement*). (I must plead guilty not only to falsehood, but *pardessus le marché*[36] to plagiarism, anent this terminology: Catullus speaks thus in one of his odes to his beloved Lesbia, the infamous Clodia who stank in the nostrils of the Rome of Julius Caesar, though her brother, Sextus Clodius, later slain by Milo, was an unprincipled but useful henchman of the future dictator still absent on his campaigns in Gaul.)

"I don't believe you," replied the Old Buddha; "but come again and don't overdo your immoral *capers*; or you will die young of *Fang Shih Kuo Tu* 房事過度, surfeit of copulation. Farewell."

Thrice I *K'ou Shou*[37] 叩首 and humbly withdrew. On return to town, I duly called at Kung Wang Fu 恭王府, the original of Jung Kuo Fu[38] 榮國府, appertaining to the Chia 賈 family in *Hung Lou Meng* 紅樓夢, and was shown into His Imperial Highness P'u Wei's 溥偉 sitting room. The strange, dingo, but beauteous young eunuch, Chu En-ming 朱恩明, of whom I have spoken was, *comme d'habitude*,[39] keeping his master (and paramour) love-breathing company. The Prince asked me awkward questions about the Empress Dowager and myself: naturally I evaded direct replies. *Hsin Pu Hsin Tsai Hu T'a* 信不信在乎他, believe it or not, as he chose. The truth was that the liaison, if I may so term it between the goddess and the man, had by constant *ébruitement*[40] become common knowledge in the imperial clan and (I fear) in less exalted circles, though perhaps the full extent of my Potemkin like relations was only guessed: saith the Odes Classic: "The secrets of the Inner Chamber, *Chung Kou Chih Shih* 中構之事, *Nan Yen Chih Yin* 難言之隱, may not be uttered aloud."

His Highness, as befitted his descent from that protagonist of homosexuality, the great Prince Kung, then started talking of strange vices and secret sins, *à la* Dorian Gray in Wilde's melodramatic novel. I fully anticipated that this was a prelude to concrete suggestions on his part, of which experience taught me that he was capable; however, just as he was preparing (unabashed by Chu En-ming's presence) to exhibit to me his redundant genital abundance, another eunuch entered with the card of

---

36 On top of it all.
37 Kotowed.
38 Prince Kung's Residence . . . Jung Kuo's Residence.
39 As usual.
40 Gossiping.

an imperial clansman of his grandfather's generation Yi Hsien 奕譞, and the Prince had perforce to go to the next courtyard to receive his elder in the main guestroom.

His temporary absence provoked the following incident, not wholly a storm in a tea-cup, *Hsiao T'i Ta Tso* 小題大作: to the chief actor *es war voller Ernst.*[41] En-ming stood with arms akimbo, looking most truculent and pent up with hidden chagrin (*Wo Nang Ch'i* 窩囊氣): "I am going to speak quite plainly (*je vais vous dire votre fait*), *Chih Chieh Liao Tang* 直截了當, *Shuang Te Kan Ts'ui* 爽得乾脆, with straight flung words and few. If the Prince likes you to possess him, in whatever form he and you fancy, I am perfectly indifferent, *Wo Wan Ch'üan Pu Kuan* 我完不管, *Sui Nin Erh Wei Pien* 隨您二位便, *Ch'ien Hou I Lü* 前後一律, the posture you two gentlemen may adopt is up to you, whether behind or before. But, if you attempt to "have" His Highness, I shall stab you dead and then kill myself. I am mad with jealousy and none, man or woman, shall interfere with my prerogative as to the Prince's sexual relations. *Wo Ken Feng Tzu I Yang* 我跟瘋子一樣, *Ch'ih Ts'u Ya Sai Pei Huo So Shao Ti* 吃醋亞賽被火所燒的. *Wu Lun Nan Nü* 無論男女, *Shei Pu Hsü To Wo Tui Wang Yeh Yin Ch'ing So Ying Hsiang Chih Ch'üan* 誰不許奪我對王爺淫情所應享之權."

En-ming was desperately in earnest and I wondered whether he might not knife me then and there, thus cutting the Gordian Knot;[42] certainly his aspect belied him, if he were indeed incapable of translating threats into deeds. I soothed him as best I might and solemnly promised him that in no circumstances would I ask His Highness' gracious permission to pedicate with my unworthy self *dans la forme active* (for the Prince) nor indeed to pose to him in any passive sense, thus poaching on his (En-ming's) private property. The latter was satisfied at this reply and signified his pleasure by displaying to me his delicately scented posterior and anus, as well as the tiny orifice (red and rather raw) where once had been, in the dear dead days beyond recall, an adequate penis and a scrotum *à l'avenant*.[43] In the stead of a lovely male organ and beautifully suspended *Hodensack* was an ugly reddish *cicatrice*,[44] clean and scented but an eyesore. All except the small cavity had vanished like the withered flower of yesteryear (*K'o Sui Huang Hua* 客歲黃花): "the glory that was Greece, the grandeur that was Rome". They were merely geographical expressions, as Talleyrand remarked of Italy at the second *Congrès de Vienne* after the Hundred Days.[45] En-ming showed no signs of ill will, allowed me to impress my lips upon his orifices, behind and before, perfumed with a delicate fragrance like reseda; while he in his turn *K'ei*

---

41 It was of grave importance.
42 Refers to the legend of Alexander the Great cutting through a knot in Phrygia that could not be untied.
43 Accordingly.
44 Scar.
45 The "Congress of Vienna" (Sept. 1814–June 1815) was a meeting of European statesmen in the aftermath of Napoleon's exile to Elba. It concluded less than two weeks before (not after) the "Hundred Days" of Napoleon's return from exile. This comment, made by chairman Prince Klemens Wenzel von Metternich and not Talleyrand, refers to the Congress' decision to divide Italy into several separately administered regions.

Wo Yen'rh[46] 撓我眼兒 (a proceeding which I have already described) and took my tool into his delicate hands, fondling it regretfully and pressing toward the urethral orifice his pomegranate lips, as if he verily loved an object whereof he was bereft.

I cannot say what might have ensued, had a larger measure of privacy been ours; as it was, the Prince's visitor had withdrawn and P'u Wei, accompanied by the *Ch'a Fang* 茶房, ganymede of the tea, rejoined us for refreshments and cigarettes. En-ming sate in amorous proximity to his master who proposed a rendezvous with me on an early evening, at the Hsin Ching Tsao T'ang Tzu 新淨 堂子, or bath-house.

Reverting to En-ming's jealous and monopolistic attributes, I must add here that in Hsüan T'ung 宣統 III year[47] Prince Kung's palace was the scene of a love tragedy which caused much sensation and certainly did not improve the slowly-dying cause of the Manchu Dynasty. Prince Kung had copulated from behind (*a tergo*) with another eunuch named Hsiao Jui 蕭瑞, and had been caught *epi autoforo*[48] (in the act, like the adulterous woman of the gospel) by his rival, now fast becoming an autumn fan. En-ming stabbed Hsiao in a vital spot under the shoulder, while the latter was actually pursuing his act of copulation. He died there and then. The Prince called out "*Chiu Jen* 救人, *Lai Tai Fu* 來大夫" *au secours, au chirurgien,*[49] but before help could arrive, En-ming had stabbed himself in the cardiac region, not before he had thrust at, and slightly wounded, the erotic princely descendant of Nurhatsi (according to Manchu spelling) or Nu Erh Ha Ch'ih 奴兒哈赤 also 奴爾哈赤 (according to Chinese transliteration)[50] – Ch'ing T'ai Tsu 清太祖, Wu Huang Ti 武皇帝.[51] The matter was officially hushed up: in other words, everyone in Peking talked about the scandal which was a nine days' wonder. En-ming nursed his wound for many weeks but ultimately recovered, only dying some seven years ago and surviving his former master and lover. It is no compliment to British morals; but Dr. Gray of the British Legation,[52] a pathic of some notoriety, had attracted the Prince's favourable attention, having been summoned to the Kung Wang Fu 恭王府 for a medical consultation respecting Prince Kung's health. En-ming told the doctor, as he had previously warned me, if guilty of pranks, that any passive action with the Prince would result in the British doctor's inevitable death at his hands; and the former *qui avait la frousse* (*Lien P'i Pu Kan Fang* 連屁不敢放, was too frightened even to *lâcher un pet*, to use a vulgar phrase)[53] was at pains never again to enter Kung Wang Fu, at any

46 Fingered my anus.
47 1911.
48 "Ἐπ' αὐτοφώρῳ" in the Greek New Testament (*John* VIII.4).
49 Help, fetch a surgeon.
50 Nurhatsi reigned from 1616 to 1626, prior to the actual establishment of the Ch'ing Dynasty throughout China.
51 **Backhouse:** Before the Mings fell, Manchus were always called in decrees 奴兒 "Slave Son" in contempt. I suggest inserting *both*, the polite being used after the Manchu conquest.
52 Dr. George Douglas Gray, chief physician of the British Legation from 1902 to 1929. His name was removed from Hoeppli's edition.
53 "Who was scared" (literally "too frightened to break wind").

rate during En-ming's regime; but I believe the Prince and the "good physician" used to meet elsewhere *pour passer une nuit d'amour de temps en temps*,[54] now and again, the latter being the obliging pathic.

Persons unknowing have said in my hearing that the eunuch (in China or in Turkey) was malodorous and urine leaking; it is not so: all the *châtrés*[55] I encountered both in Constantinople in the nineties and in China since (and I have seen and known scores) not only were innocent of any *Harngeruch*[56] – as a fact, they were cleaner than the entire male – whatsoever, but were delicately and aromatically perfumed, both as regards their frontal "void" and the erotic foyer that is their anal cavity.

The tryst at the bath-house was faithfully kept: Prince, eunuch and I reserved two intercommunicating *Ya Tso'rh* 雅座兒, private bath rooms. Kung and his catamite bathed together in one, and I in the other. The three of us, perfumed like Roman *jeunesse dorée*[57] in the days of Crassus the millionaire and Mamurra, Julius Caesar's beloved *cinaedus*,[58] so cruelly satirized by Catullus who says of him that *sa capacité évacuante en tent que fécale*[59] being limited to once a month rendered him most acceptable for *pedicatio*, – I with the violet scent that flung for me a tender memory of the divine Sarah,[60] Kung with concentrated *eau de rose*[61] and En-ming with his favourite *réséda*[62] sate together over liqueur specially ordered for the occasion, and smoking cigarettes, until passion became our master, as Cyrus spent (and diverted) the strength of the waters of Babylon.[63] We compromised in true Chinese fashion over the knotty question of procedure; in other words, Kung first worked his will with the eunuch, whilst I, who was by this time quite devoid of shame, if I ever had any, sate an admiring spectator like a tom-cat on the tiles or a reveller on *Walpurgisnacht*.[64] The rest of the comedy is easily imagined. His Highness kindly presented to me his princely buttocks and I was fain to satisfy his lust and mine, while En-ming represented a contented and applauding gallery in our passion play. Thus the eternal triangle received the consummation devoutly to be wished: the solution of the problem was obvious and might well be imitated in a more august arena, where politics, not passions, form the *tapis*,[65] say, for example, at the coming *Congrès de Berlin*, when I suppose, the carving up (like a pumpkin)

---

54   For a night of love from time to time.
55   Eunuchs.
56   Urine stench.
57   Gilded youths.
58   Passive homosexual partner.
59   His capacity to defecate.
60   Sarah Bernhardt (1844-1923), the most famous actress of her era. In Backhouse's *The Dead Past*, the author claimed to have once appeared on stage with the Parisian starlet.
61   Rose water.
62   A fragrant flower, also known as mignonette.
63   Cyrus the Great (d. 530 BC) supposedly diverted the Euphrates River, dropping it to a level that allowed his armies to cross it and seize Babylon.
64   A holiday celebrated in central and northern Europe with pre-Christian origins, usually involving bonfires and playing pranks on neighbors.
65   Topic of conversation (literally "carpet").

of *l'empire brittanique*[66] will be the main *agenda*, for the peace and happiness of the world.

So the three of us, the Aisin Gioro 愛新覺羅 prince, the eunuch catamite and the "pirate Briton" (*et penitus toto divisos orbe Britannos*, whose country was "sundered", as Vergil says, from all the human race),[67] sate in nature's garb, each fondling the other, for Kung made no objection to my amorous caresses of En-ming's fair snow white posterior.

Enter the good-looking bath attendant who saluted Kung with double genuflexion, *Shuang An* 雙安, as was the Manchu custom to members of the reigning house, and me with the usual *Ch'ing An* 請安. "Your Highness and you, M. le Marquis (*Hou Yeh* 侯爺), must be tired out: I will rub you down and ease your wearied muscles." He ignored the eunuch who glared at him, being at pains to conceal his absence of genitals by girding his loins with a towel. (Eunuchs have a superstition that it is unlucky for them to exhibit their lack of equipment to strangers; although to me they never showed the slightest symptom of embarrassment.) The masseur whose name was Jung Kuei 榮貴 (I shall refer to his brother Jung Chi 榮吉 later), obviously cognizant of our activities, paid to the Prince pretty compliments on his *banane*,[68] using a term which I had not before heard in Peking, although it was familiar to me in Paname; he also praised (as courtesy naturally compelled) my own which he likened in homely metaphor to an asparagus spear (an otiose epithet not unknown in Lutéce).[69] I think he was soliciting our favours and made the amorous eunuch frantic with jealousy. After a course of massage which greatly revived me, I bade my two companions good-night, promising to rejoin them at an early rendezvous: and shall revert to the bath-house later.

In the IX Moon, a day or so after the Old Buddha had accorded to His Highness a hereditary princedom in honour of her 70th birthday, my gate-keeper came in with the card of Prince Ch'ing's 慶 chief eunuch, Yin Hao-jan 殷浩然: "he wants to see Your Lordship on important business," said he with a partially concealed smile, – the fact being that my staff now only perceived libidinous motives in ordinary social calls or intercourse: so true is Vergil's "*Facilis descensus Averni*"[70] (but steep the ascent of Olympus, if I may add an antithetical addition to the Roman poet of empire): and yet Ch'ing and I were excellent friends – independent of any libidinous suggestions, and often foregathering at his palace, for in fact I was to him a sort of political adviser. His homosexual proclivities were as well known as his *auri sacra fames*,[71] the "accursed lust of gold": now that Junglu was gone, His Highness' palace was the goal of the office seeker and the parasitic client.

66   "Berlin Congress . . . British Empire", refers to what the author believed to be the inevitable German victory in the Second World War.
67   And Britons, from the whole world sundered far (*Eclogue* I.66).
68   Banana (penis).
69   The ancient Gallic-Roman city that would later become Paris.
70   "Easy is the descent to the Underworld" (Virgil, *Aeneid* VI.126), should actually read *Averno*.
71   Holy greed for gold (Virgil, *Aeneid* III.56).

Yin Hao-jan was shown into my reception room; he was a good-look-ing and well set up native of Tientsin *dans la quarantaine*.[72] His business was somewhat unusual: he came as an intermediary from Ch'ing to sug-gest that I should lend myself to the Prince's whims, now that M. Lessar, the Russian envoy, who had previously obliged him in both directions, active and passive, was hopelessly ill (in fact he died a few months later), and M. Pokotiloff, the distinguished director of the Banque Russo-Asia-tique and later M. Lessar's successor as envoy, though an intimate of the Prince, was not disposed to engage with him in amorous dalliance, being far too busy with his mistress and Egeria in the West City.

Yin annoyed me somewhat by tactlessly adding: "His Highness will pay generous remuneration on each and every occasion that Your Lord-ship accommodates him."

I said with some vehemence: "*Wo Ti Kang Men* 我的肛門 (*Huo Yen'rh* 或眼兒) *Pu Shih Mai Ti* 不是賣的, my posterior and anus are not in the market; *Ju Kuo Wang Yeh So Yao Ti Shih Chiao Wo Ken T'a Kan I Hsia* 如果 王爺所要的是教我跟他幹一下, *Wo Pu Chih Cho Che Ko Wei Sheng* 我不指著這 個爲生 *Yu Ti Shih Hsiang Tang Ti Jen Wu Tsu Kung Wo Yin Pa Liao* 有的是相 當的人物足供我癮罷了. If His Highness expects me to 'have' him, I am not a Professional apt in *de haut en bas*[73] and I have no difficulty in satisfying my needs among suitable aspirants to my favour. Should he desire me to be the 'horizontal', he is too old and infirm (Ch'ing was the same age as the Old Buddha, 70 years) for a concrete result. *Yao Shih T'a Jang Wo Pei T'a Chiao Kou* 要是他讓我被他交媾, *I Nien Mai Ch'i Shuai Chih Lao Sou Yen Neng Ch'eng Kung* 以年邁氣衰之老叟焉能成功? *Ch'un Ch'iu Tsui Kao* 春 秋最高, *Pei Fen Tsui Chung* 輩分最重, *Pu I Ch'ih Chih* 不亦恥之? Her Majesty calls him 'time-honoured and elder', is he not ashamed at the idea?" Naturally I did not wish the prince (with whom I had not the smallest sexual affinity) to collapse *à la* Felix Faure in a carnal compass, apart from the fact that His Highness was known to be suffering from an anal syphilitic affection and from a purulent discharge of the penis.

Yin told me that, like the last prince de Condé whose (possibly) forged will (for he hated the usurping Orléans House) left Chantilly to the Duc d'Aumale and the Russian general Skobeleff whose tragic death in a Moscow hotel was so little in keeping with much that was admira-ble in his short life of forty odd years, Prince Ch'ing was accustomed to hang himself to a beam so as to obtain an erection, naturally under the supervision of his attendants. I urged caution, and in fact Ch'ing lived till 1916, aged 81 years.

The prince and I continued on intimate social terms, so much so that on the occasion of the emperor's funeral, *Feng I* 奉移, in May 1909, a pa-vilion for the special envoys from Japan and Russia as well as for the Corps Diplomatique and foreign guests having been erected on the route of the procession near the Hou Men 後門, Prince Ch'ing left the *cortège*[74]

---

72   In his forties.
73   Haughtiness.
74   Procession.

for a moment to pay his compliments to the official guests but catching sight of his old friend, myself, who was standing in a corner of the pavilion, forgot his official duties, hurried up to me and began an animated conversation concerning *la pluie et le beau temps*,[75] much to the scandal of their Excellencies the representatives of the Powers.

Having declined Yin's request, I asked him about the *ordalie*[76] of being made a eunuch; he told me that he was aged twenty-nine at the date of the operation and still retained a measure of sexual capacity. The neighbouring region had been anaesthetized by some Chinese balsam and he felt practically no pain; a sort of tourniquet, *ou instrument pour comprimer les artères*,[77] was employed, so that haemorrhage was reduced to a minimum; the severance of the penis cost him no distress but the orchidectomy connoted a second or more of acute agony. The wound was seared with a hot iron and a styptic ointment applied. His chiefest trouble during subsequent days was in urination; as he said, he leaked like a sieve, but on the whole suffered little pain. He kindly exhibited to me his genital region: the orifice, a tiny passage not in itself unsightly nor uncomely, seemed free from inflammation and there was no oozing from the urethra which was elaborately perfumed and *on ne peut plus aseptique*.[78]

Yin and I parted the best of friends, and I asked him to convey my humble gratitude to the Prince for the signal favour he had deemed fit to bestow upon me by his suggestions, but that, viewing his high position as the chiefest representative of the Ta Ch'ing 大清 Dynasty *vis à vis* foreign Powers, I felt myself utterly unworthy of the honour which might easily involve the Prince himself in unwarranted complications, especially if the matter became noised aloud in Legation circles, when my position would become quite untenable.

It is, I think, germane to the present paper to mention a curious parallel between J.J. Rousseau (*longo intervalio*)[79] and myself: I have spoken of the severe corporal punishments of which my boyhood was victim but have not mentioned that, despite the severe pain caused by repeated floggings upon my luckless posterior, a certain sexual appetite was engendered and a pleasurable erectio penis supervened. Rousseau's *Confessions* record the same phenomenon when he received *la fessée* at the hands of his *gouvernante*,[80] admitting therefrom an aesthetic thrill.

Prince Ch'ing had a pretty wit. There was then a Scottish physician, a liar and a humbug, named Cochrane[81] in Peking, who attended Li Lienying and was currently reported to have castrated a large number of aspirant eunuchs for the greater glory of God and to his own profit;

---

75   The rain and shine.
76   Ordeal.
77   Or an instrument to compress the arteries.
78   Most clean.
79   At an immense distance (Virgil, *Aeneid* V.320-1).
80   Spanking . . . governess.
81   Dr. Cochrane accompanied Backhouse on a visit to England in 1906, when the latter supposedly suffered from a heart-related condition that required ongoing treatment.

although a missionary of the ultra-puritan type, he was known to be addicted to sodomy with a Chinese harlot named Ts'ui Hsi 翠喜, and when Ch'ing called him in regarding his anal chancre (not being a physician, nor expert in venereal diseases, I do not know the correct name for the condition but do know that His Highness' anus was foul and purulent with some kind of growth), the Scotsman tactlessly said that filthy people who commit homosexual acts are prone to contract the disease. Ch'ing who knew of Cochrane's predilections was displeased by his impudence and said very quietly: "And filthy people who commit the sodomitic act with a different sex? Do they get the disease also?" It was a palpable hit: the doctor turned green and yellow by turns and *fila à l'anglaise*.[82]

Her Majesty sent for me again before her birthday festivities in November; on this occasion Li Lien-ying wrote as follows: "*Ch'in Feng I Chih Chung Yi Hou Pa K'o-ssu Chin Wan Lai Hu Yü Pei Chao Chien Ch'in Tzu* 欽奉懿旨忠毅侯巴格思今晚來湖預備召見欽此. I have reverently received a decree from the Empress Dowager: 'The loyal and stedfast marquis Pa K'o-ssu is hereby commanded to come to the Lake (K'un Ming 昆明, Wan Shou Shan 萬壽山 – Summer Palace) and prepare himself for audience. Imperial Orders'." I noticed that the Old Buddha had accorded to me two honorific characters dubbing me *Chung* 忠 and *Yi*[83] 毅 before my title of *Hou* 侯 and felt highly honoured by the unparalleled (as far as foreign devils were concerned) favour of the new distinction. (Tseng Kuo-fan 曾國藩, the savior of the dynasty in the T'ai Ping 太平 rebellion, had been created a *Cheng Yi Hou* 正毅侯 and Li H'ung-chang 李鴻章 posthumously a *Su Yi Hou* 肅毅侯, after being a *Su Yi Po* 肅毅伯 (count) in his lifetime, it being the highest that a Chinese (Han 漢) could receive from the Manchu Dynasty; so I was in good company and felt proud to be numbered "*Tra cotanto senno*" (Dante),[84] in such an intellectual conclave.)

I faithfully did as I was enjoined and again enjoyed the old Buddha's fragrant intimacy: she limited my sexual efforts to two successions in lieu of three and I fulfilled her desires sufficiently to allay for the moment her violent carnality. The buccal[85] ejaculation (with this manoeuvre may be compared the habit of elderly debauchees to place prunes or dates inside the vulva over night and consume them next day) was once more demanded and given: I was flattered to think that apparently the pleasure, if pleasure there be, *crescit eundo*[86] increases with use. The cool weather seemed to enhance her *salacité*:[87] I am no Antonius (that essentially Asiatic nature), who, as I always feel, has been treacherously maligned by history, for we have only extant the account of his enemies who wished to stand well with Augustus Caesar, but can imagine that Cleopatra's libidinous yearnings far exceeded his by no mean's neglible

---

82 Left without saying goodbye.
83 Loyal and steadfast.
84 Amid so much wisdom (*Inferno* IV.102).
85 Oral.
86 Lucretius, *De Rerum Natura* VI.340.
87 Salaciousness.

sexual appetite. I spent most of the night with the Old Buddha who seemed unwilling to let me go. In the middle of our revels a handsome eunuch came in with *Yen Wo* 燕窩 (Salangane soup) which was very acceptable. The Old Buddha said, as was a discovery of the obvious, seeing that we were both stark naked: "*Wo Ken Hou Yeh Cheng Wan'rh* 我跟侯爺正玩兒, I am disporting myself with His Lordship," and the confidential minion replied: "*Ch'in Lao Tsu Tsung Hsiao Ch'ien* 請老祖宗消遣, Pray, Old Ancestress, enjoy your pleasuring." It was a curiously free and easy court: sovereign and eunuchs "chaffed" each other; there was no constraint, little formality. The fact was that everyone knew how far he or she could go with the Old Buddha: the slightest liberty or presumption would have meant death by flogging or possibly under the sword of the headsmen. Although for me an ill-timed word would only have connoted a wrathful dismissal, I had to be on the *qui vive*[88] and humour a temperamental old lady.

Lady Arthur Russell, a *grande dame* of the Victorian era and sister-in-law of my kinsman, Lord Odo Russell, later Lord Ampthill, British envoy in Berlin in 1878 at the time of the Congress, whom Bismark greatly esteemed, (her son Claud, later Sir Claud Russell, being a diplomatic secretary here), had visited the Old Buddha when at Paotingfu 保定府 in the previous year and remarked to me at the time, with her vast experience of courts at home and abroad, that she had never known an atmosphere of greater *sans gêne* and *camaraderie*.[89] Naturally, she was only admitted to observe one side of the old Empress' complex character, that which (I believe) Lady Susan Townley had denominated "kittenish" (playful, not "feline" in the derogatory sense of the word).

On this occasion, the Old Buddha, as I half expected, promoted me to an *I Teng Hou* 一等侯, marquis of first rank, in honour of her seventieth fête: it may be imagined that the high honour did not enhance my popularity among the sycophant courtiers, though the Manchu princes and dukes all seemed genuinely pleased, and one of the latter remarked: "Love is the ladder of advancement."

Perhaps I say it who should not, but I fancy that, had the Old Buddha lived some years longer, I should have attained the first class rank of nobility, *Kung Chüeh* 公爵, even if a princedom were beyond my deserts or expectation. And today my Manchu title is even as the shop-sign of a long extinct firm, like my Saxon-Coburg barony, my title of Russian nobility, two dormant British peerages through the distaff side which pace the Committee of Privileges of the House of Lords may be mine, and it may be my baronetcy from the House of Windsor, scarce other than bills of exchange *en souffrance*.[90] "Silence: *aux faits*."[91] Well, well: 'ifs' and 'maybes' would maintain Paris in *coutellerie* and *vaisselle*.[92] This humble

---

88   Alert.
89   Openness and friendship.
90   Past due.
91   Let us come to the facts.
92   Cutlery and dishes.

effort is only *une chronique scandaleuse*:[93] so I pass over of set purpose the dignified festivities which accompanied the 70th anniversary of the Old Buddha's birth, how the emperor at the head of the imperial clansmen and court functionaries kotowed thrice in the P'ai Yün Tien[94] 排雲殿 before Her Majesty seated on the throne of state in the glory of her resplendent court robes, ablaze with jewels and gems, radiant as Hera on Olympus, a veritable incarnation of the *P'u Sa* 菩薩 (Avalokitesvara of Mercy – literally one who hearkens to prayer). She received me in a separate audience as a sovereign toward a vassal, devoid of the intimate badinage that marked the periods of those diviner, if desultory, hours, *quas meminisse juvabit*[95] till the end of my course. As I think today of her incomparable grace and charm, "sweet as remembered kisses after death", I wonder if she did not outvie a Cleopatra or a Catherine in their amorous hey day; truly "age could not wither nor custom stale her infinite variety". Today only the recollection remains: "Fond memory, fond memory: when all things fail, we fly to thee." *Revenons à nos moutons*[96] and to the eunuchs.

After the court's return to town Li Lien-ying asked me to call at his mansion near the Catholic Cathedral. Thither I repaired, and he showed to me the pathetic relics of his "jewels", of his lost virility, preserved in ardent spirit – *Shao Chiu* 燒酒, a penis which must have aforetime been shapely and delectable, testicles of ample compass, ready to be sewn again upon his person after decease.

Li was as "ready" as a he-goat, insisted on my undressing and exposed his beautifully scented person for my admiring contemplation, while handling mine with poetic fervour. I was reminded of the ditty of the "nineties": "he wanted something to play with . . . something to love and adore," but felt nervous as to his intentions, for it is the simple truth to say that, had he demanded from me a copulation to his intention, I should have humbly pleaded *Non possum*[97] although once, when in my cups, dear Chan 占 and I both gratified him with labiation. However, I thank Buddha for it, he limited his needs to a request that I should titillate his anus and fondle the environment; while he repaid me in kind by wanting to masturbate my *Ch'iao Tzu* 巧子 which I declined. He declared that the tickling of my middle finger afforded to him the equivalent of an orgasm: sure enough there came a definite discharge of fluid which brought to him the consummation of his lubricity.

Li Lien-ying then unveiled what he called a programme of love, *Ai Ch'ing Ch'eng Hsü* 愛情程序; now that he was back in town, if the Old Buddha granted him a short *congé*,[98] he proposed to invite the best looking eunuch catamites of the staff to his house for a sort of carnal soirée for my benefit. I was to take them by turns on successive dates, say once

---

93   A scandalous chronicle.
94   Cloud Forcing Hall, Summer Palace.
95   Which it will one day be a pleasure to recall.
96   Back to the point.
97   Not possible.
98   Leave of absence.

a month, according to their place in the *Po Chia Hsing* 百家姓, catalogue of surnames dating from Sung 宋 Dynasty, Chao 趙, Ch'ien 錢, Sun 孫, Li 李 etc. or as we should say, after the order of the alphabet. They were all eager, he said, to "play" with me and, as far as in them lay, to participate in an active sense. The fee would be Taels 200 on each occasion, plus a "nominal" gratuity for Li's servants of Taels 30 for *Hsiao Fei*[99] 小費. There would be an extra charge of Taels 25, if the eunuch wished of his own volition, *passer par les verges;*[100] the other items, *Ling Sui'rh* 零碎兒 *y compris.*[101]

I asked him: "Did the Old Buddha know and approve?"

"Her Majesty has no objection to a moderate self-indulgence but commands sober-minded limitation" (as Plato said, *Sophrosune*). And so it was arranged that on the following 25 of X Moon the selected team of eunuchs and I should foregather for an introductory interview in the evening at Li's hospitable house.

When the day came, I found the Chief Eunuch and (if I remember rightly) twelve minions (if not more) awaiting my arrival. They were all charming young men, were dressed and scented like a perfumer's in the Rue de la Paix and united in expressing the wish to *Chan Yang*[102] 瞻仰, gaze upon the "devil's" private parts which had been signally honoured by the Old Ancestress, *Shou Lao Tsu Tsung T'ê Ta Chih Chih* 受老祖宗特達之知. I was fain to allow each and all to handle me *ad libitum*, feeling complimented (albeit *chansons que tout cela*)[103] by them: *Chen Hao Kan* 眞好看, how pretty it is; *Pu Han Ch'un* 不憨蠢, not ill-looking; *Yu Hsiu Wu Chih Ching Shen* 有修武之精神, it is full of martial spirit; *Yüan Pu Tê Lao Fo Yeh Ai T'a* 怨不得老佛爺愛他, no wonder the Old Buddha loves it; *Pu Shih Wei Mei Wu* 不失爲美物, quite a pretty thing; *Chen Pai* 眞白, truly white. I could not help recalling Oscar's[104] compliment: "You have quite a charming tool!"

After they had minutely examined my whole apparatus, *Ch'ien Hou* 前後, both behind and before, Li said: "Tonight we will begin with Chao Chih-an 趙芝庵, as he's the first in the order of surnames; the rest of you can go and await my summons in (say) monthly turns." So Chao, who was really only a partial *châtré* and was ardent with salacity, passed with me a delicious night; details were mostly as already recorded for previous exploits: he desired and received a dozen severe strokes with the *discipline* which he seemed to revel in, repaying them to me with compound interest. He told me that I was born in the Mansion of the T'u Hsing 土星, Saturn, seeing my homosexual predilections; it is strange that my horoscope, cast by a German astrologer long ago, disclosed the "fatal influence" of Saturn on my life. I thought was it not Uranismus, reminding Kraft Ebing's treatise on Urnings and their

99 Tip.
100 To be whipped.
101 Included free of charge.
102 Look up respectfully.
103 Mostly falsehoods.
104 Oscar Wilde.

exotic habits![105] And so there was another item to my debit of Taels 255 *pour une nuit d'amour*.[106]

Plus ça change, plus c'est la même chose:[107] I do not know that I have much to add. The schedule was faithfully followed in the ensuing months (with a summer recess) during the intervals when I was not summoned for "audience" by the All Highest Despot dame. The eunuchs attended in the order of the *Po Chia Hsing* 百家姓, so far as their surnames allowed, Sun 孫, Feng 馮, Ch'in 秦, Ts'ao 曹, Wu 吳, Wei 魏, Tou 竇 and several more. They were all passionate and responsive to caresses, *on ne peut plus*;[108] some enjoyed the *Masochismus* and physical pains of the whipping, others renounced it for themselves and the extra Taels 25 *récompense* but were very glad to chastise me until my posterior really did become hard as iron, as my table domestic had said. Nothing could have been more seductive and more appealing than those perfumed elegant Gitons;[109] add the fact that they had charming manners, were folk of humour and zest; and I have said all that need be said in their favour. About half of them were definitely castrated but were not without strong sexuality; the remainder, like Lien Tzu-yen 連子延 whom I have already described, possessed a complete *verge* and were capable of intromission, although, unlike him, there was no ejaculation, only a moisture at the urethral orifice which, I suppose, was prostatic fluid. Whether that which we did was natural or not, nothing could have compassed the naturalness and ease of their bearing; everything seemed to be a matter of course, let the world say what it will. I shall always think affectionately of Li Lien-ying, a much maligned protagonist of the twilight of the dynasty. *Sit tibi terra levis;*[110] he lived till 1911, the year before the Revolution which he had repeatedly foretold, so soon as the Empress Dowager was removed from the helm of state. Perhaps he felt with her and with Louis XV: *Après moi, le deluge!*[111] and rather welcomed the prospect of his enemy, the Regent's fall.

It is well known that in the palace the eunuch staff was always spoken of as *Ching Shen Chê* 淨身者, persons with pure bodies, as opposed to the generality of "entire" males who were polluted by their sexual appurtenance, *Cho* 濁, impure (turbid). I should certainly consider that the many fair eunuchs of my predilection and libidinous fancy were not inferior in fragrance and bodily delectability to the patricians and gilded youth, the professional actors and catamites, with whom I had so many hundred (perhaps a thousand) love affairs during those wild erotic years, *moi allumé comme toujours avec ce rut de satyre inépuisablement*

---

105   Richard von Krafft-Ebing (1840-1902) was a German psychiatrist and an early pioneer in the study of human sexuality. In his best-known work, *Psychopathia Sexualis*, he writes extensively about homosexuals or Urnings (Uranians), as they were sometimes called at the time.

106   For a night of love.

107   The more things change, the more they stay the same.

108   But no more.

109   Giton is the handsome youth lover of Enclopius in *Satyricon* (1st century AD) by Gaius Petronius.

110   "May the earth rest lightly upon you", a traditional funerary inscription.

111   After me, the flood!

luxurieux,[112] between 1896 and 1925, not to mention similar incursions of my Don Juan self to whom love is, and was, lord and king (and love treats statistics as vain things), in Europe and in Africa, London, Paris, Vienna, Rome, Naples, Madrid, Seville, Lisbon, Constantinople, Athens, St. Petersburg, Moscow, Buda-Pesth, ay, even across the tideless sea to Algiers and Cairo; all, all recall fond memories that shall not die.

112 I am always illuminated by the inexhaustible lust of the satyr.

CHAPTER VI

THE HAMMAM
AND THE INTRUSION

THE Hsin Ching 新淨 Hammam,[1] once fashionable among the Manchu aristocracy but now long closed, was situated in a lane parting east of the Hou Men Ta Chieh[2] 後門大街. It was really more a male *bordel*[3] for the imperial clan than a resort of the ordinary public; the manager, as usual among the bath-house guild, was a Tinghsing[4] 定興 man whose family had been established in Peking since Ch'ien Lung's 乾隆 reign; the attendants were all natives of Chihli 直隸 like the good-looking myrmidon, yclept[5] Jung 榮, whom I have already named. Private rooms, or *Ya Tso* 雅座, were reserved in advance; the usual programme being gossip and scandal in the large social hall with tea and cigarettes, the hot bath with the attendant ministering to the bather's needs and not infrequently offering his services, for those who had made no other trysts, as a catamite (he never took an active part), for a fixed fee of Taels 50 divisible between the manager and himself. Then after ablutions and perfuming on an elaborate scale, we engaged in dalliance with the pre-arranged partner, sometimes three in one inextricable bout of love, usually reciprocal, accompanied by the regular gamut of lascivious manoeuvres which were followed, when lust was sated and the fires of passion had cooled, by an adjournment to the main room for gambling, chess or *contes grivois*,[6] particularly the latter. The evening was often wound up with a course of massage and abundant drinks: the establishment was really a social club and in fact I do not know if casual clients would have been admitted without due introduction. The attendants were of a lower class than the staff of the Hall of Chaste Pleasures but were one and all well endowed sexually, prepared to stimulate out-worn passions as when one of them helped Prince Ch'ing 慶 (Yi K'uang 奕劻) to a desired orgasm, such as it was, by performing osculations[7] on his inert organ.

---

1   "Newly Cleansed" Turkish-bath.
2   Rear-gate Avenue.
3   Brothel.
4   A city in Chihli Province (now Ho-peh), approximately 90 km southwest of Peking.
5   **Backhouse:** N.B. *yclept*: named; Anglo-Saxon *gecleopod*, from *cleopian*, to call.
6   Bawdy tales.
7   Kisses.

None who has perused this salacious chronicle of an abnormally constituted sexualist, endowed in earlier life by an unkind nature with anomalistic didymism[8] or should it rather be fateful dualism, like a new disease unknown to men, the torment of a twofold obsession which preoccupied him, even as a thief in the night pauses in perplexity on his adventure at the parting of the ways; such a one, I say, shall not be astonished to learn that in this dissolute company of ancient debauchees and youthful profligates I was among the foremost in unbridled libertinage, perhaps (in my case) not wholly unaccompanied by literary allusion and poetical parallelism. It may seem strange to one who knows not Victorian society; but I was irresistibly reminded of another Hammam, not a hundred miles from Saint James' Piccadilly, where in the early nineties a congenial clique foregathered, rivalling its Manchu compeers in aesthetic sexuality and unbridled exercise of unchaste instinct, the archhierophant Oscar Wilde, Lord Alfred Douglas, Henry Harland, Lord Drumlanrig, Douglas' brother, the secretary of Lord Rosebery whose suicide by shooting caused such a scandal a year or so later, driving the prime-minister, his chief, to a temporary retirement at his Neapolitan villa (given by his testament to the Italian government), Aubrey Beardsley, the poet Lionel Johnson, my old school-fellow, opium smoker and a lover of beauty, a devout Catholic. With Willie Eden (father of Anthony) an occasional visitor and Henry James, urbane and cynical, contemplating the coterie's activities as a neutral observer who held nothing human alien from his theory of life, Henley, the poet, Lord Beauchamp and Lord Balcarres the artistic debonair pederast. Later events made Wilde the *bouc émissaire;*[9] largely because Lord Rosebery, burdened with an uneasy conscience after Drumlanrig's suicide, desired, and found, a means of arresting public suspicion by having Wilde arrested and tried. I think the parallel worth mentioning and, as Lord Cromer would have said "luciferous", between the drab Victorian *devanture*[10] of shop-front prudery and hypocrisy and the undisguised attitude toward life of a decadent imperial aristocracy. Equally could I tell tales out of school of Le Hammam No. 18 Rue Neuve des Mathurius or No. 63 Rue du Cardinal Lemoine with the white letters on blue lamps where *bains maures*[11] were subsidiary features. Junglu's degenerate adopted heir, Liang K'uei 良奎, P'u Chün 溥儁 the dispossessed heir apparent to whom I duly gave Tz'u Hsi's 慈禧 message regarding his whipping as recorded in the chapter on Messalina's pastimes, Jung Ch'ing 榮慶 the libidinous Grand Secretary, several ministers of the Nei Wu Fu[12] 內務府, Prince Su's 肅 second son who was afterwards shot, perhaps by accident, at a Japanese Aix-les-Bains[13] by a

---

8   Though this word seems to be the author's invention. The Greek *didymium*, meaning "dual elements", is likely the origin.
9   Scapegoat.
10   "Window". Many of the personages mentioned here feature prominently in Backhouse's autobiographical work about his life before China, *The Dead Past*. Whether Backhouse actually knew all, or any, of them is unknown.
11   Moorish baths.
12   Office of Internal Affairs.
13   French region famous for hot-spring baths.

Chinese general, Prince Kung 恭 and his jealous eunuch, all were regular clients; while Prince Ch'ing's youngest boy, Tsai Lun 載倫, would appear there on days when he knew that there was no danger of his father finding him in an ambiguous horizontal posture. A number of prominent eunuchs, meticulously concealing their nakedness if really and truly *châtrés*,[14] Li Lien-ying 李蓮英 himself who was a general favourite from his apparent *bonhomie*[15] and real courtesy, several Banner Tu T'ung 都統 and Fu Tu T'ung 副都統 including my friend Pa Ha-pu 巴哈布, General Chang Hsün 張勳, devotee of passive copulation and favourite of Tz'u Hsi, the tall Chiang Kuei-t'i 姜桂題 who was also *persona grata* to Tz'u Hsi and, if common report may be believed, bound to her, like myself, by an intimate tie, P'u Lun and his brothers, Tsai Ying 載瀛, the brother of my old acquaintance Tsai Lan 載瀾, the paramour of Cassia Flower, all were members of our circle; so much so that on some evenings I have known a quorum of over forty more or less prominent aristocrats, military men and eunuchs, so that the business flourished exceedingly, even as it did in the days of Ch'ien Lung when that monarch would pay incognito visits.

The police in those days, which was quite inefficient, winked at our proceedings and never, to my knowledge, intervened even in the not infrequent case of fighting between the retainers in waiting on their masters at the gate; but I imagine that the proprietors had to pay away large sums for the Censorate and the Peiyamen 北衙門 of the Gendarmerie. The usual fee for clients was Taels 10 a visit, plus Taels 25 commission when actual sexual congress took place, that is among the clients themselves; for, as I have stated, the services of the bath house catamites were charged extra. In case of triangular coition, the fee was increased to Taels 40, each party having to pay one third, but Prince Kung always paid his eunuch's proportion. Li Lien-ying was an honorary member and was charged no fee whatsoever, as behaved his unique position with the Old Buddha, since a word from him might have closed the concern.

Prince Ch'ing renewed his carnal overtures to me on more than one occasion, and I always said that such an unheard of honour would be like an overflowing goblet that is spilled.

"What about those higher than I," asked the prince, "what they ask, you give!"

"Only what the five cardinal duties (*Wu Lun* 五倫) require, Your Highness.[16] I am not your subject, son, wife, nor brother; as to the relation of friend, I dare not arrogate to myself such a place, *Pu Kan Kao P'an*[17] 不敢高攀. T'would be like a barnfowl's vain attempt to rival the phoenix's flight. But I am deeply honoured by your deigning to desire my cooperation and in all other matters will serve you while breath remains in my

---

14 Castrated.

15 Good-naturedness

16 The Five Relationships and their proper characteristics are as follows: between ruler and minister, rectitude; between father and son, affection; between elder and younger brother, precedence; between husband and wife, distinction of tasks; and between friends, trust.

17 I would not dare clamber so high.

body." So Prince Ch'ing had perforce to content himself with his boy attendant and the masseurs of the bath-house; he presented a pitiable spectacle of unsatisfied desire and of impotent concupiscence. He was *infect et impur*;[18] so much so that the labial or anal contact which the decayed libertine sought was fraught with very real risks of contagion.

One evening, I think that it was the 24 of XII Moon, Chia Ch'en 甲 辰 year (about February 1, 1905), I had gone to the Hammam early and Li Lien-ying (who seemed rather preoccupied) was the only other client present. We had a confidential chat and I asked him about the Old Buddha's previous amours; he mentioned a European, apparently a protégé of the French Legation, named Wallon (?), aged at that time about twenty-three, who had been working at the Chung Hai 中海 at the time of the *désaffectation*[19] of the old Pei T'ang 北堂 or Catholic cathedral in the Palace grounds. Li was then a young man and was accustomed to accompany the Empress in her peregrinations in the lake enclosure. She caught sight of "Wa Lun" 瓦倫 and admired his wellset figure, eyes which cast amorous glances, *Sung Ch'iu P'o* 送秋波 "autumn waves", and sensuous mouth. Li accordingly arranged for him to be received on the following evening at Ch'ang Ch'un Kung 長春宮 in the Forbidden City (the Empress at that time not being resident at the Lake Palace). The tryst was duly kept and the Empress did to Wallon very much what she did to (and expected from) me except for the tragic *dénoûment*[20] which I was spared: she made him reveal his nakedness, caressed his parts probably with even greater zest (seeing that she was still under fifty) than her decided passion in my unworthy direction connoted, and made him perforce effect coition with her (so Li said) five times in one night. Before leaving her presence, she had an "invigorating" drug prepared for him (which he took) and arranged for a second visit; whether it was sexual excess or the effects of the *Mei Yao* 媚葯, M. Wallon only lived a few hours, heat apoplexy being given by the Legation physician as the cause of death. Li did not himself believe that poison had been administered, at any rate he did not admit it to me. I do not perceive her object in poisoning him so early in the liaison, if poison him she did. He added, naïvely enough, that the Old Buddha had said of me: "He's not perhaps as good looking as Wa but is infinitely more fascinating and has really something to talk about."

As to the other paramours of the Empress, their number was legion and must have run into many scores: those of low birth – *Hsia Chien* 下賤 – had not been allowed to live after enjoying the favours of the Old Buddha who had to *Mieh K'ou* 滅口, or suppress their talk; but the number of sudden seizures that had occurred to pastry cooks, waiters, barbers and tradesmen's messengers, either in the Palace or immediately after leaving it, had been so large that sinister rumours became prevalent, till

---

18 Filthy and impure.
19 Decommissioning.
20 "Outcome", correctly written "*dénouement*".

at last a censor had impeached the *dérèglement*[21] of the Empress' morals. This bold man was given a provincial appointment and was commended by the Empress for his frankness, although she naturally did not admit the truth of his allegations. "It will be my duty," announced her decree, "to be henceforth more circumspect than before; if I have erred, it is my wish and pleasure to amend any moral lapses; if I am free from offence, I must see to it that I give no colour whatsoever to criticism. It is my wish to hearken to admonition and I hereby transmit to the censor my sincere recognition of his outspokenness." Obviously, she spoke with her tongue in her cheek; and I could well imagine her sardonic smile as she dictated the decree to the Grand Council; but I suspect that she sought an early opportunity of wreaking her vengeance on the courageous memorialist.

Regarding Junglu, Li was non-committal and bade me judge for myself; he admitted that General Chang Hsün 張勳 had had intimate relations with her, also the late Grand Secretary Ê Lo Ha Pu 額落哈布 and a certain Ts'ung Yin 從印 whom I did not identify. He fully confirmed the rumours concerning the "eunuch" who was no eunuch, An Tê-hai 安德海, in the early years of the Kuang Hsü 光緒 reign (but I have written about him elsewhere).[22] She enjoyed "playing" with the good-looking eunuchs, especially the tribadistic acts and the pleasurable titillation of her clitoris slightly inside the anal cavity of the favoured one. A reason of her inveterate hate of the Chen Fei 珍妃 or Pearl Concubine could be found in the fact that the latter had repaired to salute Her Majesty at an inopportune moment and had seen more than was good for her chance of survival.[23]

Li then excused himself, as he had a few words to say to the Hammam manager and was due "to report" (I could not guess what about) at the Ning Shou Kung 寧壽宮, Palace of a Peaceful Old Age, where the Old Buddha intended, according to her custom, to pass the New Year, it being a time when many sacrificial ceremonies which could only take place in the Forbidden City required her presence, the New Year homage of the court to Her Majesty being also performed in the Huang Chi Tien 皇極殿. He thought that she would summon me "for audience" *Chao Chien* 召見, before the end of the year, now only a few days distant, and warned me to be in readiness "at any moment of the day or night". In the Cheng Yüeh 正月, or 1st Moon, sexual intercourse is usually eschewed, at any rate so far as coition with outsiders is concerned, but I do not imagine that the inhibition applies to married couples. In fact, both the Hall of "Chaste Pleasures" in pre-Boxer days and the Bath House of the "Renovation of Cleanliness" deliberately limited their programmes to tea, conversation, card-playing, gambling, cigarettes or drinks, such a

---

21 Corruption.
22 See *China under the Empress Dowager* (Ch. 7-8), published in 1910 with co-author J.O.P. Bland.
23 The Pearl Concubine (1876-1900) was the favorite of Emperor Kuang Hsü. The story of her murder by the Empress Dowager, who had her thrown into a well in the Forbidden City, is recounted earlier. The corroboration for this story, however, comes from a forged document used in Backhouse's earlier work with Bland *China under the Empress Dowager*, so questions still remain as to the exact circumstances of the concubine's demise.

thing as sexual commerce being wholly debarred: it would have been regarded as contrary to etiquette.

So Li returned to his official duties, it being now about nine o'clock. Members of our circle began putting in an appearance and we had the fullest house in my recollection, partly owing to the proximity of the New Year as the establishment closed from the 1st to the 16th of the Cheng Yüeh after the manner of the more fashionable business-houses, curio dealers, tea merchants, jewellers – ordinary bath houses and shops generally opening on the 6th day. By ten thirty p.m. we had between forty and fifty clients present, including some I had not met: Prince Ch'ing was not present but two of his worthless sons, as usual, were *Yen Chung Ting* 眼中釘, or *bêtes noires*,[24] to the rest, *Hu Chia Hu Wei* 狐假虎威, the fox borrowing the tiger's prestige, what the Japanese call *Haikara* (high collar) or foppish. The late Grand Councillor Ch'i Hsiu's 啓秀 son, Heng Yü 恆虞, came that night and greatly attracted me; his father had been executed in January 1901 as a Boxer leader by order from the Old Buddha, then in Hsian 西安, under pressure from the allies. I had witnessed the decapitation which was carried out under the superintendence of foreign troops! He had died very bravely, asking if it was indeed the Empress Dowager's order and, on being told that it was so, exclaiming: "Be it so, if Her Majesty ordains." His two sons had arranged with the headsman, Li 李, that the head should be sewn on to the trunk without a second's delay, and this had been skilfully done. Heng Yü was extraordinarily seductive and I count myself fortunate in that he and I bathed together, enjoying post-balneal reciprocal coition and accompanying manoeuvres which seemed to afford to us equal satisfaction. He declared that it was his initial effort either as pathic or "uppermost", but do not think that he expected me to believe him.

After our prolonged *délices*[25] we adjourned to the reception room; I thought that the proprietor seemed unusually on edge as if he were expecting something to happen; he came in several times and took stock of the company which was in unusually gay spirits, as is natural when youth and pleasure meet to chase the winged hours. We were all *en déshabillé*,[26] some in fact almost naked. I was chatting with Prince Kung and his eunuch and the former had proposed a rendezvous for homosexual purposes one evening before the New Year.

Suddenly a peremptory voice shouted from the foot of the short flight of steps: "*Kuei Hsia* 跪下, kneel down."

The tones were imperious enough to command obedience, but Tsai Fu 載扶, Prince Ch'ing's wayward boy, shouted back: "*Fang Ni Ti P'i* 放你的屁, a fig for you." I had an inkling what was afoot and complied; so did Prince Kung and the eunuch as well as most of the party. (I heard later that it was an officer of the Guards, Shih Wei 侍衛, in attendance, who had given the order.) Who should enter the reception room but Her

24 Nuisances (literally "black beasts").
25 Pleasures.
26 In undergarments.

Majesty who had disguised herself with a *Feng Ling* 風領 or windproof cape round her head and was wearing a yellow riding jacket with masculine trousers and wadded shoes! Li Lien-ying and Ts'ui Tê-lung 崔德隆 supported her, more for appearance sake, as she walked with a firm step. She seemed very angry: "Who dared to say '*Merde*'?" (*Le mot de Cambronne* at Waterloo is not the literal translation but gives the sense.)[27]

Tsai Fu looked frightened out of his wits, and several of the company obligingly replied for him: "It was Tsai Fu, Old Buddha: please forgive him."

He kotowed several times and the Empress reviled him as a conceited puppy. "Your father shall hear about your insolence: leave the premises with your brother at once, but it is cold and I advise you to put on some clothes first. You are indecent: *T'ai Pu Ch'eng Shih T'i*[28] 太不成事體, it's too improper."

I knew the Old Buddha's caprices well enough by this time to perceive that her anger was largely feigned despite the gross rudeness of Tsai Fu's "*réplique*"[29] given, of course, in ignorance of Her presence and that she was glad to snub the Ch'ing family for which she had no love. We remained on our knees, until Her Majesty who was sitting on a low arm-chair bade us rise and accorded to me the favour of a few words, thus giving me momentary precedence over Prince Kung despite my much lower rank: "Well, Pa Hou 巴侯, it was you who told me about this 'literary' resort! It is, as I expected, chiefly sleeve cutting, *Tuan Hsiu* 斷袖, and peach remnant, *Yü Tao* 餘桃" (euphemistic for active and passive male relations).

"Yes, Your Majesty; it does not lay claim to a high moral status, but it is great fun."

"Well, I forbid *you* pleasuring anyone or anyone pleasuring *you* for this evening: if you disobey me, I shall tell Li Lien-ying to chastise you in my presence and that of the company, *in partibus posterioribus*."[30] Then turning to Prince Kung: "So you and your precious eunuch are as usual amorously reclining side by side."

Said the Prince: "Old Buddha, he has been helping me in the bath, when I really need him."

"I quite believe that he is most useful to your special tastes but don't overdo it." (*Pieh Kuo Tu* 別過度.) "What does your wife say?"

Tea was then brought in for the Empress. She bade us all be seated. She said: "I am not here as an inspector of morals nor as a government censor, but I want to *K'ai Yen* 開眼, open my eyes or initiate myself: how does your homosexual dalliance begin and end? You really all deserve to be castrated or else to have the cavity of your hinder parts (*P'i Ku Yen'rh*

27   **Backhouse:** *Braves Français rendez-vous* said the English ensign: *Merde* Vis Cambronne. [This refers to Viscount Pierre Cambronne, commander of the last of Napoleon's army after Waterloo, who supposedly replied "*Merde!*" (Shit!), when the British demanded his surrender. The expression became known as "*Le mot de Cambronne*" (the word of Cambronne).]
28   There is no order in it.
29   Reply.
30   In the rear parts.

屁股眼兒) blocked against intrusion (*Tuan Ch'i Ying Sung Chih Lu* 斷其迎送之路); however, that cannot be, so you are, at least some of you, now commanded to give me complete demonstrations of *la chose dont il est question*."[31]

Then Li called one of the good-looking bath attendants Jung Chi 榮吉: "The Old Buddha bestows Taels 100 upon you and orders you to *Wan'rh* 玩兒 (play) with that young eunuch." This was not Prince Kung's favourite but, as I later found, a nice boy of twenty or less, in attendance on P'u Ch'ün 溥儁, the ex-heir-apparent, who seemed decidedly nervous knowing the Old Buddha of old and perhaps mindful of his past whippings. I admired the self-possession of both parties and was glad that she had not assigned this honourable duty to myself, particularly as I had already done what in me lay *vis-à-vis* Heng Yü. We explained to the Empress, who perhaps was more *au fait*[32] with the *modus operandi* than she admitted, that there existed *Hang Hua* 行話, slang expressions, for the divers ways and means. The person on top was called *Ch'o Chin* 擢進 or "prick advance" and the pathic *P'o Ch'eng* 破承 (an allusion to the now extinct *Pa Ku* 八股 of the old literary essay), "break-reception". If the latter *Chüeh P'i Ku* 撅屁股, offered buttock presentation leaning forward, the act was designated as *Ch'i Hsiao Lü'rh* 騎小驢兒, ride the small donkey; if, on the other hand, he lay prone and supine, the term was *T'ao K'u Lung* 掏窟窿, open out a hole (*T'ao Ch'u Ting Ta Ti K'u Lung* 掏出頂大的窟窿 is a common expression for "got myself into a big hole" or "run myself into a debt"), also *Ch'ü T'ao'rh* 取桃兒, to obtain the peach. Triangular simultaneous copulation was known as *I T'uan Mi Chien Kuo* 一團蜜餞果, compote of candied fruits, and *Ch'uan T'ang Hu Lu* 串糖葫蘆, stringed crystallized fruits, also by the more obvious name of *San Pu Fen* 三不分, an indistinguishable trio; the central party who enjoyed favour from above (*Ch'eng Shang* 承上) and imparted it below (*Ch'in Hsia* 侵下; encroach underneath) was called *Wei Yang*[33] 未央, two characters which mean the direction of the centre, *Chung* 中, also *Liang Fang T'ao Hao* 兩方討好, winning twofold pleasuring. The term "cinnamon leaves" for anal osculation has already been given; another expression is (or was) *T'ao Chih'rh* 桃汁兒, peach juice. Lascivious stroking of the anal cavity was denominated *Shou P'iao* 手票 or *cédule* note of hand (why, I do not know. *Cédule* or *billet sous seing privé*,[34] perhaps because the act is essentially private, although on this occasion decidedly the reverse); persistent nuzzling of the posterior region, *Wu Hua Yeh* 無花葉, fig leaves. This particular feature seemed to give to devotees more pleasure than any, as it did, Buddha forgive! to me.

The above details diverted the Empress and Li kept nodding a condescending assent; as if he were thoroughly *Hang Chia* 行家 or *Ko Chung*

---

31 The subject in question.
32 Familiar.
33 Not yet halfway through; not yet exhausted.
34 Note of private agreement.

Jen 個中人, one *di color che sanno*,[35] of those who are in the know, as he doubtless was, as I have the best reason to aver.

The eunuch of P'u Chün 溥儁, who was named Ju Hsi 茹席, elected to present his shapely posterior, *Chüeh P'i Ku* 撅屁股, to the bath attendant who performed the requisite evolutions with admirable calmness, as if he was unembarrassed by his august spectator, and seemed greatly to please the Old Buddha with his very long *membrum virile* which she had contemplated with libidinous interest. (In fact, knowing the Empress' little ways, I trembled for his future prospects.) Everything went swimmingly (like a fish in midstream) and in due course ejaculation into the pathic's rectum was faithfully accomplished. This achieved, both parties rose and kotowed to the Empress who was graciously pleased to accord the same largess of Taels 100 to Ju Hsi the pathic; and P'u Chün, as in duty bound, duly kotowed to thank the Old Buddha for her generous bounty toward his "small servant", *Hsiao Chieh* 小价, all unworthy of her high condescension.

After a short interval, the Old Buddha, as I expected, demanded a further concrete display; this time she required Lun Pei Tzu 倫貝子 to copulate with a younger imperial duke of the Yü 毓 generation, whose second name (perhaps Chien 朘) escapes me: "Let it be the *T'ao K'u Lung* 掏窟窿, 'hole opening out' type; as I want to see a practical demonstration of both methods." So Duke Yü, who was no novice but *Ching Kuo Shih'rh* 經過事兒, had experience, lay prone but slightly *Chai Wai Cho* 栽歪著 or sideways, and P'u Lun, whose constant abuse of the sexual function had rather impaired his virility, after displaying his small, but still erect penis to the Old Buddha (who fondled it maternally), managed to penetrate Yü's yielding rectum and after palpable effort to effect the desired result. He had not achieved much of an entry, when Duke Yü's buttocks were thoroughly wetted with seminal fluid. This seemed to amuse the Old Buddha, who called one of the attendants: "Get a hot towel, *Na Shou Chin Pa'rh* 拿手巾把兒, and rub his posterior dry." Lun Pei Tzu and the duke both thanked the Empress who said to the former: "*Yu Lao Wu Kung* 有勞無功, you have taken trouble without much result," and to the latter: "I suppose you derived little pleasure; as P'u Lun's *Ch'iao Tzu* 巧子 is scarcely that of a *Chiu Chiu Wu Fu* 糾糾武夫, a stalwart warrior."

Then addressing me: "I suspect that your royal princes could accomplish better results?" I replied that I rather doubted it but had no opportunity to judge. "But one of them indulges in *Ts'ao P'i Ku* 肏屁股, anal copulation, does he not?"

"Madam, I am really not competent to reply but have heard that the late Prince Eddie (duke of Clarence, obit 1892), who might have been one day king, did have this *P'i* 癖 or predilection and was involved in a notorious London (Cleveland St.) scandal some fifteen years ago,[36] but things were hushed up and no action was taken. Your Majesty doubtless knows

---

35 Dante (*Inferno* IV.131) discussing Aristotle.

36 "The Cleveland Street Affair" revolved around a high-class male brothel, whose clients were said to include Prince Albert "Eddie" Victor, raided by London police in 1889.

that by our laws in England sodomy which results in a definite penetration *Ch'o T'ung* 擢通, so that a lesion is visibly and palpably caused to the patient's rectum, is punishable by 20 years imprisonment and less than a century ago by hanging. Ordinary sexual intercourse between males *inter crura*[37] or on the surface outside the anus is punishable, if detected, with two years imprisonment."

"How absurd," said the Old Buddha; "if people prefer to *Ts'ao P'i Ku* 畬屁股, let them do so. What if husband and wife do it?"

"It would be difficult to prove, but I imagine that the penalty would be less: there is a religious aspect, part of our Occidental hypocrisy."

Judging from appearance, I thought that the Empress Dowager's passions, never far below the surface, were being rapidly stimulated by this sequence of lascivious spectacles and was not greatly surprised when Li called me aside, with a "The Old Ancestress commands your attendance at the Ning Shou Kung 寧壽宮 after the party here breaks up at about the hour of the Ox, *Ch'ou K'o* 丑刻, 1 a.m. You will stay all night with her."

I bowed assent, wondering whether my physique would stand two (or more) copulation efforts after my erotic (if congenial) feat earlier in the evening; it was impossible to refuse or to suggest the appointment of another day especially with the New Year at hand, "when no man can work"; for excuses of this nature are never accepted at their face value in China any more than they would be in our barbarous Occident with our "I regret that I am unavoidably prevented from the acceptance of your kind invitation."

Next, the Old Buddha commanded Prince Kung and the Duke P'u Chün, who was as lustful as a buck-rabbit, to exhibit to her their respective *verges*, both of which soon developed an ample state of erection well over the normal length; neither appeared otherwise than self-satisfied but the prince's eunuch looked, as he doubtless felt, the picture of misery. He recovered his spirits somewhat on learning that the Empress Dowager only required reciprocal *P'in Hsiao* 品薰, carried on simultaneously, both parties being ordered to swallow the ejaculated semen of the other. Accordingly, they assumed the requisite posture not without difficulty, for "69" *soixante neuf* (*crede experto*,[38] for I know whereof I write) is only easy when the parties are of the same length, whereas in their case P'u Wei 溥偉 (Prince Kung 恭) was six inches taller than the slightly built P'u Chün, his cousin. However, each managed to accomplish the necessary buccal contact (*gamme bouche*) and after what seemed an infinite delay the voluptuous expression on their faces seemed to indicate that ejaculation was nearly achieved. P'u Chün made a wry face as if the savour did not greatly attract him, while his own discharge followed more slowly. Then the two rose from their ungainly recumbence, saluted the Old Buddha and exhibited to her, as if as a guarantee of good faith, their "tools" now flaccid and with semen still exuding from the urethral orifices. The Empress made each apply his lips and tongue to the other's moist *Ma*

---

37 Between the legs.
38 Believe one who has experience (Virgil, *Aeneid* XI.283).

Yen[39] 馬眼 and remarked: "*Hao La* 好啦! *Yu I Ssu* 有意思; *Wo Man I* 我滿意. Good: quite amusing; I am satisfied."

Then the Old Buddha called up two very comely dukes of the clan, whose names I do not know for certain, except that one was of the Heng 亨, and the other of the Ch'i 啟 generation, bidding them exhibit to her their genital apparatus which was not unhandsome, and distinctly on a large scale, while she contemplated their pearl-white buttocks. She made them open up (*Pai K'ai* 掰開) their anal cavities and gazed with renewed pleasure on the fair line and curve of their posteriors, *Ch'ü Hsien Mei* 曲 線美. She did not insist upon copulation but told them to perform mutual osculations upon the anal region. One of the lads (they were aged about twenty, I fancy), yclept Hsien 佽, Duke Ch'i 啟, seemed to demur slightly; poor boy, perhaps he was not yet wedded to this exotic posture, *Mei Na Ko Fu Ch'i*[40] 沒那個福氣, (of course, they were all exquisitely perfumed); at any rate, he had to obey and started the "peach juice" (*vide supra*)[41] manoeuvres on the region indicated. Unfortunately, the pleasurable titillation caused Heng to ejaculate, like Onan of old, upon the floor.[42] "*P'ao K'ung La* 跑空啦," said the Old Buddha, "you have cast your seed upon the void," then to the attendant "*Pa T'a Ti Kou Sung Ts'a Ching Liao* 把他的狗 鬆擦淨了, wipe up his 'spunk'," the Chinese expression being very vulgar.

Duke Heng expressed his regret for *Pu Ching Chih Tsui* 不敬之罪, *lèse majesté*,[43] and the Old Buddha good naturedly replied: "*Pu Te I Ti Shih Chen Pao Pu Ch'i* 不得已的事真保不齊, accidents will happen; it can't be helped."

Duke Ch'i then knelt to the Old Buddha: "Your Majesty, may I copulate with Heng, riding over him (*Ch'i Hsiao Lü'rh* 騎小驢兒) the small ass (*vide supra*)?"

"By all means if he is willing (*T'ung I* 同意); you will be giving to him from behind what he has just lost in front."

Li Lien-ying applauded his mistress' wit: "*Lao Tsu Tsung Tou Ken* 老祖 宗鬥艮: the Old Ancestress is indeed humorous." Accordingly Ch'i duly climbed upon Heng's upturned buttock and achieved a singularly complete and satisfying consummation.

"*Tao Liao'rh Ni Shih Ko Lu Tzu* 到了兒你是個爐子, so after all you are a regular catamite," said Her Majesty to the duke who had previously *fraudé*[44] so disastrously upon the floor (the Chinese *Pai Lu Tzu* 白爐子, ordinary stove used in poorer circles, being of a shape slightly suggestive of coitus from behind). It was now approaching midnight and I managed to convey to Li Lien-ying, not in the Old Buddha's hearing, that I trusted to him to prepare for me a stiff dose of *Mei Yao* 媚藥 on my arrival in the Palace, since otherwise, I should surely be found wanting.

---

39 Urethral opening.
40 Did not yet have the good fortune.
41 Literally "see above".
42 From *Genesis*, Onan is asked to impregnate the widow of his older brother, but each time ejaculates on the floor before consummating the act. In consequence, God smites him.
43 An affront to royalty.
44 Defrauded (his partner).

The Empress said: "Well! I have seen what I wanted; it seems just to suit your tastes – *Heng Shu Che Shih Shun Ni Men Ti Hsin Ssu* 橫豎這是順你們的心事; but don't forget your conjugal duties. I suppose the tickling is unbearable with such large anuses as you are endowed with. *T'ao Ch'ê* 套車, get the cart ready." (She had come in an ordinary *Hung T'o Ni Pu Chê* 紅托泥布車 or official cart, with, as I have said, one *Shih Wei* 侍衛 as escort.) "You are none of you to see me off: it will only attract notice. You will all attend at the Palace to see the old year out (*Tz'u Sui* 辭歲) and for the New Year congratulations. Till then, *Tsai Chien*[45] 再見." She nodded meaningly to me, put on her face concealing cape and outer jacket and left supported by Li and Ts'ui as she had come. She left Taels 100 for the bath house staff as new year largess. We stayed a few moments longer, while Prince Kung asked me if my queen would have come out incognito on such a visit! I replied that customs differ and that such spectacles, though existing in London and Paris, were concealed from publicity by the cloak of hypocrisy, though equally libidinous. Then we all went our several ways homeward; none of the imperial clansmen had brought any retinue and even Prince Kung had only his carter awaiting him. I hurried home keeping my programme secret from the sodality to prepare for my next rendezvous. Naturally, it would have attracted too much attention at so late an hour to order my chair, so I contented myself with the Peking cart which, thanks to my gold tablet, was able to take me right up to the entrance of the Ning Shou Palace of which I have already written. It was just 1 a.m., and Li was waiting for me with the philter which I drained. Her Majesty was not ready to receive me, and the respite brought surely enough an invasion of enhanced sexual excitation.

I think it was in the year 1894 that I heard Maurice Barrès remark at one of our reunions *dans ce beau jardin de la rue d'Éperon* with its blue camelias in full bloom: "*Nous avons tous notre talon d'Achille; il n'est donné à personne de rester toujours intéressant.*"[46] For Maurice Barrès *la religion du Moi, le divin égotisme*[47] was all that counted: his elegant *dévouement*[48] seemed to say: "The outside world is *le grain d'opium que je fume et tout ce que je vous montre n'est que la fumée de mes songes.*"[49] Nothing is so *embêtant*, he asserted, as *la redite d'une sale histoire*, unless it be *des propos médisants sur un grand personnage.*[50] Faithful, then, to the *obiter dictum*[51] of the master, who, more than any I have ever known, except perhaps *ce prodigieux savant qu'était Gaston Boissier,*[52] the Gamaliel at whose feet, like a Saul of Tarsus, I once sat, or Walter Pater, the gentle

---

45 Goodbye.
46 In this beautiful garden on Rue d'Eperon . . . Everyone has an Achilles heel; not everyone can be interesting all the time.
47 The religion of the Self, divine egotism.
48 Devotion.
49 The grain of opium I smoke and everything I show you is the smoke of my dreams.
50 So "boring" . . . as "the repetition of a dirty story" . . . unless it be "slanderous remarks about a great man".
51 Remark.
52 The amazing scientist who was Gaston Boissier.

homosexualist and Epicurean, my Oxford tutor, lived in intimate relation *avec la muse hellénique et la muse latine*,[53] I do not propose to descant again, and yet again, upon the loves of Tz'u Hsi, except (if possible) to throw a fresh light upon that enigmatic personality, whose faults were neither few nor small but who, equally with Catherine of Russia, possessed an incomparable state-craft and a fascination that perhaps not half a dozen men and women in history have equalled. Even in the debauched excesses of the Hammam which I have attempted to narrate, she preserved quite unimpaired her imperial dignity, the while she contemplated – what? – the unconscionable, boyish *Gitons*[54] of the imperial clan indulging in libidinous osculations of each other's hinder parts!

Li Lien-ying informed me that the maids of honour in attendance, after helping Her Majesty to her rest, always remained in the adjoining apartment until her breathing seemed to indicate that she was asleep: "*Lao Fo Yeh Shui Chao La* 老佛爺睡著啦, *Tsan Men Tsou Pa* 咱們走吧,"[55] when they retired to rest.

After a somewhat lengthy wait which gave the *Mei Yao* 媚藥 more than ample opportunity to provoke my *T'a* 塔 (pagoda) to a new climax of erotic dimensions, Li left me to inform his mistress of my due arrival and came back, saying eagerly: "Be quick! she's expecting you and cannot wait any longer. *Pieh Tan Wu La* 別耽誤啦, waste no time, and stand not upon the order of your going."

It was a bitterly cold night, but the *Ning Shou Kung* 寧壽宮 was equipped with a hypogeum[56] which assured a high temperature; the electric lights were turned on in full, as if *une nuit de noce*:[57] I suppose that our *liaison* was now an open secret and that the time to dissimulate had passed. Crossing in a freezing temperature the open and exposed vestibule leading to the inner boudoir, where today are displayed on exhibition Her Majesty's chopsticks and *cosmetiques*, pathetic (for a Manchu) reminders of a buried epoch, I at Li's direction undressed and stood, *sans cacher ma nudité*,[58] till I heard the familiar falsetto accents: "*Ni K'uai Lai* 你快來, *Teng Cho Kan Ma* 等著幹麼! *Wo Chi La* 我急啦. Hurry up; what are you waiting for? I am impatient."

Unembarrassed and aflame with exaggerated sensuality – towards what? a man of 32 before an ancient dame of 70!! – I entered the inner bedchamber, which may have been (and in fact was) well shielded from noise but was certainly lacking in ventilation, and knelt down before the newly acquired phoenix bed of "empire" style: "Your slave is here, awaiting Your Majesty's good pleasure, eager and expectant."

53   "With the Hellenic and Latin muses". The characters mentioned here also feature in Backhouse's *The Dead Past*.
54   Pathics.
55   The Old Buddha is sleeping, we shall leave.
56   An underground chamber or vault.
57   A wedding night.
58   Without hiding my nudity.

"Good," said Her Majesty, "I am glad you are feeling erotic. Tell me if I am right: I suspect that you have already *Tsou Shen Tzu*[59] 走身子 before I arrived at the Hammam?"

"Yes, Your Majesty; I cannot *Shuo Hsia Hua* 說瞎話, tell to you an untruth. I had a very pleasing hour with the late Grand Councillor Ch'i Hsiu's 啓秀 son, Heng Yü 恆虞 early in the evening."

"You foreigners made me order the father's execution, so the son ought to regard you as his dearest foe, *Pu Kung Tai T'ien* 不共戴天."

"He bears to me no malice, Your Gracious Majesty, and is most fascinating and delectable."

"Well, well; naturally you did not know I was coming nor" (said archly) "that I was expecting you tonight."

"No, Your Majesty: I dared not dream in my wildest thoughts that you would tolerate my presence when Your Majesty was pre-occupied by New Year Preparations."

Speaking as usual straight and to the point, the Empress Dowager said: "*T'o Ni Ti T'a*[60] 脫你的塔" (as a fact I was standing by the imperial bedstead *Fen Ssu Wei Chia* 分絲未加, without a loin cloth to cover me, so the word *T'o* 脫 expose, was not *le mot juste*[61] for what was already palpably evident). "Let me feel your *Ch'iao Tzu* 巧子 (tool): Good! I see it is firm as steel." Then she began caressing my private parts with her hands before applying her lips toward my undeserving member. Once again we rehearsed the mutable game of love; once more she bade me kiss the large clitoris and play with it until a paroxysm of concupiscence compelled her to seek a further erotic attraction, so that I had (as she expressed it) to *Chüeh P'i Ku* 撅屁股, present my posterior in upward posture; whilst she inserted the passionate *partie du corps*[62] which Marie Antoinette so loved in the hapless Louise de Savoie, inside *le trou fignon* and titillated it with all her might for a very long time. After obtaining the desired emission issuing (I imagine) from the mucus of the vulva, she sate upon my lap, conscious of the tumefaction of the *verge* which, thanks to the potent aphrodisiac, remained unmoistened by *Yin Shui*[63] 陰水 or inconvenient prostatic discharge. "The dry and the wet" said the Old Buddha, reminiscent of a lewd passage in the *Liao Chai* 聊齋 which she so admired; "just put your finger inside my vulva (she said *Pi* 屄 which is more vulgar than *con* or the unprintable English equivalent):[64] it is simply saturated." Then began she to discuss the 22 *Tzu Shih* 姿勢 or postures of the sexual congress; they are all depicted realistically in the *Ch'un Kung* 春宮, or lascivious collection, literally *Palace of Desire*. I do not recall many of the suggestive names for those varying feats of love: for example, *Lao Han T'ui Ch'e* 老漢推車, the old fellow plies his wheelbarrow, which is a metaphor for the female remaining seated while the *Yang*

---

59 Reached climax.
60 Expose your pagoda.
61 The right word.
62 Body part.
63 The same word used earlier to describe the Empress Dowager's discharge.
64 To disprove the author's contention, the correct translation is "cunt".

陽 element stands to perform the act of sex; *Lao Ho Shang Pao Ch'ing* 老和尚抱磬, the old Bonze[65] claspeth the temple gong, to indicate that the lady bestrides the male; *Ko* (*Chieh* in vulgar pronunciation) *Shan T'ao Huo*[66] 隔山討火, he tends the fire across the barrier (mountain), which implies coition from behind; a fourth, *Tao Kua La* 倒掛臘, the candle suspended in the wrong direction, the positions reversed where the *Yang* element undertakes rectal intercourse or *pedicatio*, *Ts'ao P'i Ku* 肏屁股, which on another occasion Her Majesty bade me perform to her. It was indeed a case with me of *Wang Nien Chih Chiao*[67] 忘年之交, I ceased to remember the disparity of age and my relative indifference to feminine charms and the goddess Aphrodite. Remaining obstinately erect as a ramrod, I manoeuvred again and yet again to the infinite satisfaction of my queen who uttered half audible (but heartfelt) cries of: "So be it. Do it again: you are ravishing tonight."

I blessed Li, the Chief Eunuch, in my heart for his admirable drug and felt as he whose faith can remove mountains or as fed horses in the morning when each adulterer neighed after his neighbour's wife. When Her Majesty "mounted" me, as Nana says in the novel of that name, I felt a careless (of Shelley's "Ode to Skylark": "first fine careless rapture") rapture that is *indicible* and *indescriptible*:[68] she kissed my lips times without number, saying the soft nothings that lovers are wont to utter in lands of many a speech. "Always, always, you belong to me – *Yung Yüan Ni Shih Wo So Yu* 永遠你是我所有; you may roam like a wild beast from love to love, where your own fickle sex is concerned; but of my sex I am the one and only, *Tu I Wu Erh* 獨一無二, *Shih Pu Shih* 是不是? Is it not so?"

"For ever and for ever, thine alone, Your Gracious Majesty, my goddess of love."

After an elaborate orgy (I cannot devise a better word for such extravagant erotic favours) Her Majesty, whose clitoris had again become erect and her vulva like a lily drenched with rain, commanded more oscular attentions toward her secret parts, while she titillated my anal cavity and even insisted upon imprinting on so ignoble and unworthy a *Pu Fen* 部分 (part) kisses without number attended by the exclamation: "*Hao Hsiang* 好香! fragrant indeed!" (naturally the usual perfuming had not been neglected either in Her Majesty's case or my own). *Shih Tao Chi Tien* 事到極點, things had attained a climax, and she exacted the first copulation (*Chiao Kou* 交媾) which took an enormous time (owing to the action of the drug) but which ended in a simultaneous consummation which greatly coincided with our desires.

It was now nearly 3, and Li who, I fear, passed a vigilant night, entered with tea for Her Majesty and dose number 2 of the aphrodisiac for me. "We are having a glorious time," asseverated Her Majesty, and Li

---

65   Buddhist Monk.

66   *T'ao* does not typically mean "tend" as the author seems to understand it. The phrase is similar *Ko An Kuan Huo* 隔岸觀火, meaning "to watch someone's house catch fire from across the river" (i.e. not come to someone's aid in a crisis).

67   A friendship that spans the difference in ages.

68   "Unspeakable" and "indescribable".

replied: "I can see that you are, Old Ancestress, and rejoice that the marquis is acquitting himself to your content. Please give the drug the time to work and he will again comfort *Tz'u Huai* 慈懷 your bountiful desires with the plenitude of his militant person."

Once more I was bidden to walk slowly up and down the bedchamber my *Ch'iao Tzu* 巧子 quiescent and drooping, while Her Majesty sipped her jasmine scented tea. Li had evidently given me a double dose, as the orgasm returned very speedily (in less than half an hour) and I humbly memorialized the Old Buddha: "Your servant has *Shang Wu Chih Ching Shen*[69] 尚武之精神, martial ardour to strengthen his humble effort for Your Majesty."

Li retired for a mouthful of opium, *I K'ou Yen* 一口煙, and we re-enacted our carnival of lust which exceeded, if possible, the previous manifestation. It seemed to me that the Old Buddha would never be satiated of her erotomania: for all I know, she may have had other amorous rendezvous ahead of her during the day, although, woman-like, she protested her eternal constancy and devotion to myself. On this occasion, she again exacted that I should, as the supreme moment arrived, place my membrum in its entire length inside her mouth and she applied with considerable zest her luscious tongue to the glans penis, swallowing in due course the late coming and abundant ejaculation.

The Empress' numerous clocks had just stopped chiming 6, when the eunuch Ts'ui came in with tea for the Old Buddha and a bowl of birds nest soup for me which she graciously permitted me to partake of in her presence. "If you are finished with Marquis Pa, Old Buddha, *Ju Kuo Pa Hou Yeh Ti Shih Suan Wan La* 如果巴侯爺的事算完啦, it is nearly time for the audience of the Grand Council and Your Majesty's chair is in waiting to convey you to the *Ch'ien Ch'ing Kung* 乾清宮 Palace of Celestial Purity, as usual."

"Well," said Her Majesty, "we have had a full night of it and I have thoroughly enjoyed myself despite the loss of sleep. What of you?"

"Your Majesty, it has been to me heaven on earth, the fair beginning of a time."

"I excuse your attendance here on the last night of the year to *Tz'u Sui*[70] 辭歲, but come to offer congratulations early on New Year's day: be sure to wear your gala robes and to come in your chair."

Then to Ts'ui: "Tell Li Lien-ying to bring his clothes or at any rate some of them as at present he is ashamed of his nudity; and I permit him to dress as a special favour, *Chia En* 加恩, in the outside *Chien* 間 (apartment). He had best wait until the Grand Councillors have all arrived in their chairs and you are to send a message to his house to command his chair and bearers' immediate attendance outside the Ning Shou Kung's main entrance. I won't allow him to lose face, *Kuang T'ien Hua Jih Chih Hsia* 光天化日之下 in the garish light of day, by returning in a shabby old cart to his residence. Let people gossip, as they may, but let them beware

---

69   Still without spirit.
70   See the old year out.

of saying anything disrespectful of me or of him in my hearing. Also bid Li Lien-ying send Taels 1,000 as New Year presents for Pa Hou Yeh's 巴侯爺 servants and chair-bearers." Then to me: "*Tsai Chien* 再見: come again for private audience after the 'Cheng Yüeh' 正月 is over, when I shall return to the Chung Hai 中海 for the spring months."

Her Majesty graciously kissed me upon the lips, caressed my *verge* and posterior as an affectionate parting gesture and bade to me an apparently regretful *au revoir*. *Quant à moi*, I felt completely exhausted and just managed to totter into my chair, *une ruine*[71] like Racine's Marius before the walls of Carthage: "*Ces deux grandes ruines se regardèrent l'une l'autre*."[72] Recovery, however, came with rapid strides.

---

71   As for me . . . a wreck (ruin).
72   These two great ruins looking at one another.

CHAPTER VII
UNDER THE MULBERRY BUSH
THE SECRET TRYST

THE Old Buddha's sentiments towards me, which I flattered myself to be warm, more perhaps from the novelty of the relationship and the comparative freedom which, as an alien, I was able to allow myself both in word and in deed, than that she really felt toward me a deep or a lasting ecstasy of passion, invited like a magnet many approaches from Manchus, and sometimes even from Chinese, demanding my service as intermediary. It always seems to be that our decadent Europe, now in the death-throes, might well imitate the practice of requesting the intervention of a third party in a delicate negotiation: the habit *T'o Jen* 託 人, that of entrusting a common friend with the manipulation of a complicated business, obviates possible causes of friction and maintains a friendship intact through the changes and chances of time, the destroyer. I was no Potemkin (could not have been, had I wished) and sought no political power; for myself I can say truthfully that the intimacy, like Fersen's for his butterfly queen,[1] brought to me no *great* nor spectacular increase of income, though it certainly profited my entourage to a high degree. It is probable that I could have obtained substantial fees and commissions, or at any rate, valuable presents in kind, but actual pecuniary advantage has never attracted (and never will) one of my temperament[2] and in fact might have paved the way to loss of favour and a falling from my high estate, like Lucifer "never to hope again". Men said of me: "*T'a T'i P'i Ch'i T'ê Pieh* 他的皮氣特別, *Yin Wei T'a Pu Hao Huo* 因爲他不好貨: *K'o Shih T'a Chen Shuo Tê Chin Ch'ü* 可是他眞說得進去, *Shang T'ou Chen Cheng T'ing T'a Ti Hua* 上頭眞正聽他的話, *Hen Tso Ch'ing T'a* 狠作情他. He is peculiar in disposition, in that money has no charm for him: all the same a word from him carries great weight, for the highest quarters really and truly do what he asks of them and greatly favour the fellow."

---

1   Count Axel von Fersen (1755-1810) was a Swedish aristocrat and supposed lover of Marie Antoinette.

2   This comment seems well founded. Although Backhouse did have trouble managing his finances throughout his career, none of the scandals he was entangled with ever seem to have benefited him monetarily in any significant way. His work as an informant and translator for G.E. Morrison of *The Times* was also unpaid.

Especially did Manchu military men of the Guards or Wei Tui 衛隊 come to me with their *curriculum vitae* beautifully written in a model (*K'ai Shu* 楷書) hand, with the request to buttress up (*Ting Li* 鼎力) their claims by my powerful support for special service or promotion. They would offer me sums ranging from Taels 5,000 to Taels 50,000,[3] according to the importance of the position sought, money payable in cash and guaranteed by a responsible money shop or *Lu Fang* 爐房, on the day that the appointment was gazetted. It was a favourite practice of the Empress both towards me and the leading eunuchs to sound the person to whom she was speaking as to sundry high officials' reputation, i.e. of those to whom she was personally unfriendly, for she would hear no word against her favourites such as Jung Ch'ing 榮慶 or Chang Hsün 張勳. "Tell me: what do men say outside about Grand Secretary Ch'ü Hung-chi 瞿鴻磯? *Jang Ni Ming Pai Hui Tsou* 讓你明白回奏, *Ch'ü Chung T'ang Wai T'ou Ming Yü Tsemmo Yang* 瞿中堂外頭名譽怎麼樣. *Yu Jen I Lun T'a Mo Yu* 有人議論他沒有?" Or perhaps: "They tell me that Chang Po-hsi 張伯熙" (a Hunanese at the head of the *Hsüeh Pu* 學部 and popular in educational circles; he had been selected as special envoy to convey the condolence of the Court on the death of Queen Victoria, but had been refused by the cabinet of St. James' on the ground of his rank being too low) "entertains revolutionary sentiments and is at heart anti-Manchu.[4] You know him, I understand: what have you heard him say about our dynasty and especially about me personally? Dares he to use wanton criticisms?" *Yu Jen Shuo Chang Po-hsi Pao Ts'ang Huo Hsin* 有人說張伯熙包藏禍心, *Hen Yu Ko Ming Ssu Hsiang* 狠有革命思想, *Hsin Chung Nan Ts'ê* 心中難測, *Tui Wo Ch'ao Yu Pu K'an Shê Hsiang Chê* 對我朝有不堪設想者. *T'ing Jen Shuo Ni Ken T'a Hen Shou* 聽人說你跟他狠熟: *Chiu Ni So Chih Tao* 就你所知道, *T'a Tui Ta Ch'ing Ch'ao Yu Ch'i* (especially) *Tui Wo Pen Jen'rh* 他對大清朝尤其對我本人兒, *Yu Shemmo I Lun* 有什麼議論: *T'a Kan Wang Chia Yüeh Tan Mo* 他敢妄加月且麼? *Ni Man Shuo Ch'u Lai* 你滿說出來, *Wo T'ing I T'ing* 我聽一聽.

Et moi de répondre:[5] "Madame, I know him very well: his Hunanese accent makes it very hard to understand him, but I never heard him say a word that Your Majesty could object to. As to Ch'ü Hung-chi," (also a Hunanese) "he is not popular in Peking, but I must not criticize him for he offered me a post as adviser."

"Did he," said the Old Buddha: "and you refused it?"

"Yes, Your Majesty, because I doubted if you would approve my working for a *Tou P'i'rh* 豆皮兒" (bean-curd peel, a derogatory term then in use for southerners).

"You showed your usual circumspection. I may tell you that he will not remain as Grand Councillor much longer." (As a fact, he was dismissed summarily in 1907 on the nominal pretext of entertaining too

---

3 £800–£8,000 based on the author's previous estimate.
4 After this sentence is the following line, which the author has neglected to translate: "His [Chang's] mind is hard to fathom and this could have unimaginable consequences for our court." The Chinese also omits "and is at heart anti-Manchu".
5 And I replied.

intimate relations with venal and disreputable press-men; the decree administered to him a considerable snub in bidding him leave the capital forthwith and behave himself in his native place. His career was finished.)

Li Lien-ying 李蓮英 and Ts'ui Tê-lung 崔德隆 must have made a huge income through fees from high officials (particularly Chinese and not Manchu) who engaged a word of commendation, *Shuo Hsiang* in their favour. (It is said that certain functionaries at the Court of Versailles used similarly to supplement their income by apposite remarks apparently dropped casually in the king's, and under Louis XVI, particularly in Marie Antoinette's, hearing.) If I remained generally popular with men in the highest places, I attribute it largely to the fact that I was scrupulous in voicing no criticism of my own, always explaining that, as a foreign devil, I was incompetent to judge. *Hsiang Hsi Ch'ing Shih Shih Tsai Fei Wai Jen So Neng Chih* 詳細情事實在非外人所能知: *Yin Tz'u Chih Ku* 因此之故, *Pu Kan Tsou Yu Lao Fo Yeh Chih Ch'ien* 不敢奏於老佛爺之前.

I do not recall the date, but memory points to the 31st year of Kuang Hsü, 1905, early in summer, when Tuan Hsü's 端緒 card was brought in one morning, not an unusual hour for social visits. He was a younger brother of Tuan Fang 端方, at that time Viceroy in Nanking, a Manchu notoriously unpopular in his own clan, who had, however, when Governor of Shensi in 1900 saved the lives of many foreigners by his courageous defiance of the Empress' orders to spare neither chicken nor dog, *Chi Ch'üan Pu Liu* 雞犬不留. Later, as Viceroy of Chihli, 1909, he incurred the displeasure of Kuang Hsü's widow for allowing cinema operators to record the obsequies of Tz'u Hsi and was dismissed from office with degradation of his official rank for *lèse-majesté*. Recalled from retirement after outbreak of revolution, he was barbarously murdered early in 1912 by Szechuanese under General Yin Heng 引衡. Tuan Hsü, my visitor, had been my colleague at the university, where I was professor of law and he proctor: he had a pronounced craving for opium, *Shih Hao Shen Shen* 嗜好甚深, not perhaps a desirable quality for a disciplinarian post, and later, after his brother's downfall and heroic death, fell upon evil days. The family mansion in P'u Kai Shih'er[6] 鵓鴿市兒 (as it is mispronounced, for it should be "Dove Market") was disposed of, and the last I heard of him was that he was destitute and depending upon the eleemosynary grants of friends like myself.

His business was unusual: a son of the Grand Secretary K'un Kang 崑崗 named Chan Wei 占偉 (I am treading on familiar ground in mentioning that the Manchu custom employed then – but not now – the personal name for the surname, so that it was very difficult to identify family relationships) had a love affair with a lady of the household named Lien Yü 連郁; but her parents watched her with a cat's persistence toward a mouse, so that it was impossible to arrange a rendezvous on the rare occasions when the Old Buddha granted her leave of absence. Chan Wei,

---

6   *P'u Kai*: pigeon.

knowing of my intimacy with the Old Buddha, *Ch'i Hsiang T'ien K'ai* 奇想天開, hit upon the brilliant notion of soliciting my good offices in the following manner. Next time that the Old Buddha desired my attendance, which Tuan Hsü euphemistically denominated *Chao Chien*[7] 召見, although as I suggested to him, it was rather a case of *Hua Liu Kuan Hsi*[8] 花柳關係, asking the flowers and soliciting the willow catkins (a pleasing metaphor for sexual intercourse, just as the Elizabethan "gather the rosebuds while ye may"), could I not oblige Mr. Chan Wei (*Kao Ch'ing Yu Chia* 高情優加) by smuggling him into the Lake Palace, where Her Majesty was then staying, and taking him out in my cart on my return next day, the desired consummation duly achieved and the harvest of love fully reaped?

The prospect did not seem particularly alluring, but I thanked Tuan Hsü for his too high estimation of the possibilities of my intervention and asked him to invite Chan Wei to come and see me. On the day following an exceedingly attractive young Manchu, aristocrat to the fingertips, whose inviting manners suggested to me, as in the case of Saint-Simon's beloved dauphin, another *penchant assez fort*,[9] duly appeared: he made me promise not to let his father know (in fact I had only a slight acquaintance with K'un Kang) and then explained the depth of his passion for the lady Lien Yü, with whom he had hitherto never had sexual commerce. Would I, in the midst of my own sensual pleasure, not give a thought to his amorous distress? I never saw a more love-sick swain, but have good ground for belief that his tastes inclined (no less than mine own) toward (what we will euphemistically denominate) "bi-metallism".

"You know," said I, "that for an outsider, even one so highly placed as yourself, thanks to your father's influence, a liaison with a concubine or even a handmaid in the palace connotes death. The punishment would extend to His Excellency; you would *Yen Huo Ling Tsun Ta Jen* 延禍令尊大人, bring woe upon the honoured sire; *Ch'iao Tzu* 喬梓 (euphemism for father and son) would perish together, *T'ung Kuei Yü Chin* 同歸於盡. But, if I can help you, I will, *Chin Li Erh Wei*[10] 盡力而爲; only remember that my influence with the Old Buddha is comparatively recent. I don't see how I can possibly suggest to her, *Kuang T'ien Hua Jih Chih Hsia* 光天化日之下, in the garish light of day, a sexual assignment for you and Lady Lien Yü: whatever is done would have to be accomplished to her privity. Would you wish the Chief Eunuch's aid to be invoked?"

"I think not: he would tell my father."

"Very good. Then please enlighten me as to your plan of campaign."

"It is this: I can accompany you next time you have a literary seance, *Wen Hui* 文會 (at the word "*Wen*" he smiled slightly, for *Wen* has divers connotations); let me go as your *Koshihhu* 戈什戶, Manchu attendant;

7   Summons to audience.
8   *Hua Liu* can mean "romantic" on the one hand and "lascivious" or "frequenting of prostitutes" on the other.
9   Strong leaning.
10   To the utmost of my strength.

there should be no difficulty in entering the Hsi Yüan Men 西苑門 and I don't think that Li Lien-ying would recognize me. I shall wait as an attendant outside the gate of the Yi Luan Tien 儀鸞殿, Palace of Empresshood and Motherhood: Li will probably come out and escort you to his room, awaiting the Empress' pleasure. My sweetheart helps Her Majesty to her rest, often reads aloud to her and sometimes has a game of elephant chess. When the Empress dismisses her, she is wont to retire to a small apartment in the Yen Ch'ing Lou 延慶樓. The moment you are introduced to the Empress' presence" (here he laughed pleasantly) "for audience, she will have no eyes and no ears except for you. I shall be able to pass a night of love with my dear Yü; while you dally to your heart's content with the Old Buddha. The latter does not ordinarily summon Lien Yü on rising, but she has to be in attendance after the Morning Council. By then, you will be on your way back and I should return in the same way that I came. How say you?"

"Simply that I think the plan very hazardous but not impossible of success. Failure will mean that the two of us will eat gall and drink wormwood; our lot will be of the bitterest and mine offence scarce less (nay greater) than yours by the doctrine of responsibility: he who prompts the crime is more guilty than he who accomplishes it, in that I shall have introduced you into the palace for an unlawful and lustful purpose. However, I like your delectable personality and am ready to run the risk. Await then my next communication, when I will inform you the day that Her Majesty may be pleased to appoint for our next rendezvous. But in the meantime, *Pieh Sheng Chang* 別聲張, keep absolute silence."

Dear Chan Wei insisted upon kotowing, much against my will. He said: "*Tsai Sheng Chih En* 再生之恩, your kindness is of a second father; *Yung Pu Kan Wang* 永不敢忘, never shall I forget." Perhaps the reader, knowing my proclivities, may suppose that I demanded a *quid pro quo*; and the reply must be "not at the time"; but I am free to confess that on a later day I found in Chan Wei everything that ardent sexuality could require or burning passion batten upon.

It was a week or more before I received the "Dine and Sleep" (as Queen Victoria called it – especially "Sleep"!) command from the Old Buddha and I laid (or tried to lay) my plans accordingly. I was by this time well known at the gate, but Chan did not look the part of an attendant, however good-looking the latter: he was palpably the patrician, the scion of a great house, a *Kung Tzu Ko'rh* 公子哥兒 or young swell, a perfumed exquisite, a Ganymede beloved of Zeus of whom the Old Buddha spoke as if he were a contemporary monarch, ready for an amorous adventure, be it with his own sex or as one who follows the beaten track, the way of a man with a maid. It seemed to me that Li would be sure to enquire of me the antecedents of my handsome footman when I would perforce have to make belated confession, and I decided, despite Chan's strong appeal to the contrary, to take Li into my confidence, because in the event of miscarriage, he was the one man who could appease the

Old Buddha's wrath; and he would assuredly blame me for not having forewarned him. So Li came to dine with me, and, in the intervals of the opium pipe, I adumbrated to him the possible situation, explaining that I only desired to oblige the young Manchu without ulterior motive.

To this Li replied, "Not so fast, my friend: you have a motive and that is, that you want to ingratiate yourself with a very beautiful youth with a view to future activities, such as . . . . . ; well, I know where your tastes lie! Should Her Majesty discover the intrigue, we shall all be like the unhappy denizens of the ninth Buddhist hell. We must hope for the best. You have been frank in unbosoming yourself to me, *K'ai Ch'eng Pu Kung* 開誠佈公; and I think, perhaps, if you arrive in the gathering dusk before the lights are on (*Chang Teng* 掌燈), this elegant young catamite (excuse me) will be able to pass unnoticed to the gate of the Old Buddha's palace. For the rest, I cannot say: Lien Yü's bedroom is quite near Her Majesty's. You will have to charm her with your conversation, your wit and your sexual industry, so that she has no need to summon Lien Yü during the night, as indeed would be contrary to her custom. Well; so be it then! *Mou Shih Tsai Jen* 謀事在人, *Ch'eng Shih Tsai T'ien* 成事在天, *l'homme propose et Dieu dispose*.[11] I shall be waiting, then, in my room inside the palace about the hour of the Dog, after 7 p.m.; when your cart is announced, I shall come out to meet you."

"I thank you from the heart: as I promised Chan not to inform you, I shall have to tell him that second thoughts proved wisest."

"Why should he be unwilling to confide in me?"

"He feared you might inform the Grand Secretary K'un Chung T'ang 崑中堂."

"What a young fool he must be in thinking so; if I did, the latter would be one to tell the Old Buddha of his boy's insensate folly and the fat would be in the fire for your dear Chan Wei."

So Li left in a pleasant state of *griserie*:[12] opium and alcohol do not appear to blend well (as Chang Hsüeh-liang 張學良 once found, when he vomited in the French Embassy's dining room). Li was in no sense *arsouille*,[13] but a little alcohol seemed to go to his head. As a matter of fact, *le vin de Marsala* with which I regaled him was exceptionally *capiteux*.[14]

Chan was horrified, when I confessed my breach of promise. "How could you tell the chief eunuch? My father will certainly flog me till I stream with blood."

"Believe me, my dear Pao-ch'en 寶臣 (his courtesy title; we were on the road to a pleasing intimacy which waxed to plenitude in the future), it was the only possible course; I know the chief eunuch's temperament, and it was imperative for us, you and me, to have a friend at court."

"Very good, then; I see that you have taken a liking for me and must just follow where you lead."

---

11   Man proposes and God disposes.
12   Intoxication.
13   Loutish.
14   Strong.

Accordingly, on the trysting day, Chan joined me early in the evening, arrayed like the "glass of fashion and the mould of form", wearing half a dozen rings of great price. Certainly, none could have mistaken him for a *laquais*,[15] for he looked what he was, a knight errant on a love adventure. I do not think that since dear Cassia Flower I have seen so delicious a youth, perfect in courtesy and charm, a "young Harry with his beaver off" (Shakspere, *Henry IV*). And so, as the shades of night were gathering fast, we fared palacewards. The dusk mercifully concealed the super-elegance of my "footman" and none questioned us at the gate, Hsi Yüan Men 西苑門, whence the distance via the Ch'in Cheng Tien 勤政殿 along the Chung Hai 中海 shore to the Empress Dowager's abode is only a few minutes drive. I was duly announced: Li came out to greet me; and Chan Wei to Ch'ing An[16] 請安, making the Manchu salutation *avec plus d'empressement*[17] than an outrider would normally employ, even to so powerful a personage as the Chief Eunuch. (I understood from Chan that his *inamorata*[18] had consented to the proposed night of stolen love and that he would have to wait outside with the cart for some hours, since the Old Buddha did not retire much before the Hour of the Rat, 11 p.m.) Li, however, obligingly undertook to facilitate the programme by emerging with a lantern as the signal that I had been summoned by the Old Buddha and that the road was clear.

So I left Chan, who was erotic as a fed stallion in the morning and impatient to begin his love congress. There is no need for me to repeat a thrice told tale as to my own love adventures. Once again, Li had prepared a Lucullan[19] banquet and we sat together recounting one *sale histoire*[20] after another. He was full of a *bon mot*[21] of the Empress who began (and ended) an anecdote as follows: "Once upon a time there lived a eunuch", and then paused, as if wondering how to proceed. "Well, Old Buddha, this eunuch, what of him? *Ti Hsia* 底下, literally 'underneath', *Tsemmo Yang* 怎麼樣, please continue: how does the story end?"

"*Ti Hsia Mei Yu La* 底下沒有啦, he had nothing underneath, that's the end of the story" – using a play of words which is not readily rendered in English but which in Chinese is made plain. We might paraphrase: "He had no lower parts, neither has the anecdote any continuation." Li looked in upon the Empress, who was enjoying her nightcap of opium, and Lady Lien Yü was reading to her. She asked if her "tame" foreigner (*Shu Shih Kuei Tzu*[22] 熟識鬼子) had arrived and told Li to make the inevitable love philter. Soon afterwards, she summoned me. I had a cloak over my shoulders and wore a pair of *babouches*,[23] or *Hsieh T'a La'rh* 鞋踏

---

15 Servant.
16 Pay his respects.
17 With even more readiness.
18 Sweetheart.
19 "Lavish", relating to Lucullus (118-57 BC), a wealthy Roman statesmen famous for extravagant banquets.
20 Dirty story.
21 Witticism.
22 A foreigner whom one knows well.
23 Turkish slippers.

拉兒, which Li kindly lent. I passed into the Empress' bed-chamber with my guilty secret heavy on me, feeling unusually self-conscious. Perhaps the Old Buddha noticed a lack of freshness in my manner, but the potent drug soon stirred me to the wanted activity of my *pendule*[24] big with animal desire and she played with me to her heart's content, particularly affecting for that evening the *Tao Kua La* 倒掛臘, the candle hung reversewise, which represents the feminine element riding uppermost over the man's orgastic ecstasy. Her Majesty required no love potion and was in a particularly salacious mood: she was fain to insist upon commerce from behind as well as the usual manoeuvres with which I was familiar, thanks to her "expertise" and wider intimacy with the *Ch'un Kung* 春宮 – technique of love and lust. Unless my memory deceives me, the date was early in June, just before the court's annual migration to her beloved Summer Palace; the short summer night soon passed, but the Old Buddha was still unsated and in fact insatiable. She rebuked me in a semi-maternal way for my homosexual diversions as a young man devoted to strange pleasures and impossible beliefs; thought it would end for me by *Chê Shou* 折壽, shortening my longevity, perhaps induce blindness, there being a superstition in China that habitual or professional pathics (not that I was purely and simply a passive "rabbit") finish by acquiring an eye affection fatal to the sight. There is a similar popular belief that coitus from behind will cause septicaemia, if the passive element should (during the contact and especially at the time of ejaculation) *lâcher un pet*, or discharge a *flatus*.[25] The late Herr Doctor Krieg once told me of a Briton named Seymour, a patient of his own, who had pedicated with a female prostitute in Peking, contracted blood-poisoning and died in three days. However, silence, *aux faits*.[26]

Dawn was breaking and the Old Buddha had exacted from me the last copulation effort (both exhausting and painful) of the present rhapsodic occasion; she had had no sleep, nor I either, and it was palpable that she had *mis son bonnet de travers*,[27] and was rather irritable and crotchety, not toward me but toward things in general, particularly to the Grand Council soon arriving for the morning audience.

To my horror, she rose from her phoenix couch, saying: "You can stay where you are. Put your cloak over you, for it is cool, till I return. I am going to call Lien Yü to help me to dress. As soon as she comes in, you can take leave of me and dress in the outer chien."[28] *Certes, l'impératrice avait une mauvaise inspiration: qu'y faire?*[29] Helpless now, man to the might of the Gods must bow, as Schiller says in the song of the Bell *"die Glocke"*.

Exit the Old Buddha. She had only some fifty yards to traverse to the maid of honour's room from which in ordinary circumstances any happenings would be within ear-shot. By some unlucky decree of the gods

---

24   Penis.
25   Break wind . . . fart.
26   Let us return to the facts.
27   Assumed a foul mood (literally "Wore her hat off-kilter").
28   Room.
29   Clearly, the Empress had an evil inspiration: what to do?

always fain to turn awry the schemes of "mice and men", it pleased Her Majesty to walk right in to her maid's room, to discover – what? My dear Chan and his adorable Lien Yü were literally caught in the act; he told me later that he was bestriding her not after the use of men but of beasts, and his orgasm was precisely reaching the supreme moment. No holding back, no reining in, was possible and he completed the act, with the Old Buddha standing grimly, like one of the Furies, at the vestibule, but saying nothing, perhaps because at such a moment silence is golden and the Empress, after her love bout with me, had pity for another's needs.

Although I was some distance away, I could follow the greater part of the Empress' tirade which proceeded on the crescendo gamut. "Have you mistaken my palace for a brothel?" (to Chan). "You wanton girl" (to Lien), "you receive your paying clients here, barefaced, in the light of day, beneath the chariot-wheels of the Throne? Do not you both know that the death penalty is ordained by law for those discovered in the palace precinct and guilty of unholy, unbridled lust? How came you here?" Then I heard Chan explain, as I expected he would (poor boy!), for he was distraught with pallid fear, that the Yang Hou 洋侯 (foreign marquis) had brought him in. The Old Buddha seemed perfectly beside herself at this rejoinder. "Yang Hou, indeed; well you name him Hou, foreign ape: he *is* a Yang Hou'rh 洋猴兒" (*Hou* means in sound monkey as well as marquis). She moved rapidly across the court and hailed me in no friendly terms: "What do you mean by your dastard presumption in introducing your lascivious boon companion into the profound seclusion of my Palace? Your offence reeks to heaven: beware lest you forfeit my favour for ever. You take too much upon yourself: your tail is fast becoming too big to wag. Answer me, Pa K'o-ssu 巴恪思; justify your conduct if you can find words, glib tongued as you are: I think you will find it difficult to explain away."

I knelt and kotowed till the blood appeared on my forehead. "Old Buddha, I deserve the death, nay, nine deaths at your almighty hand. It was the thought of your bounty toward me, and, forgive your servant from a far land for his presumption, my love for you, my queen and my goddess, my star, the harbinger of my sunrise and the glow of my evening calm, the hallowed joys of this exquisite union which your royal grace accords to me all unworthy, it was this thought, I say, that made me, wretched man that I am, connive at this base deception. I am guilty and none other: let Your Majesty visit your condign wrath upon my unhappy person and shut me out from the portals of Paradise henceforward; but I entreat Your Majesty and if it were with my latest breath, I would entreat you, to spare these two hapless lovers and allow Chan Wei to return home without informing the Grand Secretary his father, K'un Kang, who would certainly flog him to death; while as for Lien Yü, she is guilty, ay nine times nine, guilty of death. But Your Majesty is the goddess of mercy incarnate in the world of men: I beseech you to let the light of your holy favour shine upon us three guilty people, so that we may bask again in the share of your gracious favour and win a forgiveness that we assuredly deserve not."

The Old Buddha seemed moved by this appeal which, as spoken, was more convincing than it reads on paper. "Presumptuous boy, must I forgive you? I cannot strike where I have so often kissed."

At this moment Li Lien-ying made an opportune appearance. I think he heard the impassioned tones of my appeal; at any rate, I congratulated myself that I had wisely bespoken his help: it would have been fatal to keep him in the dark.

Her Majesty, anger somewhat abated, turned to Li: "This is a pretty state of things, *Pu Ch'eng Shih T'i*[30] 不成事體. I suppose you will tell me that you know nothing about Pa K'o-ssu's most presumptuous breach of court etiquette in smuggling this young fop into the palace?"

"No, Your Majesty, I knew of it, because he told me: my guilt, *Wo Ti Tsui, Wo Ti Tsui* 我的罪,我的罪. Knowing that Your Majesty loves a lover, I thought that your soft hearted nature would forgive these two young people indulging in their pretty carnival of love."

"Did you mean to inform me, supposing I had not by accident discovered them in the 'clouds and rain' *Yün Yü Chih Chung* 雲雨之中?" – a quotation derived from Mengtzu's 孟子 "*Yu Jan Tso Yün* 油然作雲, *P'ei Jan Hsia Yü* 沛然下雨," clouds gather in density and a downpour of rain ensues, in reference to the sensual act.[31]

"No, Your Majesty, I did not", said Li, with an admirable dexterity and foresight, "because I know that the Old Ancestress loveth to do good by stealth, without letting her left hand know what her right may perform."

As soon as the Old Buddha started making quotations, I knew that the storm was about to cease and that the waves thereof were still; her wrath was in measurable distance of being allayed. Once more, I kotowed until my forehead was literally covered with blood. "Foolish boy," said the Empress, "your handsome (!) face will soon be a spectacle for gods and men to deride. Well, I will pardon you all three and shall not visit his and her offences on any one. *Ch'eng Shih Pu Shuo* 成事不說, *Chi Wang Pu Chiu* 既往不究, *Sui Shih Pu Chien* 遂事不諫 (*Lun Yü* 論語), let bygones be bygones and do not rake up old scores nor rebuke past errors."

Li and I prostrated ourselves; further kotowing was beyond my power, but he amply made up for my shortcomings in that regard. "The Old Buddha *Yu K'ou Hua'rh*[32] 有口話兒, is beginning to relent; we thank Your Majesty's gracious mercy and, although we live for nine existences, *Shih Shih Sheng Sheng* 世世生生, in whatever existence we may find ourselves (in allusion to Buddhist metempsychosis and transmigration), our gratitude for Your Majesty's bounty shall never diminish nor fail."

---

30   There's no order to it.

31   The Meng Tzu (Mencius) quote here can be found in *Meng Ke*, 孟軻, *The Chinese Classics, vol. II, The Works of Mencius*, trans. by James Legge, (I.I.4.), but it has a different meaning unless it has been censored or misunderstood by Legge.

32   Speaks with intent.

"Summon the lovers, but tell your friend Chan Wei to dress himself, for he was quite naked just a few moments ago; but I suppose the wave of his swelling passion has calmed down by now?"

Li and I found them petrified with terror, huddled together in an alcove of the maid's small chamber, like two hares hiding from the hounds of fear and horror. "Come with us: the Old Buddha forgives you, and you" (to Chan) "are free to return home, while Lien Yü is to wait on the Old Buddha as heretofore." They scarce believed their ears: our voice recreated them; our hand set them free.

So we returned to the Presence: the Empress being still *en deshabillé*,[33] but even so her imperial dignity was not a jot nor a little impaired. Almost naked, she was still the power riding the storm and controlling the whirlwind. They kotowed to her times without number and thanked her sovereign grace while Li and I knelt, with tears welling from our grateful eyes. "My Yang Hou has taken the whole blame; he deserves to be flogged forty strokes for his temerity, but he is fluent of tongue and I have forgiven him, as I forgive you. As for you, Lien and young Chan, I authorize your marriage and shall act as *Mei Jen* 媒人 (matchmaker, she used the phrase, but in her case it would be *Shuan Hun* 拴婚, "tetherer" of the marriage, as the sovereign, decreeing wedlock for a subject, is termed) to your parents, who will, I think, accept my choice of a wife, without, however, divulging to them your latest school-boy's prank."

Each of us exclaimed in unison: "Your Majesty's grace is even as the ocean; you have bestowed upon us all a new life. May Your Majesty live ten thousand times ten thousand fruitful and auspicious years!"

The Old Buddha, quite recovered in spirits, bade the rest retire from her bed-chamber; while she commanded me to kneel down, naked as I was but for the saving cloak, over the edge of the imperial bed; "*Chüeh P'i Ku* 撅屁股, let your buttocks be presented upward", said she, according to me about a dozen sharp cuts with a *badine*[34] conveniently at hand.

Li was waiting for me in the outer room: "*Ni Shou Hsün* 你受訓," said he; "you have been reprimanded!"

"Yes and *Ai La Ta* 挨啦打 received a whipping *par-dessus le marché*."[35]

"*Ch'ien* 欠, you deserved it, *Kai Cho La* 該著啦, and I too, *Huo Kai* 活該, for my collaboration. But you were very adroit (as usual) in extricating yourself from the terrible consequences. Never argue with the Old Buddha, but just plead guilty of your offence (as the famous lawyer, Sir John Simon, once said at Oxford in regard to suits at law). *Chieh Ling Huan Shih Hsi Ling Jen* 解鈴還是繫鈴人: the man who tied the bell into a knot is the man to untie it!

"Dress yourself quickly, as the Old Buddha is going to the main hall for audience, and the Council is in attendance. You can wait in the side apartment where we lunched some years ago and then leave after Her Majesty's return. Chan can sit on the shafts of your cart and I will send

---

33 In her undergarments.
34 Cane.
35 On top of it all.

for your own *Koshihhu*: now that all is forgiven and forgotten, the Old Buddha would not like him to pose as your servant, son as he is of the Senior Manchu Grand Secretary."

Her Majesty was now ready to leave her bed-chamber; I knelt in the outer *Chien* and she smiled affectionately: "I forgive you, but don't do it again: *K'o I Erh Pu K'o Tsai* 可一而不可再, once is allowable but not a second offence." The admonition was needless, for I felt that my heart had once again prevailed over my judgment and that I had erred from a selfish desire to gain Chan's good graces for future erotic occasions which, in fact, did not fail to confront me.

"Give the marquis some salve for his poor bleeding forehead", called out the Old Buddha as she passed toward the main hall. The numerous mirrors disposed at different angles reflected in me a sadly changed physiognomy; for there was considerable bleeding from the repeated bumping of my head on the brick floor. However, my zealous kotowing had not been in vain, as it moved the Old Buddha's heart in showing the desperate sentiments of love which animated me toward her!

After a short wait, Chan and I returned home; he was naturally radiant with happiness and animal spirits, asking how he could return my kindness and gracious protection. *Yang Ch'eng Pao Yu Yen Tê Ta Pao* 仰承保佑焉得答報, *Kao Ch'ing Jo T'ien Chih Kao Ju Ti Chih Hou* 高情若天之高如地之厚: lofty as heaven, solid as earth.

"In the simplest way possible," said I, "by allowing our intimacy to expand and consummate itself at intervals in a delectable union of two bodies ineffably locked, of two hearts that beat as one."

"I ask for nothing better," said Chan; "just now we are both of us tired out by love, but we will appoint an early rendezvous for our reciprocal play of passion." And so in fact we were at pains to accomplish. We embraced each other upon the lips with lascivious earnestness as a pledge of the excellent days to be, when love should take all that love can claim.

So in fact it befell and for me it was the fair beginning of a heaven-sent time. Of all the Manchu princes, patricians and *jeunesse dorée*[36] that I have known, and I have known many, none charmed me more than Chan. He was to me as a second Cassia lost but to memory dear. We used often to meet at the Hsin Ching 新淨 Bath-house circle and at a club for the *Kuei Tsu* 貴族 (aristocrats) to which he introduced me. With me this form of love had (and has) a poetical aspect: where there was, or is an affinity, *T'ou Yüan* 投緣, all things were possible; but I could not understand the spirit of the British teacher lately dead, like a wild beast roaming from love to love, who gathered from the highways and hedges the lowest dregs of the population, *Hsia San Lan* 下三濫, fain to minister to his pathic proclivities for a $5 recompense (per head or rather per time, as $10 was expected for duplication), relieving his itch-ridden lubricity with their orgiastic abundance and plethoric (if mercenary) lusts.

36 Gilded youth.

Chan's marriage which took place about six months later was ideally happy; fortunately the *Pa Tzu'rh* 八字兒, or conjunction of characters,[37] were found in harmony; the Old Buddha showered rich gifts upon the pair; his tastes in my regard did not mar an exquisite conjugal bliss. Lien Yü brought up a family of six or seven children, all of whom, I believe, are today living. She always regarded me with a special favour for what she called my presence of mind in soothing the Old Buddha (*Tui Ching Sheng Ch'ing*[38] 對景生情), for none knew better than she that the Empress' rages were paroxysms resembling a cataclysm or visitation of nature, and that, once her dignity was insulted (or so she fancied), nothing could move her to mercy. "None could rival her for good nature when she was in the mood; none could equal her for ferocity when she was roused to wrath." *Elle faisait patte de velours,*[39] a gauntlet in the velvet glove.

My intimacy with Chan Pao-ch'en 占寶臣 endured for a quarter of a century; in fact, I was in my sixtieth year and he over forty-five when we had our last delight-begetting erotic congress which at my last hour (*Haec olim meminisse juvabit*)[40] I shall love to remember, across the sands of time. He was leaving for Manchuria to take up an appointment at Hsinching 新京 in the Imperial Household under him whom he regarded as his lawful sovereign.[41] Since then I have not set eyes on him nor on his wife, *Yin Jung Liang Miao Mang*[42] 音容兩渺茫, as Po Chü-i 白居易, *Shih Sheng*[43] 詩聖, divinest of poets, writes: "he has passed out of my ken, I know not whither." Shall I see him again? My heart has no knowledge, my faith no presentiment. Meantime, I linger on in dolorous death-bringing old age, watching the amateur attempts of my "heroic" compatriots playing the game of war with mighty Germany. But I am ready to wager that occasionally Chan Pao-ch'en and his lady-wife gladly recall a certain dawn in June, thirty-eight years ago, as we three knelt together in abject fear and trembling, to implore pardon for our amorous excesses in the Hall of Motherhood and Empresshood, when the Old Buddha still reigned in time-honoured secular Cambaluc,[44] in the days of our vanity. "It passeth like a shadow and we are gone."[45] Lord Buddha, forgive us all!!

---

37 The combination of the eight Heavenly Stems and Earthly Branches that tell the time, day, month and year of a person's birth; a Chinese horoscope.

38 To manifest a feeling that accords with the circumstances.

39 She switched on the charm (literally "She was smooth as velvet").

40 These memories, too, may one day be a pleasure (Virgil, *Aeneid* I.203).

41 Hsinching (now the city of Changchun), literally "New Capital", was the capital of the Japanese puppet state of Manchoukuo, nominally ruled by China's last emperor, P'u Yi.

42 *"Both voice and countenance have become remote and vague." Yin Jung* refers to the voice and features of someone deceased.

43 *Shih Sheng* is a "Saint of Poetry", an honorific title.

44 Capital city of the Mongol Yüan Dynasty (1271-1368) that later became Peking.

45 **Backhouse:** Psalm.

CHAPTER VIII

THE VAMPIRE PRINCE

"Par quelle parole magique, clef des sentiers inexplorés, pourrai-je descendre au fond des abîmes l'amour?"[1]

Judith Gautier.

I am writing in the sombre close of that voluptuous day which it has been my pleasure to adumbrate, without the skill of a Bourget or a Barrès[2] which allures the reader to pursue the same path, or (to vary the metaphor) to sound the depths and shoals of exoteric passions. But for me the savour, the zest, abides.

> "You may break, you may shatter the vase, if you will;
> But the scent of the roses will hang round it still."
>
> *Moore.*[3]

He who wrote "O! death in life the days that are no more" may have been *attristé*[4] by his own experience (Tennyson); but, in my judgment he erred, if he was delivering himself of a generality or aphorism.

Memory and imagination; the first counts as nothing without the second which is verily the ode of the agnostic to immortality and gilds old age with the after-glow of youth. These dear phantoms of the past, if they cannot restore happiness to one who moveth in what is certainly not an ampler ether, a diviner air, at least make life easier to be borne. *"Ich habe gelebt und geliebt"*:[5] is there more to say?

The Sage (*maestro di color che sanno*)[6] asserts: "*Ch'iao Yen Ling Se Hsien Yi Jen* 巧言令色鮮矣仁, a glib tongue and an attractive manner seldom connote goodness", but with all respect to K'ung Sheng Jen[7] 孔聖人

---

1   By what magic word, key to unexplored paths, can I get to the bottom of the abyss of love?

2   Paul Bourget (1852-1935) was a French novelist and literary critic, popular during Backhouse's lifetime. Maurice Barrès (1862-1923), another popular novelist and political writer, is best remembered today as a proponent of anti-Semitic French nationalism.

3   Thomas Moore (from "Farewell!—But Whenever You Welcome the Hour").

4   Saddened.

5   I have lived and loved (Friedrich Schiller, *Piccolomini* III.VII.9).

6   Master of those who know (Dante, *Inferno* IV.131).

7   Confucius.

the converse is equally true. Monosyllabic, dour, disagreeable folk; are they not *rabat-joies* (wet blankets, to use a vulgar Englishry) whose use in life is to wound their neighbours' feelings? This grave defect makes of them a byword adown the ages, just as Fox's memory bids fair to outlast Pitt's,[8] for the former had charm and the latter alienated people by his *gaucherie*[9] and gratuitous rudeness.

In the years between 1902 and 1908, Kuang Hsü 光緒 28-34, my boon companions, princes or patricians, mostly young and all drifting with every passion of the soul, jaded perhaps but "still pursuing" as Solomon remarks in Proverbs, would frequently foregather at the Ch'ing Ho Yüan 慶和園 (theatre) in the Flesh Market, Jou Shih 肉市, to wanton with the comely mimes in unrestrained and unconscionable frolic, plunging in a sea of vinegar (jealousy) whence storms were seldom absent. Till Tz'u Hsi's 慈禧 passing in November 1908 (XXXIV, 10.21) when music was hushed in the land for the twenty-seven months of Court Mourning, we were as gay and as unbridled as the Mohocks[10] of eighteenth century London presuming (some of us) like the grand dukes of Tsarist Russia on rank or influence at court and in my case known to be the Old Buddha's familiar.

He who frequented an English public school can picture conditions in an environment confined to male persons but who were emancipated from the disciplinary treatment meted out to any caught in the act. The relentless *fouailleur* or *fesseur*[11] in those days spared us not, and although we professed to belittle the severe chastisement, the discipline was a real deterrent despite the multitudinous erotic ventures on which we embarked. I remember a case which was elaborately hushed up in the press, for in those days the so-called "halfpenny" papers (now, of course, the half-penny as a coin exists no longer though the name endures) were not with us to ventilate scandals where vested interests were concerned. The editors of the *Times* and leading London journals were public school men and too loyal to Alma Mater to promulgate derogatory episodes. Two boys, aged 18 to 19, were rivals for the affections of a ganymede of 14 who (it was ascertained later) was wooed and won by both on dozens of happy occasions, apparently without fore-knowledge of either aspirant that his "*Ch'ing Ti* 情敵" (rival) had attained successful consummation, each believing in his own monopoly. Catching the catamite redhanded in ardent contiguity with a boy named Comber, the opposite party, Ward, stabbed his rival in the buttocks appositely presented with a large-bladed knife and thus terminated, *ipso facto*,[12] the consummation devoutly to be wished. There was a school enquiry not unaccompanied by manifold savage floggings (worthy of priests of Cybele),[13]

---

8   Backhouse's oft-mentioned faux-relative, statesman Charles James Fox, and his political rival, William Pitt the Younger (1759-1806).
9   Awkwardness.
10   A violent street gang.
11   Coward or spanker.
12   As a direct result.
13   Cybele, the Greek earth goddess, was the center of a popular cult in ancient Rome. Priests of Cybele would perform ceremonies involving flagellation and self-castration.

but in hypocritical England all newspaper comment was successfully suppressed; the protagonists were expelled, but Ward's father paid out a considerable sum for wounded Comber's benefit in the understanding that the matter should not be taken into court. The pathic was allowed to remain in the school and to make wicked lightning of his eyes to all and sundry, a sort of tolerated or licensed bane to his fellows; for, whether it be a monastery, a seminary or a public school, the prairie fire of lust cannot be controlled and must needs rage till the embers cease to smoulder, inevitable as war after long peace, or as the lesson which history teaches us that we learn therefrom no lesson whatsoever.

To return to the Ch'ing Ho Yüan, the Garden of Congratulatory Peace, I must be fair to myself and explain that, in referring to myself as a Mohock, I would limit my personal activities to a gaiety of word and gesture untranslated into deeds or at least deeds of ill repute. Some of the young bloods[14] were fain to insult respectable women, like the abandoned rakes of the London of the Regency who made public resorts such as Vauxhall or Ranelagh places to enter at one's peril, *Shih Wei Wei T'u* 視爲畏途. In particular Prince Ch'ing's three sons, Tsai Chen 載振, Tsai Fu 載扶 and Tsai Lun 載掄 literally stuck at nothing, secure, as they believed, in their father's influences. The former, now hereditary prince Ch'ing, had acquired an evil notoriety in London on the occasion of Edward VII's coronation in 1902 owing to his non-appearance at a court dinner, as he had a pressing engagement with a reigning beauty at the Alexandra Hotel and was roundly taken to task by King "Bertie", of all libertines the prince paramount. The Old Buddha was informed of her special ambassador's conduct in a letter which I had the honour to translate, for his father, as head of the Foreign Office, would have suppressed it from her knowledge, had it gone through official channels. The letter asked Her Majesty to reprimand him as a dissolute rake who had (as the Sage says) *Yu Ju Shih Ming* 有辱使命, disgraced his mission, in running after strange flesh and made China appear ridiculous, besides proclaiming himself as Crown Prince to the press, although he was quite ineligible to succeed to the Throne. I never saw (except on the occasion of Ts'en's 岑 hairbrained conspiracy) the Old Buddha so angry, and she threatened to dismiss his father from office. Prince Ch'ing had to pay enormous sums to both the Old Buddha and to Lien-ying 蓮英, as well as to Junglu 榮祿 (who was then, 1902, still living) in order to hush up the affair. It must have cost the old prince several million Taels before Her Majesty allowed the matter to drop.

The Old Buddha allowed me to take a copy of the royal missive which I lost along with other papers; I only roughly remember the contents which indicated that Edward VII wrote in a furious temper. It was holograph in the King's bad handwriting, dated November 1902, and began "Great and Good Friend and dear Sister," ending "Placing my homage at Your Majesty's feet, I remain, Your Good Friend and Brother, Edward."

---

14   Members of the Mohock gang.

Autant que je puis m'en souvenir,[15] the King thanked the Empress for sending a special envoy and for the beautiful presents that she had so graciously made to him, regretted that his illness had curtailed the state visits of all representatives of Foreign Powers, thanked Her Majesty for her messages of sympathy. But he had learned from his former Prime-Minister, Lord Salisbury (who had resigned in July 1902) that H.H. Prince Tsai Chen had failed to appear at a court function for a discreditable reason. His Majesty therefore requested the Empress never again to send that prince to his capital on a court mission. (It is illuminating to note that this request was disregarded by the new regime after the Old Buddha's death and that the prince was again sent to London for George V's coronation in 1911, when he (as the late Sir Beilby Alston, G.B.E., who was attached to his suite) acted little better than on the previous occasion.)

There was a very beautiful actor Yü Kuei-fang 喻桂芳, then playing at the Ch'ing Ho Yüan, with whom we were all greatly enamoured. I am not sure of the date, probably Kuang Hsü 31, V (1905). The mime had repulsed the attentions of the three Ch'ing brothers, particularly the afore-said Tsai Chen, for a sufficiently strange reason which is suggested by the title of this paper. The latter, in the excited paroxysms of his advanced eroticism, had developed vampire habits: during, or after, copulation from behind he was fain to bite some portion of the pathic's anatomy, usually the nape of the neck, for he copulated in the prone posture, not as "the small donkey rider", the former known as *Shang Wei* 上尉 or *Ta Wei* 大尉, topmost, highest place, also jocularly Captain, also *Ting Shang* 頂上 (topmost) and *Ch'ao Shan* 朝山 (pilgrim up the mountain, *P'a Shan Hu* 爬山虎, mountain scaling tiger, used for litter referring, I suppose, to the posture). In case of triangular (or rather triple storied) coitus, the party simultaneously partaking as giver and receiver is called *Lien Huan* 聯環 (link), *Fang Chung* 方中 (right in the centre, a quotation from the *Shih Ching* 詩經 or *Odes*, *Ting Tsai Fang Chung* 定在方中,[16] the Ting constellation, the Scorpion and especially the red star Antares, being just in the (south) centre of the sky, as is the case in July), also *Ssu Kou'rh* 死扣兒, a tangled skein, *Chia Pan* 夾板, median disposition, *Chung Wei* 中位, middle place, or jocularly First Lieutenant, *Te So* 得所, the ideal position to occupy, *Shui Chung Yü* 水中魚, fish in its element, the water. The pathic's place in the lowest order is *Hsia Tsou* 下走, or *Tsou Hsia* 走下; the underneath one; *Shan Ku* 山谷, the mountain vale; *Mo Wei Tzu* 末尾子, the remainder or balance still due, *Hsia Wei* 下位, lowest place or, by jest, second lieutenant. I record these names for purposes of reminiscence, seeing that they have lived their life and are today out of currency. They have had their day and cease to be, like the "touch of a vanished hand and the sound of a voice which is still" (Tennyson). *Hélas*.[17] Whether the practice of pederasty endures, I cannot say, at any rate in the higher strata of society for, I suppose, the lower classes are available for hire;

---

15 As far as I can remember.
16 Actually called *Ting Tsai Chih Chung* 定在之中.
17 Alas.

but probably other appropriate nomenclature has been devised *Chuang Hsieh Liang Ch'an* 莊諧兩攙, combining *le sérieux et le comique*,[18] a talent of which Chinese are past masters, and in fact Japanese no less so. The English are supposed to be good punsters, but I know of no *calembour* to equal Voltaire's *jeu de mots*,[19] when he remarked to a lady, his neighbour, as they partook of tea and she persisted in dropping into his teacup tobacco ashes: "*j'amaivais mieux mon thé que des cendres (monte . . . descendre)*".[20] It is a perfect specimen of wit and without a vestige of the humour incident in a normal pun.

To resume after this digression: the three dissolute brothers, attended by a large and truculent escort who blocked the entrance to the theatre one afternoon in June and prevented theatergoers from purchasing admission, marched up to the Green Room, and Tsai Chen, regardless of the large numbers of visitors, including myself and a dozen or more young Manchu patricians, demanded of Yü Kuei-fang to undo his trousers and present himself in the necessary posture on the bench to minister to his needs. Yü refused, and we all backed him up: he was due to appear on the stage in a few minutes and Tsai Chen's vampire predilections made of him a most formidable operator. The triumvirate forced him to the ground, and I suppose that the inevitable would have happened; but Providence directed to the theatre the censor Chiang Ch'un-lin 江春霖 who afterwards impeached Yüan Shih-k'ai 袁世凱 in a secret memorial after the Empress' assassination at his Yüan's hands. Chiang was a fearless, upright man, who demanded for Yüan the death penalty; but owing to the intervention of the British Minister *Yüeh Tsu Tai P'ao*[21] 越俎代庖 (metaphor from sacrifices, literally "to cross over the sacrificial utensils and take the place of the kitchen superintendent"), failing to mind his own business, the Grand Councillor escaped with no punishment but was commanded by the Regent to vacate his posts and return to his native province. The memorial of impeachment was a powerful, cogent document which was never officially published: it accused him among other events of aiming at the Throne and of high treason not only in assassinating the Old Buddha but as regards future designs. On another occasion he was to impeach (unsuccessfully) Prince Ch'ing, and when he wrote that the old prince gave to his sons full rein to break the law by riding rough-shod over the commonalty, he may well have been thinking of this incident at the Ch'ing Ho Yüan of which he was eye-witness. One of us managed to send word to Chiang Ch'un-lin and ask his presence in the Green Room on an official errand. As he entered, the three brothers and Yü were wrestling on the floor, the latter struggling terror-stricken to avoid having to assume the "horizontal" and the risk of the vampire's sanguinary designs.

---

18   The serious and the comic.
19   Pun . . . play on words.
20   "I would rather have my tea (*mon thé*) than some ashes (*des cendres*)". *Mon thé* being a homonym for *monter* (ascend) and *des cendres* for *descendre* (descend).
21   This phrase from Chuang Tzu usually refers to someone acting on another's behalf and whose actions exceed his or her proper role.

Without losing his self-possession, Chiang peremptorily said: "*Che Ch'eng Shih T'i Ma* 這成事體麼, a most improper conduct, *Kuang T'ien Hua Jih Chih Hsia* 光天化日之下, in the broad light of day, you three young princes are *Pu Ch'eng Chih T'u* 不逞之徒, lewd fellows of the base sort, *Kan Chang Wei Feng Ch'i Ya P'ing Min* 敢仗威風欺壓平民, venture to presume on your high rank to browbeat the common people: *Ming Jih Pen Yü Shih Ting Chiang Tsou Ts'an* 明日本御史定將奏參, tomorrow I, the censor, shall certainly impeach you to the Throne."

The brave trio, knowing that Chiang would be as good as his word and fearing their father's wrath, since by the doctrine of responsibility the Old Buddha would certainly deal hardly with him, took to their heels and the performance was able to proceed. So far, so good; but Tsai Chen was like a tiger (on paper) balked of his prey; for apparently this vampire tendency was a real *P'i* 癖 inveterate habit, with him, a craving that would not be denied, and rumours declared that he sucked a considerable quantity of blood from the patient after performing the act of sex.

We were congratulating ourselves prematurely on the happy outcome, for I never dreamed that Tsai Chen after the censor's menaces would dare to proceed further until things had settled down. Yü Kuei-fang returned to his home near Hua'rh Shih 花兒市, Flower Market, outside the Hatamen; some of us spent an hour or so in friendly intercourse and left him, as we thought, in perfect assurance. About nine o'clock that evening a number of Tsai Chen's hirelings and local bad characters, *Ta Hsien'rh Ti* 打閑兒的, idlers, led by the three debauched princes, arrived at his gate, forcibly entered the small courtyard and kidnapped the unfortunate actor whom they gagged and bound. The Old Buddha was at the Summer Palace: the city gates being closed, I doubted whether my gold *laissez passer*[22] tablet would be effective for leaving the city, though, once arrived at any of the palaces, I knew that the guards would admit me. I trembled to think of Yü's sufferings and greatly feared that Tsai Chen might murder him after intercourse, disposing of the body and denying all part or lot in the business, for the police were still practically non-existent where a member of the imperial house was involved. I left for the Wan Shou Shan 萬壽山 before daybreak next morning and arrived there while the Old Buddha was holding Council. I told Lien-ying the whole story and he relished the fact that Prince Ch'ing would suffer on Her Majesty learning what had occurred: "If Yü is murdered," said he, "we shall make such a scandal of the tragedy that the Old Buddha will be forced to promulgate a decree dismissing Ch'ing from all his offices, never to be again mentioned for employment."

Eunuchs are not, by dynastic tradition which wished to preserve the Manchu regime from the abuses of the Mings 明 and preceding dynasties whereby the "rats and foxes of the altar" had so much voice in state affairs, supposed to be present at audiences of the Council, but Lien-ying frequently knelt behind a screen and heard all that passed. He handed

---

22   Free pass.

from his place of vantage a slip of paper to the Old Buddha recounting what I had told him and asked her not to let Prince Ch'ing return to the city without making him accountable for Yü's safety, explaining that the latter was held a prisoner in Tsai Chen's house. The Old Buddha read the memorandum with an expression, so said Lien-ying, that augured ill for the Ch'ings, *père et fils*,[23] for she had no love for either. She completely took the former by surprise (for he had no knowledge of his eldest son's most recent misdemeanour) when she mentioned that Yü Kuei-fang, now staying at Tsai Chen's mansion, was to attend at the Summer Palace before noon; as she desired him to perform before her that very evening. "How is your slave to produce Yü? I have no knowledge of his whereabouts."

"No, but your eldest son has. Mark my words, if he is not produced or if he has suffered hurt, I shall visit your insolent boy's offences on your person. Be warned in time."

The audience was over and the Old Buddha sent for me immediately: I told to her the whole story and she particularly applauded the courageous censor Chiang Ch'un-lin. "What unheard of audacity to kidnap your 'friend'! it makes my hair stand on end with horror. You had better remain here till Yü arrives, as he will feel less nervous if he sees you and you can bring him in to tell me the whole story." So I waited and met Yü at the gate: he had been cruelly maltreated and Tsai Chen, faithful to his predilection, had bitten him, leaving a horrid mark in the nape of the neck, draining him (so Yü said) of a quantity of blood which the prince had drunk with gusto, ghoul that he was. But for Ch'ing's intervention, poor Yü thought that he would never have escaped alive. The marks of the teeth were perfectly visible and his white appearance suggested to a layman like myself a large loss of blood, but I fancy that the pallor was due to fright.

The Old Buddha sent a special imperial messenger to order Ch'ing to attend with his three sons that afternoon; she bade me not to show myself on their arrival, for she was aware that we were friends and did not desire to create ill-feeling between us. According to Lien-ying, the prince accompanied by the *Ch'üan Tzu* 犬子 (puppy sons in conventional disparagement) kotowed thrice, exclaiming, "I take the blame."

The Old Buddha, who was in a towering rage, reviled him roundly: "You can't even manage your own household, how much less affairs of state. I am going to fine you Taels 100,000 as a slight punishment and Tsai Chen Taels 10,000 which he must pay to Yü Kuei-fang as compensation. Furthermore, I order Tsai Chen to receive thirty strokes with the *Hei Pien Tzu* 黑鞭子, a formidable long thonged whip, upon the bared posterior in your presence and that of his brothers who must pay a fine of Taels 5,000 for their participation in the outrage. Tsai Chen is to give to me the names of the leading ruffians who performed the kidnapping, and I hereby order that they shall be decapitated, *Ch'eng Yi*

Ching Po 懲一警百, as a salutary example, by punishing one a hundred are warned."

Tsai Chen was ushered into the presence and whined for mercy, proving himself a *froussard*[24] of the lowest and most despicable type. "Spare me, Your Majesty, from this humiliation of a flogging in public, *T'a Chih Yü Shih* 撻之於市, hit in the market place (a classical quotation from the *Li Chi* 禮記, *Book of Rites*). It will be to me an indelible disgrace to expose my nakedness in Your Majesty's holy presence." And he began to wail and howl for mercy, like the school boy who screams before the birch-rod strikes his hindermost.

The Old Buddha smiled grimly, "You cause pain to others and now you shall *Ch'ang Na Ko Tzu Wei* 嘗那個味, have a taste of it yourself. Call the court wrestler (*P'u Hu* 撲戶, a Manchu word) let him bring the black whip with him. Call Yü Kuei-fang: he shall be present and confront you, Tsai Chen, who are the culprit."

Enter the court flogger with his formidable *sjambok* (Malay for leather thonged whip, used by the Boers). Poor little Yü, shaking like a rat, was brought forward: "Do you recognize the prince who assaulted you?"

"Yes, Your Majesty, please forgive him; it is the stoutest of the three princes who . . . . . . "

"What did he do? Speak!"

"Your Majesty, he copulated with me from behind three times *Ts'ao P'i Ku* 肏屁股, and I am very sore."

"What else? Speak out."

"After the first coition, his excitement seemed to wax and he bit me cruelly on the neck, till blood came, and he kept sucking the wound."

"Very good," said the Old Buddha, "take the whip and give to the prince six strokes as a beginning, that you may *Ch'u Ch'i* 出氣, vent your anger."

Lien-ying said that Yü hesitated before lightly applying the scourge (as if he were using a lily) on Tsai Chen's posterior. Then the *P'u Hu* did his duty in the Old Buddha's presence, belabouring the prince in good earnest with the superabundance of good will that an English pedagogue would display in chastising his pupils, as if he thoroughly enjoyed the carnival of sadistic cruelty. Tsai Chen, in the intervals of his poltroon-like groans continued to shout: "Mercy! *Lao Fo* 老佛, *Ch'iu En* 求恩, I implore you, Old Buddha, to have mercy." The flogging was evidently severe (it will be remembered that I am not writing as an eye-witness but recording Lien-ying's impressions); but none could have failed to be struck by the young prince's abject lack of valour such as most school-boys would have been ashamed to exhibit. I can veraciously affirm that in all my multitudinous castigations at school, despite the intensest pain, I never once gave to my *Plagosus Orbilius* (Orbilius, the flogger of Horace's school days) the satisfaction of seeing one flinch or of hearing from me a cry of distress. The chastisement over, Tsai Chen rose and kotowed to the

---

24 Coward.

Old Buddha, while his father, according to etiquette, returned thanks to Her Majesty for sparing to him and his sons *Kuo Shen Chih Chü* 過甚之舉, the extreme course (of decapitation). The list of the accomplices' names was handed to the Old Buddha and she ordained that six should be decapitated, *Chiu Ti Cheng Fa* 就地正法, and that four others should *P'ei Pang* 陪綁, be bound and taken that afternoon to the execution ground but with their sentence commuted to perpetual imprisonment. On my way home that evening, I encountered the two open carts, like tumbrils, which conveyed the doomed felons. The legend writ on the *Chao Tzu* 招子 or narrow strip of long white cloth inserted in the manacled hands (which were tied behind their backs) and attached to a *Kao Liang*[25] 高粱 stalk read as follows: *Ch'iang Tsou Liang Min Jen Fan* 搶走良民人犯, felon forcibly kidnapping honest people. In those days, the term *Pang P'iao* 綁票, "bind the ticket", so common under the Republic, for holding to ransom, like *Ssu P'iao* 撕票, destroy the ticket, euphemistic for taking the life of the kidnapped person, was not known.

Before leaving the presence, the Old Buddha again required me to "pleasure" her twice in succession, thanking me for giving to her the congenial occasion of "wiping off" old scores with the detested Ch'ing house. I asked Her Majesty not to acquaint the old prince of my share in the transaction, because I did not desire to *Shang Kan Ch'ing* 傷感情, harm friendly relations which, in fact, were not impaired so far as His Senile Highness was concerned. But unfortunately, the theatrical management and Yü's own immediate fellow-mimes were informed by him of the part I had taken (*quorum pars magna fui*)[26] and the former, like the majority of their compatriots, the most grateful people in the world, unlike our western barbarians who regard benefits as a good reason for calumniating the giver, *I Yüan Pao En* 以怨報恩, insisted upon offering to me rich gifts which I refused and a tablet inscribed *Hu P'i Liang Min* 護庇良民, protector of worthy folk, which I could not but accept, besides sending to my household a large pecuniary recompense. Yü and I had a long and delightful love affair over many years. As is known, he became famous as a leading actor.

I am under the impression that Tsai Chen, who after his sire's death in 1917 succeeded to the princedom, bore to me a decided grudge for my "unwarrantable" intervention, although he remained outwardly cordial. On the occasion of the ex-emperor's wedding ceremonies in November 1923, I had the honour to be invited. After P'u Yi 溥儀, Hsüan T'ung 宣統, had mounted the throne to thank us for our attendance, Tsai Chen took it upon himself with unparalleled audacity to follow his emperor's example and solemnly to salute us, as if he were only second to the emperor himself, when His Majesty's uncles refrained from exhibiting their pride of place. After the ceremony, Tsai Chen stopped me to ask how my actor friends were just now faring: *Ming Ling Chieh Chung Ling Yu Mu Hsia Tsen Mo Yang* 名伶界中令友目下怎麼樣?

---

25   Chinese sorghum.
26   In which he himself acted so conspicuous a part (Virgil, *Aeneid* II.5).

And I to reply: "They are flourishing under Your Highness' protection, *T'o Wang Yeh Ti Fu* 托王爺的福, *T'a Men Tao Shih Shang Shu Pu Ts'o* 他們倒是尚屬不錯. Your Highness and I have similar tastes! how fortunate are we! *Wang Yeh Ken Wo Suan Shih T'ung P'i* 王爺跟我算是同癖! *Ho Ch'i Hsing Yeh* 何其幸耶!"

CHAPTER IX

THE FIRE FROM HEAVEN
OR
THE LOVERS' DOOM

MY friends not infrequently ask me why I am nervous during electric storms, or rather during lightning. The answer can be found in the narrative which follows. "To have seen what I have seen; see what I see" (*Hamlet*).

> Memo: The lady is called Yü T'i 毓琕 and Shu Tê 淑德, *Yü* being her name, *T'i* a kind of jade and *Shu* chaste; the Old Buddha's petname also Tai Yü 黛玉 after the novel's heroine.

I have recounted *tant bien que mal*[1] the reactions of the Old Buddha toward my audacious connivance in furthering the love affairs within the palace precincts of two young people: it was not that Her Majesty looked askance in the abstract at the natural outcome of an affair of the heart, but she objected to the *entremise*[2] of a third party without her privity or consent. In the late summer (according to the Chinese calendar) of Kuang Hsü 光緒 31, early in August 1905, Her Majesty commanded me to arrange to bring to the Wan Shou Shan 萬壽山 an extremely beautiful and charming young actor named Liu Ch'ang 柳昌, a player of *Hua Tan* 花旦 parts[3] but as yet having developed no particular histrionic talent. The boy greatly attracted me and I rather resented the Old Buddha's latest interest; it seemed to me that in this matter Her Majesty might well have required his presence direct through a eunuch in her confidence. However, I could only obey orders and set about ascertaining from Li Lien-ying 李蓮英 when and how I was to bring him as it appeared to be an unusual personally conducted tour; at that time, actors were still regarded as a caste with whom respectable people would not publicly associate: it is true that the rule, or custom, was "more honoured in the breach than the observance" (*Hamlet*), but even so the Old Buddha was such a stickler for etiquette that I did not see how I could proceed to the palace in my official chair (as she now expected of me)

---

1 As best I could.
2 Intervention.
3 Comedic female roles.

with a catamite actor in my train, the observed of all observers, who would certainly draw uncomplimentary conclusions, alas! not by any means devoid of a solid basis of fact! Li Lien-ying's ready wit solved the problem by directing us (Liu and me) to foregather at the temple Wan Shou Ssu 萬壽寺 on the banks of the Ch'ang Ho 長河, a canal leading from the Hsi Chih 西直 gate to the K'un Ming 昆明 Lake, where I should leave my chair and travel the rest of the way by one of the Empress' launches in Liu's delectable company. A crowd had gathered at the temple gate, the temple at which the Old Buddha invariably burned incense on her pilgrimages to and fro the Summer Palace. I heard much naive admiration expressed for the mime's beauty; the opinion was broached: "*Lao Fo Yeh Yao Hsiao Ch'ien* 老佛爺要消遣: *T'a Na Lao Mang Tsai Kuo Shih* 他吶老忙在國事, *Ying Tang Yang Shen Tê Hsiu Hsi Ti Shih Hou'rh* 應當養神得休息的時候兒. The Old Buddha needs recreation; she is forever busy with state affairs and really requires some relaxation for her mind."

Liu was distinctly nervous and continued to ask me what the Old Buddha required of him: I had no answer ready, although my own experience left me in little doubt. Why she brought me into the picture seemed far from clear: it might be that in her superabundance of salacious desire the cooperation of two males was indicated. Wishing to save my face as arch-performer, was she allowing me, of my own volition, to provide the understudy ready to step on the figurative stage and retrieve by his active functioning the tired protagonist? Liu took my hand in amorous pressure: "If she makes me share her couch, promise me that you will be near; for I am *Na Yü K'ou* 吶於口, slow of utterance (he was really a glib talker) and you can be ready to supply my deficiencies *K'uang Ch'i Pu Tai* 匡其不逮 with your gift of language, while I can then *Ts'ung Jung Chiu Shih* 從容就事, composedly proceed to the matter in hand." I assured him that I should endeavour not to fail him, but up to the present the Empress had not suggested triangular unions, still less granted permission for a *tertium quid*[4] to assist as prompter. The truth was that, as we fared across the smooth waters of the K'un Ming Lake, watching the not unimposing vista of the high walled background of the P'ai Yün Tien 排雲殿 "Cloud Forcing Hall" (built after the model of the Dalai Lama's Potala palace in Lhasa), I felt completely at a loss, *Tsai Wu Li Wu Chung* 在五里霧中, befogged and in the clouds regarding the mysterious workings of the Old Buddha's mind.

As we left the launch, the lake-side was alive with attendants, eunuchs and women of the court, but I perceived no familiar face. The unexpected arrival by the lake entrance had attracted much attention, as it was only the Old Buddha who journeyed to the palace by water. Liu Ch'ang and I marched through the curious crowd which did not stint its admiration of his comeliness.

"Who's the young man wearing the red jewelled button?" I heard a lady in waiting ask; the reply from a eunuch being: "Do you really not know or are you just pretending?"

---

4   Intermediary.

"Please tell me who he is."

"Oh! he's the Old Buddha's private astrologer!" I felt rather more elevated in my own estimation by this appellation but half fancied that it might be euphemistic.

After walking towards the chief eunuch's apartments, we at last discovered the confidential chamberlain Ts'ui Tê-lung 崔德隆 who welcomed us warmly. "Oh! there you are; the Old Buddha is taking a siesta (it was then about 3 p.m.) and the chief eunuch is enjoying his pipe. But come to my room till the latter has *Kuo Yin* 過癮, satisfied the craving." Despite the vicinity of the lake, the weather was as sultry as I have ever known in Peking: gathering storm clouds in the south east presaged a thunder storm.

Ts'ui who was a lover of beauty paid considerable attention to Liu, flirting with the mime in the most approved fashion. "Her Majesty is going to take you, Liu, and her favourite maid of honour, Shu Tê 淑德 (Yü T'i 毓琪), probably also Li Tu Tsung Kuan 李都總管 chief eunuch Li, to the shrine across the lake for tea and cigarettes. You will both remain overnight, but here comes Li himself who will explain." The latter was, as usual, most cordial, invited us to a collation in his apartments; he explained to me that the Old Buddha desired Yü Shu Tê to "amuse" herself with Liu over at the shrine, while the former was "enjoying" my conversation in the main (northwest *Chien* 間) chamber which was set apart for her to rest in on the occasion of her not infrequent excursions. After our return, the usual routine, so far as I was concerned, was to be followed, but the Old Buddha might summon Liu for a private audience during the night, as she had heard so much of his rare beauty. It seemed a *partie carrée*[5] in itself perfectly normal; but I could not envisage the part I was expected to play with Yü Shu Tê. Perhaps her share in the programme would be limited to the afternoon picnic; while Liu and I should minister to the Empress' requirements during the night *à tour de rôle*.[6]

A eunuch came rushing in: "The Old Ancestress is calling you; she asks if the marquis has arrived; if so, he and the actor are to come immediately."

We entered the presence and kotowed thrice. The Empress was in radiant spirits, caressed me in an affectionate way, remarking of Liu: "*Ming Pu Hsü Ch'uan* 名不虛傳, he's as good looking as people say. Yü Tê is in luck this afternoon. But afterwards I must let him play with me, and you can reassure him, if he's shy." I could see that the Old Buddha had taken a liking to Liu: his manner, half deferential, half challenging, was what appealed to her. She detested servility, but exacted a deference to which she was entitled, but which did not exclude a timely repartie, or even a contradiction if discreetly worded. I do not suppose she would have relished any more than Queen Victoria, who remonstrated with her secretary, Sir Henry Ponsonby, for saying that some suggestion emanating from her was "perfectly absurd", "You must not speak of US as capable

---

5   Wife-swapping party.
6   In turn.

of an absurdity", a flat negative; but if it were put in the form of a question leaving the decision to Her Majesty herself, she was more amenable to a convincing argument than most monarchs of history. Above all, she had the saving sense of humour and in fact often talked with her tongue in her cheek, laughing at herself in her most impassioned moments. Her rages were sudden and she was undoubtedly capricious, but for those who understood her, such as Junglu 榮祿 or Li Lien-ying, it was not difficult to restore calm when her wrath seemed most formidable to those who did not know her.

The Empress fondled Liu's shapely, artistic chybre with lascivious delight. "Don't be jealous, *Pieh Ch'ih Ts'u* 別吃醋," said she; "he's here for Yü Tê and you are here for me. But I cannot resist touching the secret parts of so exquisite a youth. What was the name of the beautiful actor and singer mentioned in the *Lun Yü* 論語, of whom the Sage said that such as he had more influence than himself in the state of Lu 魯, while deploring the degradation of morals then prevalent? *Shui Chih* (whose?) *Mei* 誰之美, *Wo I Shih Hsiang Pu Ch'i Lai* 我一時想不起來, the handsome looks of whom? his name (said Old Buddha) escapes me at the moment." (She meant *Sung Chao Chih Mei* 宋朝之美 of the *Analects*; the play on words *Chao* 朝 morning and *Ch'ao* 朝 dynasty was one reason why the founder of the Sung 宋 Dynasty who had his fief at Sung Chou 宋州 in Honan 河南 adopted the dynastic style of Ta Sung 大宋.)

It was intensely sultry (*lourd comme le nuit òu Saint-Avit tua Morhange*[7] in Benoist's novel *L'Atlantide*), but the Empress' boudoir was cyclonic with multitudinous fans. Li came hurrying in to say that Yü Tê 毓德 asked leave to enter; she was sister of the Yü Heng 毓恆 of whom I have spoken in the adventure of the Baths and daughter of the Boxer leader Ch'i Hsiu[8] 耆秀. Knowing her brother's rare charm and grace, I was not disappointed in the dark, stately beauty with the delectable hair, clad in grass-cloth; large lustrous sparkling black eyes with delicately pencilled eye brows, exquisitely shaped hands, a patrician's daughter to the fingertips, delicate lithe body. The Old Buddha called her Shu Tê 淑德 and also Tai Yü 黛玉 after the heroine of the *Hung Lou Meng* 紅樓夢, and I thought it an illomened appellation, recalling that hapless girl, in whom the course of true love certainly did not run smooth, doomed to an early death, even though a creation of fiction. The Empress introduced me as the "foreign professor" who, as she put it, "*Ken Wo Hen T'ou Yüan* 跟我狠投緣, with whom I have an affinity," and Yü Tê, who was not in the least shy, bowing pleasantly to me, replied: "How hard you work, Old Buddha! You never allow yourself a moment's pleasure!"

"Well," said the Empress Dowager, "not entirely so; for we are going to amuse ourselves now: here's a charming boy, a *Hua Tan* 花旦, Liu

---

7   "Sultry as the night when Saint-Avit killed Morhange". Though the author correctly attributes the source, the 1919 novel *L'Atlantide*, the name of the author (Benoit) is misspelled.

8   There appears to be a slight confusion here. In the chapter dealing with baths ("The Hammam and the Intrusion") the author speaks of Heng Yü 恆虞, son of Ch'i Hsiu 啓秀. The names of both men are written differently in this instance.

Ch'ang, whom you will love to talk to. We are going across the lake to the Hsiang Chieh shrine 香界祠 and the shrine to the Dragon King 龍王祠 and, after I have burned incense there to Maitreya Buddha, we can all follow the dictates of our hearts, untrammelled by court or any other etiquette. The launch will be here at once. I shall only take Li Lien-ying besides you three."

To my delight, Liu seemed quite at home even in the Old Buddha's presence and began chatting gaily to Yü Tê: although an actor, he came of a respectable family and was endowed with manners that an emperor (especially yokel mannered Kuang Hsü) might have envied. I assumed that Yü Tê had been informed by the Old Buddha of the love carnival that awaited her.

Life is sad and so is this narration. But I must not anticipate and will recount this painful, ineffably tragic event which memory, like my conscience that never lets me be, has etched even as a corrosive acid into my quivering brain, so that to speak of the occasion is to live it over again. Like Aeneas recording the fall of windy, towered Ilium to the Carthaginian queen, I must not pause nor leave the tale half-told but must needs go bravely on to the end. The great Empress, the all powerful eunuch have for a generation been denizens of the world of shadows and foregather, it may be, by the Yellow Springs;[9] of those who were "mutes or audience to this act" only I remain, like a poor actor who has outstaged his welcome but who still persists in strutting his brief hour upon the stage, surely knowing better than to exclaim, like the great Augustus *à son lit de mort*,[10] "*Acta est fabula, plaudite!*"[11] That incomparable, ideal boy, that fragrant dainty girl born for the luring and the love of man; as I think of their mortal hour and the blow from heaven, I thank a kindly Providence for the gift of tears, idle tears perchance but which cause the purgation of the passions by pity and fear, according to the principle enuntiated by the Stagyrite 2,300 years ago,[12] words true now as they were then, in the midst of our vaunted, material civilisation dying, thank God, before our eyes.

"Silence," as Paul Bourget says in his psychological romance *André Cornélis*, "*aux faits.*" So the launch awaited us at the landing stage, and the Old Buddha walking with unusual vigour despite her 70 years (perhaps the congenial handling of Liu Ch'ang's admirable *Ch'iao Tzu*[13] 巧子 – tool – had rejuvenated her) took her seat in the poop, while we sate at her feet. Even on the water the heat was almost insupportable and I remember thinking that on such a day sexual commerce was indeed a crime inviting from the three Fates the chastisement of *un coup de sang*.[14]

---

9   The Yellow Springs, in traditional Chinese mythology, refers to an underground gathering place for the souls of the dead.
10 At his deathbed
11 The story has been acted, applaud!
12 The most influential of the Greek philosophers, Aristotle (384-22 BC), is sometimes referred to as "the Stagyrite", after his hometown, Stagira.
13 **Backhouse:** The vulgar word for *penis* or *tool*, *Ch'iao Tzu* is always written in the 金瓶梅 [*Ch'in Ping Mei*] 巧子 "cunning" thing. Also, I think, in the other famous novels. Of course 雀子 [freckle] is the same sound.
14 A stroke.

The breeze, such as it was, blew from the southeast, always a storm laden quarter in North China, and the launch attendants, who were quite at ease with the Old Buddha, much as Victoria's Scottish coachman and grooms would talk to Her Majesty in a dour tone of voice such as none of the queen's children would have dreamed of adopting, remarked: "Old Buddha, you had better not go ashore at the island: you'll be caught in a terrible *rafale*."[15]

"What if I am," retorted Her Majesty, "don't you know the Buddhist proverb: *Chiang* (*K'u* 苦) *Hai Wu Pien* 江海無邊, *Hui T'ou Shih An* 回頭是岸? The boundless waters encompass us: just turn and perceive the shore." It was not likely that the launch hands would be familiar with that famous *verse*[16] that portrays the boundless mercy of Avalokitesvara, the goddess who hearkens to prayer; but, as I have said, when the Empress started quoting, it was a sure sign of good humour. She continued: "We shall be under cover at the shrine; you may return to the launch-house and come to meet us, say about sunset or a little later."

It appeared that eunuchs had already brought refreshments, not forgetting the Old Buddha's opium pipe and an ample supply of cigarettes and drinks, to the so-called *Hsing Kung* 行宮 or Imperial Lodge whither we were bound. I noticed that Yü and Liu seemed to be *en train d'évoluer une étroite amitié*[17] and he was clasping her lovely hand in erotic passion. Alas! *Dis aliter visum* (Vergil):[18] their love was too briefly tried; let us trust that in the Elysian fields, like Dido and Telamon in *Aenead* VI, they are able *amorem reddere amore*[19] and to speak of their undying love.

So we landed. Li and I assisted the Old Buddha to ascend the short acclivity to the shrine and lodge. The rain still held off, but ominous rumblings were audible. "Are you afraid of thunder?" asked Her Majesty.

"No, Your Majesty, not if I hear the thunder, but I fear the lightning. Once the clap is audible, there's no danger. It's like a bullet overhead; if you hear the whistling, you know that it has passed over of you."

"Don't I know it? In the 21. VII. 26 (August 15, 1900) we were just ready to leave the Forbidden City and your foreign devils began fire and whizzing bullets were just at their worst, *Cheng Nao Te Huan* 正鬧得歡. Only those who have offended heaven are ever struck by lightning (*Huo Tsui Yü T'ien Wu So Tao Yeh* 獲罪於天無所禱也; He who has aroused heaven's anger, has none to whom he shall pray – Confucius). I rather enjoy a thunder storm, but they tell me to shut off electric lights and fans for fear of being struck, *Pei Tien So Ta* 被電所打."

Naturally, I did not mention the circumstance nor the superstition, but as to the latter there is a persistent belief not only in China that it is bad people who are struck by lightning. (Sixty years ago I remember being out in a terrible storm near Grenoble and La Chartreuse and

---

15 Blast.
16 Verse.
17 "Developing a close friendship". Correctly written *"En train d'évoluer vers une étroite amitié"*.
18 The gods have judged otherwise (*Aeneid* II.148).
19 To return love for love.

being assured by my coachman who piously signed himself: "We are safe, as we have both heard Holy Mass today".) As to the former, Her Majesty had perhaps forgotten, or did not wish to recall, the end of the great-grand-father of the reigning emperor, Chia Ch'ing 嘉慶, in September 1820, while staying at his Jehol *villégiature*,[20] what time the "fire" from heaven visited the Pi Shu Chuang 避暑莊 or Summer Residence. The facts are well known, in fact are chronicled by a Lazarist father then living in Ch'eng Tê 承德 (Jehol), but bear repetition since they may (*quien sabe*)[21] be unfamiliar to some readers. The Emperor Chia Ch'ing, Yung Yen 永琰 (then written 琰 as a forbidden character 敬避廟諱),[22] as his portraits which would normally present him in a flattering aspect, indicate, was a cruel, blood-thirsty, vindictive despot, whose cold-blooded murder, after a concocted travesty of justice, of his sire's favourite minister, Ho Shen 和珅 (I call it murder, though actually Ho Chung T'ang 和中堂 was "allowed" to commit suicide) made him hateful in the eyes of gods and men; in that he infringed the sacred Confucian canon that a ruler may not dismiss (let alone punish) the favourite minister of his father until three years had elapsed from the latter's death, whereas Chia Ch'ing only waited ten days before decreeing Ho's death penalty. Hence, Chia Ch'ing's death which I am about to recount appeared to his contemporaries as the just vengeance and retribution of offended Heaven. I may criticize his barbaric blood-lust but have no justification (being what I am) to impugn his morals; he was *on ne peut plus homosexuel*[23] in either aspect, but perhaps more particularly revelled in the passive or pathic ecstasy. It was said at court that ten stalwart males a day would still find His Majesty demanding more; while vulgar gossip asseverated that "*Tang Chin Huang Ti Yen'rh Chen Ta* 當今皇帝眼兒眞大, *P'i Sui Ch'ou I Sheng Pu Fa* 屁雖臭一聲不發, His Majesty the ruling emperor hath an enormous anus, his flatus is most foul but quite inaudible". *Le gaz qui sort du fondement impérial, quoique putidissime, n'a point de bruit.* (Here I am reminded, willy nilly, of the *bon mot*,[24] the T'ung Yao 童搖, regarding Cardinal Richelieu, "*Le cul putidissime de l'éminentissime*, the stinking hinder parts of the most eminent cardinal". Richelieu died, I believe, of a malign condition of the rectum, carcinoma perhaps.)

It used to be a common joke among the Turks of the house of Othman, if an aristocratic guest were to *lâcher un pet*[25] at a dinner or public gathering (not deemed a breach of manners), to retort: "I am glad to see that we still have a 'virgin' present with us", i.e. one whose anal cavity is not so much distended by incessant "pricking" from without that escaping gas is no longer audible.

---

20 Resort.
21 Who knows?
22 A character tabooed after the death of an emperor whose name contained it.
23 Homosexual through and through.
24 Witticism.
25 Break wind.

To proceed, Chia Ch'ing had one catamite named P'ang Shao-lien 龐韶濂 who was admittedly the Antinous[26] of the day. It was the emperor's wont to proceed with his idol who was said to penetrate the Son of Heaven's rectum to the depth of eight or more (Chinese) inches, to a certain T'ing Tzu 亭子 or Kiosque in the palace grounds, as umbrageous as Milton's Vallombrosa in Tuscany from whence I believe that the Great Uebermensch[27] and patriot Duce Benito Mussolini has decreed the removal of a memorial tablet "All'illustrissimo poeta inglese, Milton"[28] because Englishmen of even three hundred years ago are as invisi a Dio ed ai nemici suoi, hateful to God and to the enemies of God,[29] as the doomed Arch Angel, Lucifer, to the Almighty, against whom he waged a temporarily successful war.

It was a day as lourd[30] as the August evening, 1905, which witnessed the tragedy unfolded in this narrative; emperor and catamite (or should I not rather say P'a Shan Hu'rh 爬山虎兒, the hill-climbing tiger, litter or improvised chair, a slang term for the uppermost participant in the pedicatio) walked in the early afternoon to the place of love. There were no witnesses, but I do not think it illegitimate to infer (and here the Lazarist priest's narrative bears me out) that the two indulged in reciprocal coition to their hearts' content. Chia Ch'ing was in his fifty-eighth year, a heavy drinker, almost arsouille,[31] whose active force may well have been beginning to decline, but his passive recipiency was unabated and fain to take all that the "small donkey rider" had it in him to give. As I say, in the absence (natural enough) of témoins oculaires,[32] neither the good Lazarist father, a contemporary, nor I, writing 123 years after the event, being in that category, it is only feasible to indulge in speculation as to the exact course of events. A thunderstorm of almost unparalleled violence broke over the imperial villégiature; the Kiosque, embossed as it was in dense foliage and affording an ideal attraction for the fire from heaven, was struck by lightning and burnt to the ground. When the terrified eunuchs and courtiers, after a lull in the storm, arrived at the place of death, they found among the blackened debris a heap of whitish ashes, "un tas de cendres quasi blanches ou plutôt blanchâtres qu'on n'en pouvait même pas distinguer en constatant à qui elles appartenaient"[33] (writes the Father), all that remained of the pathic Son of Heaven and his adored Antinous. There being no possible means of distinguishing to which of the adulterous pair the ashes appertained, they were meticulously wrapt in a silken white Pao Fu 包袱 or roll-bundle and reverently placed in the

26   Antinous (111-30 AD) was the beautiful lover of the Roman Emperor Hadrian. Hadrian deified Antinous following the latter's death, and his image was widely reproduced throughout the Empire.
27   Nietzche's "overman", someone beyond the limitations of humanity.
28   To the most illustrious English poet, Milton.
29   Dante, Inferno III.63.
30   Heavy.
31   A lush.
32   Eyewitnesses.
33   "A pile of ashes almost white, or rather whitish, that one could not even distinguish to whom they belonged". Correctly written "un tas de cendres quasi blanches, ou plutôt blanchâtres, dont on ne pouvait même pas distinguer à qui elles appartenaient".

Tzu Kung 梓宮 or Palace of Catalpa wood, as the imperial coffin is denominated, in readiness for the day when the funeral cortège borne by 128 bearers should start on its slow progress to Peking, pending inhumation at the Western Ling or Mausolea. The latter were never desecrated to the extent of the Eastern Tombs; but the mausoleum of Chia Ch'ing known as Ch'ang Ling 昌陵, illustrious sepulchre, was opened and the imperial coffin rifled of the treasure (*Hsün Tsang* 殉葬) buried with the dead. The contents, so far as human remains were concerned, were, as I have set forth, a little heap of ashes, *sic transit gloria mundi*:[34] but the fair P'ang Shao-lien is fortunate in his burial place inextricably mixed with his sovereign, whose function is idiomatically but unelegantly known in the "profession" (shall I say "our" profession) as *Hsia Tsou* 下走, the underneath one, which seems a discovery of the obvious.

The digression will be pardoned as not wholly inapposite; at any rate, the Old Buddha had conveniently forgotten a not very credit-bringing (however illuminating) episode in the Ta Ch'ing 大清 dynastic history, although officially (it is needless to say) the Son of Heaven died of a sudden seizure, while actively engaged in business of state, *Wan Chi Chih Yü* 萬機之餘, amidst a myriad crowding duties. Well! I suppose that when M. le Président de la République, Félix Faure, passed away in a scarcely less laudable environment, the French Government was fain to speak of *une apoplexie foudroyante*[35] occurring after a too hearty *déjeuner* on that February day, 1899.

To resume. We disposed ourselves, after burning incense at the shrine, the result of which pious gesture was scarcely as efficacious as we might have expected from him who hearkeneth to prayer, *Yu Ch'iu Pi Ying*[36] 有求必應, in the Old Buddha's temporary boudoir, Liu and Yü engaged in intimate conversation and the Empress asking me questions about my latest homosexual "conquests" (as she termed them) and in particular about my dear Chan Pao-ch'en's 占寶臣 welfare (*vide*[37] "Mulberry Bush"). *Après une plantureuse collation*[38], Her Majesty said: "I and Pa Hou Yeh 巴侯爺 are going to have a little private transaction of business (*Yao Pan I Tien'rh Ssu Shih* 要辦一點兒私事); you two young lovers may go and *Hsiao Ch'ien* 消遣, amuse yourselves, in the side *Chien* 間 or apartment" (the shrine being in the centre, while we were immediately north, divided only by a *Ko Shan* 隔山 or partition but without intercommunicating door). "Li Lien-ying, you have your room on the east side and are hereby permitted to indulge your craving which, I can guess, is heavy on you."

Li had forgotten to give to me the habitual *Mei Yao* 媚藥 or aphrodisiac; *par conséquent*,[39] I had not arrived at a well organized state of sexual excitement. The Old Buddha was disappointed and said so, as she took

---

34 "So passes the glory of the world", a phrase used during papal coronations until 1963.
35 A sudden apoplexy.
36 To answer prayers; grant wishes.
37 "See", a direction to the reader.
38 After a generous meal.
39 As a consequence.

between her fingers my partially erect *Yang Wu* 陽物 or male organ: "I should like it to be harder," said she; "I can imagine" (said archly) "if you exchanged places with Yü Tê, the *Ch'iao Tzu* would become as firm as lacquer. But you must do your best, as I am in need of your ministration."

Meantime, the storm had broken, the waters of the lake were lashed to fury and it was fortunate that the launch had by this time safely returned to the *Ch'uan Wu* 船塢, or boat-house. Thunder gave blow on blow: the whole heaven was rent through by a blaze; earth groaned and seemed to come to the birth throughout the length of the Western Hills, now visible and now shrouded in an uncanny blackness as of Erebus.[40] Then it suddenly grew so dark that one could scarce have conjectured there was any earth or world at all. I had never known such a storm and am bound to confess that the Old Buddha, who seemed to regard it as a huge joke, showed far higher courage than the effete Briton, who fancied himself one of the latest sons of time, the heir of all the ages. (He does not fancy so in this year of grace 1943, for obvious reasons.) We heard through the incessant crash of the thunder and the fitful lightning flashes the voice of Yü Tê: "It's delicious: *Chen Hao Shou* 真好受; *Ni Hai Tei Lai I Tz'u* 你還得來一次: you must do it again. *Shih Tsai Yao Shu T'an Ssu* 實在要舒坦死: I shall die of the pleasure" ("die of a rose in aromatic pain" – Shakspere).[41]

Then we heard Liu say: "*Wo Ch'iao Tzu Shang Yu Tien'rh Hsüeh Yin'rh* 我巧子上有點兒血印兒, there's a little blood on my glans penis. *Tang Jan Ni Shih Ch'u Nü* 當然妳是處女, obviously you are a virgin. *Yung Pu Chao Ch'i Ma Pu* 用不著騎馬布, no need to apply the cloth beneath your private parts", which, if bloodstained, proves to the pleased mother-in-law that the bride is really and truly *intacta virgo*.[42]

The Empress remarked: "You see, they are busy at their pranks, *Cheng Tsai Wan'rh* 正在玩兒; do thou do likewise and insert your tool (which seems to be fuller and larger than just now: perhaps the thunder is acting as an erotic stimulant), further inside, so that you can *Tsou Shen Tzu* 走身子, ejaculate to the deepest extent possible."

I was trying to do her bidding, when suddenly there broke upon our darkness the most awful flash I have ever witnessed, unaccompanied by the expected instantaneous thunder reverberation. Li asserted that he saw a "ball" of fire fall into their chamber. Through the thin partition we heard an appalling, blood-curdling shriek or as it were a double voiced shriek; no words can describe it, at least none at my command, though I doubt not but that Dante or Shakespere would not be found wanting. It was the cry of the doomed in hell, the last appeal of a lost soul or rather of two lost souls; it seemed to be something outside the volition of the hapless victims, a sort of ultimate protest of nature against inexorable fate. The lovers had been struck by lightning in the twin shock (I suppose) of two opposing electric currents. As I have said, neither the Old

---

40 The darkness that exists between the earth and Hades in Greek mythology.
41 Actually Alexander Pope, *Essay on Man* I.I.200.
42 An untouched virgin.

Buddha, Li, nor I heard any explosion of thunder, but I felt what seemed to be a blow across the nape of the neck and Her Majesty (so she told me afterwards) a tingling of momentary violent pain.

The side *Chien* was on fire; further flashes continued; it was pitch dark save for the recurring lightning. It was pouring with rain or rather *il tombait des hallebardes*.[43] What in China is called *Ch'ing P'en* 傾盆 or *Ta Yü Pang T'o* 大雨滂沱, rain that causeth the pots to overflow. The little courtyard was several feet deep in water, but even so the unexampled force of the rain sufficed not to extinguish the fire, although the roof had fallen in with a crash. The flames were already burning the partition and approaching us.

"We must *Mao Yü* 冒雨, brave the rain, Old Buddha; *Nin Tei Shang Lien* 您得賞臉, *Chun Yüan Ch'en Pao Nin Na* 准遠臣抱您呐, you must honour your foreign servant by allowing him to take you in his arms; otherwise, the fire will overtake us and we shall be burned to death." She was very light to carry and practically naked (imagine if I had dropped her!); while I had previously discarded my long gown of *Hsia Pu*[44] 夏布 which later disappeared in the fire as it reached our room, and stood up in my grass-cloth undercoat and trousers. I had not difficulty in carrying my august burden to the court, wading through an expanse which reached nearly to my thighs but did not wet her person except for the rain. Li came out to meet us, speechless and like one with a palsy except that he had not lost the power of locomotion. Perhaps fortunately, the Old Buddha had fainted: I felt her pulse which seemed hardly perceptible except that I am unable to judge, being a layman. I placed her on the *K'ang* 炕 in Li's room and forced some liqueur down her throat. Meantime, the fire raged in the opposite *Chien*: it would have been death to enter it and quite unavailing, for the lovers' lives had terminated when we heard that heartrending cry. It grew lighter, I mean as regards the heavens, for of course, the raging fire lit up the whole environment. 'Twas like a foretaste of hell fire. I could faintly imagine the horror with which the inmates of the palace (except exulting Kuang Hsü 光緒 and his adherent eunuchs), the imperial guards, the huge staff of gardeners and domestics, must be watching the conflagration, "*Ko Chiang Kuan Huo* 隔江觀火", in this case across the lake, not the river, a phrase which, *en tout cas*, would be woefully *mal à propos*[45] in the present predicament, since it connotes an indifference to a situation which concerns others, but not oneself.

The rain was ceasing and the lightning flashes were becoming remote; evidently the storm had abated. The waters of the lake were still rising high, and no launch could yet make the crossing. We sate there for perhaps an hour: the Empress had rallied and regained consciousness. "*P'ien I* 便宜," said she, "we are well out of it. *Ju Kuo Tsamen Pei Lei So P'i* (the classic word for death by lightning is *Chi* 極) *Ssu* 如果咱們被雷

---

43 It was raining cats and dogs.
44 Linen; light cloth (literally "summer cloth").
45 In any case inopportune.

所劈死, *Jen Chia Kai Shuo Wo Yu La Pao Ying* 人家該說我有啦報應. *P'ien I Huang Shang Chiu Shih La* 便宜皇上就是啦. Had we two been struck dead by thunder (sic) people would have said that I had received retribution (from Buddha) and the emperor would have been in luck's way."

"But, Old Buddha, what of our ill-fated companions? Both are dead: what on earth are we to say?"

Tears were in my eyes and I am happy to think that the Empress burst into hysterical weeping: like summer tempest came her tears. "It is all my fault: I am a miserable woman, but who could have dreamed of such a terrible ending to our little excursion?"

"Your Majesty, it is heaven's inscrutable will: let us thank Buddha that your devout burning of incense has, at least, avoided the calamity from your sacred person. Let us bend in obedience to the decision of heaven."

Presently three launches arrived. The sun was just setting, an angry red, behind the clouds. About two score eunuchs and soldiers rushed up the ascent.

"*A Mi T'o Fo* 阿彌陀佛, Buddha hail," they shouted; "the main building is standing. We saw the fire and thought that harm had come to the Benign Mother. Buddha be praised." They rushed in; each and all kotowed to the Empress: "*T'ien Hsiang Chi Jen* 天相吉人, God helps the favoured of heaven." Change of raincoat had been brought for the Old Buddha; as for me, I was so saturated that I obtained Her Majesty's permission to strip naked in the chill evening air except for a towel round my loins. The opposite *Chien* had now nothing left to burn: it was level with the ground except for the *adobe* (*adobe* is Spanish for unburnt brick dried in the sun) *K'ang* on which (as it seemed to us from the opposite room) were two tiny heaps of grey-white ashes,[46] all that remained of so much beauty and gracious charm. I do not think that a single eye was dry: Li himself, the imperturbable, lifted up his voice and wept. Loving Liu as I did, I felt that I had lost my better self; while I grieved for him, I mourned for Lady Yü Tê and thought of her dear brother Yü Heng's sorrow with whom I was so often bound and locked in reciprocal homosexual conjunction.

There is little to add and in fact a postscriptum would sound as an anticlimax. I stayed by Her Majesty's order at the palace till the morning; need I add that the Old Buddha did not summon me again for any love carnival, although she entrusted me with a present of Taels 25,000 from the Privy Purse for dear Liu's family. I have ground for the belief that for the Lady Yü Tê her benefactions were on a much vaster scale:

---

46 **Backhouse:** N.B. In the sinister illumination of the fire which was then still burning fiercely and the lurid rays of an angry sunset, like a lost soul that shall always suffer, the light, so far as our eyes affected by the glare, and in my case blinded by my tears, could see, there seemed to be a mass of "white" ashes on the remains of the *K'ang* intermingled apparently with charred remnants of a darker hue which I took to be of the rafters. Next morning, the eunuchs brought over a sack containing these pitiable *restes* [remains]; we took them out and found divers fragments of calcined bones and a satchel full of grey white ashes. The Old Buddha divided the heap into two parts and bade me convey to Liu's parents a half portion, without, of course, knowing whether the ashes were Liu's or his sweetheart's.

the funeral ceremonies were elaborate and graced by many priceless imperial gifts. It was not feasible to hush up the tragedy: a young actor had been brought to the palace to perform before the Old Buddha who had taken him on a water excursion prior to his giving an exhibition of his talent "*Hsien Yi* 獻藝" at the lodge across the lake. In itself, this explanation was plausible; that it was believed I am disposed to doubt. I blamed myself, ay, and blame myself today, for bringing Liu on an errand of death, even though I was obeying my mistress' high command and could do no other.

CHAPTER X

LE "CABINET SECRET" DE LA VIE

In writing these papers, I have not dissembled regarding my own amoral proclivities, being frank and exact, even when I may be counted blamable, for candour seldom pays, although in this case the commercial aspect enters not into my thoughts, but in what follows, observation, not participation, is the burden of my song. The subject matter is alien from my taste and mentality: I can only faithfully record what confronted my eyes, as a phenomenon, but not as a reality to beckon me by its incompatible lure. The subject, as with pederasty, is divisible into active and passive moods; the phases and developments, *mutatis mutandis*,[1] are equally similar. I have mentioned elsewhere the erotic goat in the Museo Borbone degli Studi;[2] nothing could surpass the salacious expression conveyed in the turning of its head toward the man, loving and inviting, as consummation is effected by him. The late Lord Justice Vaughan Williams told me (when I was a law student) that on assize in country districts of England he frequently had cases of "bestiality" with their flocks by shepherds but never inflicted a severer sentence than two years imprisonment, although the law allowed twenty years as the penalty; while less than a century ago death by hanging was regularly imposed.

My knowledge (for I cannot say whether shepherds in China are addicts) is limited to the court, the aristocracy and eunuchs: I shall begin with the latter, wishing that I possessed a Lombroso's or Nordau's skill to present an abnormality, not indeed as a criminal instinct, but merely as a psychological study.[3]

The eunuch's erotic *foyer*, supposing that castration is complete, is in his anal region, immediately outside and inside the cavity: labial applications give to him an intense satisfaction, especially if the tongue

---

1   Necessary changes being made.
2   A reference to the "Secret Cabinet" (mentioned in the title) at the Museo Borbonico in Naples, which contained a collection of erotic works, some depicting acts of bestiality, recovered from Pompeii.
3   Cesare Lombroso (1835-1909), Italian doctor who believed in a phrenological connection to criminality. Max Nordau (1849-1923), Hungarian social theorist whose work *Degeneration* examined moral decline in modern society.

is inserted well within the orifice and maintained there for a considerable number of minutes. In a lesser degree, the cavity at the mouth of the bladder, even though shorn of vestige of sexual apparatus, imparts a pleasurable sensation, if touched or titillated for a considerable time. The eunuchs were amateurs of Pekingese pugs (*Chin* 狆 in Japanese) and sleeve dogs which were their inseparable companions night and day: it was usual to train them, especially the males, when puppies, to lick their masters' pudenda (or the debris thereof) and anus; while on his part the eunuch would caressingly fondle the little dogs and rub his frontal orifice against the animal's anus, producing a pleasing friction equally agreeable to both parties. A trained dog would not resent his master putting the former's male organ in his mouth: it was not customary, in the case of labial contact to swallow the semen, as would be normal when humans were the opposing party.

I believe that the female sex in several European capitals is notorious for its employment of *chiens d'agrément*[4] upon their private parts; on the other hand, the monster that was born to a lady of the ancient Scottish family of Bowes-Lyon Earl of Strathmore and Viscount Glamis (kindred to the present Queen Elizabeth) is erroneously believed to have been the fruit of a sexual union with a boarhound, her adored pet, and gave to that honoured and noble house a singularly unpleasing advertisement for the proletariat's hatred of high rank.

Apart from small dogs, it was a favourite eunuch predilection to take a male fowl, duck or gosling by the wings and to apply vigorous friction with the frontal vacant cavity to the bird's cloaca, truly a case of *Chi Chien* 雞姦 (Chinese penal code term for sodomy: "fowl copulation"). While treaty port gossip often alleges that in consummating the act the perpetrator simultaneously decapitates the fowl or duck, I am dubious regarding the fact: the birds are tame and trained to co-operate in apparent appreciation. I once heard it said by the French *littérateur*[5] Pierre Louys at Voisin's in the Rue de Castiglione that the duck was an unclean bird in China owing to its habitual employment as a passive participator: "*ex Africa semper aliquid novi.*"[6] The same thing was announced in England in connection with the importation of supposedly unclean Chinese hams and bacon and solemnly asseverated by that imaginative pseudo-omniscience which argues from an isolated particularity to a universal practice! If they were unclean, it was due to their filthy feeding, not to human sexuality, which would in any case scarcely affect the character of the meat, except sentimentally!

I remember the Old Buddha once saying to me in connexion with her suggestion that I should enjoy carnal relations with a beautiful lady in waiting: "Be careful not to apply your lips to any part of her person, which I forbid you to do, because her pet dog Hei Hsiao'rh 黑小兒 is used

---

4   Pet dogs.
5   Writer or literary scholar.
6   "Always something new out of Africa" (Pliny the Elder, *Natural History* VIII.18), refers to the supposedly promiscuous habits of lions and panthers.

regularly by her both behind and before and she takes the canine *verge* into her mouth. I should not wish you to be infected: you may 'possess' her, but only in the normal way, and must scrupulously cleanse your tool after the act. Li will see to it for you." The Empress recognized that her eunuchs were (some of them) prone to this predilection and seemed to know the addicts by name, bidding me eschew them in my erotic commerce. In fact, Lien-ying, cross-questioned by Her Majesty regarding those *auxquels j'avais affaire*[7] made it quite clear that none of the dozen or so on familiar terms with me were "steeped" in animal contacts.

Lien-ying took the view that, while men were available, there was no cause to have recourse toward animals; he was devoted to dogs and sacrificed himself to their well-being, but I can positively assert that they aroused in him no sexual interest. He said that he had bought a "red" Pekingese named Mu Kua 木瓜 or "quince" (*coing*) from a British lady once well known in the Legation Quarter, for she was returning home and did not desire to expose her pet to the discomforts of quarantine; lying down on his back stark naked one night in the height of summer, he was a little astonished to find Mu Kua licking his anus with considerable gusto, for *Hsi Kuan Ch'eng Tzu Jan* 習慣成自然, habit is second nature, and the dog could not in a moment wean himself from the former *goûts*[8] of his ex-mistress, if she really indulged in them. She certainly loved the Lesbian affinity and with zest licked her *adorées'*[9] vulvae, being a byword among young women.

Li said that an enormous monkey, or *Ma Hou'rh* 馬猴兒, named San'rh 三兒, common name for apes, a type whose habitat is, or was, the wooded region adjacent to the Tung Ling[10] 東陵, developed an amazing plethoric sexuality and would regularly gratify one of the imperial concubines (perhaps Chin Fei 瑾妃, sister of the Pearl Consort). Naturally, the union proved unproductive; fortunately so, for the birth of a monster would have meant the consort's execution; but, so Li assured me, the great monkey, *Fan Lien Pu Jen Jen* 翻臉不認人, oblivious of the hand that fed him, turned upon his *maîtresse de passage*[11] and bit her most savagely in the neck during his sexual act. As in the case of the unfortunate accident from monkey bite of the late Alexander, King of the Hellenes, in 1920, I believe that serious septicaemia developed. It occurred to me that the biting might be a symptom of affection not unknown among human beings in their orgasm: but Lien-ying said that San'rh had been very tractable in his youth but that old age affects the temper of monkeys and makes them incurably vicious. (I possessed a pet monkey who developed in old age signal animosity toward myself and bit me in the hand.) I suppose that there was nothing unusual in a small marmoset whom I once saw masturbating a Manchu duke of my

7　I was involved with.
8　Taste.
9　Lovers'.
10　"Eastern Tombs" of the Ch'ing Dynasty.
11　Passing mistress.

acquaintance: the tiny creature seemed to know exactly what was expected of him and delayed as long as possible the process of titillation; so that it was a case of *Chien Ju Chia Ching* 漸入佳境, bliss gradually attained (originally said of a person sucking the sugar cane and gradually reaching the luscious juice). Several eunuchs of my intimacy had pet monkeys; but I never associated any salacity with their animal-loving pastimes. It was said that nurses (never called *Amahs* 阿嬤 by persons born in the North, but – politely – *Chieh* 姐 or sister, pronounced in this connection in the *Ch'ü Sheng* 去聲, 4th tone – impolitely – *Lao Ma Tzu* 老媽子; *Ama* 阿瑪 in Manchu = father!! just as *Mapha* – grandfather, so no Manchu would ever speak of a *Mafu* 馬夫 or groom, owing to the similarity of sound, still less of *Ama* which is a southern appellation) in great Manchu families which possessed monkey pets encouraged them to play with their charges' tools so as to quiet them when irritable by the delicious titillation.

There was in France, I think about 1885, a case which attracted the attention of experts interested in *soi-disant*[12] perversion: a young farmhand had developed a strange affection for a young white steer of great beauty; the beast, curiously tractable, seemed to reciprocate the affection and allowed his human paramour to handle the enormous pizzle, to titillate the member and even (it was said) to apply to the urethral orifice his lips, till ejaculation ensued. Fellow labourers on the farm (I believe that it was situated in the Beauce County) affirmed to have been eyewitnesses of this unusual exhibition of *galanterie: si je ne me trompe pas*,[13] the case has become classic in the records of "bestiality". The *dénouement* is sensational: the sagacious animal, habituated as he was to the pleasing contact, arrived at the *époque de rut*,[14] *Chiao Wei Ch'i* 交尾期, and a heifer was available for his service, but had not yet been introduced into the farm-garth. According to the cowherd's own deposition *in articulo mortis*[15] before the local *gardien de la paix*,[16] he was *en train de remplir un besoin naturel*[17] and his posterior was necessarily exposed for the purpose. Suddenly, the steer, which was not tethered as it never strayed from the beloved hind's (hind, antique term for farm servant, *Nung Fu* 農夫) sight, if he were present, made an amorous rush toward the latter's buttocks, in some way achieved the requisite posture (I should imagine that the quotation *"hoc opus, hic labor est"*[18] in *Aeneid* VI. 129 is not inapplicable to the situation thence arising), and drove his Gargantuan pizzle up the man's rectum with penetration to the hilt. The cries of his agony brought other farm-hands to the garth: they found the steer busy in the sexual congress and were afraid to interfere, since he was lowing and roaring

---

12 So-called.
13 Gallantry: if I am not mistaken.
14 Mating season.
15 At the point of death.
16 Police officer.
17 Relieving himself.
18 In this the task and mighty labor lies.

literally like a bull of Basan (who is mentioned *dans les saintes Écritures*.[19] Basan was a kingdom east of Jordan in Joshua's time under King Og, famous for its breed of bulls). Ejaculation being at long last achieved, the erotic monster withdrew his now flaccid pizzle from the man's anus: perforation of the bowel ensued and he died within twenty-four hours of this (from the steer's point of view) successful coitus. His deposition received no credence, as it was taken for granted that he had profited by the advanced state of rut to present his willing anus to the steer's genital organ. It is a pity that Zola did not introduce this true incident in his exaggerated novel, *La Terre*, which deals with the countryside.

I have ventured to record at some length this episode, because *Yi Ti T'ung Ch'ing* 異地同情, circumstances differ not, despite change of sky ("*caelum non animum mutant qui trans mare currunt*",[20] as old Horace the wise says in the satires). My reason for an apparently otiose description of an event in Sunny France is that an almost exactly similar love-affair occurred (as I believe) here in Peking between a *Tsung Shih* 宗室, imperial clansman, named Yi Hsün 奕洵, aged over fifty years, and a pet young bull. I did not know him personally, but had met his son, Tsai Tsung 戴 涂, at the baths. In this case, however, the bull was more tractable and was induced, by the aid of gardeners armed with *P'a Tzu* 耙子, rakes, to desist from further activities, and no harm, except to the bull which went to the butchery, resulted, though his pizzle had actually entered Yi Hsün's anus which was notoriously on a Brobdingnagian scale, *vu ses instincts pédérastiques*.[21] As I can only *affirmer tenir le fait d'un témoin oculaire*,[22] not his son who was too filial to *Kan Fu Chih Ku* 幹父之蠱 (*Yi Ching* 易經, *Book of Changes*), betray his sire's (norms) defects, but from a near relation who actually saw the bull and *la bête humaine*[23] interlocked in carnal communion, I can naturally not guarantee its truth, while not for an instant doubting a matter regarding which falsity, or even hyperbole, would have been unfruitful *surérogation*.[24]

I was on visiting terms with a cousin of P'u Lun 溥倫, named P'u Chi 溥佶, a handsome youth of 23, with whom I could have sought, and probably attained, a closer intimacy, *ne fût-ce le dégoût que m'inspirait son penchant décidément un peu anormal*,[25] although heaven knows that I am no prude and ever ready to enter into others' feelings in affairs of the gratification of the sexual instinct.

It must have been in 1903, before my nearer intimacy with her whom Sir Edward Grey called *l'innommable*[26] (using French, though rather ignorant of that tongue), that I called one afternoon at his small *Fu* 府 (he

---

19 In the Holy Scriptures.
20 They who run across the sea change the sky, not their mind (*Epistles* I.XI.27).
21 In light of his pederastic instincts.
22 Affirm that I heard it from an eyewitness.
23 The human beast.
24 Overindulgence.
25 Except for the disgust that his slightly abnormal inclination inspired in me.
26 "The Unnameable". Sir Edward Grey (1862-1933) served as British Foreign Secretary from 1905 to 1916. Backhouse frequently writes of their close correspondence, but there is no known record of any direct communication between the two men.

was a *Pu Ju Pa Fen Kung* 不入八分公, i.e. of the minor nobility, ineligible for court duties, duke of the lowest rank (*déclassé*) and a descendant of one of K'ang Hsi's 康熙 undutiful – or said to be so – sons, I think Yün T'ang 允禟 who perished at the hands of his brother, Yung Cheng 雍正, and had become a Catholic, probably for the purpose of carrying on political intrigues with Jesuit fathers, of whom I have written elsewhere); some lack of coordination on the part of the *Men Che* 門者 or *Ssu Hun* 司閽, gatekeeper, caused my card (followed, as is customary, by myself, the caller, in its wake, the while the announcing servant holds the *bristol* (at that time the red strip of paper which was *de rigueur*)[27] bearing the visitor's name, over his left shoulder with the ideographs turned toward the caller and the gatekeeper's head slightly inclined with respect in the former's direction) to be taken in too soon. It was an unusual sight that met my startled vision: a small donkey and P'u Chi were both lying on the ground, the latter on a strip of *Liang Hsi* 涼蓆 or summer matting and the former in an advanced state of erection which exhibited a penis not inferior in length and thickness to that of Apuleius' ass. (It will be remembered that the story related to an amorous swain turned by enchantment into a donkey, whose sexual plenitude gained for him the love of many women; until the magic ceased to work and the beast reverted to his human state, whereupon the human lost his attraction and women became frigid in his regard.) P'u Chi was busy performing *P'in Hsiao* 品蕭, labial contact, with the ass, apparently to mutual satisfaction. The posture he had to assume impressed me as uncomfortable; but he had perforce *Pan T'u Erh Fei* 半途而廢 to stop halfway or *Kung K'uei I K'uei* 功虧一簣, to cease operations when on the verge of completion, as the Sage remarks in *Lun Yü* 論語 (literally: "the work only lacks one more basket of earth", a phrase which has become a household word). Naturally, what else could he do? The poor boy was bound by dictates of politeness to do no other than rise to receive me with a smiling welcome worthy of the Manchu aristocracy, for *le sang d'azur*[28] would not be denied, and he displayed the patrician's divine *insouciance*;[29] whatever his thoughts may have been I suspect that he said a good deal to the gatekeeper after my departure; but he carried off an embarrassing *impasse* with admirable sang-froid: "Glad to see you after so long; I was playing with my donkey: excuse me". He had risen (as I say) from the mat, and the ass marked the occasion by a very copious ejaculation, while we entered the guest-room. I often encountered P'u Chi thereafter, but, as I say, any sexual appetite, that might have been latent in my decidedly erotic dispositions, vanished for good and all. *Chacun son goût*[30] is as true now as on the day when Voltaire said it: probably my taste in love may seem as strange to the average reader as P'u Chi's so-called perversion of appetite appeared to myself.

---

27 Obligatory.
28 The blue blood.
29 Recklessness.
30 To each their own.

Another Manchu princeling, a relation of Prince Ch'ing, exchanged amorous affinities with a he-goat whose salacity (which is saying much) greatly exceeded the average eroticism of his libidinous species: goat and man regularly interchanged carnal association and apparently the process went merry as a marriage bell, without undue delays or otiose preliminaries, except that perhaps the initial stages in a love congress are the most intriguing of all; even more so than the supreme mood of passion, the desired, the desirable. P'u Huang (that was his name, 僙) was as comely as his ass-enamoured kinsman, P'u Chi (the house of Aisin-Gioro, so far as I knew them, and I knew many, perhaps sixty or more, was remarkable for the attractive looks of its members, particularly the men; but perhaps my idiosyncrasies make male beauty more noticeable in my sight). As a special mark of favour which I appreciated without sympathy for the *P'i* 癖 or proclivity, P'u Huang graciously allowed me to witness his copulative fervors which took place in his study at the back, the gate of the courtyard being barred with the *Men Shuan* 門閂. The animal's expression prior to the sexual act suggested to me the painting in the Naples Museum to which I have made allusion; it was exultant and expectant, much like a dog awaiting his dinner. Its sexual organ was as erect as P'u Huang's, which is saying a good deal: the latter, undeterred by my presence, took the goat's member in his hands and sucked it for a while without however bringing about an ejaculation. Then he inserted his comely penis inside the hircine fundament as far as the former's measure (of considerable longitude) permitted, proceeding with the act of sex from inception to consummation, the while the "randy" goat turned his eyes in his lover's direction with palpable appetite for more. After ejaculation had duly and more than adequately supervened (naturally I did not time the process but should guess that it occupied some six or seven minutes), the animal, as a mere man might have done, licked the now flabby *verge* with lustful ardour. Then he jumped upward and appeared to entreat the imperial duke to meet him half-way, in other words to present his libidinous buttocks and anal cavity in the posture which should facilitate the next development. Down went P'u Huang on the carpet, exhibiting his handsome posterior and enormous hairy anus, resembling rather a woman's vulva than the excretory orifice. The road was evidently familiar to the goat, for with obvious rapture he occupied the necessary strategic position and without let or hindrance pursued his rampant course to the end, not without, upon completion, copiously befouling P'u Huang's anal region with his thick, viscous sperm that had escaped back from the latter's rectum. I noticed that the young prince did not imitate the goat in licking the latter's *verge*: perhaps he did not savour it or, maybe, he thought that such a "sideshow" might not appeal to my critical tastes. The whole affair had little, to my thinking, of the *Mei Shu* 美術 or aesthetic aspect: perhaps I am a philistine, as in the Oscar Wilde trial the counsel for the prosecution, Sir Frank Lockwood (a friend of mine who, in my judgment, discredited himself by his merciless virulence in the trial), exclaimed in his violent peroration: "But men say that we are philistines in these matters: Let us thank God, gentlemen of the jury, that we are philistines, Men with honest and pure minds", *etcetera, ad nauseam*. No British jury, composed as this was, of petty and unimaginative small tradesmen, could possibly resist such an appeal and it faithfully convicted Wilde of "unnatural" offences, never having known Terence's immortal maxim: "*homo sum et nihil humanum a me alienum puto*:[31] I dare do all that may become a man." Both goat and prince had spent themselves: the former was fain to quaff a copious draught of water and the latter to open a bottle of sweet champagne, called by Britons in China the Taot'ai[32] 道台 brand, which I shared with him. He was quite frank and unashamed: told me that he had weekly (or more) congresses with the goat of his affections, that his wife was suspicious of their exact relations. "Mind you don't *Hsieh Lou* 洩漏, *éventer la mèche*,[33] when you meet her," said he. I could not help wondering what the duke could have believed of a foreign devil's capacity for unseemly indiscretions, in laying upon me so unnecessary a charge.

To the Old Buddha these practices were, I should think genuinely, uncongenial, although their exhibition did not fail to amuse her. After all, they only represent one facet of the many sided crystal of human vagaries. One evening, it may have occurred in the autumn of 1905, I had been pre-occupied in dalliance with Her Majesty, when she suddenly rose, saying: "I am about to take you to the bedroom of Yüan Yüan 瑗琬, of whom (though she defies even 'US') I am very fond, but her particular form of animal love disgusts me. She has a pet fox, about a year old, and I always call it Hu Hsien 狐仙, saint vulpine, for I really believe it possesses her and is endowed with spiritual qualities. I shall command her to play with Hu Hsien in erotic dalliance: you shall see the form in which her pronounced lust seizes her." So we to the fair one's room, and Her Majesty to introduce me. "We want to see you play with Hu Hsien: this 'devil' is of scientific taste, and would like to *K'ai K'ai Yen* 開開眼, gain initiation."

Yüan Yüan did not seem embarrassed and delivered to Her Majesty what I thought was a clever, if audacious, *réplique*.[34]

"Certainly, Old Buddha: *Shih Hao Pu T'ung* 嗜好不同, tastes differ: some people like intimacy with devils" (meaning me); "some with saints" (meaning the fox).

"You talk in riddles, my child, and have evidently been reading the *Liao Chai*[35] 聊齋. This gentleman is my professor in law but takes an interest in the world of spirits. Come! let us see you gambol with your fairy fox." Foxes are dangerous pets; the fifth duke of Richmond Charles

---

31 *Heauton Timorumenos* I.77.
32 Magistrate.
33 Reveal the plot.
34 Reply.
35 *Liao Chai Chih Yi* 聊齋誌異 (*Record of the Extraordinary*).

Gordon Lennox, descendant *de la main gauche*[36] of Charles II's beloved Nell Gwynn, died of rabies, after being affectionately licked, not bitten, by his pet animal.

She took off all her clothes and displayed herself in the fullness of her radiant unveiled beauty which appealed to my normally unsensitive (where women are concerned) habit of mentality. The fox crouched at her side and allowed the Old Buddha to stroke him, but was definitely hostile to me, the interloper. He jumped on to her lap and, as she opened wide her fairy legs, licked with evident savour her beautiful clitoris and vulva.

I know not whether the vulpine tribe is normally lascivious but can vouch for this particular member of the fraternity, be he saint (as the Old Buddha declared) or beast, as no less erotic than Her Majesty herself. He ejaculated in moderate profusion on and around her pudenda, then descended from his tactical position and crouched once more at his dear mistress' feet, growling (if which is the right word or should it be murmuring) menacingly, as I sought to pet him.

"Thank you," said Her Majesty; "your predilection is really *I Lu Ping* 一路病, a pathological affection; but *Pu Tê I* 不得已, *Shih T'ien Jan Ti* 是天然的, you cannot help it, it is natural to you. What will your fiancé say if he hears of it? Will he not *Tui Hu Hsien Yeh Ch'ih Ts'u* 對狐仙爺吃醋, be jealous of the sainted animal?"

"A man," said Yüan Yüan rather archly looking toward me, "has no call to be jealous of a divinity; if my future husband disapproves, *Tsai Chi Ch'i Shen* 災及其身 (as the Classic has it),[37] he will invite misfortune on himself." Then, to the Empress with whom she was evidently quite at ease, and in fact the Old Buddha rather appreciated a certain kind of jest which did not infringe on her imperial dignity: "Suppose Your Majesty, which is not the case, had an erotic passion for anything, I presume that you would keep it secret from the *Wang Kung Po Kuan* 王公百官, princes and high officials? Even so I am not bound to explain to my betrothed the intricacies and recesses of my inmost soul, *le fond et le tréfond de mon âme*."

"Well, well," said the Old Buddha; "people speculate about me, as it is, giving full rein to their imaginations and perverted fancies. I regard their chatter just as the east wind in a horse's ear, *Ma Erh Tung Feng* 馬耳東風, with unabated indifference; but, if they compel me," (which was said in a menacing tone) "I know how to deal with them, and my hand is heavy. Come, *Pa Hou Yeh* 巴侯爺, we will return. Good night, Fox lordship, and good night, Yüan Yüan: we leave you to your diversions."

"I humbly thank Your Majesty for the signal honour of your visit. *Sheng Chia Tz'u Lin* 聖駕慈臨, *Kan Hsieh Wu Ming* 感謝無名, *T'ien Kao Ti Hou* 天高地厚, *Yung Pu Kan Wang* 永不敢忘. Your favours are all embracing and unforgettable."

---

36 On the left hand.

37 *Hsün Tzu* 荀子, a Confucian text written around the 3rd century BC by the philosopher of the same name.

UN TRAIT ORIGINAL

My pages deal more often with homosexuality than with the *soi-disant* normal intercourse between man and woman. Among the many Manchu princes and aristocrats for whom sexual gratification chiefly connoted *coitus a tergo*[38] preferably with males, however necessary normal commerce might be for the purpose of procreating an heir, I found it an almost invariable custom to preserve in a sort of *reliquaire pour les choses laïques*,[39] like an amulet or talisman, specimens of pubic and anal hair from the *Luan T'ung* 孌童 (*Kagema* 陰間 in Japanese, "Behind the scenes", or male prostitute, also *Wakashu* 若衆, *Jigo* 稚兒, "something young") or of those admitted to their intimacy. Prince P'u Lun once proudly exhibited to me a gold casket which contained perhaps a score of such amorous trophies beautifully mounted on cloisonné plaques and neatly labelled according to their *provenance* together with the date of the event. It was his predilection to savour with nose and lips *ces trophées d'amour*,[40] even as one who fights his battles o'er again and handles in old age the claymore that none save he once could wield. Equally did sundry of these carnally minded exquisites love to retain as cherished souvenirs strips of silk (ay! and less savoury relics with excremental traces, unlovely manifestations of poor humanity's elemental needs) which had served their purpose to wipe away the residual sperm dripping from urethral and anal orifices subsequently to completion of *jouissance*.[41] It is, of course, known that the Dalai Lama's solid excrements are powdered and preserved by the devoted faithful in tiny, gold cases inscribed with *Dharani* or incantations to Buddha. But this custom belongs to religion, not to love and lust. These pious relics were often known as *Hsi Shih Chih Pao* 稀世之寶, *rarissime*[42] jewel; and I would not doubt but that their loss would have entailed very genuine grief to the possessor; recalling as they did a fond memory, sweet as remembered kisses after death; even as in Europe it used to be the custom (perhaps is still) to place a dead parent's or lover's hair in chased gold or jewelled locket to be worn on the watch-chain.

"*Ohimé!*"[43] what a subject for a Juvenal or a Martial satirizing for posterity the *luxure* of imperial Rome *et les moeurs de la décadence*.[44]

---

38   Intercourse from behind.
39   Shrine for secular things.
40   These trophies of love.
41   Orgasm.
42   Extremely rare.
43   My goodness.
44   Lust . . . and the mores of decadence.

CHAPTER XI

A HAIR-BREADTH ESCAPE

(WEI CHI I FA 危機一髮)

IT must have been early in August 1906 (by the Lunar Calendar 6th of VII Moon) that the Old Buddha, who was rapidly acquiring the habit of exacting from me onerous, if honourable *corvées*,[1] sent Lien-ying 蓮 英 to request my attendance for the following day, the 7th, at the Summer Palace with an actor named Hsing Chüeh 幸玨 (Hsing was his *nom de guerre*, but his *nom de famille*[2] was Yin 殷), then appearing at the San Ch'ing Yüan[3] 三慶園 in Ta Cha Lan'rh 大柵欄兒 (or Ta Shih Lan'rh[4] 大 事欄兒) outside Ch'ien Men 前門 in feminine parts, like my dear Liu Ch'ang 柳昌 of great beauty and charm, the desired of many Manchu patricians, one whose heart was all a flame, whose soul was all a lust. The Empress wished him to *Hsien Yi* 獻藝, present his art; while obviously desiring his nearer and more intimate association. In her letter of command she bade me prepare a private "rehearsal" before her of *Kuei Fei Tsui Chiu* 貴妃醉酒, Yang 楊 the imperial consort of Ming Huang 明 皇, overcome by the winecup; Fa Men Ssu 法門寺, the temple of Buddhist law; and *T'ien Ho P'ei* 天河配, *the Union of the Milky Way*, usually played on Ch'i Yüeh Ch'i Hsi[5] 七月七夕; but I was to *Fan Ch'uan* 反串, reverse my usual part, representing His Majesty the emperor instead of his adored consort, – Liu Chin 劉瑾, whose fortune, when confiscated after his death, was found to amount to over 60 million Taels, the notorious eunuch of the eccentric Wu Tsung 武宗 or Cheng Tê 正德 (as his reign was entitled), a *Hua Tan* 花旦 or semi-comedy, half burlesque,

---

1   Chores.

2   "War name" or pseudonym . . . "family name".

3   "Three Celebrations Theatre". The San Ch'ing Theatre was an expensive venue, popular with Peking's literati in late Ch'ing era China. The scholar Shen T'ai-mo (1864-1924) described the atmosphere as follows: "The little boy-actors from the San Ch'ing, Ssu-hsi and Ch'un-t'ai troupes usually participate in three sessions, after which they stand stage right and left, and gaze toward the balcony. If they notice familiar guests they hurry upstairs to sit with them . . . these parties are not interested in theatre, and before the second to last act ends they leave for restaurants with their favourites." It should be noted, however, that the San Ch'ing troupe did not perform exclusively at the San Ch'ing Theatre.

4   A commercial district outside of the Ch'ien Men, which began to flourish in the Yung-lo period of the Ming Dynasty (1403-24).

5   "The Seventh Day of the Seventh Moon", a Chinese holiday celebrating the annual union of the cowherd and the weaving maid, normally separated by the Milky Way.

part instead of the injured female whom he rescues – and the amorous cowherd in lieu of the weaver-maid; while Hsing played the female part. As the court custom of "command" theatricals was time-honoured and would create no comment, Hsing and I were to present ourselves at the Palace gates in the capacity of mimes: it appeared somewhat farcical, since I was well known to the guards and eunuchs on duty not as an actor but as Her Majesty's supposed professor of the Law of Nations, as well as her recognized *Ch'ung Ch'en* 寵臣, favourite. However, my moral reputation probably had not much further to sink, as naturally the worst interpretation appealed to scandal-mongers; in fact, César Borgia or the Marquis d'Ancre[6] were nothing compared to me; so Hsing and I started next afternoon in Peking carts with *Hsing T'ou* 型頭 or the theatrical appointments on a limited scale and the necessary troupe of players and *comparses*[7] who travelled separately. It was to be an entirely private representation on the Empress' miniature stage and not a court function in the imperial theatre to which princes and high officials were formally invited. Hsing was of exceptional beauty with a lovely olive complexion, eyes which simply radiated desire, the most adorable mouth in the world, moth eyebrows, a delicate nose with the least little delectable tilt and a musical voice which demanded, and inspired, love and lust.

I had no doubt about the Old Buddha's welcome to Hsing: her standards of male beauty were by now familiar, my own attraction to her was independent of physical considerations and was due to her wish to be amused. We were received in her outer boudoir, where later Ts'en Ch'un-hsüan 岑春煊 was to tremble before the infuriated despot. She asked Hsing many questions about the stage, with which she had an exceptional acquaintance. Then, dismissing Lien-ying but bidding me remain, she made the actor undress and present his comely nudity to her doting, abundant expectancy. "You shall stay, Pa Hou 巴侯, and prevent him from feeling nervous." This desire for publicity in sexual relations seemed to be a *réversion au naturel de l'homme.*[8] At least, it did not embarrass Hsing who at once achieved a supernormal erection and proudly exhibited to the Empress that something attractive and pretty wherewith she wished to play. She allowed to him full play of his fancy, in fact asked him "*Na I Chung Shun Ni Hsin* 那一種順你心, which form (of amorousness) do you affect?" exactly as a prostitute arranging an erotic programme with a client. Answering her own question, she started by slapping his capacious buttocks, then presented to him her clitoris to titillate. Naturally, the schedule had no novelty for me, but, when the moment of achieved copulation was near, I asked Her Majesty if I should withdraw and leave them alone in their glory.

---

6   Cesare Borgia (1475-1507), son of Pope Alexander XI, was a Catholic cardinal turned soldier and statesman. Marquis d'Ancre refers to Concino Concini (1575-1617), a prominent Italian politician in the court of Louis XIII of France, later assassinated on the king's orders. Both Borgia and Concini had a reputation for treachery and were posthumously vilified.

7   Extras in theatrical performances.

8   Reversion to the natural state of man.

"No," she said, "*Wu So Chü Ni*[9] 無所拘泥, there's no cause to feel uncomfortable"; and in truth there was not, for Hsing played his part to perfection, slowly and in measured cadence, exactly what Her Majesty desired in those admitted to her favours.

I admired Hsing's sang-froid and thought him a promising pupil, having told him not to be in the least disturbed by the unusual nature of the honour. He timed his ejaculation to a nicety and the Old Buddha exclaimed: "*T'ung K'uai Chi La* 痛快極啦, tis most pleasant."

"I congratulate you," (to me) "on your adept: he is a worthy *Men Jen* 門人 or disciple. Well, now I am satisfied, *Chih Tsu* 知足, for the moment and am going to regale myself with a few whiffs of opium. Call Lien-ying." Then she directed him to take us to the stage and to begin preparations for the rehearsal, promising not to fail us a little later.

Hsing was a professional and I a mere amateur; he was, however, a most convincing and helpful partner and, as we started going over the *Kuei Fei Tsui Chiu* 貴妃醉酒, I could see that his histrionic range could partly cloak my obvious defects, although perhaps for an amateur I was tolerably efficient, but not outstanding by professional comparison.

The Empress, like Queen Victoria, was an ideal personage to play before: she knew the "business" well, in fact had the "book" by heart and was most generous in awarding applause. There were only a few court ladies and eunuchs present; but we none of us felt that we were playing to empty benches and Her Majesty complimented me on my rendering of Liu Chin 劉瑾 with his sardonic humour.

Much to my delight, after the three plays had been presented, the Old Buddha announced for the *bouquet* her intention of taking the part of the weaver maiden in *T'ien Ho P'ei* 天河配, *the Union of the Galaxy*, with me as the swain. It reminded me a little of Marie Antoinette playing at the Salle de Spectacle de Trianon *Le Devin du Village*[10] and modestly apologizing to the audience for her deficiencies; for at the end Her Majesty expressed to the small audience her regret that her histrionic ability was not up to the measure of her desires.

Among the audience was the lady in waiting Yüan Yüan 媛婉 of whom I have spoken – the Empress, after ordering a feast for the performers and bestowing on the professionals a liberal endowment, bade Hsing Chüeh, after the unsightly coats of stage paints and bedaubment had been removed, come to the "front" and be presented to the eager maid of honour. What the Old Buddha could not forgive in me, when I smuggled the fair Chan Pao-ch'en 占寶臣 into her palace, she looked at with indifferent eyes when herself the dispenser of favours. "Yüan Yüan, you are often lonely and I have brought to you a beautiful boy to share your couch. He has my leave to spend the night with you." Yüan Yüan, nothing loth, thanked the Empress and the two took leave of Her Majesty, both on pleasure bent; while she called to me to accompany her for a trip on the lake which on this occasion was calm and unruffled as a mirror.

---

9   *Chü Ni* can mean hemmed in by convention or precedent; it also can mean slow-witted.
10   Jean-Jacques Rousseau's *Village Soothsayer* at Salle de Spectacle de Trianon (Versailles Palace).

At that time, owing, I fancy, to Flammarion, and the novelist Wells' predictions,[11] there was a great deal of interest manifested in court and literary circles in Peking regarding a possible invasion of the earth from Mars. The Old Buddha had taken the *chimera* rather more seriously than I should have expected from one of her astuteness. "You know," said she, "that you are my loyal admirer; please tell me what the position in International Law would be if 'Martian' airships invaded China?"

"I assure Your Majesty, *sauf votre respect*,[12] that such a possibility does not exist; it is a case of *Tsui Chung Shuo Meng Hua* 醉中說夢話, the ravings of one overcome with wine, to write as my compatriot does in his novel. But, should the invaders indeed come, they would be free-booters like the Angles who invaded my country after the Roman evacuation some 1,500 years ago, sea-pirates who, however, achieved their purpose, whereas 'over-planetary' bandits, owing to atmospheric conditions, could never possibly attempt the inter-spatial journey."

Then Her Majesty changed the subject and spoke of Hsing Chüeh and Yüan Yüan: "I suppose they are gambolling together at this moment. He's a delicious boy; but don't be jealous, for I must have for constant 'use' (she used the expression *Yung* 用 which, though not very polite, exactly savoured of her mind) someone like yourself who has *K'ou Ts'ai* 口才, is quick of tongue. By the way," to Lien-ying who was kneeling at her feet, "see that the two lovers have a good meal and you may order for them champagne which Yüan Yüan affects and plenty of cigarettes. I shall expect you, Pa Hou, as usual about midnight and we will amuse ourselves, as befits the occasion of Ch'i Yüeh Ch'i Hsi 七月七夕, 7th of VII Moon, to the heart's content till dawn summons me to the meeting of the Council."

I asked the Old Buddha whether the family into which Yüan Yüan was going to marry would not be irate at the discovery that she was not *virgo intacta*.

Her Majesty to reply: "Doubtless her *P'o P'o* 婆婆, mother-in-law, will make the usual test with the *Ch'i Ma Pu*[13] 騎馬布 and be annoyed to find no blood on the cloth after the first conjugal night; but I shall rectify that possible cause of misunderstanding by saying: *Shen Kung Chih Shih* 深宮之事, *Ni Huan Pu Chih Tao Ma* 你還不知道麼; *Shih Wen Nan Tzu Tsemmo Hui Ju Nei Ts'ao Wo Che'rh Ti Kung Nü* 試問男子怎麼會入內裔我這兒的宮女? Surely, surely you can't be unaware of things in the profound seclusion of the palace. Pray tell me how could a male find means of entering and of possessing my maids of honour!"

The Empress asked me whether European practice permitted copulation between affianced lovers before marriage.

I replied that it was not the custom, but, in Mephistopheles' words, "Custom or not, it happens though."

---

11 Camille Flammarion (1842-1925) was a French astronomer whose book *La planète Mars et ses conditions d'habitabilité* suggested the existence of a life form on Mars superior to humans. "Wells' predictions" refers to H.G. Wells' *War of the Worlds*, where Earth is attacked by Martians.
12 With all due respect.
13 Horse-riding blanket.

"Yes," said the Old Buddha, "we call it *T'an Tao* 探道, ascertaining the road, preliminary survey."

Again changing the subject, the Empress asked my opinion about future flying possibilities. (At this time, a few sensational experimental flights had been made; but beyond that the prospect seemed fantastical.) As I am, so to say, kneeling at the confessional and recording that which I must in bounden duty admit before the priest, namely my long chapter of sins against the divine law, I may as well not deny my want of perspective, proving myself a sorry prophet indeed, in saying to the Old Buddha that I did not believe in practical flight ever becoming more than a dream of wild imaginings!!

Her Majesty, treading on delicate ground, begged me to define the exact nature of the pleasure derived to the "pathic" by pedication (I might, knowing the Old Buddha's tastes in this connection, have made an obvious retort, but reverence forbade). "I can comprehend," said she, "that the tightness (*Chin* 緊) of the hinder orifice affords superabundant satisfaction to the giver, but wherein lies the gratification to the recipient of being possessed *a tergo*?"

"I suppose, Your Majesty, people are differently constructed, just as one person relishes caviar and another mite-ridden cheese" ("I hate cheese," exclaimed the Old Buddha); "what is one person's ecstasy is another's agony. But, as the 6th Prince, Liu Yeh 六爺 (Prince Kung 恭) once said, the pleasure to a male in being possessed from behind is not other than the happiness of its *essor*[14] to the bird or the roaming of the fish in the sea, gaining, as the Sage saith, its natural element, *Te Ch'i So* 得其所. Nay, 'tis even as the flower which owes its beauty to the grower, even as the gem its lustre to the miner, as the ship with the winds over her, with the waters under her, so is it with him to whom is accorded this esoteric bliss."

"Did Yi Hsin 奕訢, Kung Chung Ch'in Wang 恭忠親王," (Chung 忠 was his canonized name of Loyal) "really say that? He was, as I know well, speaking from a tried and lengthy experience, for he was even more enamoured of the practice than you yourself, old Pa!" And Her Majesty laughed, as did Lien-ying, for they invariably found my frankness disarming and somewhat ridiculous; although Lien-ying was fully sympathetic toward the abnormality. I wondered how much the launch attendants, who were looking on open-eyed with a broad grin on their faces and drinking in every word, comprehended of this conversation. The Old Buddha asked me, as she had heard from her minister in Seoul, whether it was true that Sir John Jordan, the British Minister to Korea, now appointed to Peking, was, as she had heard, an ardent pederast.[15]

"Rumour's many-tongued voice makes free with his name, Old Buddha; but when in Seoul he was like a fed horse in the morning (*Chao*

---

14 Taking flight.
15 Here, as elsewhere in his writing, the author attacks a former business associate. Foreign Minister Jordan regrettably involved the British Government in an elaborate arms deal during the First World War, using Backhouse as the intermediary with Chinese partners. The weapons never materialized and Backhouse was suspected by Jordan of inventing the whole scenario including the Chinese partners, though Backhouse never benefitted materially from the transaction.

Chung Pao Ma 朝中飽馬) where women are concerned, as is Your Majesty's Inspector of Customs, Ho Te (Hart),[16] who has been caught in the act times out of number."

"You 'devils' seem all devoid of moral sense: I heard of a Protestant missionary, who contracted blood-poisoning from possessing a third rate prostitute in *pedicatio Ts'ao P'i Ku* 肏屁股. Well, it is time to go back. I shall have supper and a short sleep after my opium pipe, and then . . . . . and then . . . . . !!"

As I looked at the lake which reflected the latest rays of the setting sun, I thought of the fatal cataclysm of the previous year when the forked levin suddenly enlightened the face of the waters, till then blacker than Erebus in their cimmerian darkness,[17] and they became (an instant!) white as a ghost disshrouded and stript bare of its cerements in that infernal convulsion. So we reached the landing stage, half expecting that Hsing Chüeh and his lady friend would be there to meet us. "*T'a Men Mang* 他們忙, they are busy, *Pan Li Ssu Shih* 辦理私事, over their private affairs, *Pu Pi Ching Tung T'a Men* 不必驚動他們, don't disturb them," said the Old Buddha.

So sovereign and subject went their several ways. I was pleased, on entering my room, to meet again the fair misnamed eunuch Lien Tzu-yen 連子延 with the large tool but somewhat subtracted testicles, of whom I have written a description on the occasion of our very erotic night at the Pi Mo Yen 碧默巖 Temple. He had been away on leave, seemed really pleased to see me; unbeknown to Her Majesty, with Lien-ying's obliging cooperation, we passed a joyous hour and I marvelled at the plenitude of his cyclopean *rigida* (to quote Cicero's letter to Atticus)[18] as of a *conviva nunquam satur*, one who can never take enough, and at the dauntless virility which came and came again. He told me that the Old Buddha made him titillate her *alauda*[19] (again Ciceronian for *Yin T'i* 陰蒂 or clitoris) and that Her Majesty found his male colossal development as welcome a phenomenon in the palace environment (*rara avis in terris*)[20] as it was gratifying to her sexual obsessions. Very surely, I needed no artificial stimulus in this glorious dalliance; but the time soon passed, ay, all too soon for us, and the Empress called me once again to her couch for night duty.

I am not going to rehearse, like an actor never weary of what he falsely terms his "farewell" performance, the path of true love on that auspicious 7th of VII Moon; for I have a sadder duty to perform in recounting what befell in the bed-chamber of the fair Yüan Yüan only one courtyard

---

16   Sir Robert Hart (1835-1911), an Ulsterman popular with British and Manchu officials, served as the head of the Chinese Imperial Maritime Customs Service for many years. Backhouse sometimes did translation work for the Customs Service under Hart.

17   Erebus is the darkness between Earth and Hades in Greek mythology and the Cimmerians the people who dwell there.

18   "Rigidity" (penis). This is not actually from Cicero, but most likely from Catullus 56: "*hunc ego, si placet Dionae, protelo rigida mea cecidi*" (and, so please you, Dione, for lack of a weapon I slayed him with my own rigidity. [Smithers]).

19   The name of a species of lark.

20   A rare bird on the earth (Juvenal, *Satires* VI.165).

to the west from the Old Buddha's boudoir. It was about 3 a.m.; the latter and I were indulging in our usual tactics interspersed with occasional variations of theme that Her Majesty's fertile invention suggested. Suddenly, we heard an awful shriek and then another.

The Empress was startled and angry: "This is really insupportable, it sounds to me like nightmare, *Sa I Cheng*[21] 撤嚜症. I am going to see what is afoot; you are to attend me." The sounds came from the west, but I did not at the moment apprehend that it was poor Hsing Chüeh's voice raised in frantic pain. Her Majesty's ears were quicker than mine: "I am certain that the shrieks are from Yüan Yüan's room, but it is not her voice. It must be *your friend*" (I thought this thrust to be rather unfair, as after all I was only indirectly responsible for Hsing's introduction to the "profound seclusion of the Palace"); "really, it is too much; you seem to bring trouble in your train." The Old Buddha was in an exceedingly irritable temper; her nerves were on edge and she always hated sudden noises. On we went toward Yüan's bedroom, where a light was burning; heartrending groans were audible, and to my horror I recognized the dear catamite's accents which seemed to be growing feebler, as if he were overcome by the pain and were about to swoon. "What on earth is the matter?" cried the Old Buddha; "*Ni Men Pa Wo Hsia Ssu* 你們把我吓死, you have frightened me out of my wits; *Che Ch'eng Shemmo Chü Mien* 這成什麼局面, this is a pretty state of things; *Shen Ching T'ien'rh Huan Yao Na Mo Jang Ma* 深更天兒還要那麼嚷麼? what does this shrieking mean in the dead of night?"

"Oh! Your Majesty! forgive me; it is Fairy Fox, Hu Hsien 狐仙, he has bitten poor Pao-shan 寶善 (Hsing's courtesy name) right on the *Yang Wu* 陽物, penis, close to the *Ma Yen* 馬眼, meatus, and he is dripping with blood. It was the pain that made him shriek and see, Old Buddha, he has fainted away! I think he is about to die. Oh! Old Buddha, have pity, I love him so dearly."

Hu Hsien was crouching in the corner; his eyes did not look natural to me; there was an unhealthy redness apparent in his stare and he was making strange guttural noises. Poor Hsing was in a dead faint and bleeding profusely from his urethral orifice. With Lien-ying's timely aid (he had heard the cries and hurried to ascertain what had occurred) I managed with a kerchief of Yüan Yüan's to make a sort of clumsy bandage and to stay the flow of blood. Of course, there were no competent doctors nor anyone with surgical training available, and I am as helpless as a newborn babe in such emergencies.

Yüan Yüan, through her copious tears, explained what had happened: they had passed a rapturous night and after several copulations, Hsing was "airing his tool" *Liang Ch'iao Tzu* 晾巧子 in proximity to her *Pi* 屄, vulva. She said that she had completely forgotten Hu Hsien's presence, but he had refused food and water on the previous evening and had spent the night on his mat in the corner. All of a sudden, he had rushed forward and jumped at Hsing's penis which he held on to and

---

21 Talking, tossing and turning in one's sleep.

seemed to tear viciously. (The wound was jagged and reminded me of a bite I had two years previously received on the wrist of which I still have the scar from a "pet" monkey.)

Said the Old Buddha: "Bring *Shao Chiu* 燒酒, ardent spirit, and I'll bathe his *Ch'iao Tzu* 巧子, tool, because your 'fairy' saintship's bite may be poisonous."

After she had suited action to the word, the intense pain aroused poor Hsing Chüeh who said: "Oh! Your Majesty, I am going to die, the pain is more than I can bear."

The Empress patted his head: "Poor little boy, make your mind easy. I shall see that you have proper treatment at the *Kuei Tzu I Yüan* 鬼子醫院, the devil's hospital," meaning (I found) what was then called the Lock-hart Hospital near the former Ketteler Memorial *P'ai Lou* 牌樓. "You will require to have at least a month's rest, and I shall present you with Taels 3,000 over and above the hospital fees for your loss of time. Meantime, I am going to wrap a rag soaked in kerosene round your poor *Ch'iao Tzu* which only yesterday I loved to fondle and play with." Kerosene is often used by Chinese as a specific for scorpion stings; there seemed to be no carbolic preparations available, for I remembered that my intense pain from the monkey's bite had been relieved by a weak carbolic solution.

I felt extremely uneasy about the consequences of the wound, for, ignorant as I was, I thought that Hu Hsien was suffering from rabies and the apparent difficulty in swallowing seemed to confirm my lay diagnosis. Yüan Yüan bade her lover recline on her settee; he took a glass of champagne and some potion produced by Li Lien-ying which certainly revived him. Her Majesty decided that I should take him with me to the city and arranged that a eunuch escorted him to the hospital with an imperial order that all expenses would be provided by the Privy Purse.

The Old Buddha and I left him to rest undisturbed, so far as the pain permitted. Arrived at her boudoir, I went on my knees and implored Her Majesty to pardon me. It seemed that there was a relentless curse in my wake: Liu Ch'ang 柳昌 had been struck by lightning and now the equally beautiful Hsing Chüeh had been bitten by a fox, which, as I told Her Majesty, I believed to be mad. I mentioned that the head of the house of Gordon Lennox, the duke of Richmond and Gordon in England, had died from the saliva of a rabid fox which licked, without biting, His Grace's hand. She asked me if there were no cure, and I informed her that the Pasteur treatment often succeeded but that I believed it was not available in North China. The Old Buddha was alarmed when I pointed out that the bite of a rabid animal was normally fatal, also that the beast's saliva was poisonous, so that its proclivities in applying its tongue to Yüan Yüan's private parts must be ruthlessly checked.

"May I implore Your Majesty," I proceeded, *avec des larmes dans la voix,*[22] God knows genuine and heartfelt, "not to command of me again to bring actors or beautiful youths into the palace."

---

22 With tears in the voice.

"Stop a moment," interrupted Her Majesty; "who brought Chan Wei 占偉 to the Lake Palace?"

"But to make arrangements according to your *bon plaisir*[23] through the Chief Eunuch? I am very guilty in regard to Chan, but Madame, you forgave me; and it is borne in upon me that disaster after disaster will occur, if I am again the intermediary. I am of a superstitious nature and it is some *influence néfaste*[24] that emanates from my person and is due to that dreadful influence of Saturn at the hour of my birth, *Ch'u Tu* 初度 (the actual hour of birth, in my case, the hour of the Monkey 猴 *Hou*, thus foretelling my future marquisate or 侯 *Hou*).

Her Majesty acceded to my prayer though ridiculing my *craintes de surérogation*[25] and bade me prepare to return to town after the audience to the Council, for she disliked my being seen by the officials of the latter. I was on the verge of exhaustion, but her activities had in no way abated; so that I had perforce once again to strain my tired energies and give to her the sexual collaboration that she so salaciously sought.

To conclude the story on a happier note, Hsing Chüeh was duly admitted to the hospital and his frightfully torn and lacerated *Ch'iao Tzu* gradually healed. Despite my advice to chain him, Hu Hsien bit two eunuchs and one maid-servant. My prognosis had been correct, like the *Hsia Mao Chuang Ssu Hao Tzu* 瞎貓撞死耗子, *Chuang Shang La* 撞上啦, the blind cat lights upon a dead rat, a lucky find; or, in this case, an (unlucky) fluke or *raccroc*: the beast *was* rabid, but, being supposedly divine, was left to its own devices, dying some days later. Of those whom it had bitten, one of the two eunuchs and the maid both developed hydrophobia[26] and died in agony. The other eunuch, Hsing Chüeh, and Yüan Yüan whom it had habitually licked, escaped scotfree.

After Hsing's discharge from the hospital (he did not know that the period of incubation might be as long as a year or even more, but as a fact no sinister consequences ensued) he came to see me, exclaiming ruefully: "My tool is sadly disfigured and the scar will be with me for life. For one of my profession an injury to the private parts is as serious as the loss of voice to a singer or the amputation of a hand to the fiddler or artist."

"But," replied I, "you must be thankful that your hand escaped any hurt: it is such a useful organ!"

"So is the *Ch'iao Tzu*," rejoined Hsing. "Mine was ornamental and artistic (he proceeded) into the bargain, and today it is scarred and hideous, *Sed Fortuna fuit*;[27] *Pu Sheng Chin Hsi Chih Kan* 不勝今昔之感, things are sadly changed."

We were standing in my second courtyard, and I was escorting him, *Pu Yüan Sung* 不遠送, towards the gate. There was a wonderful lunar rainbow, and as I looked at him, I exclaimed: "How fair thou standest in

---

23 Good pleasure.
24 Nefarious influence.
25 Fear of going beyond the call of duty.
26 Rabies.
27 "But fortune has been" (Virgil, *Aeneid* VII.413), i.e. is no more, has passed away.

the moonlight! Your fair face never was more fair. If much is taken, much abides; let us thank Buddha that your charm will not pass with the long years away. Every day that you were in hospital was an age to me: *I Jih Pu Chien Yen Jo San Ch'iu*[28] 一日不見儼若三秋. How like a winter hath thine absence been!"

"Well," said Hsing, "I must not let clients see nor touch the attraction that once was mine; it must remain a mystery except to such as you who knew it in happier days; and after all its activity and usefulness are unimpaired despite the jealous fox of the Wan Shou Shan 萬壽山. But you know that a one-legged man discards ornament because his personal appearance lacks attraction, *Chieh Che Ch'e Hua Wai Fei Yü Yeh* 介者撤畫外非譽也." (*Chuang Tzu* 莊子.)

He left for Wuch'ang 武昌 in 1907 and achieved a considerable reputation in Hupei 湖北.

CHAPTER XII

THE MANTLE OF CAGLIOSTRO

THE Taoist pope, Chang T'ien Shih 張天師, whose position is hereditary,[1] arrived in Peking from Kiangsi 江西 during the summer of 1906 (Kuang Hsü 光緒 32) and was, as his rank in the hierarchy befitted, accorded an audience by the Old Buddha.[2] In his suite was a *Lin Ch'iung* 臨邛 (Szechuan 四川) itinerant Taoist named Hsing Hsüan 幸玄 (In those days Hsüan was written 玄 or else changed into 元 owing to it being K'ang Hsi's 康熙 personal name, *Miao Hui Ching Pi*[3] 廟諱敬避. He was also called 星玄 "astrologer" and sometimes, why I do not know, *Hsing* 幸 which is a surname but also in his case implied a "lucky" significa-tion, as *Hsing* means "good fortune" which is what one wants from an augur!! But he also used the patronymic of *Jen* 任, why, I do not know), whose physiognomy was that of an ascetic Brahmin and I believe that he came of Indian stock. He was a Sanskrit scholar and spoke Parbuti or Nepali more fluently than Chinese. It had become the use and wont of the Empress to summon me for multifarious honorary duties[4] (when I say honorary, she always indemnified me, not in lucre[5] but in rich gifts, for my loss of time, and generously recompensed my retainers), so that it was no great cause of astonishment to receive an order to ar-range for a "secret" (in so far as anything the Old Buddha might be preoccupied with could be called secret) séance at which only she, Li Lien-ying 李蓮英, Ts'ui Tê-lung 崔德隆 beside Jen Hsüan 任玄 and myself would assist. A great believer in omens and soothsayers, like Henriette Marie de France, wife of Charles I with her Lady Elinor Lennox, or still more Catherine de Médicis with her dear Ruggieri (*Caro Cosimo Mio*),[6]

---

1   "Heavenly Master Chang", a highly elevated and exclusive title.
2   Some Chinese sources, not beyond reproach, claim that Chang T'ien Shih was denied an official audience with T'zu Hsi but it is possible that he was given a private audience.
3   More commonly translated as "temple name" (the name of the deceased Emperor).
4   **Backhouse:** Occasionally, I thought that she was retaliating in a playful way for my audacity in introducing the fair young Chan Pao-ch'en 占寶臣 into the palace for his love affair with the lady for whom the Old Buddha graciously *"Shuan Hun"* 拴婚 brought about wedlock, after chastising my luckless naked buttocks with a switch, in order to hurt my "face" rather than my body.
5   Money.
6   "My dear Cosimo", the Italian astrologer and soothsayer Cosimo Ruggieri (d. 1615), brought to the French court by Catherine de Médicis as an adviser and a spy.

being also uneasy about the future, she was determined to consult him in the Tung Yüeh 東嶽 Taoist temple, outside the Ch'i Hua 齊化 Gate. On the rare occasions (I fancy only five in all since the death of Hsien Feng 咸豐) that the Empress Dowager visited the Eastern Tombs in full state and pomp, it was her custom to take a rest and refreshment at this temple; but for the visit now projected she required a strict incognito and planned to go late at night, the city gate being specially opened for Her Majesty, attended only by a single *Shih Wei* 侍衛 or officer of the guards. It appeared to me that these excursions of a very active and inquisitive old lady, whose face was of late years as well known as that of the late Kaiser Wilhelm II in Berlin, to the people of Peking, since her photograph was everywhere obtainable, were not devoid of risk; neither did I relish the new responsibility placed on my shoulders.

Howsoever, my despot mistress called me: I must not say no and at once visited Hsing Hsüan who was staying at the Po Yün Kuan 白 雲觀, White Cloud Taoist Temple of which I may write again. Learning my mission, he naturally received me with *empressement*[7] which was enhanced when he found that I knew Sanskrit and Nepalese (the latter slightly).

He was curiously modest respecting his qualifications, while admitting that the future was revealed to him, as well as past incidents in the careers of those who consulted him with absolute sincerity (*Ch'ien Ch'eng* 虔誠) and a spirit of devotion. But, as to the future, he drew a metaphor from a sailing ship which ran somewhat as follows (the original being in doggerel I have rendered it in equally trivial verse): "Two ships fast sailing, one east, one west, but the wind's toward the sunset blowing. Tis the set of the sail and not the gale, in home port both safely bestowing" (i.e. fate can be averted by human effort: there's no such word as inevitable, which was an *obiter dictum*[8] of the greatest man who ever lived, Napoléon). He took my horoscope, spoke of the "dreadful influence" of Saturn ascendant at the hour of my birth, made several prophecies which have been remarkably fulfilled, besides one (I think now that he meant death: like Spencer's "Death is the end of woes; die soon o Faery son") which I cannot so far explain: "Out of fortune misfortune; out of misfortune fortune," which resembles an epitaph in Bourg cathedral on the tomb of a Duchesse de Bourgogne, fair but *infelix*:[9] "Fortuna Infortuna Fortuna", although I believe that in this case Fortuna is an elision for *Forti una*, "To the brave fortune and misfortune are one".[10] Certain adventures of my life prior to meeting him were accurately described, particularly an incident in Russia (wrongly named by him Persia) which was extraordinarily vivid and gave to me an uncanny weird sensation, as of one rising from the dead to revisit the glimpses of the moon.

---

7   Eagerness.
8   Remark.
9   "Barren", referring to the childless Margaret of York (1446-1503), sister of Edward IV and Richard III, and a staunch enemy of the Tudor King Henry VII.
10   Alexandre Dumas, *The Companions of Jehu*.

The Empress had selected the day for her visit: he said that her horoscope had already been told by several eminent astrologers and that he proposed, subject to Her Majesty's high approval, to employ the method of crystal gazing at which he was adept. I anticipated no objection from her.

The interview was accordingly fixed and I lost no time in going to the Summer Palace to report the result of my mission. The Old Buddha bade me attend at the main gate of the temple at 11 p.m. but not to come in my chair. In due course two official *Hung T'o Ni Pu* 紅托泥布 (the Empress used red rather than yellow, the imperial colour, to attract less notice) mule drawn carts arrived; as I expected, the visit had not been kept secret and there appeared to be at least a battalion of Manchu troops surrounding the temple area. Reports of revolutionary activity were at that time rife in Peking, and in fact only nine months previously the Anhui student, Wu Yüeh 吳樾, had caused consternation to the Old Buddha and still more to the courtiers, by throwing a bomb at the members of the Constitution Mission just as the special train was about to leave, perishing in the attempt. I was delighted to notice the vigilance of the authorities on the occasion and felt relieved of the greater portion of my responsibility.

Her Majesty graciously bowed on seeing me and motioned to me not to kneel, while allowing me to support her up the entrance steps and into a sequestered courtyard, where the soothsayer awaited us in a small room lit by a solitary green-shaded lamp of old fashioned make. The four of us entered, and Jen Hsüan, though kneeling to the Empress, remained religiously silent and appeared in a sort of waking trance or *Dhyana*, an ecstasy of contemplation, which, I suppose, is the correct attitude for a seer wrestling with the secrets of the future or lifting the screen from past events previously unbeknown to himself except by revelation. Her Majesty took her seat on the only chair in the room, while we knelt on hassocks (*P'u T'uan* 蒲團) disposed below the chair where she sate. On the table in front of her immediately under the lamp was a crystal ball about the size of a Seville orange. I was reminded of Marie Antoinette's first meeting with Cagliostro[11] on entering French territory in 1770 for her wedding with Louis Auguste the Dauphin; there was the same darkened room but in her case no witness was present till her cry of terror at what she saw in the crystal ball, namely the representation of her own severed head falling into the basket from the platform of a ghastly *machine à bascule*,[12] at that date still unknown in France, though used in Italy, brought in her retinue to the swooning princess' aid.

I hoped that Hsing Hsüan in his revelations and prophecies would not be called upon to introduce the subject of lightning, for the Empress, especially since the scene of which she and I had been terror-stricken

---

11   Giuseppe Balsamo (1743-95), alias Count Allessandro Cagliostro, Italian adventurer, alchemist, sorcerer and confidence man, best known for his alleged role in a fraudulent diamond sale that greatly (and probably unjustly) damaged the reputation of Marie Antoinette.
12   Guillotine.

eye-witnesses that summer's day a year or so ago, was on that score "like sweet bells jangled, out of tune and harsh", *difficile*[13] and crotchety, as during the past years both the Ch'i Nien Tien 祈年殿 at the Temple of Heaven (the northern hall where the emperor proceeds, or proceeded in dynastic days, early in the year to pray for a prosperous harvest) and the T'ai Ho Tien 太和殿, the main throne hall in the Forbidden City, had been destroyed by lightning which is regarded as a sign of divine displeasure toward the throne. I do not imagine that Tz'u Hsi regarded her own morals as setting a bad example: it all depends on the point of view and as long as scandal was not caused, her private life concerned none. Unfortunately, just at present, rumours were busy in her regard and I blushed to think that I was partly to blame, for, of course, our liaison was freely talked of. Favourites of reigning sovereigns (sometimes, like Essex, during the despot's life), minions or *Ning Ch'en* 佞臣, are of necessity unpopular and have been known to die on the scaffold after demise of the throne, although I kept in the background and was no Sir Reginald Johnston, most overweening of Scotsmen, who loved to blazon his position abroad, under a phantom sovereign, as Hsüan T'ung[14] 宣統 was, during the time that his British tutor taught bad habits, as well as an English pronunciation with the affected Oxford drawl, as irritating as the Parisian accent to a Provençal or a Bordelais.[15]

What I am about to describe may seem incredible, *Jan Hu* 然乎, *Ch'i Ch'i Jan Hu* 豈其然乎, "Tis so, tis indeed so", saith the Sage in the *Lun Yü* 論語 (for some there are who would not be persuaded, though one rose from the dead), although I trust, perhaps too confidently in the light of painful experience of doubting Saint Thomases, that my own *bona fides* will hardly be impugned; I shall say the same, when Yen Wang[16] 閻王, Hades, calls me to himself; but it might be that a reader shall think I was the dupe of an optical delusion. It is not so: I know that my record is true. Were it otherwise, may High Heaven destroy Me! *Sui Fu T'ien Chu Yi Shu So Yüan* 雖伏天誅亦屬所願. I believe that Ts'ui Tê-lung is still living and he would corroborate the accuracy of my narration; albeit, as a man without culture, he would naturally have retained a fainter impression of details which are burnt like a corrosive acid into my keener (may I say it without false modesty), if quivering, brain. I presume that Hsing Hsüan, by some psychic control, forced the Old Buddha to recall salient events of her past; but, as regards his forecast of the future, my imagination pauses in silent wonderment and awe: "There are more things in heaven and earth, Horatio, than are dreamed of in your philosophy."[17] I can offer no

---

13 Difficult.
14 China's last emperor, P'u Yi (1906-67), reigned under the name Emperor Hsüan T'ung during the years of his actual reign (1908-12).
15 Sir Reginald Johnston (1874-1938) was one of Backhouse's contemporaries in Chinese scholarship, the tutor of Emperor P'u Yi in the Forbidden City from 1919 to 1924 and later Governor of the British-controlled port of Weihaiwei. It appears that the resentment was mutual: Johnston notes, in a 1934 letter to J.O.P. Bland, that he "had [his] reasons for disliking the man" (Backhouse), but does not elaborate further.
16 Yama, the God of Death.
17 Shakspere, *Hamlet* I.5.

explanation, any more than I can for the "rope trick" which, almost alone of white men, I saw performed in India, or the Mysore Yogi's forecast of the date of my father's death which he wrote that day in 1909 in the Bangalore temple in Mysore in Pali, placed in a sealed cover and bade me open it as soon as I learned that my father had passed away. Allowing for the difference of time between India and England, the hour, 1:45 p.m. was exact to the minute, the date being July 27, 1918.

It is only a personal matter and, as such, devoid of the interest which any fact concerning a great historical figure must naturally arouse; but the Yogi foretold to me that my brother, Roger Backhouse, then a humble naval commander, would one day rise as Admiral of the Fleet, 1st Lord of Admiralty, Sir Roger Backhouse G.C.B., G.C.V.O.,[18] to the supreme place in His Britannic Majesty's navy, which once ruled the seas, that my sister's husband would become a Lord Lieutenant and Baronet of the United Kingdom but would die comparatively young (64), both the above-named honours duly falling to his lot. As to the conundrum, *"Fortune, Misfortune, Fortune"*, which I have mentioned, the elucidation is on the lap of the gods, *"epi gounasi theon"*, as Homer says, and remains to me an enigma. But I think it means the happy release of death; for it is written:

> "Peace after war, port after stormy seas:
>   Ease after toil, death after life, doth greatly please"
>   *Faery Queene*

(if death be not the solution of the puzzle). Peradventure, the reference is to current events and to good emerging out of evil: *Sê Weng Shih Ma* 塞翁失馬, *Wei Ch'ang Fei Fu* 未嘗非福, as the adage has it: The old gentleman outside the Pass (Mongolia) lost a horse, but it turned out to be a blessing in disguise. (The new owner of the animal had a bad fall and broke his thigh in consequence.) The Japanese have the same saying: *Ningen Banji Saioga Uma, Jen Chien Wan Shih Sê Weng Chih Ma* 人間萬事塞翁之馬.

The scene was eerie, macabre, such as a Dürer might have delighted to portray: the dim religious light (both the eunuchs and myself felt as if we were attending a Buddhist service and were awed in spite of ourselves, Li and Ts'ui being the most materially minded of men); the figure of the Empress, expectant, almost suppliant, for I knew that she hankered after auspicious prognostications, sitting with hands clasped in an attitude of prayer and contemplation, evidently hoping, by a last minute devotion to deceive the immovable *Soeurs Filandières*[19] and to turn back the hands of time; the magic worker apparently unaware of the Empress', still more of our presence, developing a state of ecstasy which reminded me of the Yogi I had seen in Mysore,[20] his eyes open but quite expressionless, foaming at the mouth like an epileptic, muttering

18 G.C.B.: Grand Cross of the Order of the Bath; G.C.V.O.: Grand Cross of the Victorian Order.
19 "Sisters of Fate", the three Fates of Greek mythology, who respectively spin, measure and cut the thread of life.
20 This comment seems somewhat confused as, earlier on this page, the author mentions that his meeting with the Yogi was in 1909, three years after this anecdote takes place.

incantations and evoking, like another Pythonisse of Endor, the spirits from the land where all things are forgotten to lend their harmonious cooperation at his divination; our three mundane presentments adding a Euripidean touch of common things obtruding upon the mystic and the sublime, thereby enhancing by the contrast the things, exalted and spiritual, that are not seen but are eternal. I heard the Old Buddha mutter: "*Nan Wu* 南無" or "Hail", part of the invocation to Amitabha, repeating it many times over, like the Catholic telling his beads! She was paler than usual, but it may be that in the uncertain half light the powder of her widowhood appeared more amply applied, giving to her an uncanny ashen tint.

We waited, speechless except for the Old Buddha's and the adept's whisperings, for a great while, till at last the latter addressed Her Majesty in Chinese: "Old Buddha, look into the crystal ball: Old Buddha what do you see?"

She gazed with strange intentness and a look of incredulous amazement: "I see a girl kneeling in the court of a modest mansion and kotowing to a messenger who bears a writing engrossed upon thick apricot yellow paper. She prostrates herself again and rises from her knees. The girl is myself, the courtyard is that of my parents' home in Hsi La 錫拉 Lane (near the Tung An Men 東安門); the picture in the crystal is exact and recalls to me the well-remembered day when I, a girl of sixteen, received the imperial mandate of His Majesty Hsien Feng 咸豐 to enter the palace as a concubine of the lowest rank, *Kung Feng Wen Tsung Hsien Huang Ti Ts'e Ming Pei Wei Kung Wei* 恭奉文宗顯皇帝冊命備位宮闈."

The vision is blotted out, but Tz'u Hsi trembles with wonder and expectation. More than before she engages in prayer, and I am fain to confess that, carried away by the wonders of her description, I too proffer a petition to High Heaven for, even from the selfish aspect, on the Old Buddha's happiness mine greatly depended, but my devotion was really and truly selfless.

Li and Ts'ui exchanged to one another the words: "*Pien Hsi Fa'rh* 變戲 法兒, it is conjuring".

But I doubt if the saint heard the ill-timed interruption. He is wrestling in prayer and a stranger to the environment, seeming to hear and to see nothing save the crystal ball on which he concentrates his gaze. There is a pause as in a theatre, when one scene yields place to another. Once more he says with tremulous accent: "Old Buddha, look again into the crystal: what do you see?"

I could see from her bewildered expression and the fear apparent in her eyes ever sparkling with zest of life that the buried past was rising from its cerements ("Thy canonized bones hearsed in death have burst their cerements," said by Hamlet to his father's ghost) in concrete form: "I see the dragon couch in a vast chamber richly carpeted and equipped; there are many jades, vessels of gold, tapestries and ceramics. A man reclines on the couch in the death struggle; as it seems, he calls hoarsely and beckons to two princes in court robes kneeling at the foot of the bed (I cannot hear his words but his gestures are plainer than speech): 'Put Yehonala to death: the Ta Ch'ing 大清 house law prohibits a member of her clan becoming empress or empress dowager. *Wo Chen* 我朕, the imperial We, nominate you two as Regents. Summon Su Shun 肅順: write my valedictory decree.' The empress (afterwards Eastern Empress Dowager) enters the room weeping: the man on the bed has departed on the far journey." The Old Buddha speaks more to herself than to the seer: "It is the occasion of Hsien Feng's death at Jehol 熱河 in 11 Year Hsien Feng (Hsin Yu Nien 辛酉年, 1861): the princes are the regents Prince Yi 怡 and Prince Cheng 鄭. They were legally nominated but we two, as empress regents, overcame their ill-laid plans and assumed the supreme power. Su Shun was decapitated in Peking by my orders."

"Look again into the crystal, Your Majesty: what do you see?"

"I see a young officer of the Imperial guards in amorous union with a woman of great beauty, whose white powdered face shows that she is a widow. There is ecstasy written on the man's face but no words are spoken."

"Can you recognize the surroundings, Old Buddha?"

"Yes: the officer is Junglu 榮祿 who was bound to me by the closest of ties; the scene is still at Jehol: he is pledging to me his aid to place me firmly on the Throne and to protect the child, now emperor, my son Tsai Ch'un 載淳." (Written during imperial days 淳 in respect for the personal name, *Yü Ming Ching Pi* 御名敬避, respectful avoidance of the imperial name.)

The Old Buddha's hands are tremulous, though usually so firm; she says: "These pages from the past are painful: what I require of your marvellous magic is the future."

"Old Buddha, to reveal the coming events I must first present to you the past. If what the crystal shows to you is truly historical fact, you will be disposed to believe the truth of my prophecies and to guide your future course accordingly. Fate may write the scroll; but man has power to modify and even to shape coming events."

"Be it so, then: go on evoking these phantoms; and if they lie not, naturally I shall allow my judgment to be swayed by your divination."

He waited a great while, concentrating on some inward struggle which barred the gates of speech. "Old Buddha, look once more into the crystal and say to me what you see."

"I perceive the dissipated pox-ridden features of a youth of nineteen indulging in sexual intercourse with a drab in a low-class bawdy-house. I recognize the features of my son, the late emperor, T'ung Chih 同治; although I never visited the house of ill-fame, it is the case that he died of *Tsang Cheng Hou* 臟症候 or syphilis. He was a bad, undutiful son, but he was Son of Heaven. Your record is once more true: I was to blame for his death: *Shan Fo* 善佛, *Pu Yao Kuai Tsui Wo* 不要怪罪我! Holy Buddha, let not the guilt fall on my head!"

The emaciated face of the ascetic, whose eyes were as full of life as his frail body, *à deux doigts de la mort*,[21] was devoid of it, seeming to belong already to the world of shades, lit up for an instant with unimagined fire, as he listened to the Old Buddha's pious apostrophe to the world-honoured one. "Aye! Your Majesty, whatsoever in another creature might be reckoned a sin, Buddha will forgive to one of your exalted station.[22] Statecraft may demand a course of action from a ruler from which are eliminated the words 'guilt' or 'crime'; mercy and justice, what are they but shibboleths or high sounding platitudes for imperial decrees to employ? Does not the Sage himself ride in the court procession behind the notorious harlot and mistress of the prince of the Wei 衛 State? 'Lust in front and victim at the rear', as his disciple, Tzu Lu 子路, when remonstrating with K'ung Tzu[23] 孔子 remarked to his master, and the latter accepted the blame asking pardon of High Heaven for the offence, if offence it be. The Lord Buddha reminds us that a *nénuphar*[24] of purest hue may rise majestic out of a pool of filth, *Ni Chung Lien* 泥中蓮. Regard not the past, Your Majesty, with remorse, save as your guide for the future: think of your dynasty and its future interests which should be, and are, paramount in your mind. *Shih Chih Tung Yü* 失之東隅, *Shou Chih Sang Yü* 收之桑榆: what is lost in the region of the east may be retrieved in the quarter of the sunset. But look again, Old Buddha, at the crystal and tell me, the humble adept, what you see."

The Empress scrutinized the round ball on which the ineffectual lamp-light seemed to throw an unearthly light. "I see a young woman wearing mourning, a recent widow, paler than death, of rare beauty, kneeling before me: she points weeping bitterly toward her pregnant body, *Tzu Kung*[25] 子宮 (the palace of children), and craves piteously for a respite, so that the child in her womb may yet come to the birth. But I am inexorable, since in the event of a male child (the foetus was male of about eight months' gestation; the Old Buddha caused the womb of A-lu-tê 阿祿德 to be ripped open after death) being born, he would be emperor (superseding the infant Kuang Hsü), and A-lu-te, now known as the Chia Shun Huang Hou 嘉順皇后, laudable and excellent empress,[26] would be regent; while I and my colleague, the Eastern Empress Dowager, would be relegated to the lower room of dignity without power. So she must die for reasons of state: pity shall be a stranger and the milk of human-kindness shall be banished from my breast. I command her to *Shang Tiao* 上吊, hang herself; she hesitates to carry out the fatal order; I summon An Te-hai 安德海 and another who execute the doom even as my imperial will decrees. The vision is true."

---

21 On the brink of death.
22 **Backhouse:** Note: A convenient doctrine for kings and queens, a "flattering unction" (*Hamlet*) for their soul. Not otherwise did Louis Le Bien-aimé persuade himself that the virtues of Saint Louis assured to all his descendants, whatever their crimes, eternal bliss at the Throne of God.
23 Confucius.
24 Lotus.
25 Womb.
26 The author seems to over-translate here. *Chia Shun* was simply Lady A-lu-te's title as the Empress Consort.

Again, a long interval: we had been assisting for more than two hours and a half at this psychic séance: my patient knees, and probably those of the eunuchs also, though more habituated than I to lengthy genuflexions, were benumbed, *Ma Mu Pu Jen* 麻木不仁, and I suffered from violent cramps in the thighs. Then the Yogi in an apparently agonizing convulsion managed to find words: "Old Buddha, look once more into the crystal: what do you see?"

The Empress needed not the admonition, as she was already engaged in a fixity of contemplation. "I see a beautiful youth made for love and its ineffable rhythm, wearing the five-clawed imperial dragon robes as if he were Son of Heaven; he is in a barge flying the dragon flag, being towed by a gang of haulers on the banks of a river. I recognize the adored, love-inspiring lineaments of my dear, dear, unforgettable favourite An Te-hai, foully murdered by Hsiao Chen 孝貞 (the Eastern Empress) and that traitor, the Prince Kung 恭."

"The scene is about to change: look again, Old Buddha and tell me what you see."

"I see my own face, in disordered rage and frenzied horror, as I revile my colleague with the language of the gutter for her treason to me in slaying my paramour and menace her with death; Prince Kung kneels to me in penitence and shame, but I avert my face and refuse to be entreated. Once again, your magic power brings back the ghosts of bygone years; the seasons have come and gone in their sequence for a generation. It is terrible, but I bow to, and acclaim, your wonderful magic: it subjugates and compels me."

"Wait a while, Your Majesty, and I will show to you another picture of fancy, or rather of fact: perchance, it may awake in you a fresh recollection of great events." Once more he uttered the formula: "Your Majesty, look into the crystal and tell me what you see."

And she to reply: "I see a slightly built fair round faced woman of some thirty-eight years writhing in agony on a settee; the features are distorted and horrible; it is the Eastern Empress Dowager in her death throes. I had given to her *P'i Shuang* 砒霜 (arsenious crystals) in revenge, at long last, for my adored one's murder. She is dying: nay, she is dead. Buddha be thanked." Her Majesty seemed to be living over again the hour of her magnificent vengeance: exultation, not as previously a sort of passive remorse, was written in her eyes and in every feature. Li, who remembered the occasion as a young man, trembled violently and looked stedfastly at Her Majesty, as if to suggest that these past revelations were too poignant to pursue.

The next reminiscence visible in the crystal ball was the death of Yin Liu 陰劉 (the character *Yin* has a double meaning, one referring to his taciturn and secretive nature and the other to his large penis), the pastry-cook, Liu 劉 of the large tool; that is to say, the saint asked the Old Buddha if she recognized the pain-ridden face of the beautiful Adonis, and she replied without swerving a muscle: "It is Yin Liu, whose mouth I had perforce to shut. I have not forgotten his comeliness and sexual unabated zeal. When are you coming to future events, wonder-worker Jen Hsüan 任玄? I am all ears to hear and eyes to see."

"Nay, Your Majesty, be patient: there are still three scenes from the past for the crystal to present to your august memory. I entreat you to look once again at the crystal ball, what do you see?"

"I see myself playing elephant chess in my boudoir at the Wan Shou Shan 萬壽山: I am happy and free from the cares of state, having handed over the government to the emperor. Suddenly a young man of about thirty-six enters; he appears excited and uneasy in my presence; he craves an audience. For the moment, I recognize him not, but now I perceive that he is Yüan Shih-k'ai 袁世凱 fresh from an audience with the emperor who has given to him orders to place me under arrest and to go at once to Tientsin in order to put the viceroy Junglu to death. He shows to me the imperial order signed with the seal, *Feng T'ien Ch'eng Yün Chih Pao* 奉天承運之寶, the jewelled mandate of him by God's grace invested with imperial authority. I thank him for his loyalty to me and promise to act with resolution and despatch; for the occasion brooks no delay." (This event was in the 8 moon of the Wu Hsü 戊戌 year (two signs in the *T'ien Kan* 天干 and *Ti Chih* 地支, heavenly stems and earthly branches of the *Chia Tzu* 甲子 or Cycle of Cathay, *Wu* 戊 representing the central place and *Hsü* 戌 the year of the dog, i.e. Kuang Hsü 24, 1898, year of the *coup d'état*).)

"Once more, Old Buddha, look into the crystal and tell me what it discloses."

"I see myself wearing the dress of a peasant woman: a young girl insults me and charges me with harlotry. I command her death: she is pushed by two eunuchs into the well behind my palace. It is the Pearl Concubine: she deserved to die a thousand deaths. How say you, Lien-ying?"

"Ay, Your Majesty: it is so." (What else could he have said!)

"Old Buddha," said the Yogi, "we are coming to the end of the historical portion and the crystal is about to reveal the future, as Your Majesty desires. But first let the Old Buddha look into the crystal and say what you see."

Her Majesty looked and seemed distraught with anger: "I refuse to tell you; what your crystal shows has offence in it."

"But, Your Majesty, if you do not speak, I cannot protect your sacred person as regards the future in store for the Old Buddha."

"Well, then: I see the late Grand Secretary, my loyal servant (Junglu, but she does not name him), in amorous congress with myself. I do not deny, neither do I admit, that the crystal speaketh truth."

"So be it," said the seer: "it is as your good pleasure directs. But look once again into the crystal ball and inform me what confronts your benevolent gaze."

"I see a band of ruffians invading the palace precincts, but the issue is not revealed."

"Then, Old Buddha, be prepared to take occasion by the hand and nip future conspiracy in the bud. Be warned, for Your Majesty has many enemies of your own house. Look yet again into my crystal: what see you there?"

"I see a eunuch running toward me as a herald who bears auspicious news; his face is lit up with joy, but I know not what he says."

"Concentrate your attention to the crystal ball: you shall see more yet."

"I see myself seated on the Throne while my council kneels to receive my mandates. There is a vacancy of the imperial throne and I am appointing the new emperor. The vision fades and melts into air, into thin air."

"But look again: what see you?"

"Ah! I see myself still on the Throne, while two men entreat me urgently and presumptuously. I rebuke and threaten them. One points a revolver at me *à bout portant*:[27] does he wound me? I cannot say."

"Do you recognize the faces of the two men, Old Buddha?"

"If my eyes deceive me not, one is Yüan Shih-k'ai 袁世凱, the other I cannot perceive in the dimness."

"The séance is drawing to an end, Your Majesty: pray be patient and look yet again into the crystal."

"I see a vast cortège passing the gate of this very temple: the great sarcophagus is carried by 128 bearers: the long snake-like procession is several *li* in length. May it not be my own funeral obsequies?"

"Buddha send a far day," said Jen Hsüan; and we all responded like a Greek chorus: "And may your servants not live to see it!"

"*Wan Wu Tzu Jan Chih Li* 萬物自然之理, we all have to pay the debt of nature; but tell me, saint, when will these things be?"

"If Your Majesty will be circumspect and deal resolutely and pitiless-ly with a man whose name is neither Yü, nor Jen, nor yet Liu (俞任柳, the three characters above being allusion to the *Po Chia Hsing* 百家姓 or *Recueil*[28] of surnames, the names in the thirteenth verset of four characters being *Yü* 俞, *Jen* 任, *Yüan* 袁, *Liu* 柳, thus leaving no doubt to a Chinese or a Manchu, even the illiterate who are all familiar with the 'hundred surnames', that Yüan was the name referred to, although the prophet shrank from the risk of naming it for walls have ears and Yüan's spies were everywhere; just as the saying in the time of Edward IV of England cryptically declared how 'G. of Edward's sons the murderer shall be', G. being Gloucester, the wicked uncle, later Richard III, but also stood for George duke of Clarence who was drowned in the Malmsey Butt for suspected treason),[29] then the sinister omen can be averted. Man is the

27 At point-blank range.
28 Collection.
29 King Richard III of England (1452-85) and George Plantagenet (1449-78), Duke of Clarence, were the younger brothers of King Edward IV (1442-83). The Duke of Clarence helped temporarily depose Edward IV and, when the latter returned to power, was imprisoned and executed. Legend (and Shakspere) has it that Clarence was executed by drowning in a butt (about 500 litres) of Malmsey wine.

master of his fate and is the captain of his soul. Above all, can the super-human wit and energy of Your Majesty successfully cut the gordian knot by shortening the life of your deadliest enemy whose vaulting ambition knoweth not gratitude nor duty toward one who has loaded him with benefits. But, Your Majesty, I entreat you for the last time to look into the crystal and tell us what you see."

The Old Buddha gazed intently, changed countenance and collapsed on the chair in a dead faint. We rushed forward, so far as our numbed limbs would permit, and supported her on to her seat. She could not speak for a while, but at last exclaimed: "The horror of it: ask me not what I saw: no nightmare ever approached this spectacle of death."

"Your Majesty, there is no need to recount the vision; but I implore you to take time by the forelock, or it will be too late."

"One question before I dismiss you: will the Dynasty endure after my death?"

"Your Majesty, Fate doth not answer yea nor nay. In any event its unscrutable decrees can, and may be, averted if Your Majesty's dynasty itself takes heed and profits by warnings of history. *Yin Chien Pu Yüan* 殷鑒不遠, *Fu Chü Tsai Ch'ien* 覆車在前. The example of the Yin Dynasty is not remote, the overturned chariot is just ahead."

The Old Buddha was trembling all over and her hands were like ice; for in helping her to her chair, I had touched them. With queenly dignity she thanked the saintly Yogi, bestowing upon him Taels 5,000 in recom-pense and an equal sum to chant daily masses for her longevity and, when that day comes which comes to all, for the repose of her soul in heaven, *Tsai T'ien Chih Ling* 在天之靈. Lord Buddha! Mercy! So mote it be!

A chilliness in the air showed us that dawn was about to break; it was nearly four o'clock. We were all worn out by our vigil; the seer bowed courteously to me, saying: "You will find that my horoscope regarding yourself will be true to the letter. Let us pray whatever gods there be that the crystal may have lied concerning Her Majesty's future." He kotowed thrice to the Old Buddha and asked leave to retire, proposing to take a brief rest in the Tung Yüeh Miao 東嶽廟 prior to returning to his official duties with Chang T'ien Shih, the Taoist pope.

Her Majesty took my hand in affectionate pressure: "Some day per-haps I shall tell you what I saw: it frightened me worse than death, which indeed I do not fear; as what must be, must be." I asked no questions and never learned from her dear lips what the lastest vision of the crystal had revealed. Mayhap it was the sight of her own desecrated remains hud-dled in the courtyard of the vast mausoleum. Perchance, 'twas a vision of the tortures of the damned in hell! Who shall say? Perhaps I shall know in another world and in another life. Till then, live on!

> "Absent thee from felicity a while,
> And in this harsh world draw thy breath in pain
> To tell my story."
>
> Hamlet, *last scene.*

"There may be heaven; there must be hell." Meantime, we have our weary life here, as we "grunt and sweat" the hours away. *Car tout est vanité*;[30] or as Lord Byron said, when asked if he had enjoyed his life: "Yes, except that I would rather not have lived at all!"

ONE WORD MORE

Regarding the death of the fair A-lu-tê 阿祿德, canonized as Hsiao Che Chia Shun Yi Huang Hou 孝哲嘉順毅皇后, empress widow of T'ung Chih 同治, Li Lien-ying, who however was not then in the palace nor had in fact as yet "left the family", *Ch'u Chia* 出家, so that his evidence is not infallible, told me that poison by arsenic was the cause; equally, the "anonymous" letter (of Chin Chih-ch'üan 金芝泉), quoted in the chapter on the conspiracy, definitely accused the Old Buddha of poisoning her, so as to prevent the possibility of a posthumous heir being to T'ung Chih and causing dynastic complication owing to Kuang Hsü's illegal accession (as being of the same generation with T'ung Chih). But in the séance of Jen Hsüan, the adept Yogi, Her Majesty herself stated, on gazing into the crystal ball, that A-lu-tê met her death by hanging; naturally, she had the best reason to know the facts, so that the common tradition of poisoning by arsenic (*Hsin* 信) must be abandoned. I can positively asseverate that the Old Buddha admitted having commanded An Tê-hai and another eunuch to adjust the cord round the widowed empress' neck, till she was dead. Perhaps this may account for the blackened tumefaction of her face, when the courtiers entered for the *Ju Lien* 入斂, or encoffining of the body. Weng T'ung-ho 翁同龢 mentions this fact in his diary; especially that her tongue was protruding and the eye-balls starting out of her head. Arsenic (I presume) could not have had this effect. Perhaps Her Majesty had intended to use poison but thought better of it; as she gave out that A-lu-tê had committed suicide by hanging herself and commended her in a glowing eulogy for her wifely devotion to her late lord's memory just as in 1901 she praised the Pearl Concubine for her "noble suicide"!! The removal of the foetus was done secretly, and Weng does not mention the facts: I suppose it was burnt, but *quién sabe?*[31] for it would have been treason to do so.

---

30 For all is vanity.
31 Who knows?

CHAPTER XIII

THE LETTER AND THE JUDGMENT

Having lost all my private records at the time of the anti-British boycott in August 1939, I am unable to date exactly the letter of which I had a copy and am now going to speak: it certainly reached me about June 15, 1907 and was from the British Foreign Secretary, Sir Edward Grey, later Viscount Grey K.G., dated early in May and marked "Confidential: Burn after perusal". It ran practically as follows (for 'tis writ upon the tablets of my memory):

My dear Backhouse,

> As an old friend of your family and also a neighbour, I am writing to you in a private capacity but yet not wholly so. I have greatly appreciated during the sixteen months since I became Secretary of State your confidential reports which show insight into, and also a real sympathy with, the Manchu Dynasty from within. But I am frankly a little concerned at your very close relations with that enigmatic personage whom it is best not to name. Your life is of value to your family and to us: be at pains not to tilt against windmills! I should be unwilling to believe that you are being played with; but your position as an alien favourite, an Axel Fersen, as it were, at the Court opens up the avenue of crime to those who (as you tell us) are definitely *not* on the side of the *Innomable*.[1] It happens that those who have the greatest intimacy with a situation fall the readiest victims of an intrigue. Let me end by thanking you now (at long last), for I only sent a formal acknowledgment at the time, for your very kind sympathy with me in the sad event at Fallodon (the death of his wife in a carriage accident in January 1906). Your father also wrote most kindly."

This note is almost *textuelle*, especially in the metaphor. I fancy that there was a sentence (P.S.) about British influence and *izzat* (prestige) in

---

Unnamable.

China which is not germane to the subject of this paper. I give this letter, although marked "Secret", as Lord Grey has been dead ten years or more and there is nothing to injure his posthumous reputation. Else I should not reveal a letter marked "Secret".

By a coincidence, I had recently been warned by several Manchus and Chinese, personal friends and in more or less prominent official positions, that Tz'u Hsi's 慈禧 "secret" or more accurately open relations with me were generally known; but I had gone so far that *Ch'i Hu Nan Hsia* 騎虎難下, dismounting from a tiger's back is no easy business. Events would have to take their course; since I could not say to Her Majesty "I am never coming to see you again" and it seemed to me highly problematical that the Old Buddha would be off with the old love and on with the new despite her manifold "ofs" and "belongings", as Cleopatra who passed from Pompée to César, from Hérode to Antoine, from one affection to another.

I pondered Grey's letter many times in my heart and came to the conclusion that there was more in it than met the eye. He was ten years my senior but the product of the same school, Winchester, where he was head of his house. In the war of 1914 he was regarded in Germany as Machiavellian and was considerably *maltraité*[2] by the press. In fact, he was an unimaginative Englishman, a member of a great Whig House, whose forbears had "done the State some service" (as Coriolanus says), a clear-cut and not unimpressive speaker, who rather gloried in the fact that he had never been out of England, unsophisticated, a lover of birds and angling. He was borne into the vortex of great events, but his niche in history will not be that of one who was lord of his event, no rider of the whirlwind. I knew that the British Legation, blissfully ignorant but sure, as always, of its omniscience, would be at pains not to mention me, since relations between S.S.[3] and official departments are notoriously like fire and water. It seemed to me that the Chinese Minister in London might have heard some gossip about the Old Buddha and her *Yang Hou Yeh* 洋侯爺, foreign marquis. What I did was to engage some of the best detectives in the city to frequent the tea shops, houses of ill fame, bath houses and theatres in the hope of picking up some "spider's thread" which might furnish a clue. The Empress, as usual, richly indemnified my large outlay. Their investigations were not particularly helpful, but one of them, *Ma Yü-lin* 馬玉麟 who since became famous in criminal enquiry, brought me news that men were talking in whispers of a coming *coup de main*[4] with which was connected the name of Ts'en Ch'un-hsüan 岑春煊, the president of the Board of Communications, who had offended the powerful Canton clique in that Ministry, especially Liang Shih-yi 梁士詒, "the god of wealth", for his announced intention of "purging the Augean stable". I knew that he had made an enemy of Li Lien-ying but fancied that this was due to failure to disburse the prescribed fees which Li regarded as his apanage.

---

2   Abused.
3   Secretary of State (Foreign Secretary).
4   Surprise attack.

The long arm of coincidence brought to me a week or so later an anonymous letter of extreme indecency and violence. It accused me of "Ni Lun 逆倫" relations (contrary to nature) with the Old Buddha whom it named, used of her language that would have caused Wu Tse-t'ien 武則天 to blush or Agrippina[5] to bow her head in shame. It gave a long list of Tz'u Hsi's paramours, a sort of *Who's Who*, with references or *Pei K'ao* 備考: "poisoned", "murdered" next day, "fell dead in the palace precincts", went back a great number of years and named several (such as Junglu) of whom Li had not spoken to me. The letter ended: "You will be the next victim: even if the *Tsei Hou* 賊后 (the usurping empress) spares you, others will not, and you and she will perish together, just as when the fire rages on the K'un-lun 崑崙 range, pebbles and jade are equally victims of the flame. *Huo Yen K'un Kang* 火炎崑崗, *Yü Shih Chü Fen* 玉石俱焚 (*Shu Ching*[6] 書經)."

Carefully meditating on this threat which, but for Grey's note, I might perhaps have disregarded, I decided to write to Li Lien-ying, then at the Wan Shou Shan 萬壽山 with the Old Buddha, who was (as I have stated elsewhere) my usual intermediary and to ask him for an appointment. He arrived punctual at the tryst, seemed a good deal perturbed before I had touched the subject and produced a letter likewise in exquisite *K'ai Shu* 楷書, copper-plate,[7] which the Empress had received, identical with mine except that her name was in the second person and my own in the third. It was written in a cultivated style suggestive of an official in the *Nei Ko* 內閣, Grand Secretariat, but, of course, a subject has only the right to memorialize the sovereign by official channels and apparently this communication had been smuggled into the Summer Palace with some edibles that Her Majesty affected. The restaurant in question had been able to throw no light on the origin of the letter, of which the staff professed entire ignorance, and the Old Buddha had accepted their assurance. She at once ascribed this act of *Majestätsbeleidigung*[8] as being due either to the *Komingtang* 革命黨 or revolutionaries, or else to the machinations of that imp of mischief, *Yao Kuai* 妖怪, Kuang Hsü 光緒 and his faction. I told Li what I had heard from Ma Yü-lin 馬玉麟 regarding the tea shop story of Ts'en Ch'un-hsüan 岑春烜 and he was much impressed, especially as Ts'en and he were enemies.

Li said that he would post certain private detectives of his own on watch and, as he knew Ma Yü-lin of old, I raised no objection to his getting in touch with the latter with a view to cooperation. He bade me not to preoccupy myself with regard to expense, as the Old Buddha would gladly be responsible for all charges. Meantime, he advised me to await the issue before again attending at the Summer Palace, unless the Old

---

5   Empress Wu Tse-t'ien (625-705 AD) was China's first official female head of state. Empress Julia Agrippina (15-59 AD) was the highly influential wife of Emperor Claudius and mother of Emperor Nero. Both of the women have been accused of being ruthless and of questionable moral integrity.
6   *The Book of History*, one of the five Confucian classics.
7   More commonly translated as "regular script"; *K'ai Shu* is a much more orderly, angular script than "copper-plate" would suggest.
8   Maligning the sovereign.

Buddha should send for me. I left it at that, felt I could do no more and wondered if the whole affair were not a bluff, although the perpetrators might have known that Tz'u Hsi was not easily intimidated, nor one to let the grass grow under her feet, especially in regard to the denunciation of her morals as to which she was as *susceptible*[9] as Le Roi Soleil to a mention of smallpox, fancying an allusion to his own royal visage *maltraité par la petite vérole*,[10] a disfigurement that artists of the time were at pains to conceal in representing his dignified countenance, unlike Oliver Cromwell who bade the painter faithfully to depict his unsightly wart on the forehead.

The very able detectives now at work soon furnished us with valuable material *qui donnait à penser*.[11] To begin with, it appeared established that the ring-leader was Ts'en Ch'ün-hsuan, but the aged Grand Secretary Sun Chia-nai 孫家鼐, once imperial tutor and a known sympathizer with Kuang Hsü, a man of high moral virtue, a sort of Cato standing four-square to all the winds that blow, who despised the *déreglement*[12] of Messalina's morals, was undoubtedly privy to the plot, thus lending to the proposed *coup de main* the prestige of his unblemished reputation even though a *magni nominis umbra*.[13] The scheme was as follows: some traitor eunuch, Li thought he could guess his identity (but I never learned it), was to inform the conspirators regarding the Old Buddha's next "dine and sleep" appointment with me; how they were to be admitted into the palace was not yet clear, but apparently the guards were to be suborned at a figure surpassing avarice's fondest dreams. Sun did not desire his name to appear, but Ts'en, who was certainly a brave man, announced his intention of presenting a sealed memorial in person at the office of the Grand Council just before day light. His retainers would all be *sicaires*, hired assassins, whose duty it would be to surround the Empress' bed-chamber and to catch her *epi autoforo*, in the act, like the woman taken in adultery of the *Écriture*.[14] The next step was to confront her, Messalina, in dalliance with her paramour (my unworthy self), with *un fait accompli*,[15] compel her to issue a penitential decree and to hand over the reins of government to the emperor, who would order her to commit suicide. My punishment was that I be handed over to the Legation for deportation from China. The plotters were prepared to use violence if necessary; and it had been arranged to take Li alive for summary trial and decapitation, also, I think, the eunuch Ts'ui Te-lung 崔德隆.

Li displayed remarkable coolness, more in fact than I. He said: "We will thwart their treason yet once more. Now I am going straight to the Old Buddha and will notify you of the day and hour on which she

---

9   Touchy.
10   Suffering from smallpox.
11   That implicated.
12   Disorder.
13   "The shadow of a great name" (Seneca Minor, *Octavia* 70-1); an unworthy descendant of an illustrious family.
14   Scripture.
15   A known fact.

commands your attendance. You need not come armed; we will do all that is required. In the meantime, just forget it and leave it to me."

My household staff, loyal but certainly not courageous, seemed to have an inkling that strange matters were afoot, but affected an indifference that they were far from feeling. Li had said that he should be at pains to promulgate the day fixed for my rendezvous (contrary to his usual custom) well ahead of time. I well remember that it was on July 10, 1907 but forget the lunar calendar equivalent. Apparently the Kuang Hsü emperor was fully aware of the proposed happenings, but the empress, loyal to her mother-in-law, was in blissful ignorance. I was carefully intimated not to come in expectation of erotic manoeuvres: once the *spadassins*[16] were disposed of, Her Majesty would appoint for me another *nuit d'amour*, where we could both be *T'ai Jan Tzu Jo* 泰然自若, calm and self-possessed, *T'a Shih* 塌實 or *recueilli*, so far as the things of Eros make for *recueillement*.[17] I thought to myself: "No need of the aphrodisiac, then: so much the better to avoid exertions in this hot weather." It is only candour to affirm that I was distinctly nervous: Ts'en was a man of intrepid resolution and I was not perfectly sure that the palace guards, like the pretorians of old, might not be won over to the cause of the emperor and bring about the deposition of the Empress.

It was obvious that hired assassins could not succeed in any *attentat*,[18] unless the imperial guards on duty at the palace held aloof. Ts'en Ch'unhsüan must have reckoned on the attendant circumstances, the discredit of the Empress Dowager's love intrigue with a European, her bare-faced effrontery in admitting him to the imperial couch, the lovers caught redhanded in the most ambiguous of situations more worthy of Sardou or of Dumas the younger than of punctilious dynastic etiquette, the natural anti-foreign sentiments such as would be imitable in any country (what would the good people of Aberdeen-shire have said if Queen Victoria and a Manchu noble were discovered in bed together?), the definite sympathy felt by a minority for the hapless emperor, the strong undercurrent of disapproval, latent but present, in the imperial clan and among the public of Peking (still more so in the rest of China) at Yehonala's defiance of the conventional code of morality in introducing, *Ming Mu Chang Tan* 明目張膽, openly and unashamed, a barbarian to the profound seclusion of the palace (as she loved to call it in her decrees), above all the loss of face for the Ta Ch'ing 大清 Dynasty, a rank offence that "smelled to heaven"[19] and demanded retribution. The actual armed strength of the assassins *soudoyés à gages* mattered little: what Ts'en reckoned upon was the assured repercussion, the spark of fire which starts a vast conflagration, *I Hsing Chih Huo* 一星之火, *Shih Ch'eng Liao Yüan* 勢成燎原, or as a new disease unknown to man which carries all before it like a mountain torrent in spate. I asked myself had the Old Buddha sufficient self-control

---

16   Assassins.
17   Contemplative ... contemplation.
18   Attack.
19   "O, my offence is rank, it smells to heaven" (Shakspere, *Hamlet* III.3).

Mien I Yin Huai 勉抑淫懷, to keep forcibly under her strong concupiscence, for it seemed to me that, if she gave rein to her desires and introduced me to her couch, there was no certitude that even she could palliate or explain away this *amour de passage*, worthy of Le Parc aux Cerfs,[20] the love of a goddess for a "devil", like the moon in the ancient myth who loved a mortal!

As I, like Faust, a man without a fear, without a hope, evoke, even as *la pythonisse d'Endor* Samuel's ghost in King Saul's trembling presence,[21] these phantoms of a generation ago in my artless, but truthful narration, I marvel at these ingenuous doubts of my great mistress' indomitable will. In love she was as burning as Cleopatra; but in craft she surpassed England's Tudor queen. Like the great cardinal whom, *mutatis mutandis*,[22] she greatly resembled, she excelled in taking time by the forelock, *pour déjouer les complots des grands*.[23] I might have spared myself the preoccupations, but am free to admit that, had the usurping regents of 1861 (Hsien Feng 咸豐 11. IX) Princes Cheng 鄭 and Yi 怡 with their colleague, Su Shun 肅順, astute as Mazarin and cunning as Burleigh,[24] been confronted with such a situation, or had a Prince Kung 恭 (Yi Hsin 奕訢) and still more a Junglu 榮祿 been supporters of the emperor against the Old Buddha, the conspiracy might have been consummated with success. *Avec des si on mettrait Paris en bouteille*:[25] these historical ifs are fascinating to dwell upon but wholly futile, like the ode of the agnostic to immortality or the amorous yearnings of a nonagenarian.

The mandate which summoned me to the Summer Palace was differently worded from the phraseology of previous occasions: "*Ch'in Feng I Chih* 欽奉懿旨, *Cho Chung I Hou Pa K'o-Ssu Li Shih Ju Yeh* 著忠毅侯巴恪思立時入謁, *Yu So Ch'ui Wen* 有所垂問, *Ping Cho Hsieh Tai Kuan Yü Hsien Cheng Shu Chi Shu Chung* 並著擕帶關於憲政書籍數種, *Ch'in Tz'u* 欽此. I have reverently received a decree from the Empress Dowager: The Marquis Pa K'o-Ssu is ordered to enter my presence immediately in a matter whereon I design to consult him and is to bring with him sundry volumes dealing with Constitutional Government." (Her Majesty had in the previous autumn promulgated a mandate governing the eventual grant of a constitution to China after a preparatory period of nine years.)

Li Lien-ying also wrote bidding me attend in my summer court robes and *Liang Mao* 涼帽 (cool summer hat) and to be sure to come in my chair with outriders. This procedure was quite novel, as in previous

---

20 "Passing love . . . the Deer Park", refers to a mansion in Versailles Palace, where Louis XV would meet his lovers.

21 "The Witch of Endor", who channeled the ghost of the prophet Samuel in presaging Saul's impending defeat.

22 The necessary changes having been made.

23 To foil the conspiracies of the great.

24 Cardinal Jules Mazarin (1602-61), the Italian protégé and successor of Cardinal Richelieu, was a gifted statesman serving under the French Kings Louis XIII and Louis XIV. Lord W. Cecil Burleigh (1520-98) was one of England's most powerful statesmen under Queen Elizabeth I. For an in-depth account of the coup described here, see Backhouse and Bland's *China under the Empress Dowager* (Ch. 3).

25 If ifs and buts were pots and pans, there'd be no trade for tinkers (literally "With ifs and buts, one could put Paris in a bottle").

instances I had been at pains to dissemble my arrival, but on this occasion everything was to be performed in the garish light of day and I was to be received in my capacity of adviser on law of nations, *Kuo Chi Kung Fa Ku Wen* 國際公法顧問. And so my chair entered the *Yi Ho Yüan* 頤和園 gate, while the lieutenant on duty remarked: "It's the foreign scholar. How the Old Buddha spends herself in toil, labouring all night and fasting the livelong day! *Hsin Kan Chih Lao* 昕肝之勞, work before the break of day and after sundown." As enjoined, I brought with me a dozen tomes on law and the constitution, Grimm, Dicey, Bryce, Holland, Anson and others. Li came out to meet me, bidding a comely young eunuch carry with the sweat of his brow the ponderous volumes to Her Majesty's boudoir. I did not greatly envy myself the task of exposition of the contents, especially as the subject was a virgin furrow for Her Majesty and in itself dry as dust to the layman, but knew that she was a past mistress in the art of make-believe, full to repletion of platitudes and shibboleths, "phrases of little meaning, though the words are strong".

Li Lien-ying informed me that the *spadassins*, about thirty in all, were coming disguised as workmen, with the character *Chiang* 匠, a workman, on their badges of identity. The guards at the gate and inside the grounds were presumed (Li did not seem absolutely certain on this point) to be heart and soul with Her Majesty; but the fact is, in China as elsewhere, *Shang Chê Wang Hou Pai Chê K'ou* 勝者王侯敗者寇, the conqueror is ennobled, while the conquered is a felon. Treason doth never prosper, what's the reason? Why, when it prospers, who dare call it treason? *Ni Chê Pi Pai* 逆者必敗, *Ch'i Ku Ho Tsai* 其故何在? *Ni Erh Ch'eng Kung* 逆而成功, *Shu Kan Yüeh Ni* 孰敢曰逆? And I still believe that the coup would have succeeded, if the Old Buddha and I had been "discovered" (in the theatrical sense) stark naked on the phoenix couch, indulging in libidinous antics worthy of the times of Martial when Domitian was on the throne of the Caesars. "*Paedicare negas, uxor . . . . . Sempronia Graccho, Julia Pompeio, Portia, Brute, tibi grato animo dabant . . . . .* Wife, do you refuse copulation from behind? Sempronia gladly accorded it to Gracchus, Julia to Pompey and Portia to thee, O Brutus . . . . " (i.e. the chastest Roman matrons granted favours *a posteriori*).[26] Neither do I see how Her Majesty could ever have regained her loss of prestige, less from the act itself than from the nationality of the actor.

I was shown on the instant into the Empress' presence; she greeted me with a cordial but royal reserve in the presence of two beautiful ladies in waiting. "Well: so you have come to enlighten me on the rudiments of constitutional government. *Tun K'ai Mao Se* 頓開茅塞, my benighted ignorance will have light shed upon it." She was never so great as when face to face with a crime or in the presence of imminent danger, *Lin Ta Chieh Erh Pu Pien Ch'u Chih* 臨大節而不變初志, and in this regard she merits comparison with the greatest characters in history, a Napoleon after Moscow or a Henri Quatre at Ivry: "*Ralliez-vous à mon chapeau*

---

26   From behind.

blanc: vous le trouverez toujours au chemin de la gloire et de l'honneur."[27]
Then she dismissed her maids of honour with a gracious gesture, afterwards saying to me: "This time, you will have to content yourself
by dispensing with 'rose petals', 'peach juice', *Chi* 繫 (or 紀) *K'ou'rh* 扣兒
(tying the knot, a 'technical' phrase for the inextricable union of copulation, with male or female), the 'old Bonze'[28] (alluding to the female
element being uppermost *au moment du commerce sexuel*)[29] with gong in
his arms. These lewd fellows are insupportable and waste my time and
yours. But I have made assurance doubly sure and you shall see one
more 'fiasco' performed in your presence like a poor actor strutting his
brief hour on the stage. Love shall come into its own later.

"Well now, forget all about it: I permit to you a cup of tea in my presence. Don't stay kneeling there, as if you had never cast eyes on me
before; I know that it is useless to offer to you a few whiffs of opium, but
you may smoke your favourite Russian 'gold' *Papirosi* (cigarettes). I am
going out on the lake in the launch: it will be cooler in half an hour with
the evening breeze. You and Li shall accompany me, but none else. Li
will give to you your cue for this night performance, so that you will be
able *prendre la parole en temps et lieu*."[30]

So we enjoyed *une promenade sur l'eau*,[31] the Old Buddha's calm self-
possession communicating itself to me. "I warn you, you will have a vigilant night, for you are here to expound constitutional principles, starting
at midnight until the psychological moment, probably before dawn." I
assured Her Majesty that I had brought with me enough textbooks to provide material for a dozen lectures if she possessed the requisite patience.

"This constitution," said she, "is going to bode no good for the Ta
Ch'ing Dynasty, but Japan seems to have continued very well in main-
taining the time-honoured theocracy" (that was the word she used) "in
the face of a representative government and the so-called popular will."
Then she asked me about the libellous letter and laughed sardonically at
the long list of her paramours. "The writer knows too much but it will be
his own irrevocable ending."

"Does Your Majesty guess the author?"

"No, I am only convinced that he is a secretary of the *Nei Ko* 內閣: not
only the calligraphy but the phraseology are reminiscent of stereotyped
Grand Secretariat formalism. But I shall ascertain the perpetrator's name
and by tomorrow at this time he will have 'lived'." (Compare Cicero's
phrase *Vixerunt*[32] when he announced to the people of Rome the death of
the Catilinarian conspirators.)

I asked Her Majesty why Ts'en Ch'un-hsüan was so ungrateful.

"Because he loves notoriety, *Ai Ch'u Feng T'ou* 愛出風頭. As you know,
he was very unpopular in Canton when viceroy of the Two Kuang 廣;

---

27 Rally to my white hat: you will find it on the path of glory and honor.
28 Buddhist monk.
29 In the moment of sexual commerce.
30 To speak in the right time and place.
31 A ride on the water.
32 They have lived (Plutarch, *Cicero* XXII.2).

it is a fact that the people of Kuangtung 廣東 detest their neighbourers of Kuangsi 廣西 who speak an entirely different dialect even more than they hate our Dynasty. He showed himself bloodthirsty but competent in suppressing local rebellion; I had accorded special favour to his brother Ts'en Yü-ying 岑毓英 and brought Ch'un-hsüan 春烜 up to the capital, because I know the corruption that prevailed in the Cantonese gang which controlled the Ministry of Communications, *Yu Ch'uan Pu* 郵傳部, and practically gave to him *carte blanche* to make a clean sweep with his new broom. He is a Hanlin 翰林 graduate[33] but not really a great scholar like Chang Chih-tung 張之洞 or Li Hung-chang 李鴻章. Yes; he attacks my morals, but my private life is not his affair, if in public life I am recognized, as I am, by the world as the ruler China needs. I am not pure as ice, nor white as snow, but what I have done, I have done."

"We have a saying, Madam, that the venal, infamous tribe of calumniators calls not Sir Galahad clean, nor Lancelot brave, although the former was a saint in purity and the latter a veritable incarnate Kuan Ti 關帝, the God of War."

"Take your Queen Victoria; when her favourite, Brown, the gillie (Gaelic for servant), to whom she erected a statue, died, did people accuse her of murdering him?"

"No, Madam; it was recognized as a natural death."

"Well, in the same way, I say that Wa Lun (Wallon) also died from natural causes: it is well known that *Mei Yao* 媚葯 (aphrodisiacs) sometimes provoke the rupture of a blood vessel. But I admit nothing and disavow nothing. Shall I forsooth blazon evil deeds or consecrate a crime? Never!! As to Kuang Hsü, may he pass thirty million Kalpas, *Chieh* 劫, (one Kalpa = forty-three thousand and twenty million years), roving, a disconsolate ghost, from one hell to another!"

"How will Your Majesty deal with the assassins?"

"*Il faut voir venir.*[34] You know that *Hao Ch'i Chê Shou* 好奇折壽, curiosity shortens life. Wait and see! But I can promise you that there will be no half measures, any more than there were in 1861 or 1898. As to Ts'en 岑, the arch-offender, he will live to regret his treason in a way that he shall most feel both in person and in pocket."

Talking of other monarchs' private lives, Her Majesty asked me some pointed questions about Edward VII: she had heard of a scandal in Denmark, where the King had won huge sums at baccara from an admiral who could not discharge the debt of honour and had blown his brains out in Edward's presence. I told her again of Sir William Gordon Cumming, falsely accused of cheating at cards, whom Albert Edward, as Prince of Wales in 1890-1, had advised *se brûler la cervelle*,[35] but the Scottish Baronet (a gentlemen which the prince was not) of highest lineage replied after the classic manner of Cambronne after Waterloo, on the Guard being

---

33 The Hanlin Academy was China's most elite academic institution at the time.
34 We will need to see how it goes.
35 To shoot himself.

advised to surrender to Wellington's troops: "*Merde*".[36] I am afraid the Old Buddha thought me disloyal but a monster of Edward's type does not command loyalty. As Gordon Cumming told him many years later when Edward, now King, sought a reconciliation: "As my sovereign I respect you; as a man, I despise you."

The sun was setting as our *dolce far niente*[37] terminated: the Empress went to her opium pipe and a game of chess with a eunuch who was something of a prodigy, while Li and I repaired, as on a previous occasion, to regale ourselves al fresco on an elaborate repast. Li gave to me the *consigne*:[38] he would call for me in the dressing room I had previously occupied, at about midnight. The Empress would be waiting for me in the drawing room; all the lights would be extinguished excepting one reading lamp with a green shade on the writing table; we were to sit opposite each other: writing materials were disposed for Her Majesty to take notes like an *acroates* (hearer) at a professional lecture. A partition led therefrom to her bedchamber which naturally neither of us was to enter.

It seemed that Ts'en Ch'un-hsüan was so convinced of success that he had actually demanded from the emperor a special audience, next morning at the hour of the Hare (5 to 7) and had already sent in through the confidential head-eunuch the memorial impeaching Her Majesty and incidentally (for I was afterwards shown the document) speaking of me in terms far from flattering, "the scorn of society (*Hsia San Lan* 下三濫) *Hsing T'ung Wu Lai* 行同無賴, a regular *vaurien*, an unemployed adventurer, *Wu Chih Yeh Chih T'ou Chi Che* 無職業之投機者, absolutely penniless, *Shen Wu Ch'ang Wu* 身無長物, *Pao Ts'ang Huo Hsin* 包藏禍心, harbouring dreadly designs", and sundry perhaps not wholly unmerited compliments if only I had been a woman to whom the original quotation applies, such as *Yeh Jung Chao Yin* 冶容召淫, *Man Ts'ang Hui Tao* 慢藏誨盜, a bedizened face encourages lust and an unprotected safe invites robbery (not that I painted my face but I plead guilty to seductive ways).

Rather ruefully I thought how much pleasanter dalliance, say *Ts'ao P'i Ku* 奝屁股 or *Ai Ts'ao* 挨奝, *pedicatio* active or passive, would be than poring over miserable books; it is true that I had taken a high degree in law and been called to the bar, but the subject bored me and, I am equally sure, bored Her Majesty. Moreover, one had put one's hand to the plough and the stakes were worth playing for.

Punctually at midnight, hour of the Rat, enter Li Lien-ying with a command from the Old Buddha: "Am ready, come now." I entered the darkened boudoir, found Her Majesty already seated and by her orders took the place arrogated to me, on a level (contrary to all etiquette) with her own. We started the lesson in sober earnest; she asked an infinity of more or less germane questions and hypotheses which were unlikely to materialize either in China or anywhere else in the world. I discoursed,

---

36 Shit.
37 Pleasant idleness.
38 Instruction.

and she poured in questions, till my tongue was packed and my throat dry; with a brief respite for tea and cigarettes the comedy was played for nearly four mortal hours.

Dawn was on the verge of breaking, when I heard the confused noise of hurrying feet and a tumult of thundering voices with shouts of: "Catch them, the fornicators. Kill the harlot empress; seize the adulterous devil: take them in the act: she is probably just being 'had' by him, what fun! *Na Na Liang Ko Se Kuei* 拿那兩個色鬼; *Sha Che Ko Yin Luan T'ai Hou* 這個淫亂太后, *Chiu Tsou Che Ko Ch'iang Chien Ti Kuei Tzu* 揪走這個強奸的 鬼子; *T'a Men Cheng Tsai Jo Nao Chung Chien* 他們正在成熟鬧中間, *Hsien Tsai Na T'a Men Cheng Shih Shih Hou* 現在拿他們正是時候; *Ta Kai T'a Cheng Tsai Tsao T'a* 大概他正在�》他, *Hao Jo Nao* 好熱鬧!" About a score of ruffians armed with long knives pushed open the door which was not locked nor even closely shut, rushed in the semi-darkness, for I had switched off the light on the table and they were falling over one another in their excitement to reach the bed-chamber where the supposed lovers were disporting, being evidently acquainted with the *aîtres*[39] of the palace. Suddenly all the numerous lights in the bed-chamber were turned on, while we were still in darkness.

The Old Buddha rose from her seat: her every word cut like a knife. "I do not usually grant an audience to a rabble of ruffians, but" – (at this moment all the lights of the boudoir were opened and the guards were rushing in from the bed-chamber, whence there was a secret passage leading to an antichambre), "I hereby command your summary arrest and decree your sentence, namely that each and all of you *Li Pi Chang Hsia* 立斃杖下, be flogged to death with the heavy bamboo in the outer courtyard of the palace."

One or two tried to resist but they were promptly disarmed and implored Her Majesty's clemency.

"*Ju Wo K'uan Shu Ni Men Ts'ai Chiao Kuai* 如我寬恕你們才叫怪, 'twill be a strange state of things if I pardon you. Order the soldiers to take each man and carry out the sentence." The guards, seeing that the Old Buddha had gained the rubber, left no doubt of their loyal devotion. "Now that the assassins have been bound and conveyed to the place of death, go and place Ts'en Ch'un-hsüan now engaged on urgent business with the emperor" (splendid was the sarcasm in her beautiful voice) "under instant arrest."

Ts'en's intelligence department must have been at fault, for at that moment an excited voice, speaking *Kuan Hua*[40] 官話 in a marked Kuangsi accent, shouted: "Have you caught them? His Majesty is issuing the decree which I drafted, commanding the harlot who calls herself empress dowager to hang herself with the silken cord, *Tz'u Pai* 賜帛".

There was no answer and Ts'en came bulging in, with the expression of a man who had completed a great enterprise and was about to cull the fruits. "*Pa T'a Men Liang Ko Kuo Tsei K'un Ch'i Lai* 把他們兩個國賊綑

---

39 Various parts.
40 Court language; Mandarin.

起來, bind the two of them, traitors to the state, with cords", shouted he. We were sitting slightly aside from the direct line from the door, and he did not take in the new situation immediately. I went on my knees as etiquette required; while the Old Buddha looked at Ts'en, her face disclosing a play of feature which was new to me, accustomed as I was to the vicissitudes of her wonderful physiognomy, tragedy and comedy blended, as in Sir Joshua Reynolds' portrait of David Garrick[41] which presents the rival allegorical figures striving for the mastery over the great actor's art. But I had once seen an identical expression on a face. Where? It was in the year of the Italian disaster in Abyssinia in the middle nineties (before the *Saturnia Tellus* sought to dominate the world under a masterful dictator):[42] I was staying at hillgirt Marinata in the Campagna where the Popes once had a villa, whence there is a wonderful view of the Basilica of Saint Peter which to the devout country-folk constitutes their life, their sweetness and their hope. I had been on a visit to Lake Nemi, then almost without peer or parallel even in Italy for beauty and charm, now alas! spoiled for a generation to come by the Fascist enterprise which drained the lake and retrieved Caligula's twin barges. A diver had brought up from one or other of the insane, libidinous emperor's pleasure-ships a statuette perhaps from Tarentum by the sea or Sybaris in the Graecia Magna of Southern Italy, inscribed "Medusa". I saw a peasant woman cross herself devoutly before that pagan figure; "Santa Medusa", she said, including her in the Catholic fold! It was the image of the Old Buddha at that moment: the eyes, usually so restless and eager, were metamorphosed into a cold, cruel, death-bringing stare which, as it were, petrified Ts'en who had momentarily lost the power of movement to kneel and kotow. He resembled Thésée at the moment of learning the awful truth of Hippolyte's death and of Phèdre's incest.[43] After a space, the truculent "Canton" tiger he, who had drunk the blood of a decapitated brigand to acquire courage which he certainly lacked (even so, during the September massacres a female prisoner at La Force drank a cup of fresh blood to save her father's life),[44] rallied from his trance of terror, trembled in every limb, sank upon the floor and muttered inarticulate sounds, while the Old Buddha played with him even as a cat with a mouse or as a boa constrictor with the rabbit or *cochon d'Inde*[45] which it fascinates with that stony, basilisk fixity of gaze.

"Come here, Ts'en Ch'un-hsüan," called out the well-known falsetto; "I want a word with you before I make use of the cord His Majesty so

---

41 David Garrick (1717-79) was a prominent English actor and playwright.
42 "*Saturnia Tellus*" or "the Land of the Golden Age" was an ancient Roman name for Italy, attributed to Virgil. Italy lost the First Italo-Ethiopian War to Abyssinia (Ethiopia) in 1896. The dictator referred to is Benito Mussolini.
43 Hippolytus (confusingly, in French his name is "Hippolyte", which is his mother's name according to the English transliteration), was the son of Theseus, who spurned the advances of his father's wife, Phaedra. Phaedra falsely accused Hippolytus of raping her and, believing this, Theseus cursed Hippolytus, resulting in his death.
44 The September Massacre (Sept. 2-7, 1792) comprised of a series of violent mob attacks on Parisian Royalist prisoners during the French Revolution, where over a thousand were brutally murdered.
45 Guinea pig.

graciously accords to me. You are a traitor who deserves to die a thousand deaths. First, tell me the author of the letter which you sent to me and to my British Legal Adviser whom, I think, you have not met."

"I am guilty of death, Your Majesty; the plot was suggested by the Grand Secretary, Sun Chia-nai 孫家鼐, against my wish. The letter was written by Chin Chih-ch'üan 金芝泉, a Manchu secretary of the Nei Ko 內閣."

"Do not lie to me: old Sun is in his dotage" (he was 88 that year); "I know he is of the emperor's party but he never initiated any action in his life. I hereby order" (to Li Lien-ying) "the arrest of Chin Chih-ch'üan who will die by the Ling Ch'ih 淩遲 (lingering death or Kua Tsui 剐罪)[46] this afternoon. As for you, Ts'en, I am not going to put you to death" – here Ts'en kotowed several times – "but you are fined two million Taels payable to me within forty days. At the expiry of this délai[47] you will be relieved of your present post of Yu Ch'uan Pu Shang Shu 郵傳部尚書 or president and by my gracious clemency given the viceroyalty of the Liang Kuang 兩廣, where, if I am accurately informed, your appetite for bribing Hao Huo 好貨 will soon replenish your temporarily empty purse. But, in order to shame you in public, Shih Ni Han Ch'un Wei Chung Mu So Tu 使你憨蠢爲衆目所睹,[48] Li Lien-ying is to order two of the P'u Hu 撲戶 (Manchu word for wrestlers noted for their strength of arm) to inflict upon your naked posterior forty strokes with the light bamboo, after receipt of which you are at liberty to return to Peking with what appetite you have."

The flogging was duly carried out in the Old Buddha's presence, Ts'en behaving, as I anticipated, like a poltroon. He fainted after thirty or so stripes but received the full tale upon regaining consciousness and his thighs resembled a shapeless jelly. I heard later that his Cantonese enemies in the Ministry, for of course, despite the Old Buddha's prohibition, the news became public property, joyfully inaugurated a sort of Nunc est bibendum[49] carnival, as the Romans did, according to old Horace, after the tidings of Actium and later of Cleopatra's suicide. Ts'en never attended the Ministry again and had considerable difficulty (despite his own fairly ample resources) in raising the two million fine as he had already disbursed 1½ million to obtain his present post in Peking; but Canton bankers came to his assistance and, if all accounts be true, the Hongkong and Shanghai Banking Corporation granted to him a special accommodation. He left for Canton early in September. It would have been a shock to the Grand Council arriving for audience to contemplate the naked buttocks of their colleague when he passait par les verges,[50] had they seen him. Neither Old Buddha nor the emperor gave any more audiences that day, and the Councillors returned to their villas at Haitien 海甸.

---

46 More commonly called "death by a thousand cuts".
47 Period.
48 The characters for Han Ch'un 憨蠢, would normally be written 寒蠢.
49 Now is the time for drinking (Horace, Odes I.XLVII.1).
50 Was being whipped.

The floggings were carried out one by one and occupied the greater part of the long day. The stalwart soldiers charged with the punishment were exhausted before the conclusion; it is said that a hundred strokes from the heavy bamboo are sufficient to cause death: the Summer Palace was like a shambles and my waiting chair-bearers who had seen part of the proceedings seemed utterly stunned and aghast for after all *Ts'e Yin Chih Hsin* 惻隱之心, pity, is part and portion of human-kind. It will be inferred that I remained as far away as possible; but the shrieks of the doomed men will remain in my ears till I die. Whether all were dead, I do not know; but in each case they were decapitated and the heads suspended in Haitien, while the corpses were consigned to the common ditch. Chin's sentence of *Ling Ch'ih* was duly carried out at Ts'ai Shih K'ou[51] 菜市口 before sundown; the long strip of linen mounted on a roll or *Chao Tzu* 招子, that was placed in his bound hands during the journey to execution carried the legend for all to read: "*Mou Hai Huang T'ai Hou Chih Fan* 謀害皇太后之犯, misprision of treason against the Empress Dowager".

Her Majesty who seemed "faint yet pursuing" (in the words of the Bible) detained me in conversation and bade me remain for luncheon. She said before taking leave: "It has been a tiring night for us both, far more so than if we had had our heart's desire. It matters not, however: I shall send for you at an early date and you shall perform the various manoeuvres of which you tell me the names and with which you are so familiar. Be not uneasy: I don't fancy we shall have any more anonymous letters nor melodramatic impeachments in the near future. You did well, and I thank you once more. As to Li Lien-ying, he shall have a share in Ts'en's fine which will compensate for previous omissions toward him on that gentleman's part. I shall order the gendarmerie to prohibit all mention in the press of this unimportant incident. I am really obliged for your lesson in Constitutional Government and hope that you found me an apt pupil. But next time we won't discuss International Law but sexuality and the myriad forms of love and lust, while we exhaust the gamut of exotic emotions. What do you say?"

"What can I say, Old Buddha, what shall I say, except that you are my Aphrodite and my queen of love. Yesterday, today and forever. Forever and forever, Thine alone!"

In these papers I have been meticulous to record things actually seen and heard at first hand, *ce que j'appelle vu et non pas ce que je sais par ouï-dire*,[52] so that I refrain from chronicling conversations plausible but lacking in verisimilitude, unlike the great Athenian, Thucydides, who chronicles speeches and orations with the convenient preamble: "To this effect spoke so and so", probably reproducing the substance with a good deal of his own creation, but not the actual wording. Hence I am, in a sense, breaking my own rule, but deem it of interest to add here what Li Lien-ying told to me a few days later respecting the Old

---

51   "Vegetable Market", Peking's execution ground at the time of this story.
52   I say what I saw, not what I know from hearsay.

Buddha's conversation with the emperor, on the evening of the events above set forth. As Li was present, I consider it to be dependable and veracious. It is as follows: (I had no opportunity of asking the Old Buddha if the report is verbatim or otherwise.)

Enter Kuang Hsü who kotows thrice, then kneels: "Your Majesty, I am come into your presence with a birchrod in my hand and ask you to chastise me." (*Fu Ching Ch'ing Tsui* 負荊請罪, the phrase is historical and figurative.)

Empress Dowager: "The cup of my patience is overflowing. You little fool, *Sha Hsiao Tzu* 傻小子, do not you know chalk from cheese (lit: one kind of grain from another)? It is always the same story, disobedience, unfilial conduct, futile plots. You have no sense in you: every page of your life is a repetition, *Ni T'ai Pu K'ai Ch'iao* 你太不開竅, *Ch'ien P'ien I Lü* 千篇一律."

Kuang Hsü: "Ts'en Ch'un-hsüan brought to me what he called proofs of Your Majesty's love-adventures with a 'devil'. He forced me to seal a decree which (he said) old Sun Chia-nai had drafted. I hardly read it. This is the truth. For he blustered and bullied me till I acquiesced."

Empress Dowager: "Yes: I have to thank you for allowing me to use the silken cord for suicide (*Tz'u Pai* or *Po* 賜帛), thus saving my face. The 'devil' you spoke of is engaged by me on a regular salary through the Hsüeh Pu[53] 學部 and comes here to teach to me Law and Constitutional Reform. Love affairs indeed!!! *Fang T'a Men P'i* 放他們屁!!! *ce sont des péteurs, voilà tout.*[54] I see him at night because affairs of state detain me all day and shall continue to do so, by your leave. I warn you, Emperor, that the next time you offend me will be the last. *Wu Wei Yen Chih Pu Yü Yeh* 勿謂言之不預也 – Say not that you were not warned in time! *Kun K'ai Che'rh* 滾開這兒, be off with you" (with a vigorous gesture).

Exit Kuang Hsü after kotowing, greatly perturbed.

---

53 "Ministry of Education". This claim is technically correct. Backhouse was appointed professor of law and literature at Imperial Capital University (later Peking University) in 1903 by the Chinese government, who must have been suitably impressed with his qualifications. He held the position for ten years.

54 They are merely breaking wind (telling ridiculous lies).

CHAPTER XIV

THE DEMON-RIDDEN EUNUCH

PROLOGUE

FLAUBERT once said: *"J'ai la pensée, quand je fais un roman, de rendre une coloration, une nuance. Par example, dans mon roman carthaginois (Salammbô), je veux faire quelque chose pourpre. Dans Madame Bovary, je n'ai eu que l'idée d'un ton, cette couleur de moisissure de l'existence de cloportes. L'histoire, l'aventure d'un roman, ça m'est bien égal."*[1]

I am not writing a *roman* nor yet a *nouvelle*,[2] perhaps could not if I tried. But in the following sketch (as in all the series *sur la décadence mandchoue*),[3] I definitely have in my mind the tint of mouldiness; wherein the wood-louse thrives and multiplies. I fancy that it was one of the de Goncourt[4] who said: *"La nature pour moi est ennemie. Rien n'est moins poétique que la nature. C'est l'homme qui a mis, sur toute cette misère et ce cynisme de matière, le voile, l'image, la spiritualité ennoblissante"*[5] (the last word I would omit). Les Goncourt take a respite from the horrible spectacle of nature by contemplating humanity. Even so, Baudelaire turns toward contrasts which have naught in common with reality as usually conceived and is disposed toward creations whence nature (in its ordinary sense) is absent and which seem (but are not) purely artificial. To Gautier, Baudelaire, Goncourt, Flaubert all human life is evil: they blame nature (as normally represented) for their own bitterness and melancholy toward life. Flaubert was epileptic; Baudelaire died of aphasia; Jules de Goncourt of general paralysis of the insane.

It was Flaubert who hailed in Nero *"l'homme culminant du monde ancien"*;[6] he insisted that the artist must needs so write as to cause

---

1 My thought, when I am writing a novel, is to depict a colour, a shade. For instance, in my Carthaginian novel (*Salammbô*), I want to do something purple. In *Madame Bovary*, I had only the idea of a tone, the colour of that mouldiness of a woodlouse's existence. The story, the plot of the novel, I do not care.

2 Novel . . . short story.

3 On the decadence of Manchus.

4 The Goncourt brothers, Edmond (1822-96) and Jules (1830-70), were writers and critics. In honour of Jules, Edmond willed his entire estate to support the foundation of the Académie Goncourt, which now bestows the most revered prize in French literature, the Prix Goncourt.

5 To me, nature is an enemy. There is nothing less poetic than nature. It is mankind who puts on all this misery and all this material cynicism, a veil, an image, an ennobling spirituality.

6 "The human culmination of the ancient world", originally *"l'homme culminant du monde antique"*.

posterity to doubt his individual existence; he was the most hard-working of men, but he writes: *"quel fruit revient-il à l'homme de tout l'ouvrage?"*[7] he who worked fourteen hours a day!! Again, Flaubert in his correspondence: *"On m'a fait hier une petite opération à la joue à cause de mon abcès; j'ai la figure embobelinée de linge et passablement grotesque; comme si ce n'était pas assez de toutes les pourritures et de toutes les infections qui ont précédé notre naissance et qui nous reprendront à notre mort. Notre vie n'est que corruption et putréfaction successives, alternatives et envahissantes l'une sur l'autre. Qu'on ajoute à cela les cors aux pieds, les mauvaises odeurs naturelles, les sécrétions de toute espèce et de toute saveur, ça ne laisse pas que de faire un tableau fort excitant de la personne humaine. Dire qu'on aime tout ça! Encore qu'on s'aime soi-même!"*[8]

I can just imagine "Wit's self" (as Browning calls him), Voltaire's Homeric laughter, as he wrote: *"Il n'y a plus de Manichéens, disait Candide. Et Martin répondit: il y a moi."*[9] Even so, may I not say, in all humility, that, not indeed Voltaire, but Flaubert exists (*in petto*)[10] in these my studies, rich, according to normal conception, in human depravity but owing nought to art; since they all happen to be true. There runs through them a coherent nexus, a sympathetic coloration, whether the personages be the Old Buddha, Li Lien-ying 李蓮英, the Manchu princes and patricians, mimes, catamites, soothsayers, astrologers, eunuchs and Li Ting-kuo 李定國, the possessed maniac, the theme of this narration, who came within an ace of terminating my existence!

H.B.M.'s envoy to the Manchu Court, Sir John Jordan, that dauntless libertine who sold consular offices for the price of his staff's and their wives' favours, who was, like (in this one respect) the great Julius César, *vir omnibus mulieribus et mulier omnibus viris*, all things to all men and all women when they met his lusts half-way, *princeps et pontifex maximus generis insignissimi pedicantium*, sovereign lord and pope of the noble race of sodomites, wrote in 1908 to Sir E. Grey (as the latter informed me and in fact showed to me the letter)[11] that I was brilliant in intellect, unbalanced in judgment and amoral in character, betraying a capacity for epigram that I should hardly have looked for. It was Chuang Tzu 莊子 who said that the "poor pedestrian" worm "thou treadest on" conjectures nought of the swan's high aspiration and *essor*.[12] Jordan, petulant, irascible, vindictive, hated the rival service to which I had the honour to belong and all its works; how much he knew of the Old

---

7   From the whole work, what fruit goes to man?

8   Yesterday my cheek had to undergo a small operation due to an abscess; my face is wrapped in cloth and looks quite grotesque; as if there were not enough rottenness and infection which preceded our birth and that will take over us after our death. Our life is nothing but corruption and putrefaction, successive, invasive, alternating one after the other. Add to this the corns, the natural foul odours, secretions of any kind and any flavour, it does not fail to make a very exciting picture of mankind. And we admit that we love it all! That we love ourselves!

9   There are no more Manicheans, said Candide. And Martin replied: there is me.

10   In secret.

11   **Backhouse:** Sir E. Grey told me that Jordan, in reporting the incident to the Foreign Office in London, spoke of a revolution in embryo in the region West of Peking which had been quelled by Manchu guards who arrived in good time. Thus is history written.

12   Taking flight.

Buddha's affections toward me I know not but what he did know he resented. I would fain hope that the Goncourt *frères*,[13] Baudelaire, Flaubert, even Gautier, would have found in my narratives a certain appeal (*Bog znayet*,[14] God knows) not because of much literary skill in them inherent, but owing to *l'accent de la vérité de laquelle j'ose me flatter*.[15]

Nature teaches crime: the animals kill their kind perhaps from jealousy or without any reason except hunger. The ants are terrible in their ferocity; doe, no less than buck, rabbits eat their young; wolves devour each other; female apes and orang-outangs slay a rival. Humanity constituted justice; so that violence is the exception and crime an anomaly. It is today a morbid germ which poisons life, instead of being the "nurse" of primitive man, as Dostoiyewski perceives in *Crime et Châtiment*.[16] A Catholic priest of Notre-Dame once became insane from the thought of Judas Iscariot's sufferings in nethermost hell; because Jesus' betrayal was fore-ordained in order to fulfill the Scriptures and to accomplish the Mystery of the Redemption. And so the good father prayed at the high altar for Judas' pardon and asked for a sign. And God heard the prayer, sending Judas to touch with his warm, gentle hand the priest's forehead in benediction! The father *se releva radieux et tout en larmes*.[17] But, when he reported the miracle next day to his father superior, Holy Church *le frappa de ses foudres en l'excommuniant*.[18] Ah! what fools we mortals be!

It was, I fancy, in August 1907, Kuang Hsü XXXIII, 7, that I had been once more summoned by Her Majesty to the Summer Palace for a *nuit d'amour* which indeed I might hesitate to record in otiose detail traversing familiar ground, but for the sequel. Her Majesty had been unusually salacious, even for her *nondum satiata cupido*,[19] and the damp heat of an August night, even in the relative cool of the lake-side, did not make for advanced sexuality, where I was concerned. It is, I believe, the fact that Chinese as Manchus usually eschew conjugal intercourse during the *San Fu* 三伏, *la canicule*;[20] not so the Old Buddha who seemed to enjoy the act of sex even more in the hot weather than in winter. Of course, her apartment was as cool as a cyclone with fans overhead galore and a small one above the phoenix couch.

On this particular occasion, despite copious draughts of Lien-ying's specific *Mei Yao* 媚葯, four successive copulations, the last *pedicatio*, had completely "floored" me: my final attempt culminated, or *pour mieux dire*[21] did not culminate, in the discharge of no seminal fluid whatsoever.

13   Brothers.
14   Бог знает.
15   The ring of truth of which I dare to boast.
16   *Crime and Punishment*.
17   Became joyful and teary eyed.
18   Struck him with the thunderbolt of excommunication.
19   Insatiable desire.
20   The dog-days; warmest season.
21   To be more precise.

The *meatus* or *Ma Yen* 馬眼 was indeed slightly tinged with a sticky red material, but *à tout prendre*,[22] I was as dry as the *Sciroccacio*, Roman term for the hot and oppressive wind from the Libyan desert,[23] so that, much to the Old Buddha's discontent *questo pezzo era un fiasco completo*,[24] the performance was *une affaire manquée et j'étais allé aux cerises*.[25] In a word, *j'avais fait four*,[26] and the Old Buddha, with her habitual thoughtfulness, *avait eu la mauvaise inspiration de prendre dans sa bouche mon chybre, en le titillant d'une manière vive et d'entrain*, took it into her head in an unlucky moment to put my tool in her mouth and to titillate it back and forth with her tongue in a most vigorous manner. "There's a taste of fresh blood, *Hsien Hsieh Ti Tzu Wei* 鮮血的 味," said she; and I to reply: "*Prière de ne pas le sucer, V.M., cela me fait bien du mal.*[27] Please don't apply the *gamme à louche*[28] to it any more; it is very painful indeed."

"Ah! I see: you have been having amorous gambols again with your pet eunuch: if you go on disobeying me, I shall whip you once more. You remember the last time what happened at the Lake Palace? However, you had better take a rest now and I shall expect much better results this evening (it was now nearly dawn), for you must not return to the city today."

"Old Buddha," said I, "as always I shall do my best, *je ferai l'impossible*[29] but sexuality is not enormously pronounced in my case."

"It is all gone into your anal region; that's why you can't achieve more in front. *Ch'üan Kuei Ni Yen'rh Tso Yu* 歸你眼兒左右, *Ch'ien T'ou Pu I Ch'eng Kung* 前頭不易成功."

Thus we bandied words and Her Majesty was about to dismiss me, for the hour of audience was approaching. Enter Li Lien-ying in a terrible state of hysterical confusion, scarcely able to find words, utterance or the power of speech.

"What in the world ails you?" asked the Old Buddha; "have you seen a ghost? If not, there's one here" (meaning me; a play on the word *Kuei* 鬼 foreigner and *revenant*).

"Oh! Your Majesty, I implore you not to jest; there's terrible news from the Shih Tzu Wo'rh 獅子窩兒, Lion's Den (temple) at Ssu P'ing T'ai 四平台, where, as you know, my maniac relation Li Ting-kuo, the eunuch who some twenty years ago was Your Majesty's body servant, has his *Pieh Yeh* 別業, country home. He has been demented these years past, in fact ever since the Boxer time, when, as Old Buddha remembers, he was a prominent *Ta Shih Hsiung* 大師兄, a preceptor in the hierarchy, and its failure broke his heart. But my nephew" (*à la mode de Bretagne*)[30] "has just

---

22   All things considered.

23   *Scirocco* is more commonly used in Italy. The word used here employs the pejorative suffix *accio* and would correctly be written "*siroccaccio*".

24   This piece was a complete fiasco.

25   An utter failure and I went to the cherries.

26   I had failed.

27   Please do not suck it, Your Majesty, it does me great harm.

28   "Great ladle", presumably her mouth.

29   I will do the impossible.

30   In the British style.

arrived from the hills and says that Ting-kuo is having a most violent access of his mania: he is possessed (Fu^{31} $T'i$ 伏體) by Ch'ang Yeh 長爺, Lord Long, the mystic snake who never leaves him, and keeps on shouting with prodigious force which carries a li or more away: '*Ts'ao Lao Fo Yeh* 奅老佛爺, *Ts'ao T'a P'i Ku* 奅他屁股, *Sha Kuei Tzui* 鬼子, *Sha Chien Fu* 奸夫, *Mieh Ch'ing Ch'ao* 滅清朝, *Ta Kuei Tzu* 打鬼子, *Ko Ming Wan Wan Sui* 革命萬萬歲! F.... the Old Buddha, pedicate with her, slay the devils (foreigners), slay the adulterous paramour (meaning me!!); destroy the Manchu Dynasty, down with the foreigners, long live the revolution.' " (It should be noted that revolution was rearing its head in the capital; the Old Buddha looked black as thunder at the reference to a revolution which she hoped in her life time to avert, as the oracle had promised.)

Lien-ying went on: "Oh! Your Majesty, come and deliver me from this death in life. The Old Ancestress doubteth not of my loyalty but folks who hear the madman's ill-omened horrible frenzy will say that our Li family has joined the forces of evil to Your Majesty's detriment. Again, Your Majesty knows that a number of devils are accustomed to make Ssu P'ing T'ai 四平台 their *villégiature*[32] during the hot weather: Chu Erh-tien 朱爾典, Jordan, is staying at the Hall of Neptune, Lung Wang T'ang 龍王堂, and will certainly be told of Ting-kuo's lunacy."

"Well, well," said Her Majesty rather angrily; "what do you want of me? Do you expect me to go and heal your demented cousin-brother (*Shu Pai Hsiung* 叔伯兄)? How can I make the journey in this weather with the roads a quagmire and I *hate* this sticky heat, *T'ien Fa Nien* 天發黏, *Wo Hsien T'a* 我嫌他."

"Forgive me, Old Buddha, but this is exactly what I do implore you to do; and you will deliver me and my whole house. If we don't go, the scandal will be noised abroad and the talk of revolution will be *ébruité*[33] all over the country side, so that even the "devils" will be reporting to their foreign governments. Ting-kuo will certainly murder the unhappy family and my nephew says that a crowd of yokels was beginning to collect at the gate."

"You certainly are unfortunate and not lacking in effrontery. But in the circumstances I am willing to consider a trip to your cousin's home after audience. Pa Hou Yeh 巴侯爺 shall accompany me. I know you are worn out by too much love, but never mind: you will feel better for the excursion and shall have some *vin de Champagne* to stimulate you before we start. Don't refuse me! Be ready then, in about an hour's time. Order my chair and his; tell his bearers there will be *doubles guides* (double fees) for them as an act of grace." I felt literally dumbfoundered at Her Majesty's words, being too weak even to fling "the poor cat of the adage"[34] and could not, for the life of me, champagne or no champagne,

---

31 **Backhouse:** 伏 was used in the Boxer year of the young adepts possessed by the Jade Emperor.
32 Resort.
33 Leaked.
34 "Like the poor cat i' the adage" (Shakspere, *Macbeth* I.7). The adage referred to is "The cat loves fish but she's loth to wet her paws".

conceive how I was to support an exhausting trip which entailed much hill climbing *par-dessus le marche*[35] for a semi-impotent *débauché*.[36] But the Old Buddha willed, though I still hoped to dissuade her despite the fact that none dare disobey what is Heaven's (heaven being the Old Buddha) ordinance: *Feng Ming Tzu T'ien* 奉命自天, *An Kan Huo Wei* 安敢或違?

While I am waiting for Her Majesty's good pleasure during her audience with the Council and hoping for the cancellation of her order, I must needs say a few words anent the *Wu Ta Men'rh* 五大門兒, five great families of supernatural Beings round whom so much superstition gathers in China and partially in Japan. Certain things that I have seen lead me to place greater credence in their reality than may appear reasonable to the scientific-minded. The five great families then are: 1) Hedgehog, Tz'u Wei 刺蝟, Pai Yeh 白爺, Lord White; 2) Huang Yeh 黃爺, Lord Yellow, Weasel, Huang Shu Lang 黃鼠狼; 3) Hu Yeh 狐爺, Lord Fox, or Fairy Fox, the "*Kitsune*" venerated in Japan, which, or who, specially possesses women and is frequently named in the *Liao Chai* 聊齋 or *Strange Stories from the Library of My Love* by P'u Sung-ling 蒲松齡, as indeed are the other sacred beings; it assumes the form of a beautiful young female and bewitches men whom it allures to paths of love; 4) Ch'ang Yeh 長爺, Lord Long, Ch'ang Ch'ung 長虫 or snake, of which there is question in this narrative; 5) Ch'ing Yeh 青爺, Lord Green, or Dragon, who has his habitat in the grottoes of Chieh T'ai Ssu 戒台寺 and in whose honour the great Ch'ien Lung 乾隆 wrote a tablet of commemoration.

It is germane to the subject to record an experience of my own. Some ten years ago a friend and neighbour, who in fact occupied part of my spacious mansion, once part of a prince's palace in the West City, had remarried: his fourth wife being a Manchu named Ho 何 of the *Nei Wu Fu*[37] 內務府 whose family residence was on Hsi La Hut'ung 錫拉胡同, Pewter Lane, not far from the small house which saw the birth of the Old Buddha. The Ho family had been wealthy, as behoved officials for generations attached to the Imperial Household, but had been looted of large quantities of hoarded silver in 1916 during Chang Hsün's *opéra bouffe*[38] Restoration.

My friend, who had ample (certainly triple) experience of marital blisses (?) apart from multitudinous *Egéries*[39] of his passing fancy, can hardly have been enamoured by Ho Ta Hsiao Chieh 何大小姐, for, far from being *jolie à croquer*,[40] she was uncomely *à faire peur*,[41] a fright of stout build, huge eyes which seemed to radiate insane delusions even at first sight, with a strangely unworthy waddle appertaining to the domestic duck rather than to a woman. I am pretty sure, however, that he

---

35 On top of everything.
36 Libertine.
37 Office of Internal Affairs.
38 "Farcical", a reference to a theatrical style pioneered by the Théâtre des Bouffes Parisiens in the late 19th century.
39 Muses.
40 Pretty as a picture.
41 Dreadful.

was enamoured of her *dot*[42] and sumptuous *trousseau*, brass bedsteads *de luxe*, costly Paris furniture and exquisite porcelains of K'ang Hsi 康熙 and his two successors.

She had scarcely entered the home of her husband than her vagaries manifested themselves. A vagabond Taoist priest of the Lü Tz'u 呂祠[43] near the Liu Li Ch'ang 琉廠 had been *Mei Jen* 媒人 or matchmaker for the union, which the widowed mother, a concubine of the late Nei Wu Fu Lang Chung Ho Hao-jan[44] 內務府郎中何浩然, had welcomed; as her daughter had not been deemed marriageable, being ugly as a scare crow, and her husband to be, my old friend, was supposed to be wealthy. Incidentally, it will not astonish my readers to hear that his family by his former wife were up in arms against this new *belle mère*,[45] and a sort of *Chia T'ing Ka Ming* 家庭革命, domestic revolution, supervened. The very day of her arrival (*Kuo Men* 過門) she announced in awe-struck melodramatic tones that she had received a mandate from Ta Ch'ing Yeh 大青爺, Lord Senior Snake (the sacred Being owned to a younger brother Erh Ch'ing 二青, Junior Snake or Snake the Second) to construct a shrine for his sojourn of the most costly materials (like King Solomon about to start operations for his temple in Sion). Contractors were summoned to offer estimates and in due course the shrine alone cost to the family the pretty figure of $4,500, say at that time £500. Lavish expenditure on shrines might peradventure be justified; but unfortunately "Lord Senior Snake" was not satisfied with construction but demanded *démolition par-dessus le marché*.[46] He compelled his votary to pronounce on his behalf a series of "decrees" which enjoined the immediate levelling to the ground of many recently erected *Chien* or rooms. The demon-possessed bride found fault with the *Feng Shui* 風水 or geomantic influence in this or that portion of the house, including even my own quarters. With lurid metaphors she glibly cursed and swore at buildings in a perfect state of repair compelling their removal, insulting the family *lares et penates*,[47] even destroying the ancestral *Ying* 影 or portraits, using language that the Old Buddha herself, past mistress of lewd phraseology, might not have disowned, generally making life a hell, *Hsiu Lo Ch'ang* 修羅場 or Aceldama (Field of slaughter where Judas hanged himself: *Acts* I.19), in Japan known as *Shurajo*, a field of death, for her unfortunate husband and associates. She even shattered valuable ceramics and vases. I used to think that the paroxysms of her possession were hysterical or imaginary; but we found that violent slapping, even whipping, vigorous and implacable, across the breech (bared) passed unperceived during the convulsions, while the cold-water treatment was quite ineffective. Each attack would last half an hour or more; recovering she would utter a few words delivered like

---

42 Dowry.
43 Correctly written 呂祖.
44 Secretary-general of the Office of Internal Affairs, Ho Hao-jan.
45 Mother-in-law.
46 Destruction to top it off.
47 Household gods.

a Papal Bull *ex cathedra*:[48] "Decree reverently received from Ta Ch'ing Yeh 大青爺 (Lord Senior Green): You," to her husband, "are hereby commanded to cut down the secular sophora or acacia (*Huai Shu* 槐樹) in the north courtyard and to kill all the tame pigeons" (of which we had many trained for their whistle-equipped flights). I am glad to think that in this case neither mandate was carried out thanks to my ultimatum, viz. that I would inform the police and have her ladyship arrested as a dangerous lunatic. I can sympathize with the neighbours of the man possessed of many devils whom Jesus once "healed" in Galilée, by exorcizing the lunatic and causing the unfortunate swine in Gadara to plunge into the lake (an act unworthy of the "Son of God"). Although I lack proof, I have always believed that the murder some years later of her husband was due to this demoniacal possession which caused, or compelled, her to enter into contact with hired *apaches*[49] who duly performed the will of Saint Senior Green, Ta Ch'ing Yeh, which was perhaps not wholly unconnected with some lustful feminine desire toward a Lothario of her ken.

Li went on to say: "He wants to *Ts'ao* 姦, copulate with, everyone he sees although he has nothing to *Ts'ao* with; he is saying the most terrible things such as 'Down with the Old Buddha; destroy the Monarch; long live the revolution. *Ta Tao Lao Fo Yeh* 打倒老佛爺; *Mieh Ta Ch'ing* 滅大清; *Ta Ko Ming Wan Wan Sui* 大革命萬萬歲.' It is a dreadful loss of face for me, *Wo Chen Han Ch'un* 我真憨蠢; everyone knows he is my relation and people are accusing me (me of all people) of having anti-dynastic sentiments and of wishing to harm Your Sacred Majesty's person. Old Buddha, I entreat you once again to deliver me, *Lao Fo Yeh* 老佛爺, *Nin Shih En* 您施恩, *Chiu Wo* 救我: *Chien Chih Ti Wo Yao Feng La* 簡直的我要瘋啦, I am literally going off my head." Then he broke out in wild weeping, frenzied and seemingly on the verge of being possessed himself by one of the five Great Beings, be it dragon, serpent, hedgehog, weasel or fox. (I might mention here that, as Anatole France says in *Les Sept Femmes de Barbe-Bleue*,[50] I never reject a legend or a myth on the ground of its incredibility, *il n'y a pas à y croire ni à en douter*,[51] because my own experience of the supernatural has been distinctly abnormal; Excalibur (T'ai O 太阿) may have been *fée*, *contes bleus*[52] may be other than the "baseless fabric of a vision", Merlin may have conducted Arthur in the latter's mystic barge to the island of Avillon (Shakspere's *Tempest*) to heal him of his grievous wound: it does not sound probable nor greatly endowed with verisimilitude but is all on the same principle of credulity. I was even at pains in my walks abroad or in my own "curtilage", should I encounter hedgehog or weasel (for I never came across a fairy fox except at the Summer Palace, and he died of rabies), to accord to him, or it, right of way with a

---

48   From the throne.
49   Parisian slang for "gangster" around the turn of the 20th century.
50   *The Seven Wives of Bluebeard.*
51   There is neither belief nor doubt.
52   Faerie, fairy tales.

courtly *Tso Yi* 作揖, or bow. My Manchu friends expressed polite approval; the *Kuei Tzu*[53] 鬼子 of my acquaintance, on whom be the latest curse of Buddha, calmly concluded that I was, and am, eccentric, nay! insane, oblivious of the fact that one must first find the circle before pronouncing on its centre! *Ils estiment qu'un homme est fou quand il entend ce que les autres n'entendent pas et voit ce que les autres ne voient pas; pourtant Socrate consultait son démon et Jeanne d'Arc entendait des voix,*[54] like the hero of *le Horla* haunted by a vampire who drinks the milk *sur sa table de nuit*).[55]

After the council I once more appealed to Her Majesty for my sake, if she loved me, not to go; but Lien-ying became even more hysterical in his uncontrolled weeping. "Well, well," said the Old Buddha, "*Ni Shuo Ti Shih Shih Hua* 你說的是實話, *Feng Feng Tien Tien Ti* 瘋瘋癲癲的; *Sang Hsin Ping K'uang* 喪心病狂; *Huo Kai* 活該: *Shemmo Tung Hsi* 什麼東西; *Chê Huan Liao Tê* 這還了得; *Pu Hsü Ni K'u* 不許你哭. You are certainly speaking the truth and seem quite crazed; frenzy is dazing and stupefying you. Serve you right? What in the world are you up to? I really can't stand this. You are forbidden to weep any more. So you will take no denial! Poor Pa Hou Yeh is quite tired out and I have had a bad night" (said playfully) "thanks to his erotic attentions (!!) which give to me no peace from his amorous whims and desires. Come to the point at once: I can see you are still expecting me to take immediate action by going on this mad excursion, and to drive the nail right in, *Pa Ting Tzu Ting Ssu La* 把 釘子釘死啦."

"Your Majesty, I know old Pa is feeling the effects of his tiring night, but I venture on my knees to entreat the Old Ancestress once more to insist on his accompanying you and to go with me at once to the Shih Tzu Wo 獅子窩. It may be that the Old Buddha's miraculous power may exorcise this wretched snake; my nephew informs me that his demented shrieks can be heard a great distance away: in fact (as I said before), he is accusing Your Majesty of salacious propensities, declares that you have many secret liaisons even with 'devils' (foreigners), that you have bewitched him with your magic charms!"

"But I thought you said he was snake-ridden; apparently he is empress-dowager-haunted!"

"No, Your Majesty; I meant that Lord Long possesses him against his will, so that his mouth vomits forth filth and excrements (*étrons*)[56] against the Old Buddha's Majesty."

"Very well, what do you say, old Pa? Do you persist in saying 'nay' or shall we go with him and study Li's 'honourable relative' on the spot? You cannot refuse to lend yourself to my wishes?"

Naturally, I could not press my entreaties to Her Majesty and consequently had to feign a delighted compliance which I assuredly did not

---

53 Devils; foreigners.
54 They believe that a man is insane when he can hear what others do not hear and when he can see what others do not see; however, Socrates referred to his demon and Joan of Arc heard voices.
55 "On his night table". Le Horla (1887) is a short-story by Guy de Maupassant about a man tormented by an invisible supernatural being that subsists on milk and water.
56 Turds.

feel. So Her Majesty renewed her order (which I had besought her to countermand) for the apricot-yellow chair of state, but bade Li note that she was *Ch'ing Chü Chien Ts'ung* 輕車減從, taking very few attendants or retinue on the excursion. I still thought the whole proceeding risky in the extreme; for I was quite unarmed and we were going forth to an encounter with a maniac who, mad or not, openly proclaimed himself a revolutionary. I did not relish the possibility of an *"attentat"*[57] against the Old Buddha and the eventual intervention of foreign soldiery, since I knew that there was a small body-guard for the British envoy, composed, I fancy, of troops from a Highland regiment, stationed at Pa Ta Ch'u 八大處 quite close to the Shih Tzu Wo 獅子窩: it would be an ideal opportunity for Jordan to gain face at home and a desired decoration from the dynasty of Saxe-Cobourg![58]

My own green chair was awaiting me with a couple of outriders and the usual relief of eight bearers in their open cart; there was no course now open except to put a good face upon the matter and trust to providence. The Old Buddha was ready in surprisingly quick time for a woman; Li Lien-ying contented himself with a humble ass hired at the gate, and we started the same afternoon in the very hottest part of a hot day. The Old Buddha was fanning herself vigorously, as was her use and wont when nerves, usually so composed, mastered her indomitable, albeit frail-looking, physique. We arrived at last at a hamlet about 2 li distant from the Ts'ui Wei Shan 翠薇山, and I asked Her Majesty if she wished Li to engage three *P'a Shan Hu* 爬山虎, mountain chairs, for the ascent to Shih Tzu Wo. She declined, saying: "We had better walk, *Pu Yüan Kuo Yü Sheng Chang* 不願過於聲張, I don't want the matter made too public."

It was a longish climb and I did not see how not only she, but also Li and myself, although he had his donkey but could not well ride it in her presence, were ever going to accomplish the "round trip" of say six or seven English miles in this burdensome heat. In a moment, the Empress called a halt, her bearers and mine took a rest, and we entered a small tea shop for repose and refreshment. The Empress and Li, as I expected, needed a siesta in a tiny back room after their exertions and followed it up by *Kuo Yin* 過癮, indulging their opium cravings. Her Majesty had brought a large supply of Russian *Papirosi*, cigarettes, and a bottle of Niersteiner for me. Naturally, the apricot yellow chair made it impossible to conceal her identity. Said the Empress: "It amuses me to see and hear these honest rustics talk."

One villager said, not in the Old Buddha's hearing: "Who's that devil in the green chair?"

"Don't you know? You are really too bereft of sense: it's the foreign emperor, *Kuei Tzu Huang Shang* 鬼子皇上."

---

57 Attack.
58 The House of Saxe-Coburg (sometimes called "Saxe-Coburg and Gotha") was a royal Germanic line. In 1840, Prince Albert of Saxe-Coburg married England's ruling monarch, Queen Victoria. Their son, Edward VII, became the first Saxe-Coburg ruler of England and the family, renamed Windsor during the First World War, remains on the English throne today.

"Why is he not in a yellow chair?"

"Really, you are stupid today: are not you aware that *Lao Fo Yeh Pan Shih* 老佛爺辦事, the Old Buddha performs the government?"

"They seem very *Ch'in Jo* 親熱, on warm terms."

"Of course they are, *Shei Li Pu K'ai Shei* 誰離不開誰, they are quite inseparable!"

So we rested there for a great while, and to my relief no "devil" appeared in the vicinity. It must have been about four o'clock when Her Majesty gave the signal for us to start on our long stroll. Li looked ruefully toward me at the prospect and we exchanged commiserating glances; but the Old Buddha was adamant and seemed to enjoy making us both, particularly Li, stretch our legs. It ended in the Empress riding the ass for a short distance, and she kept on saying to me: "You must be tired, Pa Hou," and I to reply: "Yes, Old Buddha, I am indeed quite exhausted."

We encountered no aliens, only some bonzes[59] who did not at the moment recognize Her Majesty, for none kneeled as etiquette required. We reached a point more than midway up the hill and then turned along a level path eastward, with the Shih Tzu Wo in full view. We had not gone afar when a series of horrid half human (as from Charenton or Bicêtre)[60] yells greeted us; they were hardly of a nature to soothe Her Majesty's feelings on a subject regarding which she was particularly susceptible, running as follows: "*Ts'ao Lao Fo Yeh* 奓老佛爺, *Ts'ao T'a P'i Ku* 奓他屁股; *Sha Chien Fu Ti Kuei Tzu* 奸夫的鬼子; *Sao Mieh Ch'ing Ch'ao* 掃滅清朝; *Ta Hsing Ko Ming* 大興革命. F.... the Old Buddha, f.... her up the anus; slay the adulterous 'devil' paramour; sweep to destruction the Manchu dynasty, execute the great Revolution."

The Empress turned grimly to Li struggling onward on his donkey: "Your honourable relative's language is passing strange, Lien-ying: what have you to say?"

"Nothing in excuse, Old Ancestress; his speech freezes me to the ground in horror. But it is not he who is speaking, it is the demoniacal snake of his demented possession."

"I see; but it sounds like a man's voice, and your Lord Snake seems to have a good command of the vernacular. Perhaps his lordship has been a student abroad (*Yu Hsüeh Wai Kuo* 遊學外國, Her Majesty hated all foreign educated students): small wonder, then, that he wants to destroy our dynasty and raise the standard of revolution. Well, I am going straight in to reason with your 'scholarly' kinsman: you, Pa Hou, shall attend me and Lien-ying, who is naturally timorous, can remain outside on the terrace during our confidential chat."

Lien-ying looked half ashamed, half relieved; I did not enjoy the prospect of an encounter with a maniac who, for aught I knew, might be armed and assassinate the Old Buddha. I hope I was not selfish in wondering what my predicament would be in such a disastrous event; surely my enemies would say that I had lured the great Empress to her doom

---

59   Buddhist monks.
60   French hospitals that were once used as insane asylums.

and that I was suborned by the revolutionaries. However, it was no use anticipating trouble and I meekly supported the Empress for some 200 yards to the rather elaborate entrance (for Li Ting-kuo was a wealthy man, as behoved a near relative of Lien-ying). The shrieks and vociferations waxed as we advanced; perhaps the maniac's keen ears had heard the steps of undesired guests; he kept crying in ill-omened and damnable repetition: F.... the Old Buddha etc.

Her Majesty whispered to me: "Reviling ceases to be original, if heard a hundred times over; like a *Lao T'ai T'ai Ma Chieh* 老太太罵街, *Shei T'ou Wo Hsiao Mao* 誰偷我小貓, the old hag uttering imprecations up and down the street, 'who is it that has stolen my kitten?' " (I have frequently heard this selfsame gibe shouted in the lanes of Peking: the idea being that the guilty party loses face by the anonymous malediction.)

"What if the eunuch is armed, Old Buddha? Have you thought of that? Your Majesty knows that lunatics are possessed with preternatural strength and I don't feel sure that even Your Majesty, though you *Yang Ch'eng T'ien Yu* 仰承天佑, are under the aegis of divine protection and we two, your servants, would fain die for you, *Sui Fen Shen Sui Ku Shang Shu So Yüan* 雖粉身碎骨尚屬所願, have our bodies broken and our bones ground into powder, are after all two weak mortals whose will outruns our strength."

Said the Old Buddha: "I know how to manage a lunatic, ay and his precious 'Lord Snake' too. You shall see that I get the better of him and of his insolent curses. F.... Old Buddha indeed!!"

Cries of women and children were audible from the court at the back: apparently Ting-kuo's household (for he had married and begotten children before his castration) had taken refuge in some outhouse and no doubt barred the entrance with a *Men Shuan*[61] 門閂. I heard Ting-kuo cry: "I'll kill anyone who enters. Lord Snake's orders are my law." Lien-ying, to my pleased surprise, showed that his loyalty had overcome his cowardice and overtook us as we entered a lofty, airy room, the appointment of which evinced wealth and taste. The maniac was sitting on a *T'ai Shih Yi* 太師椅 black and straight backed chair; his physionomy resembled a rabid dog whom I had once seen: red swollen eyes, protruding tongue, marked foaming at the mouth, apparent difficulty in swallowing, thick confused utterance.

"Why, it's the Old Buddha herself and her adulterous lover! I'll first f... both of them, the woman to begin with and the devil next; then I'll kill them by order of Lord Snake. See, I have a kitchen knife and I am going to stab the two to the heart and then eat their livers raw."

"Wait a moment, Ting-kuo: I remember when you served me as a boy in the Yang Hsing Tien[62] 養性殿 early in the present reign. If you want to *Ts'ao* 'have' me, ay and my 'devil paramour' as you politely call him, you are welcome. But to succeed, you will have first to *T'ao Ch'u Chi Pa* 掏出肌巴, pull your tool out, for you can't accomplish much without that

---

61 Bolt.
62 Hall of Spiritual Cultivation in the Forbidden City.

useful implement. If you have *Ch'i Hsing* 起性, achieved an erection, I am ready, and my friend will be pleased to receive you in his hinder region, after you have completed your will on me. As to your relative, Lien-ying, I make bold to aver that he will be most happy if you possess him up the anus: that is, supposing you are not too tired and if Lord Snake has no objection. It is true that, to the best of my recollection, when you and I were both younger, you lacked that valuable appendage which should enable you to fulfill your heart's desire; but perchance Lord Snake is supplying your deficiency."

Ting-kuo was now making menacing gestures in the Old Buddha's and my direction with his knife; it appeared to me that, if Her Majesty continued to mock him, he would infallibly stab her, especially as he continued to revile the Dynasty and all its works. The Old Buddha apparently thought the same, for she changed her banter into a tone of peremptory command, addressing the evil spirit, if evil spirit there were: "Ta Ch'ing Yeh 大青爺, Your lordship the snake-dragon, I order you to come out of this man whose body you are occupying (*Fu T'i* 伏體): You are at liberty to take possession of the donkey which is tied up at the gate and to fare where you will."

I was again reminded of the episode in Gadara, "a thing written for our learning", when the evil spirits entered into the swine and caused their cruel drowning in the lake of Tiberias; the effect was not so rapid as Jesus' exorcism, however, and Ting-kuo, whose paroxysms had in no way subsided, opened up his trousers to disclose a eunuch's restricted anatomy and in disregard of his palpable impotence, to start rubbing his incomplete person against Her Majesty's grasscloth gown. He continued reviling the Manchus, the Empress, and myself in particular: "You should have been killed like all the devils in the 26th year (1900) when we had the chance. Drive them out, let none survive, neither chicken nor dog."

He raised his weapon and was about to strike; but Her Majesty shouted in a loud, majestic tone: "Orders have come to me from the Rakshas (*Yeh Ch'a* 夜义) themselves (Buddhist devils) to command that you prostrate yourself before me, kotow nine times and then run your knife into your own belly. As for 'his lordship' the snake, if he is as astute as I think him, he will hasten to obey my previous mandate and betake himself into the internal anatomy of the ass."

She had "called his bluff" as far as she was concerned, for his vociferous, unceasing shouts changed to a maudlin, whining voice; but he moved towards me knife in hand: "I will kill the devil and then kill my relation, so that I shall be one to the good, *Chung Jan Chuan I Ko* 終然賺一個."

So far Her Majesty's invocation to "Lord Snake" and to the Rakshas had not proved of much avail, so far as I was concerned; for the humble ass, peacefully tethered at the gate and calmly grazing, had evidently not yet been possessed by Ch'ing Yeh; while the Rakshas had not been able to obtain obedience of their orders to Ting-kuo to kotow to the Empress Dowager before he committed self-slaughter or *Hara-kiri*. On the contrary, the maniac's attentions were turned in a very unpleasant and concrete manner toward the foreign devil. T'ing-kuo was saying the regular Boxer incantations, making cabalistic signs, repeating figures apparently meaningless like the apocalyptic 666 in the Revelation, *Offenbarung Johannis*,[63] by which the words Néron César are to be understood. "Turn southward and prostrate yourselves; burn the incense; kill the devils." These were all shibboleths. (In particular did he repeat the *T'ung Yao* 童謠 or doggerel which I had often heard in 1900: "*Chê Shih Pu Suan K'u* 這時不算苦, *Erh Ssü Chia I Wu* 二四加一五, *Hung Teng Chao Man Chieh* 紅燈照滿街, *Na Shih Ts'ai Suan K'u* 那時才算苦. Things are not yet at their worst, wait for the intercalary 4th moon and the 5th moon, the whole city will be aflame: then will be the great terror." The meaning is not clear: the previous year 1906 had seen an intercalary IV moon: perhaps it referred to the revolutionary attempt of that year which heralded the fall of the dynasty. But there were no disturbances in Peking at that time.) These slogans were naturally not unfamiliar to me who had had ample experience of the events of the Keng Tzu 庚子 year (1900). Then he waved his terrible knife back and forth on my luckless head, till I felt rather like (I suppose) the unhappy Fatime, when her lord Barbe-Bleue not yet whitewashed by M. Anatole France, returned home from his journey and was about to slay his unfortunate spouse but for the timeous arrival of her brothers. My one comfort was the reflection that the Old Buddha (not to speak of Li) could hardly sit tamely by, while I was being hacked into mince-meat. The situation seemed to demand immediate action, or, as the Chinese say, 'twas like a sudden call of nature which neither prince nor peasant can ignore or postpone. The metaphor is homely but apposite to the circumstances. My chief source of comfort, apart from the Old Buddha's probable ultimate intervention, was that I had seen Boxers at their mystic "drill" and knew that the office or liturgy was long and minute. Multitudinous incantations had to be uttered, prayers to be addressed to Lord Buddha, incense to be offered by the culprit on trial, whether a Christian, a supposed Christian or a Mahommedan, in fact any person, even Buddhist, against whom the local Boxer chief (a sort of *Gauleiter*)[64] had a personal grudge. Then, if the incense only partially ignited or failed to ignite at all (as was often provided for by first dampening the incense stick), 'twas time enough to proceed to the slaughter, and the victim was stabbed by a hundred swords.

Lien-ying tried to expostulate with his kinsman in a singularly ineffective effort at persuasion: "He is my friend; the Old Buddha loves him; spare his life, etc." Not at all the arguments which were likely to appeal to a red-hot xenophobe and raving lunatic *pardessus le marché*.[65] Yet I did not feel as if my mortal hour had arrived, partly because I saw, so far as

---

63 *Gospel of John.*
64 Regional leader of the Nazi Party.
65 To top it all off.

I dared look away from my antagonist (or should it be: judge), a grim look of determination on the Old Buddha's countenance, as of a woman whose mind is made up for a desperate remedy.

I was not far wrong; suddenly Her Majesty's voice changed; it became still more majestic and compelling. She went down on her knees and began a prayer (she reminded me of that description by the *Mantovano* seer (*Aeneid* VI.46) of the Sibyl of Cumae as she felt herself penetrated by Apollo's prophetic influence and inspiration: "*Deus, ecce deus*, the God, the god is there"): "Yü Huang 玉皇, the Jade Emperor, Your Majesty who hath founded the cult of the Yi Ho T'uan 義和團 (Boxers) that are your votaries; the righteous movement against the 'devils' failed six years ago by Your Majesty's will; because the principles of the cult were prostituted by impostors and by their sordid lust of gain. Descend from Heaven, I conjure and implore Your Majesty, and inflict upon this foul madman the punishment due for his 'offence which is rank and smells to heaven' (*Hamlet*), the effluvium rising even to your imperial Throne. Descend, then, Your Majesty, and pronounce upon the vile caitiff the penalty of death. Then shall I, who on earth am indeed empress but in Your Majesty's sight am only your humble worshipper, prostrate myself nine times daily, at dawn, noon and eve, before your sacred tablet and praise your holy name for the times which are to come. Jade Emperor, hearken; a humble petition from the lady Yehonala, Empress Dowager."

Ting-kuo certainly looked alarmed by this inspiring form of conjuration but still held his knife in a way that I did not appreciate, over my apparently doomed head. Suddenly, a voice rang out, seemingly from the rafters of that lofty room, the voice of majesty and of command, compelling obedience: "Ting-kuo, you caitiff wretch, we, the Jade Emperor, command you to kneel and to drive the weapon now in your hands into your vitals, ay right to the hilt till you be dead."

As it was perfectly obvious that no deity was concealing his august presence in the rafters, even though the passage of the *Odes* quoted in the *Ta Hsüeh*[66] 大學 tells us that "*Shen Chih Ko Ssu Pu K'o Tu Ssu* 神之 格思不可度思, supernatural beings' arrival is a thing inscrutable", it was evident that the Old Buddha had shown herself a past mistress of the art of ventriloquism and equally of mimicry, for the voice from Heaven was palpably made in a deep voice, quite other than her habitual falsetto tones. Truly, the great Empress was many-faceted; many may deny to her the quality of greatness; but history will surely vindicate her. Great she was in her statecraft, her unique (or almost so) capacity to play one party against another, to inspire devotion and loyalty, to prop up, and to galvanize back into life a slowly dying cause, for her dynasty had long exhausted the Mandate of Heaven which her strong hand prolonged for half a century.

Ting-kuo, then, knelt meekly down, implored forgiveness from His Divine Majesty and placed the knife with his huge hands ventro-laterally

---

66   A Confucian text, sometimes translated as *The Great Learning* or *Magna Scientia*.

to the right of the navel, much, I presume, after the manner of General Nogi or other Japanese patriots who perform the act of *Seppuku* (*Ch'ieh Fu* 切腹) or *Hara-kiri*. He grovelled in agony, muttering indistinguishable words, but did not yet go down into the dust of death; though obviously his soul was drawing nigh unto hell.

The Old Buddha looked calmly on, as at a play: "*Cette charogne, cette lie du peuple, cette canaille,*[67] he has his deserts. *Ts'ao* 肏, f.... me, forsooth, when he had nothing to *Ts'ao* with!! Lien-ying, your relatives do to you no credit; I can't congratulate you thereon; beware lest others of them do likewise; it will then go hard with you. Remember."

Li kotowed meekly: "Your Majesty knows my devotion to your holy person. Even Ti Yü 帝禹, the Emperor Yü, had a bad sire (Kun 鯀) and Confucius' brother was a great sinner. But I shall write out Your Majesty's admonition and have it engraved in letters of gold inside my couch. I shall say it over like an incantation to be for ever repeated night and morning."

"So be it then. Go and call your kindred who, I suppose, are still in hiding on the premises: bid them attend me here at once and say that I shall not visit a maniac's crimes upon innocent folk."

Li hastened to announce the gospel of good tidings, while I knelt to thank the Old Buddha for saving my life. She smiled: "I brought you hither. What would your foreign devils have said, had Li Ting-kuo butchered you? They would have accused me of bringing an arch-Boxer who lured you to your doom. But I care not for their baseless calumnies which they vomit toward my person, and only rejoice in your safety, because you are dear to me" (she pressed my hand with an erotic gesture and kissed my lips).

Ting-kuo at this moment yielded up the ghost, as his family, like frightened rabbits, entered the Presence. "Your Majesty has brought us back into life; he threatened us and we could do nought against him. But for the Old Buddha's gracious advent, he would have slain us all, young and old, male and female. May Your Majesty live for ever!"

"Ting-kuo was long ago my servant, then loyal and faithful to me: in consideration of his past not negligible merit (*Wei Kung Pu Wu K'o Lu* 微功不無可錄), I bestow upon you Taels 3,000 for his funeral expenses. The country folk are inquisitive about matters which concern them not; you must say that Ting-kuo killed himself in an *accès de démence.*[68] The yokels hereabouts and the foreign devils are sure to learn of my visit: you must reply (if cross-questioned) that I was concerned about an old servant's disease and came to comfort him, even to minister with medicine to his frenzies."

Lien-ying and the rest of us went down on our knees, and the former appropriately thanked Her Majesty: "Your bounty is even as the Ch'ang Chiang 長江 (Yangtze) which disdains not even a tiny drop or the T'ai Shan 泰山 which refuses not one grain of sand: it is thus that the Yangtze

---

67 This scum, this lowlife, this scoundrel.
68 Fit of insanity.

and the sacred mountain have became what they are. Even so is your gracious favour, dew from heaven falling on the parched ground, rain in a land where no water is."

"A truce to compliments: *Ch'an Ch'an Mien Yü* 諂面諛, flattery to my face, as Mengtzu[69] 孟子 says. It is high time to be going; the fast westering sun bids us hasten home. Farewell!"

So we emerged into the court, followed by the benedictions of the household for the Old Buddha's magnanimity. The donkey was still tethered at the gate, and the Empress said: "It looks as if Lord Snake had disobeyed my order and preferred not to make of the humble ass his temporary tenement. Probably his Godship has returned to his haunts at T'an Chê Ssu 檀柘寺 in the hills (at T'an Chê Ssu, a well known temple, there is a tablet written by Ch'ien Lung 乾隆 himself in eulogy of the sacred serpent dragon, the denizen of a cavern behind the monastery). But look, old Pa, at the herculean sexual excitement that Li's donkey is developing. Does it not make your own organ *Ch'i Hsing* 起性, become erect? But certainly your 'jade stalk' *Yü Heng* 玉莖 must needs take second place in comparison; while, as for you, Lien-ying, the sight must cause your orifice to water with longing. *Ni Mei Ch'iao Tzu* 你沒巧子, *Shih I Ch'iao Tzu Pu I Ch'an* 是以巧子不易饞, *Nai Tang Jan Ti* 乃當然的: *K'o Shih Yu Ti Shih Yen'rh* 可是有的是眼兒! You lack the necessary implement, so your tool is debarred from desire; but you still have your hinder-cavity available for an intruding *Yin Ken* 陰根 (penis) to prick its entry into your posterior door! *K'o Jung Wai Lai Ti Yin Ken Ch'o Ju Men Chung* 可容外來的陰根擢入門中. Well, I am going to ride the donkey; ask some rustic if there is a side path down the hill. I don't wish to meet the devils who are probably enjoying the evening cool." A shortcut was indicated by a yokel in quest of faggots. I led the ass and the Old Buddha did not let conversation drop.

"You must stay at Yi Ho Yüan 頤和園 tonight and I order you to minister to me more actively than yesterday and this morning."

"Oh! Your Majesty, it was four times, was it not? I felt utterly played out when you commanded my attendance here."

"Very good: you shall share a magnum of champagne with Lien-ying, and he will see that you have at least two extra doses of the *Mei Yao* 媚葯. And I hope that your tool will be even as that of the donkey a moment ago."

We reached the hamlet and found the imperial yellow chair awaiting Her Majesty at the tea-shop. The *Chang Kuei Ti*[70] 掌櫃的 knelt to inform Her Majesty that many foreign devils and crowds of Chinese had turned his humble cabin into a sort of peep-show, pestering him with questions and asking who the foreign *Huang Shang*[71] 皇上 (!) with the green chair could be! Her Majesty did nothing by halves and commanded Li to send Taels 100 as a present to the honest fellow. She called my *Chiao Fu Pan Tou'rh* 轎夫班頭兒, the head of the bearers who walks beside the chair:

---

69   Mencius.
70   Manager.
71   Emperor.

"There's a present of Taels 250 for Pa Hou Yeh's attendants: he has had a tiring afternoon and you deserve for his sake a higher recompense than usual." (Truly, those were spacious times when "silver was nothing accounted of in the days of Solomon"; and today the man who writes these faltering lines, in a death-nearing eld, wonders whether *ses moyens lui permettront la dépense*[72] of an enhanced outlay of 50 cents for a bottle (scarcely Falernian) of local *vin ordinaire! Sic transit*: thus doth *inexorabile fatum*[73] decree. *Lo Chi Sheng Pei* 樂極生悲, weal's culmination begetteth woe!)

Then she called me, addressing me in a voice that only I could hear: "You are glad to come to me tonight, are you not? My widowed couch is lonely and needs a companion. You are not too tired? This has been a weary outing for you, but I admired your calmness and *sang-froid* when that *Hsia San Lan* 下三濫 (*la lie du peuple*)[74] toyed with his knife over your devoted head!"

"Your Majesty, it was your sacred presence that gave to me courage that I did not feel. You, Old Buddha, are as always, my light in night and lonely places, my day in day."

"We must lose no more time talking. Lien-ying, you had better ride your donkey ahead of me and let them know at the gate that I and Pa Hou are on the way back. I don't want a search party sent out, as it would attract attention, especially as there is no moon tonight. The roads are a quagmire after the rains: tell the bearers to avoid the ruts and to take the chair, where there is space along the *Kao-liang*[75] 高粱 and crops, by the banks on each side of the road, when possible, as it is easier going and I shall be able to get some sleep."

So we departed on our way, reaching the palace under the star-light; as a special favour, the Old Buddha allowed my chair to be carried right up to my room-door. I dismounted ahead of Her Majesty and knelt to receive her.

"Now I am going to have my evening meal and an opium pipe: Good appetite and good digestion. You shall attend upon me at the hour of the Rat (11 p.m.); don't forget that I expect much better results than yesterday."

"Oh! Your Majesty, my tool was dry as your own rainless Gobi desert."

"Well, we will investigate it on the spot. I will expound to you the twenty-two divers postures in the 'Clouds and the Rain', while you, in your turn, discourse to me with your inimitable humour the subject of which you are past master; I mean that puzzling vocabulary and nomenclature of your beloved homosexual and pederastic preoccupations."

---

72   He has means to allow the expense.
73   So passeth . . . inexorable fate.
74   The scum of the earth.
75   Chinese sorghum.

CHAPTER XV

THE WHITE CLOUD
(TAOIST) TEMPLE

I⊤ was in the late spring of 1908, 34 Kuang Hsü 光緒, that the Old Buddha, still mindful of Hsing Hsüan's 星玄 prediction at the crystal gazing but unhappily deaf to his admonition to keep at a respectful distance (*Ching Erh Yüan Chih* 敬而遠之) Yüan Shih-k'ai 袁世凱, whom she had brought up to Peking and placed on the *Chün Chi* 軍機 or Council in the previous year, thus stripping him of the military power but allowing to him full rein for intrigue, sought confirmation or refutal (preferably the latter) of the prophecies that had recently so perturbed her rest o'nights. It was likely that she would summon me to be present at any future spiritualistic séance; so that I was scarcely astonished when Ts'ui Tê-lung 崔德隆 (who had been with us at the Tung Yüeh 東嶽 Temple) arrived at my house with an urgent mandate from the Empress, this time, in her own handwriting: "*Cho Pa Hou Chi Shin Ch'ien Lai Chiang Fu Poyünkuan I Hsing Ch'in Tz'u* 著巴侯即時來將赴白雲觀一行欽此. Marquis Pa is hereby ordered to attend immediately: I am about to visit the White Cloud Temple."

She was staying at the Lake Palace, so that for the short distance outside the city special precautions would be necessary, since revolution was in the air. To the Chung Hai 中海 I went accordingly, found Her Majesty outwardly cheerful, although it seemed to me (wrongly as the sequel denoted) that her zest for life had somewhat diminished. She bade me go forthwith to see the Taoist abbot, Kao Jen-ssu[1] 高仁峒, the friend of Li Lien-ying and of the Russian Ministers Lessar and later Pokotiloff, and arrange with him for a séance of table turning and planchette,[2] called by the Japanese *Kokkuri*, fox, dog, wild-cat, plank divination, *Uranai Ban*. Kao Hsien Chang 高仙長, politely so denominated from his place in the Taoist hierarchy, "sainted elder", assured me that a recently arrived mendicant priest, Shih Lao Tao 史老道 from Ch'engtu 成都 was unrivalled as a medium: if then the Old Buddha would come

---

1   The White Cloud Temple under Tz'u Hsi was once presided over by an Abbot Kao, but his name was Kao Ren-t'ung 高仁峒 (1841-1907) and he died prior to the alleged time of this séance.
2   A small board used in séances to communicate with spirits, most commonly used with a Ouija board.

that same evening with Lien-ying (whom he specially invited, if Her Majesty approved), Ts'ui Tê-lung and myself, all preparations should be completed. But he asked that her visit should be incognito and that she would not return to the city till daylight next morning.

He already had the Old Buddha's horoscope but did not know the details (so, at least, he declared) of Hsing Hsüan's warnings to Her Majesty. Like Côme (or Cosimo) Ruggieri for Catherine de Médicis or Galeotti under Louis XI,[3] he had already divined from its study that the Empress would live to the age of 83 (or 82 by Western reckoning) i.e. till the year 1917, but that her star (like that of Henri Quatre before his expedition against Cahors which, however, ended successfully)[4] was momentarily somewhat dimmed. And so I hurried back to the Yi Luan Tien 儀鸞殿 and lunched there, spending the afternoon after Her Majesty's siesta and opium pipe in chatting of love and later rehearsing for her amusement "The Rainbow Jacket" in the part of Ch'ü Yang Kuei Fei 去楊貴妃. Before the hour fixed for our outing, 9 p.m., I had, *comme d'habitude*,[5] a short but blissful (at any rate from Her Majesty's point of view, as personal choice might have directed me toward my dear eunuch Lien Tzu-yen 連子延 of sadistic trends whose lascivious glances once again fanned my desire) intercourse with the Old Buddha.

She was unusually erotic, even for her; whilst I was at the supermost height, "that bad eminence" (Milton) of salacity and uncurbed, untrammelled *luxure*[6] which aye begins and never ends for one of *ma complexion perverse*[7] and ill-mastered impulse, *il fatale dono*[8] of a sinister dualism, that strange, inexplicable didymistic hovering (two loves at either blossom of the breast) betwixt male and female concupiscence, as of a forest fire, coming none knows whence, going none knows whither, other than toward a bourne of havoc and irretrievable ruin. I kept note duly of my days and nights *d'amour* with her and believe that *commerce sexuel* took place between 150 - 200 times.

On this occasion the Empress decided that our party should go in two *Hung T'o Ni Pu Ch'ê* 紅托泥布車 equipped with red waterproof cloth mudguards under the curtains, or "official" carts; but order had been sent for the Hsi Pien Men'rh[9] 西便門兒 to be kept open. I rode on the shafts of her cart, while the eunuchs followed in the second. Despite Abbot Kao's wish to preserve the incognito he had had the entrance to the temple strewn with yellow sand (as official custom required) to honour her arrival. He was waiting with the medium at the main gate, both of them kneeling as the cart drew up. There was no delay and we went through several courtyards of the capacious temple to the *Hsing Kung*[10] 行宮 at the

---

3   Cosimo Ruggieri (d. 1615) and Marzio Galeotti (1440-94), Italian astrologers and soothsayers.
4   Henri IV of France laid siege to Cahors, in southwest France, in 1580 during the so-called "Lovers' War".
5   As usual.
6   Lust.
7   My perverse nature.
8   The deadly gift.
9   The gate at the northwest corner of Peking's old city walls.
10   The Imperial Lodge, home of the Emperor while travelling.

back. The Empress preferred to alight at the gate out of respect to Ch'iu Tsu[11] 邱祖. Saint Ch'iu was the temple's founder. Over again as at Tung Yüeh Miao 東嶽廟, Her Majesty took her seat on a *Pao Tso* 寶座 or throne, north of the table to be used for the demonstration; Shih Lao Tao, the medium, was to the right, while we three, by the Empress' permission, sat (or rather squatted) on low stools at the foot of the small oblong table. It appeared that Shih had been staying on his way from Szechuan at Wu T'ai Shan 五台山 where the Dalai Lama, shortly expected in Peking, was *Chu Hsi* 駐錫, making a pontifical sojourn. Although of different faith, he had been summoned to draw the Living Buddha's horoscope and had aroused the latter's ire by forecasting with accuracy (as the event of January 1910 proved) his imminent degradation by the Manchu House, degradation which though promulgated never came to anything, since the incarnation or *Hutuktu* (Saint) cannot be "defrocked" and only Yüan Chi 圓寂 or the entrance into Nirvana can terminate his existence for the moment, pending the rebirth of the next Avatar (Avatar = Sanskrit for descent) in the ensuing metamorphosis.

The "sainted elder" was granted a seat to the Empress Dowager's left but spent most of the night hovering near the Old Buddha without, however, having part nor lot in the mystic portion of the séance, although free with his comments, mostly platitudinous, on the possibilities of future events, which saints and sinners are equally likely to forecast with startling inaccuracy as the event proves.

As I suppose to be usual in "table lifting",[12] the proceedings started with incense burning, while all of us, including the Old Buddha, kotowed in silent prayer, albeit I am not perfectly sure to whom we were praying. "The will for the deed! *Pro facto accipias voluntatem.*" Shih then developed an ecstasy or spiritual rapture; after perhaps twenty minutes the table definitely began to move of its own volition; that is to say, I can guarantee that none of us touched it in any way. Apparently, communication with the spirit world had been achieved. Shih knelt with an ink filled brush in his hand held very lightly and wrote, without (so it seemed) knowing what he was writing, the following oracular message:

1) *Chi Yüan Keng Hsin* 紀元更新,
2) *Hsi Ch'ing Ta Lai* 喜慶大來,
3) *Yün Ch'ou Sheng Suan* 運籌勝算,
4) *T'ien I Wan Hui* 天意挽回,
5) *Pu Nan Ch'eng Kung* 不難成功,
6) *Hsien Ch'u Ta Tui* 先除大懟,
7) *Chien Tsei Pu Ch'u* 奸賊不除,
8) *Sheng Ling T'u T'an* 生靈塗炭,
9) *Chin Shen Ts'ung Shih* 謹慎從事,

---

11   "Progenitor Ch'iu" (1148-1227) was a Taoist immortal from the Ch'üan Chen school.
12   The shaking and movement of tables seems out of place in this context. While table movement was a common feature of the European séances popular around the time of this story, it is not associated with Chinese spirit-writing.

10) *Mien Yu Hou Huan* 免有後患,
11) *T'ung Ku Jeng Ts'un* 統固仍存,
12) *T'ien Ming K'o Ch'ang* 天命可昌,
13) *Tung Cho Ts'uan Wei* 董卓簒位,
14) *Tsu Wei Yin Chien* 足爲殷鑒,
15) *Jeng Shih Ku Hsi* 仍事姑息,
16) *Ta Tsai Chiang Lin* 大災將臨,
17) *T'ao T'ien Chih Huo* 滔天之禍,
18) *T'ung Kuei Yü Chin* 同歸於盡,
19) *Shou Tuan Pi Tu* 手段必毒,
20) *Chung Sheng Tê Chiu* 衆生得救,
21) *T'ien I Ju Tz'u* 天意如此,
22) *Shu Kan Huo Wei* 孰敢或違,
23) *Huang T'ien Hou T'u* 皇天后土,
24) *Chün Wen Ssu Yen* 均聞斯言.

"A new era is about to emerge: great happiness is in store: victorious plans have been laid: human's will[13] can be retrieved: success is within grasp: first expel the arch-abhorred one: unless the foul traitor disappear, the people's lives will be plunged into the mire and the burning charcoal: take heed in your actions, lest there be cause for repentance: the succession will certainly be assured: the mandate of Heaven shall endure: Tung Cho's 董卓 (it was hardly usurpation, but he acted as a dictator and was assassinated) usurpation (at end of Han 漢 Dynasty) furnishes a sure warning: if you continue indulgence, an appalling disaster will befall you: in the presence of a great cataclysm, all shall perish together: you must needs employ truculent measures, and the lives of the people may be delivered: such is Heaven's will, who shall dare to disobey? High Heaven and Mother Earth, hearken ye to my words."

Oracles, as we know from Delphic precedents, are usually as cryptic as prisoners' letters in war time: it seemed to me that 11 was ambiguous, since *T'ung* 統 does indeed mean "line", and especially succession (as in *Hsüan T'ung* 宣統, succession to Hsüan Tsung 宣宗, Tao Kuang 道光),[14] but unfortunately the words for President, *Tsung T'ung* 總統, also contain this character where it means supreme chief. The same thought struck the Old Buddha who riveted her attention on the writing: "What *T'ung* does he (or she) mean?" she asked both medium and abbot; the reply was: "It must be the *Huang T'ung* 皇統, imperial succession, Your Majesty."

"I should like to be clear on this subject", said Her Majesty. She handed to me the oracle: it was written in a rather poor *Hsing Shu* 行書 or

---

13   *T'ien I Wan Hui* should be translated as "Heaven's will".
14   Emperor Tao Kuang (Hsüan Tsung) reigned from 1820 to 1850.

running hand, but was quite legible; in any case, it would not be fair to blame the oracle nor any one save the medium for the calligraphy, especially as Shih Lao Tao held the brush between thumb and finger very lightly at the top of the holder and not even perpendicularly, as the rules of calligraphy require.

The Old Buddha had a copy made after her return to Peking and graciously presented to me the original; like my other papers, including several autograph notes from Her Majesty, I lost everything (largely through my own fault) in August 1939 during the boycott. I was however, and am, word perfect and am certain that the transcript as recorded above is absolutely accurate: the style is literary and of the four character antithetical couplet type, scholarly without being very allusive nor erudite, but still definitely *Wen T'i*[15] 文體. I do not believe that the medium's scholarship, unaided by a spirit, was equal to a composition not unworthy of a graduate.

The Old Buddha also enquired regarding verse 1: did "new era" connote a new reign or a change of *Kuo T'i* 國體, regime? On the face of it, the phrase would rather indicate the passage from one form of rule to another, being applicable to the Manchu abdication in 1912. "Still," said the Empress, "the oracle speaks of great happiness: it would hardly in my presence call the overthrow of my dynasty a happy event, hence I take it to mean a change of reign which" (she added gravely) "may not be far off, even if I do have to 'take heed in my action' regarding the traitor."

None named him, not even Her Majesty; but we all knew that the *Ta Tui*[16] 大憝 implied Yüan Shih-k'ai 袁世凱: the same characters were used by the two empresses regent, Tz'u Hsi 慈禧 and Tz'u An 慈安 (Hsiao Chen Hsien Huang Hou 孝貞顯皇后) in 1861 after the first *coup d'état*, when they summarily disposed of Princes Cheng 鄭 and Yi 怡 together with the arch-plotter Su Shun 肅順, the president of the Ministry of Finance. The comparison of Yüan and Tung Cho, as was shown by the former's subsequent record when he betrayed the House of Gioro in 1912, was not inapt; it may be that the latter's assassination removed him from the scene in time to prevent his seizure of the throne, 1700 and more years ago.

Pronounced table rattling continued: evidently another oracle was due. Once more, Shih took up his pen and traced very slowly and deliberately the following characters: "The year with the cyclical characters *Ting Ssu* 丁巳 of the element earth and appertaining to the snake in the intercalary III moon, will, alas! see national mourning for the 'sainted' chariot's far journey on high. *Ting Ssu Nien Jun San Yüeh T'ung Tsao Kuo Sang Hsien Chia Sheng Hsia* 丁巳年閏三月痛遭國喪仙駕升遐." Again: "The whole world will be at war, nation against nation: the issue is uncertain." (A very oracular prediction.) "*Ch'üan Shih Hsing Chiang Kan Ko Hsiang Chien* 世行將干戈相見, *I Kuo Pu Mien* 一國不免: *Sheng Pai Pu Ting* 勝敗不定."

---

15   In a literary form.
16   Arch-abhorred one.

The Empress seemed satisfied: "Except that the date fixed for my decease is fuller, this prediction coincides with your horoscope, Abbot Kao: in other words I have ten years ahead of me and shall employ them to advantage. As to the war, I think that your oracle, with all respect, has blundered; it is a case of *Ch'i Jen Yu T'ien* 杞人憂天, the man of the Ch'i State who feared that the sky was going to fall and crush his head" (set phrase for chimerical alarms). "Shorn of its verbiage and sonorous catchwords, the first oracle directs me: 1) to appoint a new emperor; 2) to dismiss (or perhaps execute) Yüan Shih-k'ai; 3) not to be in too much of a hurry; 4) not to disdain nor reject methods savoring of tyranny. Very good: I thank you, Medium Shih, for your planchette reading, all the more so because there is no vestige of flattery in the language. Let us now all burn incense again and return humble thanks to the Lord of the Lower World, Yen Wang 閻王, if it be he who has accorded to me this inspiring message or decree of fate." The ceremony completed, the Old Buddha called for tea and cigarettes which seemed rather out of place in what savoured of a religious function.

The *Wu* 巫 or medium with his *Chiang Shen Shu* 降神術, spirit rapping, seemed greatly exhausted and in an advanced state of perspiration; he was saying in audible tones to himself: "The worst and most difficult portion of my task is ahead; it is always a great ordeal to communicate with any designated denizen of the world below, who can say what Her Majesty may demand of me?"

There were continued signs of spiritual activity, as the table never ceased rattling and moving up and down, although we were all sitting several feet away. The Old Buddha, who had the gift of inducing sleep at will even in the greatest emergencies, rested awhile and then asked the two eunuchs and myself if our hearts were pure for the reception of possible messages from the spirits. Naturally, in our curiosity, we reassured Her Majesty regarding our comparative sober mindedness (or *sophrosune* of Plato), although purity is a relative term and neither the Old Buddha nor myself, in view of our love congress of the preceding afternoon (it was now past midnight) could fairly lay claim to that ideal quality, that "strength which is as the strength of ten, because my heart is pure, *Hsin Ti Chieh Ching* 心地潔淨, *I I Tang Shih* 以一當十."

"Well then, take your seats again. Medium Shih, I command you to enter into communication with the late Grand Secretary and Grand Councillor Junglu 榮祿, *Wen Chung Kung* 文忠公 (his canonical title 'His Excellency Learned and Loyal'), that I may, as of old, benefit by his mellow counsel."

Shih at once began to invoke somebody or something; but the language conveyed no meaning to me, being a farrago of Buddhist and (I think) esoteric but unfamiliar (though I know the tongue) Tibetan incantations, strange perhaps in the mouth of a Taoist priest, except that the latter faith owes much to Buddhism and even to the debased Lama faith of the Mahayana or "Great Vehicle" of Buddhism, *Ta Ch'eng* 大乘. After a great while he memorialized Her Majesty: "There is a serious confusion of sounds: a spirit is trying to answer me, but I cannot comprehend what 'it' is saying." At long last, I heard him say: "What is your proof?" Then he addressed the Old Buddha: "There is a spirit who on earth was called Ch'en Shih-an 陳石菴 and declares that Jung Chung T'ang 榮中堂 is speaking through him."

The Empress Dowager excitedly interposed: "I know Ch'en: he was the Grand Secretary's major-domo and owned the big restaurant Fu Shou T'ang 福壽堂 in Chin Yü Hut'ung[17] 金魚胡同 before the Boxer *émeute*.[18] Bid him speak."

Shih transmitted Her Majesty's command, rapping the table violently as he spoke. Thus the spirit: "Junglu humbly salutes Your Sacred Majesty and prays daily for your longevity."

"Make Ch'en," said the Empress Dowager, "ask him what proof Jung Chung-hua 榮仲華 (Junglu's courtesy name) can give to me of his identity: name some of the event whereof only I and he have knowledge."

After brief delay came the reply: "He mentions two incidents which Your Majesty will remember: 1) When you were residing at Hsian 西安 (1901) in the governor's *Yamen*,[19] some 600 cases of silver ingots, each of Taels 53 in weight, arrived there. Your slave (the Manchus, in addressing the Throne, styled themselves *Nu Ts'ai* 奴才 or slave; the Chinese were *Ch'en* 臣 or servants) Junglu, and no other person, attended Your Majesty to count the tale of the cases. One was opened and the number had been counted as 250 in all, the figure being written on the lid before transportation. Your Majesty ordered that, in the meantime, no other cases should be opened but that the consignment be placed under lock and key. 2) On Your Majesty's progress from Hsian to Pienliang 汴梁 (K'aifengfu 開封府) where you passed your *Wan Shou* 萬壽 fêtes[20] (in November 1901) you alighted from the chair in which you were being borne, just this side of T'ungkuan[21] 潼關. Your Majesty summoned your slave to your side and gathered wild flowers on the edge of the road. You said: 'It reminds me of Jehol and of 40 years ago'. Then Your Majesty continued: 'We have been together now for over 45 years and your advice has invariably been wise; but I wish I had always profited by it.' "

Her Majesty became greatly excited: "Yes, yes: it is indeed my dear Junglu; every word that he says recalls to me those days. Now continue and ask Ch'en Shih-an the following questions for Junglu to answer: 1) Does he know the number of years I have yet to live? 2) Am I to put to death his former blood-brother (*Pa Hsiung Ti* 把兄弟) Yüan Shih-k'ai? 3) Am I to depose Kuang Hsü or to end his life? 4) Who is to be the new emperor?"

---

17 A lane very close to the southeast corner of the Forbidden City.
18 Uprising.
19 Office.
20 The Empress Dowagers' birthday celebrations. *Wan Shou* means "longevity" or, literally, "10,000 years", the symbolic reign of a Chinese Emperor or Empress.
21 The T'ung Pass between Honan and Shensi Provinces.

The questionnaire was duly sent to the spirit world; again after a long interval, a reply came through: "1) May Your Majesty live 10,000 years! (which was a little indefinite);[22] 2) Yüan's heart will never cease to be wolf-like (*Lang Hsin Wei Ssu* 狼心未死) and his plans are inscrutable (*So Mou Nan Ts'e* 所謀難測). It would be wisdom to *Ch'ing Chün Ts'e* 清君側, purify the sovereign from his environment, for he *Pao Ts'ang Huo Hsin* 包藏禍心, cherishes treachery; 3) Your Majesty should depose the emperor and confer on him some such title as *Hun Tê Kung* 昏德公, 'Besotted Duke', while sparing his life, *Tai Ch'i I Ssu* 貸其一死; 4) P'u Lun 溥倫 should be the new emperor: he is senior in the line of primogeniture from Tao Kuang 道光."

"Ask him," said Her Majesty, "how he fares since our parting."

It was an interesting séance, though lacking the thrilling element imparted by the crystal-gazing; to the Old Buddha it involved no poignant recollections and presented a much happier vision of future events. We were now not far from dawn and I knew that, according to Chinese soothsayers, the spirits cease communications after cockcrow, *Chi Ming Kuei Li* 雞鳴鬼離. After a very considerable delay Ch'en Shih-an replied for his former patron: "Need you ask, Old Buddha? There is never an hour that I do not think of you and pray for Your Majesty's perpetual happiness and peace. It is more than five years since communications ceased between us, and I am thankful indeed, as it were, to bask again in the light of your presence. Life here is much as it was, when I was still *Yang Chien* 陽間, beholding the light of the sun: I am honoured by His Majesty Yen Wang 閻王 in the world below and pass my days by the Yellow Springs, recalling dear memories. *Yin Chien* 陰間, in the world to come, your slave shall again be in blessed communion with Your Majesty and the days and nights shall not be long enough for me to kneel in worship and listen to your well-remembered accents of affection. I have for ever been bereft of the sight of the Forbidden City (*Yung Wei Kung Wei* 永遠宮闈) but my heart is always there (*Shen Ch'ih Tso Yu* 神馳左右). Your slave Junglu humbly salutes Your Majesty with tears in his eyes. *T'ung* 痛, *T'ung* 痛, *T'ung* 痛: *Chin Tsou* 謹奏."

"I recognize the words, though alas! I hear not the voice, of my dearest counsellor and thank you, Medium Shih, for conveying them to me with such speed. It is almost morning, but seek to enter into communication with my murdered favourite, An Tê-hai 安德海, that I may enquire after his welfare."

Shih Lao Tao made repeated efforts; but there was apparent (as we should say now) interruption or atmospheric interference, that is, if the lower world has any atmosphere; during this time the table seemed to be endowed with life and was extremely animated. The attempt culminated in failure; it was near daylight, the table quieted down and the Old Buddha commanded to adjourn the séance (Lien-ying's journal records

---

22   As noted, 10,000 years represented the symbolic reign of any ruling Chinese monarch, regardless of how long the ruler actually lived. The response *Wan Sui* 萬歲 ("may you live 10,000 years") is therefore somewhat evasive.

briefly a second séance, at which I was not present, when An Tê-hai achieved through Shih, the medium, spiritual connection with the Old Buddha and assured her of his welfare) to a more convenient season, not without munificent largess to Shih and a generous *Pu Shih*[23] 佈施 to the temple. Kao Jen-ssu, the abbot, provided a *repas maigre*,[24] and by the time the Old Buddha had taken a brief repose, the sun was high and we returned to the palace, an enormous crowd, as might have been expected, having collected at the temple gate, but on this occasion the Old Buddha commanded the cart to enter the inner courtyard and drew down the front curtain, *Lien Tzu* 帘子, (for I think she meant to take a siesta in the cart), leaving only the driver and me visible on the space in front of the shafts; so that the *badauds*[25] gained little by their curiosity; but every spectator meekly knelt as we passed, in accord with dynastic custom.

---

23 Charitable donation; alms.
24 Meager meal.
25 Onlookers.

CHAPTER XVI

HER LAST AUTUMN PICNIC

It was the custom of the Old Buddha to mark the festival of the last
month of autumn, Ch'ung Yang Chieh 重陽節, 9th day of 9th Moon, by
climbing a certain distance with her court in the Hsiang Shan 香山 enclosure, once K'ang Hsi's 康熙 country palace before the days of Yüan
Ming Yüan[1] 圓明園, where in fact he was staying on the eve of the Winter
Solstice of 1722, K'ang Hsi 61. XI, when seized with his mortal sickness.
The emperor had sent his son Yin Chen 胤禛 to represent him at the
sacrifice to Heaven, and the news of his desperate illness was brought
by a confidential eunuch to the Chai Kung 齋宮 or Hall of Fasting. Yin
Chen was not the man to stand on ceremony and left the prayers unsaid,
the ritual at the Circular Altar due before sunrise next morning unper-
formed, in his haste to reach the dying emperor's side, not indeed from
filial feeling but to take time by the forelock regarding the nomination
of K'ang Hsi's successor. As is well known, the rough draft had declared
Prince Yi 怡, the favourite son, heir to the Throne, but the eunuchs, well
recompensed by Yin Chen, Prince Yung 雍, opened the casket immediately the breath was out of the emperor's body, destroyed the original
slip and placed another decree in its stead, Cho Yung Ch'in Wang, Yin
Chen Ch'ü 著雍親王胤禛去, "We command Prince Yung to proceed", referring to the sacrifice at the Temple of Heaven, which was indeed in K'ang
Hsi's handwriting. It was quite irregular as a nomination to the Throne,
as Ch'eng Chi 承繼, succession, would be employed and not "proceed"
which is nonsense in this connection. However, the slip was hastily conveyed to the Grand Secretariat and the valedictory decree was drafted
and promulgated, declaring Yung Cheng 雍正, the heir. This decree was
on exhibition (perhaps is still) at the Historical Museum on the Wu Men
午門 of this city.

It was in October 1907 that I accompanied Tz'u Hsi 慈禧 on her *Teng
Kao* 登高, mountain climbing expedition (I believe her last – I do not
fancy she commemorated the occasion in 1908), and on the way we
called at Pi Yün Ssu 碧雲寺, the temple built by Wei Chung-hsien 魏忠賢

---

1   The so-called "Old Summer Palace", destroyed by British and French troops in 1860.

(whose character *Chung* "Loyal" was changed by the imperial decree of Ch'ung Chen 崇禎 into *Ni* 逆, traitor) in T'ien Ch'i's reign about the year 1628, which the all powerful eunuch intended for his place of sepulture, had not fate, in the shape of emperor Ch'ung Chen, willed otherwise. As we burned incense before the statue of Sakyamuni, the Old Buddha became contemplative: "Pity and resignation are the ends of life. Here we have the son of a king brought up in a palace, 'high walled gardens green and old', where nothing is known of the miseries of the outside world. But to Sakyamuni the harem was transformed into a charnel house and he felt that he was living in a grave-yard. He went out of his pleasure-house, just as I am doing today, met an old man and felt the decrepitude of imminent death; then he met one stricken by sickness and felt himself under its invasion; he met a corpse and felt death in life; seeing a yogi (saint), he realized that the latter's soul was at peace and determined to win the same peace for himself. As you know, he abandoned his palace and fled into the jungle, where he would have starved, had not a maiden brought to him milk and honey on the shores of lake Nairandjana. There he sate beneath the Boddhi tree during a nightly vigil and his intelligence expanded like a white lotus flower. He perceived that all our miseries are caused by desire, whereas, once we acquire knowledge, we realize that nothing is desirable, so that all our woes would end. We must destroy the passions, as an elephant overturns a cabin of reeds; because desire never satiates appetite any more than the waters of the sea can quench thirst."

Then Tz'u Hsi told to me a story of a courtisan, Vasavadatta, who fell in love with a rich youth named Upagupta in her town of Mathura in Bengal and sent to him a message to join her in dalliance. But he spurned her advances and it befell that Vasavadatta was sentenced to death for her profligacy by mutilation of her limbs, nose and ears. She was left to die on the execution ground, while a faithful attendant watched by her side, awaiting her death. Suddenly the attendant perceived the approach of the youth Upagupta who had spurned her mistress in the days of her vanity. He stood by the mutilated harlot in an attitude of deference and devotion. She recognized him and with her dying voice said: "When I was beautiful as the nenuphar and inspired desire, you never came near to me. What brings you here to contemplate my mutilated body?"

"In the days of your beauty I knew you for what you were and saw the corruption that would soon be yours. You have lost nothing and may die happy. Life is a bad dream which you need not regret. Earthly pleasures are like the reflection of the moon on the water. You desired too much: desire nought and you will be happier than the gods. Do not wish to live any longer, for life is evil. I love you: believe me, you can now with a glad heart enjoy your rest." And so the harlot died happily, quenched of desire, leaving this world of illusion and hallucination.

I was fairly well accustomed to the infinite variety of the Old Buddha, but today she exhibited herself to me, her adoring slave, in a totally new guise. That she was a devoted Buddhist in theory, I knew; equally that her nature was benevolent when not thwarted, pitiful towards others' sorrows, devoted to children and animals, one who did by stealth as much kindness as (say) Queen Alexandra or Queen Marie Antoinette. The environment of the temple and the aroma of the incense that she had just offered before the image of the Buddha had made her apparently oblivious of the world of desire which ordinarily appealed to her with so great a zest. As we walked up the hill together, Li Lien-ying toiling rather reluctantly up the slope, she seemed more inclined to hark back to mundane topics and put a question to me which was characteristic of the workings of her mind, as it were indicative of a certain jealousy. "You and I have enjoyed a pleasing intimacy. Tell me the truth: if your Queen, who is said to be, or to have been (a true feminine touch) beautiful, sent for you as I have so often done, should you obey her commands or would your affection for me constrain you to hold aloof?"

"Madam, such an event would never happen; except in the last page of a novel. There could be no question of my obeying or disobeying an order that could not conceivably be issued."

"You mean that the King would be jealous?"

"No, Your Majesty. I don't imagine that a man like Edward VII would object to his wife having amours of her own. But it simply could not happen. Your Majesty's gracious kindness to me is largely, I fancy, because I am an alien who has absorbed Manchu ideas; so that I interest the Old Buddha. But in England I should only be one in a thousand, of good family indeed and perhaps above the average in interests. But Alexandra, or Alix, as we call her as a sort of pet name, if she desired a companion, would seek such a one in naval or military circles. Your Majesty may not be aware that our Queen is stupid as an owl (except that a *hibou*[2] is not stupid!), although kind-hearted: she has none of the infinite range of Your Majesty and your width of outlook."

"Well," went on the Old Buddha, "I want you to promise me two things: firstly, that you will never have sexual relation with another woman. I know your habits and ask no promise nor resolution from you regarding your own sex; for I believe you would never keep it and, apart from that, I have no objection to your multitudinous and amorous relations with princes, actors, eunuchs and male prostitutes nor am I in the least jealous. But I should never forgive you if you married, or still more had relations with, a foreign female, or indeed with a Manchu lady."

To this question I gladly gave an unqualified affirmative. "Secondly, I anticipate another ten years of life, and by the time that day comes which comes to all, you will be not far short of 50. I want you to reside at my mausoleum in the capacity of 'tea server' to my manes, not necessarily all the year round, but at any rate on the occasion of my *Yin Shou* 陰壽, anniversary of my birth when I were gone, during the New Year and the other festivals." (This request is less extraordinary than it sounds, except

---

2   "Owl", which actually *is* quite unintelligent for a bird.

for the fact that as an alien I could hardly be entitled to such an honour. When Chia Ch'ing 嘉慶 emperor compelled the suicide of Ho Shen 和珅, his father's favourite, he permitted Fu K'ang-an 福康安, who was of Ho Shen's party, to live at Ch'ien Lung's mausoleum in the capacity of tea server to the great sovereign's spirit, with the one typically mean proviso that on the occasion of Chia Ch'ing himself proceeding to the Yü Ling 裕 陵 (Ch'ien Lung's mausoleum) to worship, Fu K'ang-an was not to show himself in His Majesty's vicinity (as he did not desire to set eyes upon a man he detested).)

The Empress seemed very anxious for my reply: naturally, I thanked her for this new honour and promised to carry out her wish, if I survived her death.

She went on: "I should gladly have nominated you one of the *Shou Ling Ta Ch'en* 守陵大臣, Custodian of the Tombs, but such an appointment would stir up frantic jealousy and I fear that your life would be in danger, although the new emperor, who will be P'u Lun 溥倫 as I have told you, would certainly confirm the appointment, unprecedented as it is." I cannot pretend that the idea of migrating to the exile of the Tung Ling 東陵 greatly appealed to my taste, and I asked myself how it would fare with my numerous amours. It would scarcely be feasible for a train of catamites to accompany me thither, as the mausolea are essentially a sanctuary which is debarred to the *profanum vulgus*[3] and is, in fact, a *Ching Ti* 淨地, unsullied earth, where mundane loves and unruly affections shall have no sojourn. "Take thy shoes from off thy feet, for the place whereon thou standest is holy ground."

The manner of the Old Buddha's passing was so utterly unexpected and so premature, while the Regent's personality was so alien from my own, that it was not feasible to carry out her wishes under the new reign, although it was my privilege to be present at her sepulture (in fact the new empress dowager Lung Yü 隆裕 recognized me at the obsequies, summoned me to her chair and thanked me for my devotion) and to pay occasional visits between 1909 and 1911. But with the revolution and the changed situation, there was no possibility of a foreigner being permitted to reside in the grave enclosure of the dispossessed dynasty. Not only so, but my chief at home, Sir E. Grey, put a veto on the idea when I mooted it to him, as my possible usefulness to the Foreign Office could only be achieved by my continued residence in Peking. I have recorded elsewhere my pathetic pilgrimage many years later in 1928 to the Old Buddha's tomb and what I saw there. Had I been faithful to her wish and remained permanently in residence as "tea server" at her sepulchre, I could not have averted the desecration when bandit troops kennelled themselves in the holy of holies, while my own inevitable murder would not have served my mistress' spirit in heaven except as a token of inalienable devotion.

"Well," went on the Old Buddha, "I know that you will keep my memory green hung round by the *immortelles*[4] of your love. But enough

3   Profane crowd.
4   Immortality.

of the future: *Chin Jih Yu Chiu Chin Jih Tsui* 今日有酒今日醉, let us make the most of the present hour." (We have wine today so today we will carouse.) "We shall soon reach the *T'ing Tzu* 亭子 or kiosque where I usually rest after the long climb; and I bade the eunuchs await us there with *Tien Hsin*[5] 點心, tea, wine and cigarettes, also opium, if desired." The Empress seemed to have thrown off, like a discarded robe, her Buddhist reflections on the vanity of desire and the emancipation from mundane entanglements. She had grown strangely old while telling the story of the Indian courtisan (reminding me of the divine Duse[6] in a scene where she contemplates herself in a mirror, envisaging the days of her old age, and she appears to the spectator by a brilliant climax of histrionic power to be an old woman riddled with wrinkles and lined with crow's feet) and seemed, for the first time since I had known her, to be bearing the burden of the years. Frivolous and pleasure loving as few great women of history, she had another side to her complex nature: "shoulders supporting a load, Atlantean, immense: well nigh not to be borne of the too vast orb of her fate", like the weary Titan looking neither to right nor to left. She was buoyed up in performing the exhausting duties of State by her stedfast conviction that she had still many years before her, a belief that was confirmed in the following spring of 1908 by the oracular séance at the White Cloud Temple. Alas! ill prophets were we all!

As we approached our destination, the Old Buddha became jocular and rejuvenated. "I have a surprise for you, something that will just suit your tastes."

Lien-ying had gone ahead, and I heard him shout: "The Benevolent Old Ancestress has arrived: everyone go down on his or her knees to receive her."

It was a pleasing sight for a lover of beauty: at least a score of court ladies and an equal number of beautiful actors, including several familiar acquaintances, were doing homage to Her Majesty at the foot of the short flight of steps to the arbour. The Old Buddha bade everyone rise: "No formality today and we are all going to amuse ourselves first here on the Hsiang Shan 香山 and later at Wan Shou Shan 萬壽山. Let us all make the most of the shining hour and we will prolong our revels through the livelong night after our return." I was reminded of Marie Antoinette with la princesse de Lamballe *et "la favorite"* Polignac making the "return to nature" at Trianon and rehearsing under Rousseau's direction "*Le Devin de village*",[7] while the Comte d'Artois was never wanting in *une pointe d'esprit*.[8] All the eunuchs except Lien-ying and Ts'ui Tê-lung who soon appeared, had been selected for their personal beauty. The Old Buddha

5   Snacks, cakes, dumplings; "Dim-sum" in Cantonese.
6   Eleonora Duse (1858-1924) was an internationally acclaimed Italian actress and a rival (personally and professionally) of Sarah Bernhardt.
7   "*The Village Soothsayer*", a one-act opera by Jean-Jacques Rosseau.
8   "A flash of wit". Marie Antoinette's co-performers in this anecdote are Marie Louise of Savoy (1749-92), Superintendent of the Queen's Household, and Gabrielle de Polastron (1749-93), Duchess of Polignac and the queen's favourite. The witty Comte d'Artois (1757-1836) was Antoinette's friend, later to become King Charles X of France.

made us all feel at ease in the most delightful spontaneity which her presence invariably imparted, always providing that none presumed on her *joie de vivre* to touch upon certain forbidden topics, especially Kuang Hsü or princess Ch'un, Junglu's daughter, who had defied Her Majesty and was never forgiven.

I suppose that there were Manchu imperial guards in the vicinity, but it always appeared to me that the Old Buddha's frequent country excursions involved a certain risk now that talk of revolution was in the air. On the occasion of our adventure with the possessed eunuch I had rather exaggerated the risk that Her Majesty ran, as it appeared that troops were available from a neighbouring encampment in event of revolutionary activity. None could have dreamed, least of all Her Majesty herself, that a near relative of Lien-ying, one who had formerly been for years in the Old Buddha's service, would dare to threaten her, to say nothing of myself, as I have narrated in another paper.

At any rate, on this halcyon day which graced the auspicious festival, no soldiers were visible during our revels. At that time, none of us believed in a revolution and in our blindness, we failed to read the writing on the wall, fondly dreaming that the old order was immutable as the hills. The grounds of Hsiang Shan are spacious and comprise a number of convenient and secluded resting places, in which actors, catamites, eunuchs and maids of honour had ample opportunity, with Her Majesty's good-natured, if tacit, acquiescence, to disport themselves.

My darling friend, Chan Pao-ch'en 占寶臣, hero of the adventure in the paper on the "Secret Tryst", had been honoured by the Old Buddha with an invitation to spend the holiday at the Court. His wife was *en couches*,[9] *Chan Fang* 佔房, and therefore unable to obey Her Majesty's commands, as Queen Victoria loved to write in the *Gazette* in recording court functions where certain of her invited guests failed her from accident or excuse. And so Pao-ch'en and I determined to engage in dalliance after our return to the palace, that is, if the Old Buddha were graciously willing: though I feared that our delicious commerce could only be unilateral on the occasion, knowing Her Majesty's exacting demands on an exhausted concupiscence. Despite the difference of time and place, our *fête champêtre*[10] reminded me of the Intendant Fonquet's magnificent reception to Le Roi Soleil at Vaux le Vicomte, where *l'appareil fastueux*[11] and the lavish sumptuosity hastened the faithful minister's arrest and perpetual confinement.[12] The actors florished with the ladies; the eunuchs amused themselves to the fullness of their *lubricité luxurieusement manifestée*;[13] the Empress who had engaged me in games of elephant chess in which I

9   Giving birth.
10 Country party.
11 Ostentatious ceremony.
12 Nicolas Fouquet (1616-80), France's Superintendent of Finance under the "Sun King" Louis XIV. Fouquet enraged the king by flaunting his wealth at a 1661 reception at his lavish estate, Vaux le Vicomte. He was later arrested, charged with embezzlement and imprisoned for the remainder of his life.
13 Lustiness expressed in a lascivious manner.

beat her, for Her Majesty, unlike our *hochseliger König*[14] Edward VII, now, I suppose, in heaven, was a good loser and resented nothing so much as being allowed to win by complaisant courtiers or maids of honour, summoned many of us to play at *Hua Ch'üan* 划拳 or wine forfeits[15] with sweet *vin de Champagne* flowing like water. Then she summoned the best looking actors to perform impromptu theatricals without the aid of cosmetics or make-up, *Hua Chuang* 化裝: making me join them in the part of P'ang T'ai Shih 龐太師 slaying his two concubines when tricked by Pai Yü-t'ang 白玉堂. The Old Buddha herself took part as Li T'ai-hou 李太后, the wronged empress dowager, in the recognition scene with the emperor Jen Tsung 仁宗 when she produces the imperial gift of pearls as proof of her long concealed identity.

I, who knew Her Majesty's moods better than most except, perhaps, Lien-ying or the deceased An Tê-Hai 安德海 and Junglu, could perceive that she was becoming salaciously minded and wondered who would be chosen as the fortunate *amant de passage*,[16] knowing well that the lot would not fall on me, as my time was due later, and I did not think that the Old Buddha, for face-saving expediency, would wish the court to know of an open-air (for the kiosque was little else) liaison with a "devil", however much uneuropeanized. I did not err: Her Majesty told us all to withdraw with a, to me, *"T'ing Ch'uan* 聽傳, wait to be summoned", with the exception of a luscious youth named Yin Tsu-wu 印祖武, but he used a different appellation in the theatrical world, *Ling Chieh* 伶界, which for the moment escapes me. "I want *you*", said she, and we all left them to their genial devices.

There were several side-shows on that auspicious day: performing apes with dogs and sheep trained by skilled Shantung mountebanks, conjurers of an art exceeding any legerdemain of the West, *Shuo Hsiang Sheng* 說相聲 or mimics, who love to introduce topical allusions and on this occasion took me off rather cleverly.

"What is the highest honour you can aspire to?" asked the leader of his *P'eng Chüeh'rh* 捧角兒 or associate whose duty is to act as a sort of provider or *pourvoyeur*[17] for his chief's sallies.

"How do I know? *Ni Wen Chao La Wo* 你問著啦我, to have two good meals a day and a pleasant night with my wife?"

"No; you have not guessed, *Mei Ts'ai Chao* 沒猜著; the highest honour is to be born a devil and to become a *Shen* 神 or 'divinity'; then such a one has reached the goal of ambition, *Cheng Tao Chi Tien* 正到極點, though he lives 1,000 years."

He meant that I, though a foreigner, had gained the favour of the highest in the land and, as it were, became one of the celestial hierarchy. The reference was obvious and the audience, including myself, were delighted; while the ever ready witted Lien-ying intercepted my own

---

14 Late king.
15 *Hua Ch'üan* is a finger-guessing drinking game.
16 Passing lover.
17 Purveyor.

intention and said to the chief mimic: "The devil, now elevated by you to sainthood, presents you with Taels 100 as his compliments."

There were blind soothsayers and open eyed diviners, one of whom told my fortune, predicting, as in the case of most human lives, fortune combined with misfortune, money gained and lost. The same adept proved himself a good prophet when he told Pao-ch'en that he would one day rise high in Manchuria, of course he did not say Manchoukuo 滿洲國, but I have mentioned elsewhere sweet Chan's appointment under the emperor K'ang Tê 康德 at Hsinching 新京.[18] There were skilled musicians manipulating every conceivable instrument (I remember the late Monseigneur Favier telling me that he could play forty odd different types and in fact he graciously discoursed on a considerable number for my benefit); at every open space in the park pedlars, hawkers, sellers of peanuts, confectionary, *Hsing'rh Ch'a*[19] 杏兒茶, delicious of manifold flavour and exotic taste: every guest took what he or she listed at the Old Buddha's expense. Some of the actors played burlesque with the court ladies, much as Henriette d'Angleterre and La Vallière at Fouquet's famous fête, when Louis XIV sheltered his future favourite under a tree from a passing *rafale*.[20] However, we had the ideal Peking autumnal glory and the North China sun bathed us in its incomparable light, surely a heaven on earth. I imagine that from burlesque the participants passed to concrete exhibitions of one another's charms: it was a delightful scene of spontaneous jollity, equalling if not surpassing, the masques of the middle ages, in the days of François I or of England's Spanish queen.[21]

Lien-ying came up to us, for the Old Buddha was still merry-making with her mime, and asked Pao-ch'en why he and I did not repair to a conveniently adjacent pleasance and beguile our appetites with sexual activities. Laughing in my direction, he said: "You know how to excite old Pa's 巴 perverted instincts: I'll bring a *discipline* and if you give him twenty strokes on the buttocks, you'll make him as salacious as a he-goat."

"Thank you for your gracious thought," we both said, "but we hope, if the Old Buddha permits, to *Wan'rh* 玩兒, amuse ourselves, to satiety tonight, and we don't want to indulge over much just now." Despite our laudable resolution, I am fain to confess that we did withdraw for a brief season and mutually embraced times without counting. Ah! the memory of those ideal days; "*o fortunatos nimium sua si bona norint*", as Virgil says: "Too happy we, had we but known our own bliss". Little more than one short year had gone and all was dust and ashes. "O memory, fond memory, when all things fail we fly to thee."

---

18 China's last emperor, P'u Yi (1906-67), nominally presided over the Japanese puppet-state Manchoukuo from 1934 to 1945 as the K'ang Tê Emperor. Hsinching or "New Capital" (now Ch'angch'un 長春) was Manchoukuo's capital.

19 Sweet almond soup (literally "tea").

20 "Storm". This refers to the grand reception of Nicolas Fouquet, mentioned earlier. The court ladies discussed are Henrietta Anne of England (1644-70), sister-in-law and suspected lover of Louis XIV, and Louise de La Vallière (1644-1712), Henrietta's Maid of Honour and another of the king's alleged lovers.

21 Catherine of Aragon (1485-1536), first wife of the English King Henry VIII.

As already more than one hour had elapsed, I, who understood better than most, the probable extent and duration of Her Majesty's carnality, momentarily assuaged but ever recrudescent, truly a case of *vires acquirit eundo*, gaining fresh ardours as it advances, thought that her séance with Yin 印 was probably terminated by this time, so repaired thither to find the screen still drawn and was pleased, as was Lien-ying, to feel that she was taking her fill, especially after her rather gloomy dispositions of the morning ramble. So Lien-ying, Pao-ch'en (who was radiant in his glorious beauty after our delicious carnival of lust) and myself took tea at a neighbouring improvised tavern, while the former who was a good player had a game of elephant chess with my adored one.

In a short time (for we were within ear-shot of Her Majesty's *Hsing Kung* 行宮, travelling lodge, as etiquette designates it) the Old Buddha's voice was audible: "K'o- Ssu 恪思, Lien-ying, come here at once: *Wo Men Che'rh Wan La* 我們這兒完啦, we here have finished!" At the same moment, Yin emerged looking as beautiful as the sun god. He told me later that he had "pleasured" the Old Ancestress four times in succession, and my own experience enabled me to imagine the details without his expatiation. Nevertheless, he presented to me the fullest picture, copulation from above and from behind, mutual labial accommodations, clitoris titillation of his delectable proctal region, not without lengthy osculation by Her Majesty of that part which particularly appealed to her aesthetic senses, swallowing of his semen which flowed in ample ejaculation, kissing his fragrant person in every possible locality, for by her order he had stripped stark naked, while she had him caress and toy with her abundant vulva as well as presenting to him her *Kang Men* 肛門 (anus) for penetrating pedication. She seemed to have beaten her own record for dauntless salacity, and I wondered whether perhaps she might not dispense with my ministration for that evening and permit me to pass an untrammelled night in endless dalliance with my angelic Pao-ch'en.

As we reached the Presence, the Old Buddha who looked sated but in high spirits, called Lien-ying to prepare her opium pipe for a short siesta. Then to me: "I shall want you tonight, as usual, but I may call Yin again before you come. So be ready to follow him." Seeing the Old Buddha so redolent with humanity and exuberance, I thought it a good opportunity to ask if she would graciously permit Chan Pao-ch'en to stay overnight with me in the room she so thoughtfully had prepared for me. "What about his wife?" asked Her Majesty.

"She's expecting her confinement, Old Buddha."

"Oh! very well then: if she doesn't mind, I don't. *Chia En* 加恩, as a special favour, he may sleep with you, but don't overtire yourself and you had better limit yourself to the passivity which you enjoy."

I thanked Her Majesty and left her to her craving: during her siesta, Lien-ying, Yin Tsu-wu and Chan Pao-ch'en lunched together in a charming café prepared for the occasion. Yin, whose frankness left nothing to the imagination, told us that Her Majesty had paid him lavish compliments on his genital organs which he graciously exhibited for our delectation: as was natural after so prolonged an exercise, his tool showed little sign of excitation, but as Lien-ying remarked: *"Jeng Pu Shih Wei Mei Wu* 仍不失爲美物*"*, it's still a beautiful object. I felt a little jealous, as Chan seemed considerably attracted by the gracious mime, and I fancy (who knows) that Lien-ying would have welcomed a prolonged titillation on his *foyer érotique*,[22] had not Yin been incapable of furnishing for the nonce a fresh militant development.

After a pleasing collation, Lien-ying thought that he and I had best return to be within call at the Empress' pavilion and we left Chan and Yin to their own devices. When the Old Buddha's siesta had terminated, she was pleased to see us kneeling at the entrance.

"Kan Ma To Li 幹麼多禮, why all this etiquette? *Pu Tsai Tz'u Hsü Li Mo Chie* 不在此虛禮末節, there is no need for so much petty ceremonial. Well, I am refreshed and am going to make a tour of the park. Better call the *P'a Shan Hu* 爬山虎, mountain litter, to be in readiness, but I mean to walk if I can all the way." Li was not much of a pedestrian but of course he would have to walk if Her Majesty insisted on doing so; if she preferred to ride in the chair, she would not object to his riding a donkey. But I fancy that the Old Buddha took a malicious pleasure in making him exercise his legs and perhaps it was a healthy change for him. So Her Majesty, Lien-ying and I (not forgetting Ts'ui Tê-lung who had been out on some errand for his mistress) started upon a lengthy ramble. We stopped at every booth and stall, while Her Majesty with delicious condescendence questioned the vendors, mountebanks, conjurers, soothsayers, magicians, blind augurs respecting their well-being, asking numerous queries regarding the cost of commodities and comparing the prices with those of her own girlhood. She remarked to us that costs had risen at least 100%: I wonder what she would have said in the present year of grace 1943?

I admired, as always, the Old Buddha's natural self-possession when, for example, we encountered her lover of the morning, Yin Tsu-wu, who was kneeling as we passed: "How do you feel?" asked she: "tired I suppose."

"Ch'en Ching Mu Lao Fo Ti En 臣敬沐老佛的恩, bathed in the Old Buddha's benevolences, *Chih Ssu Pu Wang* 至死不忘, I shall never forget while life lasts", was the apt reply. There was no false concealment nor specious prudery, such as I could imagine would be inevitable in London or Paris, especially London, once the mart of the civilised world but today the moribund capital of a tottering empire.

The afternoon passed very agreeably, as the Old Buddha led us on her peregrination: she had a word for every visitor and for every performer, petting the monkey which tried to bite her hand, admiring the pigeons with whistles attached to their tails and trained to fly in picturesque circles above each halt made by the Empress. She lavished praise (and also money) on the conjurers, once again had her fortune told by the blind augur without saying who she was: the latter, on feeling her

---

22 Erotic hearth.

hand, said "This is a great personality, like a goddess visiting the world, *Huo Shen Chiang Shih* 活神降世." Perhaps he had an inkling to whom he was speaking: anyhow he greatly gratified Her Majesty who showed her appreciation in kind. She listened with real pleasure to the vagaries of the professional mimics; but I noticed that they avoided any reference to her august presence, much as Queen Victoria objected to the minister of her religion referring in the pulpit to her presence.

Feeling weary myself, I was astounded by the Empress' abounding vitality and poor Lien-ying looked fit to drop, until Her Majesty graciously sanctioned his riding on the donkey.

The weather continued deliciously warm in the hot sun, although there was an autumn bite in shady corners. Her Majesty sat down, bidding us do likewise, before the improvised theatre and we listened with pleasure to several plays of the Three Kingdoms period, the arrest of Ts'ao Ts'ao 曹操 and the K'ung Ch'eng Chi 空城計 of K'ung Ming 孔明 and so forth. An al-fresco meal was served for all Her Majesty's guests including the actors, and the performers of humbler origin were each supplied with abundance of viands on a regal, or rather imperial, scale. The Empress herself insisted on partaking of their fare and greatly pleased us all by her natural loftiness of spirit when she said: "As a girl, I knew what hardship was: I used to go market with a very small purse to purchase comestibles for my family. In some ways, I was happier then than now when I am supposed by you all to revel in every imaginable bliss." I could imagine Napoléon speaking in such a way; but it is only a supremely great personality who can unbosom himself or herself respecting past humble circumstances.

The sun naturally did not wait for the conclusion of our long progress from booth to booth or pavilion to pavilion. "It is time for us to return to Wan Shou Shan," said Her Majesty, "but K'o-ssu (myself) and Lien-ying shall first accompany me again to Pi Yün Ssu 碧雲寺 as I wish to present incense; and afterwards we shall stop a moment at the Yü Ch'üan Shan 玉泉山, Jade Fountain, for I intend to sacrifice at the Lung Wang Tz'u 龍王祠, Dragon King's Shrine (Chinese Neptune). There's no need for all the household to accompany me if they like to remain a little later. It is getting chilly but there is, of course, good moonlight this evening.

"Some of you," said she amply, "may like to gambol a little later, so just amuse yourselves to your hearts' content." So the Old Buddha and we two left the kneeling company, *Kuei Sung Lao Fo* 跪送老佛; while she mounted the rustic *P'a Shan Hu* 爬山虎, Lien-ying and myself riding donkeys. She had no escort whatsoever, although, as I have said, guards were not far away against eventualities. We carried out the ordained programme, not without scented tea prepared with the delicious Jade Fountain water and reached Wan Shou Shan just before sunset in the promise of a glorious moon.

Up to this point, my narrative may not appear to the benevolent reader other than uneventful and hackneyed: I am glad that veracity comes to my rescue and enables me to add as a sort of dessert a somewhat strange culmination, though hardly stranger than my previous abnormal experiences. Her Majesty had been duly met at the west gate of the palace by eunuchs and maids of honour, but was much astonished (as I was) to see her younger brother, the extremely handsome Duke Kuei Hsiang 桂祥, in full court dress kneeling to await her arrival. (An attendant had gone ahead of us to announce the return.) The Old Buddha looked completely bewildered. "What in the world brings you here from the city? You look agitated: out with it. What has happened now? I suspect you have not had your afternoon bout of opium." (The craving was exceptionally strong on him, which was a pity as he was really a beautiful old man of about 66.)

"No, Your Majesty," (although a brother, he used the formal address of court etiquette) "it isn't that, but I must ask you graciously to allow your slave to memorialise you in private. But it concerns Pa K'o-ssu, so perhaps you will allow him to kneel and hear my communication."

"I suppose you are hardly going to tell me that Lao Pa is plotting against my life; if you do, I shan't believe you."

"No, Your Majesty, but be pleased to ask me no more till you have returned to your state apartment."

I could see that the Empress was on the *qui vive*[23] and felt considerably agitated. It seemed to me that my chair bearers, who like carters are an irascible race, might have had a brawl with some high official's retainers. However, Duke Kuei and I accompanied the Old Buddha who sate on her chair of audience, with the former kneeling slightly ahead of myself, as etiquette required.

This was the duke's story, practically in his own words: "Old Buddha, you always show exceptional favour to Pa Hou Yeh and order special viands for his delectation, a bowl of *Yen Ts'ai* 燕菜, swallow nest soup, *Kuei Hua Ch'ih Tzu* 桂花翅子, shark's fin in scrambled eggs, besides other dishes such as *Ch'ing Cheng Ya Tzu*[24] 清蒸鴨子. What I have to inform Your Majesty, though I deserve the death, is that a recently arrived chef in the *Yü Shan Fang* 御膳房, imperial culinary department, named Chao Jen-chai 趙仁齋, who was specially recommended by Prince and Princess Ch'un 醇 (Junglu's daughter) to the emperor for his gastronomic skill, had asked as a special favour to be allowed the privilege of preparing Pa's meal this evening, because, as he said, he knew how Your Majesty *Tso Ch'ing T'a* 作情他, favoured him. None would have raised any objection, but by the blessing of Heaven Chao drinks to excess and was heard to say, while in his cup, 'What will the Old Buddha do tomorrow? *K'an T'a Pan* 看他辦, *Chiu Shih La* 就是啦: let her manage as best she may', a remark which was as treasonable as suspicious. As Chao was very much inebriated, two of the other head cooks, alarmed by his wild words, did not encounter much resistance in searching him. Your Majesty, they discovered a packet of what the palace official apothecary says is *P'i Shuang* 砒霜, arsenic crystals, more than sufficient to cause death to several persons. This

23 Alert.
24 Steamed duck.

was at about 1 p.m., and the chefs thought, in Li Tu Tsung Kuan's 李都總管 absence (chief chamberlain Li Lien-ying) that instead of alarming the Old Buddha at your carnival, it would be well to send posthaste to the city and bring me here. I arrived an hour or more ago and at once, on my own responsibility, had Chao Yin-chai bound with cords and severely flogged, K'ao Wen 問. He had not yet fully Hsing Chiu 醒酒, shaken off his drunkenness, but under torture admitted that Princess Ch'un had handed to him the poison with orders to put an equal portion in each of the dishes for Pa K'o-ssu but to take the utmost precaution that none else (especially Your Majesty) partook of the viands. Chao also said that the emperor was privy to the plot: if it be so, Your Majesty will know best how to deal with him. Chü Chü Wei Shih 句句為實, every word is the truth. Nu Ts'ai Mao Ssu Chin Tsou 奴才冒死謹奏, your slave reverently memorialises Your Majesty, braving death for temerity."

The Empress heard him to the end with apparent imperturbability. "Why does that ungrateful wretch, Princess Ch'un, wish Ken Pa Hou Kan 跟巴侯幹, to make Marquis Pa her object of attack? She hardly knows him, Tai Wu I Mien Chih Ya 殆無一面之雅; she may consider herself dispensed from all duty to me the Empress Dowager, but I presume she has still some filial sense toward her illustrious sire who thought well, as I do, of old Pa. Answer me at once."

Kuei-hsiang hesitated a great while: vox faucibus haesit,[25] he seemed incapable of utterance. At last: "Your Majesty, your slave is uttering words that none dare utter, Yen Jen So Pu Kan Yen 言人所不敢言. Wai T'ou 外頭, outside, it is common talk that Pa Hou is Your Majesty's minion, Ch'ung Ch'en 寵臣, who (forgive your slave) has Mi Mi 秘密, secret, Hsiang Chiao 相交, relations with you, K'o Wei Tsui Ch'in Tsui Tu Chê 可謂最親最篤者, of the most extreme nature. Do not you perceive that Pa's death by poison, here in the palace, because after taking so large a quantity of arsenic, says the apothecary, he could not survive the night, would embarrass Your Majesty especially after recent events? Is it not possible that Pa's government with which he has important connection might intervene through the British Shih Ch'en 使臣, minister? In other words, the motive is the same as the traitor Ts'en Ch'un-hsüan 岑春煊 when he hoped (again forgive your slave) to 'catch you together' (Chuang Tsai I K'uai'rh 撞在一塊兒)."

The Old Buddha changed colour and her unparalleled self-possession seemed for an instant only to desert her. "It only shows me that till that accursed wretch Tsai Tien 載湉 (it was the only time that I ever heard her speak of Kuang Hsü 光緒 by his personal name which was taboo) disappears from the Throne and the world, there will be no peace for me nor for Pa Hou. Call Lien-ying, but you two are to remain here."

I rose from my exceedingly cramped position, for I am not a good kneeler, being not to the manner born as a Manchu official is, except on European religious occasions, and called Lien-ying who had evidently

---

25 Voice stuck in the throat (Virgil, Aeneid II.774).

heard the whole conversation. He came in, did not kneel (probably because Her Majesty allowed to him special dispensation), and said quite frankly: "I know all about it, Old Ancestress. It's because of the *La Pa* 喇叭 affair." (I was completely in the dark and the word *La Pa*, trumpet, conveyed nothing to me. As Li proceeded, I began to recollect a recent conversation with the Old Buddha of which I will speak in a moment.) "Your Majesty knows," Li proceeded, "that La Pa (apparently *Rab* or *Raab,* but it may not be his surname, *Rab* being Russian for slave, while *Raab* is, I believe, a German patronymic) died a few hours after leaving the Summer Palace of what the foreign doctor pronounced to be arsenic poisoning. It was known that he had passed the evening with Your Majesty" (I noticed that Li's special position of freedom and familiarity enabled him to call a spade a spade without any apology or otiose verbiage) "in erotic connection with the Old Buddha."

At this point I may interpolate that sometime in the previous August the Old Buddha had done to me the honour to discuss the *format* and appearance, artistic or otherwise, of Europeans' tools. She remarked that my unworthy organ was aesthetically pleasing, because the *Pao P'i* 包皮 or prepuce was intact. In China only Mohammedans and the small remnant of Jew religionists performed circumcision, as both Manchus and Chinese considered that the absence of the foreskin or prepuce was not only *Han Ch'un* 憨蠢, ill-looking, but greatly subtracted from the copulative ecstasy. She then mentioned that she had recently had occasion to "inspect" a Russian "devil's" penis which was large and voluble but lacking in the all important *Pao P'i* or foreskin. I think that she probably named him to me, but the circumstance of his death had not come to my ears and the matter passed from my mind.

The Old Buddha did not deny the carnal intercourse with Rab (?): "Yes," said she, "he possessed me five or six times and was very full of lust (*Shê Fei Hsiao* 色非小). I knew that he died after leaving the palace; but we need not go into details." Li continued: "The old ancestress knows that Pokotiloff (the Russian envoy) and I are very intimate: I have already memorialised Your Majesty that he was quite frank in saying that his death was attributed to poison *not* self-administered (how the doctors assigned an external cause, I know not). The tea-house gossip has been busy with the matter, and it is my duty to the Old Buddha, whose horse and dog I am in every loyal service, *Hsiao Ch'üan Ma Chih Lao* 效犬馬之勞, to tell Your Majesty that you are believed to have caused his death by poison, in order to shut inconvenient mouths. I can however assure Your Majesty that Pokotiloff is too loyal to Your Majesty to raise any question, and in any case a very long time has elapsed; though I suppose it would be possible to exhume the body and find traces of the poison, which would not matter as Your Majesty's name is not involved, except in the gossip of *la pègre et la canaille*, the scum of society and the criminal elements. The sun's eclipse is only temporary: he soon resumes his wonted brightness. So it is with Your Majesty."

"Well," said the Old Buddha, "the least said, the soonest mended. You can eat your sharks' fins in peace, old Pa, tonight, but if you are suspicious, I will share them with you from the same dish."

"Your Sacred Majesty, my daystar from on high, my gracious patroness, my giver of all good things, my Goddess of Mercy incarnate, how can you speak to your foreign slave as if I could ever have the vestige of suspicion toward your gracious, holy personality? May I not entreat you, meekly kneeling" (and kotowing till the blood came to my luckless forehead), "to banish once for all such an ill-conceived thought. Foreign devil as I am, I am not a stick nor stone: gratitude abides and heats in my heart even as it does in Duke Kuei or Li Tu Tsung Kuan himself. Were I to live a hundred lives, I could never display even the ten thousandth part of the affection and devotion that it is my dear delight to owe to my sacred benefactress."

"Rise from your knees," said Her Majesty, and she drew me toward her person and honoured me by a luxury of kisses on my mouth. "I don't mind you seeing it, Kuei Hsiang, *Ni Pu Shih Wai Jen* 你不是外人, you are one of us: Pa Hou is very dear to me and I would liefer[26] poison myself than cause to him a vestige of harm, nay to hurt one raven-black (as it was then!) hair of his dear head.

"For the present," she continued, "see that Chao Jen-chai remains bound, and in the morning, when Tsai Feng 載灃 (Prince Ch'un 醇) attends the *Chün Chi* 軍機 council, I shall cross-question him before dealing with Kuang Hsü. But I suspect that the whole plot owes its initiative to his wicked wife, that owl (*Hsiao* 梟) who pecks out her parents' eyes, the symbol of unfilial atrocity. That is all I have to say at present: you can retire but don't *Sheng Chang* 聲張, retail the matter to anyone, nor gossip, as you love to do" (to Duke Kuei who kotowed and withdrew). Then she addressed me: "I give you permission again to copulate a hundred times if your tool has the strength, in anal bliss with your darling Chan Pao-ch'en. But frankly I prefer that you allow him to minister to you from behind; and then you will feel fresh when I summon you. Lien-ying tells me that you like your paramours to chastise you on the bare buttocks, till the red blood flows. Well! you can enjoy *votre prédilection originale*[27] to your heart's content. Personally, after supper, I am going to amuse myself again with Yin Tsu-wu, for I told him at the Park to be prepared for 'another audience' some time before midnight. And you shall come in later, after you have had your surfeit from Chan's favours."

"Yes, Old Buddha," replied Li, "Yin Tsu-wu quite understands, is profoundly grateful to your divine Majesty and awaits your gracious commands."

"Very good, I am going to rest before supper. Leave me for the present."

Lien-ying and dear Pao-ch'en joined me at my repast. I need not say that the sumptuous fare was quite innocent of arsenic but was redolent

---

26   Willingly.
27   Your unique predilection.

of the unsurpassed Chinese perfection of cuisine. We *sab-lâmes*[28] with exceptional zest two magnums of the Old Buddha's incomparable *vin de Champagne* of the house of Pommery et Greno, to my mind *la marque suprême*[29] of Sunny France. Lien-ying became very salacious, insisted on us both titillating his erotic *trou fignon* and even forced us to indulge in repeated osculation on and around that lovely region. He graciously excused us from *Ts'ao P'i Ku* 肏屁股, on the ground that the Old Buddha had forbidden me to do so and that Chan Pao-ch'en would tire himself before his *nuit d'amour* with me. We were both in a state of advanced *griserie*,[30] but the condition did not impair his militance nor my unparalleled lasciviousness. He performed on my person all the manoeuvres that I have recorded elsewhere in the course of my familiarities with male persons: we applied osculations in every conceivable portion of our anatomy, he possessed me thrice or four times, if not more, in the *Ch'i Hsiao Lü'rh* 騎小驢兒 as well as the *P'a Shan Hu* 爬山虎 posture;[31] his ample, nay Brobdingnagian, *verge* penetrated my rectum right up to the hilt, even as Cassia's in years gone by, to my indelible and endless gratification. I would not deny that he did not forget to impart to me most severe and painful castigation across the buttocks; so much so that, when the Old Buddha a little later observed the laceration and bleeding, she said with consternation: "*Chen Chiao Kuai Ni Chê Ko P'i* 眞叫怪你這個癖, what a strange *P'i* 癖, or craving, is yours! *Wei Wen Chih Yu Yeh* 未聞之有也: it is quite new to me to hear of. Is it usual in Europe?"

"No, Madame, I should say, it was quite *sui generis*[32] but not unique; Henri III, *ce monarque étrangement poétique*,[33] had the same predilection."

"*Ch'ü Shemmo Lo* 取什麼樂? where is the pleasure?" And I could not answer her, not knowing myself.

Pao-ch'en's flogging was certainly the severest and most painful that I ever experienced; he said that he expected me to cry "halt" and whine for mercy, admitting, as a true sadistic disciple, that the castigation gave to him a keen sensual delight. The *discipline* was broken to pieces and numerous twigs found themselves embedded in my flesh. Pao-ch'en was also an adept of Masoch, for he demanded, and obtained, from me that I should retaliate on his posterior for which purpose I served myself of a fresh *discipline*. He stood the chastisement with admirable self-control and said that he enjoyed it at my hands, but that, if another had touched his "bottom" he would have knifed him till he died the death.

As these chronicles are veracious (however artless) from alpha to omega, I must acknowledge that, despite the Old Buddha's inhibition, I had the joy to copulate once with Chan after the habitual *modus operandi*, greatly to his dear content. Lien-ying came in with an ample dose of *Mei Yao* 媚葯; he told me that Yin Tsu-wu had successfully possessed the Old

28 Uncorked.
29 The supreme brand.
30 Intoxication.
31 The "ride the small donkey" and "mountain scaling tiger" positions, respectively.
32 In a category of its own.
33 That strangely poetic monarch.

Ancestress on three occasions, one of which was *a tergo* and the other buccal ejaculation. I wondered how he would be able to take his place at the theatre that afternoon, but Lien-ying said he had taken kindly to the *Mei Yao* or aphrodisiac, also that the Old Buddha, that inexhaustible fount of bounty, had presented him with Taels 1,000 for his distinctly titanic or cyclopean activities. And so with countless kisses on lips, posterior and urethral orifice, I bade to dear Chan good-night and obeyed the Old Buddha's summons. I confessed to her my disobedience, but happily the potent drug absolved me from blame and the desired activity was safely and fully acquired. Our congress was short but pleasurable, and Her Majesty confirmed to me that she had perforce to shut the mouth of the unfortunate La Pa or Rab, as she was convinced that he would inform all and sundry of Her Majesty's affections: "*il n'avait pas de secret*",[34] as Saint-Simon makes the valet of the duc d'Orléans say to Le Roi Soleil when the latter asks whether his brother was privy to the supposed poisoning of his beloved sister-in-law (who actually died of heart failure after bathing in cold water). I admired Her Majesty's frankness but ventured to implore her to dissemble the murder to the rest of the world, and she promised to do so "to please you", as she graciously remarked. I sometimes wonder how the Empress Dowager's habit of disposing of her *amants de passage*[35] had become so well-known in Europe: in fact, I actually heard of her in this connexion as long ago as 1890, when I never dreamed of my future briefly worn, but still distinguished, honours as an Empress' paramour to be.

Respecting the unfortunate *cuisinier*,[36] Chao Jen-chai, who, I suppose, was well paid for his part in a conspiracy which might never have succeeded, for possibly I should have detected an unusual flavour (having a sensitive *gustation*) in the delicate perfume of birds nest soup and never swallowed it at all, I left the palace early in the morning, while the audience to the Council was still continuing, but heard later from Lien-ying that Prince Ch'un denied any knowledge of the plot while admitting that his wife had recommended the cook as a *cordon bleu*[37] to the emperor. Accordingly, the Old Buddha decreed that Chao should be flogged to death at the palace gate, *Li Pi Chang Hsia* 立斃杖下, and that his decapitated head should be suspended in Hai Tian 海甸 village with the legend *Tu Sha Chê* 毒者, poisoner, although it would have been truer to write *Mou Tu Sha Fan* 謀毒犯, attempted poisoner, since none tasted his arsenic.

I ought to add that owing to the unexpected news conveyed by Duke Kuei Hsiang regarding the projected administration of poisoning, the Empress cancelled the projected theatricals for that evening but had a most elaborate celebration on the anniversary of her birth a month later.

---

34 There was no secret.
35 Passing lovers.
36 Cook.
37 Gourmet chef.

CHAPTER XVII

THEIR MORTAL HOUR

ON the morning of the Old Buddha's *anniversaire*,[1] her 74th according to Chinese reckoning, 10 day of 10 moon, November 3, 1908,[2] I was just putting on my court gala robes, amber necklace and other ornaments graciously conferred upon me by my imperial mistress, in readiness to start in my chair for the Lake Palace and then to present my homage and loyal wishes of longevity to Her Majesty. I did not anticipate that she would on this occasion grant to me a private audience, since not only the entire Manchu court but also His Holiness the Dalai Lama 達賴喇嘛, then visiting Peking, were due to attend at the Yi Luan Tien 儀鸞殿, the Hall of Motherhood and Empresshood; so that obviously an obscure "foreign devil" who was already an object of jealous suspicion to the traitor Yüan Shih-k'ai 袁世凱, the Princess (*Fu Chin* 福晉) Ch'un 醇 (daughter of Junglu 榮祿, unworthy, she-wolf hearted child of a great statesman), to Chi Lu 繼祿, the *Tsung Kuan Nei Wu Fu Ta Ch'en* 總管內務府大臣, Chief Minister of the Household, and others, including the so-called *Chün Tang* 君党, or party of the emperor.

Suddenly, a note arrived from my friend Li Lien-ying 李蓮英, couched as usual in somewhat cryptic terms: "The Old Ancestress commands your presence today. It is absolutely requisite not to attract attention. Come at the *Shen* 申 hour (Monkey period, from 3-5 p.m.). You know the name of writer: no separate card nor signature - *Chih Ming Pu Chü* 知名不具."

I hastily scribbled with the brush on my visiting card the words: "Will carry out Imperial orders, so as to obey your honourable direction - *Tzu Tang Chin Tsun* 自當謹遵, *I Ch'i Pu Fu Ya Chu* 以期不負雅囑", handing it to the eunuch Ts'ui whom I knew so well.

I wondered at the Chief Chamberlain despatching so important a messenger as Ts'ui on a fête day when he would naturally be preoccupied with Her Majesty's business, and started guessing the cause. Evidently something was afoot: in fact my confidential major-domo

---

1   Birthday.
2   **Backhouse:** Please note: I have no *Synchronismes Chinois* and cannot be sure of the date by the Gregorian calendar.

was greatly perturbed and said quite earnestly: "*Ta Jen* 大人, *Nin Pieh Ch'ü* 您別去, *Hen Wei Hsien* 狠危險. Don't go, Your Excellency, it is very dangerous." It is well known that the "man in the street" in China (*Lu Jen Chieh Chi* 路人皆知) possesses a wonderful "flair" regarding what is pending, especially at Court (after all, it is much the same in our benighted West). In obedience to Her Majesty's High Command, I dismissed my bearers until 2 p.m. and passed an unquiet morning in wonderment and perplexity. During the past six and half years I had become strangely intimate (ay, in the climax and the crown of unchaste but ecstatic communion) with Her Imperial Majesty and was devoted, as she knew, to her service, so that, as I once told her, I worshipped her very shadow. She was my goddess, my *P'u Sa*[3] 菩薩 who hearkeneth to prayer. Truly she was a compelling personality: we shall not look upon her like again. No such glamour emanates from a Hitler, a Stalin or a Mussolini, to say nothing of Britain's Welfendynastie, *incapable de gouverner et usurpatrice*,[4] although it has lavished honours on my house and I may appear ungrateful to the *soi-disant*[5] House of "Windsor", Saxe-Coburg, to accord its proper name.

So I meditated, listening the while to the hysterical appeals of my servants, some ten in number, asking me to invent some time-serving excuse for non-attendance: "You will never come out alive, my lord. Don't you know the Old Buddha by this time! There is great trouble brewing. What will happen to us if you are 'transformed into the yellow crane' *Hua Wei Huang Ho* 化為黃鶴, a euphemism for disappearing from the scene (my retainers' subjective point of view gratified my not wholly dormant humour perhaps not *typiquement britannique*),[6] to whose remonstrance I replied: "The Empress has emptied wide upon me the horn of her favour: our relations, if not secret, are at least intimate. I have already told the *Tu Tsung Kuan* 都總管 (Li Lien-ying) that I will *Ming Chia Ch'ü Fu* 命駕驅赴, *Kung Ch'ing Tz'u An* 恭請慈安 order my conveyance and hasten reverently to salute Her Benevolent Majesty. How can I compile at the last moment a pretext which would not be believed?" The chief chair attendant (who had charge of the bearers and of their relief of eight men who were accustomed to accompany me in an open *charrette*[7] in accord with official custom) was equally vehement in speaking with other voice, for the obvious reason that the Anniversary of Her Majesty's birth connoted for him and his staff an imperial largess of at least Taels 100. The bearers and the indoor servants almost came to blows over the matter; so that it was a relief for me when the time came to leave, escorted by the doubtfully genuine lamentations of my staff who expected never to see me again alive. So off I went wearing the

---

3   Bodhisattva.
4   "Welfen Dynasty, incapable of ruling and usurpers", referring to the House of Welf, known as the "House of Hannover" in England. Queen Victoria was the last of their English line, her descendents ruling as the House of Saxe-Coburg, later Windsor.
5   So-called.
6   Typically British.
7   Cart.

triple-eyed peacock's feather and the yellow riding jacket with the rest of my court robes.

On arrival at the gate, Hsi Yüan Men 西苑門, of the Lake Palace, Chung Hai Kung Tien 中海宮殿, it seemed to me that there was an atmosphere of tension despite the usual affluence of officials inseparable from the occasion of the Old Buddha's anniversary. I had little difficulty in being admitted, but the officer of the Banner troops at the gate called out: "*Chin T'ien Hen Chin* 今天狠緊: *Ying Tang Ch'a P'ai Tzu* 應當查牌子, *la consigne* is strict today: I ought to examine your *plaque d'identité*."[8] I showed him my gold tablet and he saluted, bidding me pass.

A eunuch of my most intimate and love-locked acquaintance (who had been sent to await my arrival) informed me that the Dalai Lama had not yet completed his masses of intercession for Her Majesty's long life, also that the projected theatricals which were to follow the religious ceremony would not take place. Most of the high officials had left, but I noticed that T'ieh Liang 鐵良 (Pao-ch'en 寶臣), the Minister for War, whom I knew well,[9] had his chair and mounted attendants waiting inside the gate. This eunuch, Ho Yün 和雲, who was a favourite of Li Lien-ying, and (*crede experto*)[10] as comely as Antinous, said that the latter had asked me to go straight to his room for a collation, pending Her Majesty's summons. Thither I went on foot, although I had imperial permission to move about the precincts in a chair. Li was at the moment in attendance on Her Majesty, but an elaborate feast (his hospitable idea of a "collation") awaited me. Everyone I saw seemed to be *distrait*[11] and ill at ease: none admires the Chinese so much as I, but their inveterate tendency (due perhaps to ingrained sincerity) *à eventer la mèche*[12] always mystifies me; since none is more sphinx-like, when he so chooses, in the matter of concealing his thoughts, like the Prince of Benevente, that admirable ex-Catholic bishop who betrayed three sovereigns, but died in the odour of sanctity.[13]

It must have been four o'clock when Li arrived to bid me wait on the Old Buddha in a side chamber of the Yen Ch'ing Lou 延慶樓 where 16 years later Ts'ao K'un 曹錕 was to be interned by Tuan Ch'i-jui 段祺瑞 and Feng Yü-hsiang 馮玉祥.[14] I entered and prostrated myself three times, uttering loyal wishes for Her Majesty's health and strength. She bade me with a gracious gesture rise and draw nearer, dismissing the attendant

---

8   Regulation . . . identification.

9   In a 1903 letter to G.E. Morrison, Backhouse notes: "A great friend of mine is [the Manchu army's] Colonel, and he says T'ieh is fiercely is fiercely anti-foreign besides being well acquainted with foreign ways."

10   Believe one who has experienced.

11   Distracted.

12   To uncover the plot.

13   Charles Maurice de Talleyrand-Périgord (1754-1834), French bishop turned prolific statesman. Talleyrand successfully remained in power throughout the eras of Louis XVI, the French Revolution, Napoleon, Louis XVIII, Charles X and Louis-Philippe.

14   Ts'ao K'un (1862-1938) was a Chinese warlord and briefly the nominal president of the fractured Chinese Republic. In 1924 he was betrayed by his former ally, the "Christian General" Feng Yü-hsiang (1882-1948), leaving an opening for the return to power of former Premier and fellow warlord Tuan Ch'i-jui (1865-1936).

eunuch Ts'ui Tê-lung 崔德隆. It seemed to me that the Old Buddha looked well and vigorous, except for a slight screwing up of her left cheek which made her speech, usually so clear, slightly indistinct and which I thought might be due to a seizure. She was majestic in her glory of full court robes, resplendent with jewels and wearing the famous pearl jacket.

Like Le Roi Soleil and Queen Victoria, the Old Buddha had all her life been favoured by the weather: every anniversary up to the last in 1908, was passed in the incomparable light of a Peking autumn day. But on this occasion, the clouds had gathered all day and as I entered the palace, rain began to fall. So, when I humbly offered to Her Majesty my dutiful homage and congratulations on her fête, I said: "Heaven favours you, Madame, in sending down rain in due season as a harbinger of plenty and perennial peace."

The Old Buddha said with a typical smile, half affectionate, half re-monstrating: "You know how to turn a compliment. Had the sky been cloudless, as is usual on my anniversary, you would have said: 'The glory of the azure firmament betokens Your Majesty's unending lon-gevity'.

"It must be two months since you came to 'audience' and I asked you to come at this hour, because I rely on your discretion and there are few outsiders, Wai T'ou 外頭 (i.e. other than the confidential eunuchs), who can keep their tongues shut. I will not even ask you to be circumspect, because I know you of old. If only Junglu were here – " she did not complete the sentence – "this is the reason of my commanding you. Last month, I had an attack of some kind, and Prince Ch'un 醇 (brother of Kuang Hsü 光緒 emperor) whom I foolishly put on the Grand Council, Prince Ch'ing 慶, Shih Hsü 世續 and Prince Yü Lang 毓朗 (direct descend-ant in fifth generation of Ch'ien Lung 乾隆 by the latter's eldest son Prince Ting 定, who, as son of a concubine, was excluded from the Throne) said publicly that it was time to abandon the Regency and to restore the em-peror. Tsai Feng 載灃 (Prince Ch'un) and his wife, who has persistently defied me, presuming on her father's (Junglu's) unique claims, are plan-ning a coup d'état, by which I should either be assassinated or banished to Jehol 熱河. I am not one to let the grass grow under my feet and mean to anticipate these traitors. Consequently, and Li Lien-ying is cognizant of the plan, I feel it my bounden necessity to "dispose of" (Ch'u Chih 處置) the emperor, because in so doing I shall deprive these treason workers of their puppet figurehead, K'uei Lei 傀儡, who is merely a Mu Tiao Ni Su 木雕泥塑, wooden idol and image of mud. I shall deal with each of them later", said the Empress, speaking with grim decision.

"Permit your servant from a far land to ask Your Majesty one humble question. Regarding the emperor's disappearance, how can I be of any help? Your Majesty knows that I would perform the service of Your dog or Your horse (Hsiao Ch'üan Ma Chih Lao 效犬馬之勞) for Your Sacred Per-son, but as a foreigner subject to European law .... and in any case, Ch'en Shih Ch'i Chün 臣弒其君, Tzu Shih Ch'i Fu 子弒其父 ... Fei I Chao I Hsi Chih

Ku 非一朝一夕之故. Regicide or parricide 'originates from manifold and complex reasons' " (*Yi Ching* 易經).

"No!! I am not asking you to perform impossibilities. I recognize that you are debarred from participation; what I want is that, if you hear of the emperor's sudden passing dragon-borne to Heaven, you will be at pains to let your government know that it was a natural death. I do not trust Yüan Shih-k'ai; he is as unscrupulous as he is capable: but I am forced to make use of T'ieh Liang who is his blood brother. I am going, after the emperor's death, to place P'u Lun Beitzu 溥倫貝子 on the Dragon Throne under my regency, with the reign title of Heng Ch'ing 亨慶 or Chen Ch'ing 貞慶, the *Ch'ing* being in reference to his descent from Chia Ch'ing 嘉慶, his great grandfather. That done, I shall eliminate the present Grand Councillors not by death but by dismissal, except Old Chang Chih-tung 張之洞. The air will be cleared and we shall start afresh. As you know, the séance this spring at the White Cloud Temple 白雲觀 told us that my horoscope indicates ten years more life, and, as I told you before, it has been borne on me that I shall live longer than your great queen who died at 82, I think?"

I replied: "My service is, as always, at the disposal of Your Gracious Majesty. I have no great influence with the government of Edward VII except with Sir E. Gray, but will tell the latter statesman what Your Majesty wishes and in due course will publish the facts as indicated by Your August order to the world, in such a way that none who reads shall question the entirely natural cause of the emperor's passing."

"Thank you," said the Old Buddha. "I cannot say at this moment when the event will occur, but I am going to send Yi K'uang 奕劻 (Prince Ch'ing 慶) on a mission to inspect my mausoleum which is now complete, and probably during his absence you may hear tidings which will not surprise you. So be it, then. I shall not forget your co-operation and after the new emperor mounts the Throne, I shall ensure for you his special favour; I do not say mine, of which you have, I know, no doubts and whereof you shall have further concrete proofs." (The Old Buddha directed upon me her most gracious smile which seemed to suggest the memory of old intimacies and the promise of more nocturnal raptures in the excellent days to be. *Pu Wang Chiu Ch'ing* 不忘舊情.)

"Might I ask Your Majesty to be on your guard against Yüan Shih-k'ai and T'ieh Liang? They are wolf-hearted and not men of their word. The latter has command, as Minister of War, of all Your Majesty's Manchu troops. Might it not be well that Your Majesty should take one of the generals into your sacred confidence, in case force should be needed, as when Your Majesty placed the emperor on the Throne 36 years ago?"

"It is a good suggestion; for a foreigner, you are marvellously astute about our intrigues. Perhaps I will make use of General Chang Hsün 張勳 whom I call my 'Pekingese pugdog' (*Pa Kou'rh* 巴狗兒): he hates Yüan and has no love for T'ieh. He shares your proclivities, as you probably know. Men call him the 'Rabbit general' " (i.e. pederastic in the passive "voice").

"Your Majesty, when I entered the Forbidden Precincts, T'ieh Liang's chair was still waiting: he knows me very well. I think it would be rather unwise to let him become aware that you had granted to me a special audience on this most auspicious of days."

"Be of good cheer," said Her Majesty. "I shall see that he is informed of your attendance here in order to receive from me an autograph letter for your Queen whose birthday is, I believe, next month, which I wish you to send to her direct and not through the Foreign Office." (This letter was duly sent via Siberia and reached Queen Alexandra on December 2, the day of her nativity.)

Then the Empress fell to discussing *la pluie et la beau temps*:[15] she asked me about Edward VII's well known liaison with Mrs. Keppel and desired to know what Alexandra's reaction to the intimacy was and whether the former amusing lady would be accorded rank as an imperial concubine. (It is a fact that, when the Hon. Mrs. George Keppel arrived in Peking in 1911, the Manchu court wished to despatch an apricot-coloured imperial chair to meet her and to provide for her one of the detached palaces for lodgment. But the idea, though mooted, received no official nor Legation encouragement, although Mrs. Keppel – when I told her of it – greatly appreciated the joke. She said to me: "In any other dynasty I should be a duchess in my own right, like Mme. de Kéroualle under Charles II".)[16]

The Empress graciously presented me with a pair of jade bowls with covers – the last of the many gifts I was to receive from her – and the characters *Fu* 福 and *Shou* 壽 writ in her own rather feminine but characteristic caligraphy. Perhaps she had an intention that I should not kneel at her feet again: she took my two hands and pressed them, saying: "Your hands are soft and small as a woman's. I wish we could pass this evening in unison, but my birthday festival prevents. Wait a few days, when things are settled." She added: "After we have *Yü Ch'eng Ch'i Shih* 玉成其事, consummated the affair into perfect jade (put the business through), I shall summon you again under a new reign and we shall all be much happier. The clouds will have broken and the sun shall emerge, *Yün P'o Jih Ch'u* 雲破日出. So now Fare-well!"

"Farewell, Your Sacred Majesty; and may Buddha, the source of all good, shed upon Your Benevolent Person his manifold blessings and may Your longevity ensure to us, your slaves, perpetual peace."

Then I kotowed thrice and she dismissed me with a "See Li Lien-ying before you go and await further commands".

Li was waiting in an ante-room and pretended complete absence of curiosity; although I could see that he knew everything that had passed. "Well," said he; "we are going to have some busy days ahead, *ces jours mouvementés me font bien du mal.*[17] All this excitement is very bad for

---

15 This and that.
16 Alice Keppel (1868-1947) was one of the best-known of Edward VII's mistresses. Their affair lasted from 1898 until the time of the king's death in 1910. Louise de Kérouaille (1649-1734), as indicated here, was a well-known mistress of the French King Charles II.
17 These hectic days are doing me much harm.

me, at my age, and for the Old Ancestress even worse. Whatever my enemies may say, I hate intrigue. Everything open and aboveboard is my motto."

Having received my *consigne*,[18] I returned home to find my servants immensely relieved at what they called my "resurrection". Naturally, they asked me a thousand questions with which I parried rather unsuccessfully; for I fear the matter was *un secret de Polichinelle* (public property); otherwise the issue might have been other. If mortals leave human things *epi gounasi Theion* (*Iliad*),[19] on the knees of the gods, they must cooperate in some measure by controlling their own tongues and in not anticipating events with hyperbolic *bavardage*.[20]

Personally, I felt like an accomplice before the fact; but my "faith unfaithful kept me falsely true", as Tennyson says of Sir Lancelot in *Idylls of the King*. How could I betray the Old Buddha? and in fact had I done so, I should only have encountered the fate of Cassandra as decreed by Ares, for none would have believed me.[21] The unhappy emperor was past saving; but I asked myself whether the Old Buddha would be able to bring about this her latest stroke.

Personally, I thought yes: ill prophets were we all, for she was dealing with colossal villains, *O Kuan Man Ying* 惡貫滿盈, whose cup of iniquity was full to the brim, who were detestable in the sight of gods and men, *Shen Jen Kung Fen* 神人共忿: *T'ien Ti Pu Jung* 天地不容, men outside the pale of humanity, so that even she became their hapless victim. I passed the next ten days on tenterhooks, expecting hourly to hear of some untoward happenings. My household's nerves were equally on edge and in fact the population of Peking was like him who sleepeth upon a volcano. As usual, the European legations were in blissful ignorance of coming events; "no one is infallible, not even the young", says the Persian proverb, which could be amended: "Even the diplomats don't know everything." How true is the adage of the Sage: "To know your ignorance is the beginning of knowledge." But those people were ignorant before the event and boasted thereafter that they had expected it.

Li Lien-ying called on me in the afternoon of Friday, the 20 X Moon, Nov. 13, 1908, with a decree in manuscript which the Empress had drafted in the name of the emperor, stating that the latter was sick and calling upon the physicians of the empire to heal him. As Li said: "This is the beginning of the end. A halo round the moon betokens wind; a damp pavement indicates rain. *Yüeh Ch'üan Chu Feng* 月圈主風; *Ch'u Jun Chu Yü* 礎潤主雨. It will not be long now: don't forget what the Old Ancestress told you! (as if I were likely not to remember something of which my thoughts were endlessly full). I shall sleep happily tomorrow night, when I suppose Her Majesty will be at ease again. I never saw her so

---

18 Order.
19 XVII.514.
20 Gossip.
21 In Greek mythology Cassandra is the tragic figure blessed and cursed by Apollo (not Ares as the author mistakenly states here) with the ability to see the future but have no one believe her prophesies.

perturbed, not even when you foreigners were attacking the city eight years ago."

Prince Ch'ing 慶 was returning to Peking, to the Old Buddha's annoyance, although she knew him well enough to be assured of his neutrality whatever might betide. Meantime, men talked in whispers all over the capital and P'u Lun 溥倫 was definitely named as the new emperor, thus winning at long last the place that was lawfully his by primogeniture (so far as this principle counts in China) as eldest living great-grandson in the direct line through the empress consort (and not through a concubine) of the Tao Kuang 道光 emperor, Tz'u Hsi and her sister regent having passed over his claim thirty-four years before by placing Tsai T'ien 載湉 on the Throne, despite the stringent dynastic house-law which forbids the accession of one of the same generation as the deceased emperor.

On the morning of Saturday, Nov. 14 (X Moon, 21) it was known all over Peking that Kuang Hsü had "passed to a far-off region"; but the valedictory decree had not yet been issued. What had occurred was as follows: At about 11 o'clock on the previous evening (*Tzu Ch'u* 子初, hour of the Rat) my friend, the favourite eunuch and ex-catamite, Ts'ui Tê-lung, and an older confidential attendant of the Old Buddha named Mao K'o-ch'in 毛克勤, crossed the drawbridge to the emperor's lakegirt palace, each provided with a revolver in case of opposition from His Majesty's own servants, although shooting was to be avoided except as a last resort. The sentries on duty were all General Feng Shan's 鳳山 bodyguard: they had been forewarned and were to receive Taels 50 apiece from the Empress. Feng Shan was a very intimate friend of mine, *Tu Lien Ta Ch'en* 都練大臣, inspector general of the Forces and generalissimo of the Banner armies or *Wei Tui* 衛隊 of some 70,000 men. He was assassinated in October 1911 on arrival at Canton as *Chiang Chün* 將軍, Manchu commander in chief, just after the outbreak of revolution.[22] A servant followed carrying stuffed pillows and cushions. Ts'ui bore a decree from the Empress Dowager: "The emperor is hereby ordained to take a definitive course forthwith, as a separate decree is appointing a new sovereign. Reverence this. *Tzu Cho Huang Ti Chi Shih Tzu Ts'ai Ling Yu Chih I Ta Wei Yeh Ch'in Tz'u* 茲著皇帝即時自裁另有旨易大位欽此." Kuang Hsü's bedchamber was a single *Chien* facing south, the second on the east side of the third court immediately behind the Lake terrace building later converted into a restaurant, the actual Ying T'ai 瀛台 proper, the haunt today (in the warm months) of anglers and bathers and in winter of *patineurs*.[23]

The emperor was reclining on the *K'ang* reading the novel *Chin P'ing Mei*[24] 金瓶梅 (not one of the most reputable Chinese novels) of which a wonderful Manchu translation by the brother of K'ang Hsi 康熙, Prince Yu 裕, exists. Electric light had for some time been installed in the Lake

---

22 **Backhouse:** N.B. My enemy, Daniel Varè, has stated falsely in his book *The Last of the Empresses*, on the authority of that arch-liar Morrison that the Diary of Ching Shan 景善 was not genuine but written at my dictation by Feng Shan 鳳山 who was my intimate.

23 Skaters.

24 *The Plum in the Golden Vase*, written anonymously in the early 17th century under the pen name Lan-ling Hsiao-hsiao-sheng 蘭陵笑笑生.

palaces. Ts'ui said: "Your Majesty, we are respectfully conveying to you our congratulations: we have a decree from the Empress Dowager. Please go on your knees to receive it."

Here Kuang Hsü's faithful body servant, the eunuch Chu Wei-shou 朱維壽, interposed: "The emperor shall not kneel to a piece of paper: let Her Majesty come herself at a reasonable hour of the day."

Ts'ui answered: "Our business will not wait. Either leave us alone here or prepare for the inevitable hour." Chu moved slightly to shield the emperor, and the eunuch Mao shot him dead. Why the sentries did not intervene was due to orders. Then Ts'ui read out the vermilion decree, adding: "Your Majesty had best 'Shang Tiao'[25] 上吊; we have a silken rope with us and will give you a loyal send-off to Heaven."

"Never," said Kuang Hsü; "I always knew that the empress meant to have my life. My reign has been one long agony. I only ask who is my successor."

"Lun Beitzu 倫貝子", replied Ts'ui.

"You shall inform the empress of my last wish: 'let her put Yüan Shih-k'ai to death': he betrayed me and will betray my successor as well as the empress herself sooner or later." He drew an imaginary circle (Yüan 圓 which is homophonic with Yüan 袁 the surname) and made a downward gesture to indicate decapitation. "Secondly, tell the empress not to exclude my tablet from the ancestral temple but to make P'u Lun my joint heir on a parity with my predecessor, Mu Tsung 穆宗" (T'ung Chih 同治, this was done a month later).

Then the two murderers, Ts'ui 崔, Mao 毛, with the comparse[26] (who only did what he was told), pressed the resisting but feeble emperor down on the K'ang 炕, according to Ts'ui's own account to me which differed slightly from Li Lien-ying's narrative; partially strangled him with the slip-knot; then suffocated him slowly with pillows.

The remaining attendants of Kuang Hsü were too terrified to show themselves and seem to have hidden in an outhouse beside the entrance. His wife and concubine were both in the Forbidden City. As soon as Ts'ui was satisfied of the emperor's demise – his eyes were bulging almost out of his head, mucus was flowing from his mouth, his genital organ was in a state of excitement and an emission had taken place from the Ma Yen 馬眼 or urethral orifice (despite the thricetold tale of his sexual impotence), his face was black, so that they believed life to be extinct and left him there, pressing the pillows once more on his head. It is said that after the murderers' departure the emperor's servants attempted to revive him without success. There was no time to lose: the Old Buddha was anxiously awaiting the event and in fact Li Lien-ying came to meet them as they crossed the draw-bridge.

"What a time you have been," said Li; "the Old Ancestress is almost hors d'elle[27] with impatience."

---

25 Hang.
26 Secondary player.
27 Infuriated.

"Well," replied Ts'ui, who possessed considerable humour even in a crisis, "these matters can't be done all in a moment, but he has mounted the dragon all right: we have a new emperor. *Fan Cheng Chê Lei Shih Tei Jung Kung Fu* 反正這 事得容功夫, *Pu Shih Hsü Yü Chih Chien So Neng Ch'eng Kung* 不是須臾之間所能成功, *K'o Shih Chen Cheng Yü Lung Shang Pin* 可是眞正御龍上屏, *Huan La Huang Shang Pa Liao* 換啦皇上罷了." (I was reminded of the Vatican ceremony after a new Pope is elected: "I have tidings of great joy: we have a Pope, *habemus Pontificem*".)[28]

Said Li: "The job is only half done; the decree appointing the new emperor has to be promulgated; the Old Buddha is going to have a crowded hour or two, we have to put out Kuang Hsü's valedictory decree which Her Majesty has already drafted in the rough and to declare court and national mourning for 27 months." (Actually, as far as the public mourning is concerned, "*I Yüeh Wei Jih* 易月爲日, change the number of months into as many days", for convenience sake, but the court mourning persists for the full period.) Li and Ts'ui then hurried to memorialize the Empress Dowager of the successful issue: she was beaming with satisfaction and in the highest spirits.

She said: "*A Mi T'o Fo* 阿彌陀佛, Amitabha Buddha, Thank God. I feel a new life within my veins: it's the most blessed of all events, *ich lebe bei dieser Nachricht wieder auf.*[29] *Wo Ch'ü I K'uai Ping* 我去一塊病: *Ch'i Fei Pen Shen Chih Ta Hsing* 豈非本身之大幸 . . . . Summon the Grand Council, also T'ieh Liang and Feng Shan,[30] so that everything may be in order and the accession of the new emperor be promulgated in good time."

Prince Ch'ing had, as usual, thought it expedient to sit on the fence (*Ch'i Ch'iang* 騎牆), though back in Peking, but Prince Ch'un 醇, Shih Hsü 世續, Yü Lang 毓朗, Chang Chih-tung and Yüan Shih-k'ai with T'ieh and Feng as Minister of War and Commander in Chief of the Manchu army respectively (specially summoned for the occasion to the Audience) all attended in the main Throne Hall of the Yi Luan Tien 儀鸞殿. The Old Buddha, who was wearing a sable robe, sate on the Throne, which consisted of two tiers, with a lower place for the emperor; but P'u Lun had not arrived at the Lake Palace and was said to have gone to the Forbidden City where the formal assumption of the Throne would naturally occur according to dynastic etiquette. The Empress said: "The emperor has become a guest of Heaven. P'u Lun succeeds him. Prepare the necessary decrees immediately so that there may be no delay and that the nation shall feel perfect relief. T'ieh Liang, you must prevent rumours being disseminated. Feng Shan, you must maintain order with the Manchu army."

Prince Ch'un, who looked mortified and as dumbfounded as a cicada in autumn, managed to mutter: "But Your Majesty promised Junglu that the Throne shall descend to his grandson, if my wife, his daughter,

---

28   Properly *Habemus Papam*.
29   I live again through this news.
30   **Backhouse:** Feng Shan only returned from Japan the evening before; he had been attending the Autumn Manoeuvres.

gave birth to a male heir. Can you break your promise to a loyal states-man? What feelings will animate his devoted soul at the Yellow springs, if he be conscious of this unfulfilled undertaking?"

"Yes, I can and do; because your wife has been disloyal to me, has demanded my abdication and has spoken slightingly of my morals. It is for me to make or to unmake whom I will: you had better be circumspect in your words."

Yüan Shih-k'ai approved of P'u Lun's accession, and none of the oth-er officials spoke except Chang Chih-tung who asked what steps the Old Buddha meant to take to prevent foreign governments asking awkward questions.

"I have provided for that already," said the Empress; "it is no one's business except mine."

Feng Shan, in discussing the event, told me that Her Majesty was wonderfully alert and vigorous: the death of her *bête noire*[31] had verily rejuvenated her. She announced her intention of continuing the Regen-cy with the rank of *Impératrice Grand-mère*,[32] *T'ai Huang T'ai Hou*.[33] The Council withdrew to prepare the decrees, while the Old Buddha retired for a short rest, it being now about 12:45 a.m. Naturally, in such a delicate matter, the drafting of the phraseology took some time and it must have been 4 a.m., the hour of the Tiger, when the Council sent in a message through Li Lien-ying to invite the Old Buddha to *Sheng Tien* 升殿, accord her presence on the imperial seat. At 5 a.m., the hour of the Rabbit, the Empress rose from her shortened slumbers, maids of honour being as usual in attendance by the Phoenix Bed, and ascended her yellow chair to enter the Throne Hall. T'ieh Liang and Feng Shan were not summoned to the audience, not being on the Council, but were waiting in attend-ance in a side hall. By dynastic customs eunuchs were not admitted to the deliberation, although Li Lien-ying told me that he sometimes stood behind a curtain watching developments and ready, I presume, to de-fend his great mistress in case of treachery, although physically he would have been no match against a *coup de main*.[34] On this occasion, said Li, he heard everything that passed until the *dénouement*, which I am about to describe, but apparently retired for a few minutes to take a few "whiffs" (*Ch'ih Liang K'ou Yen* 吃兩口煙) as his craving was insurmountable. So the Councillors handed the draft decrees to the Empress for approval: she read them with her usual meticulous care, altered several phrases and added a few words of eulogy toward her august self to the valedictory decree. Then she said: "So be it: let these decrees be printed and issued at noon today. The new emperor shall proceed tomorrow to the T'ai Ho Tien[35] 太和殿 to receive the homage of the officials. Yüan Shih-k'ai, you must go and tell Prince Ch'ing to notify the diplomatic corps not later

---

31 Nemesis.
32 Empress Grandmother.
33 太皇太后.
34 Surprise attack.
35 Hall of Supreme Harmony.

than this evening. He is to attend here first at the hour of the Dragon (9 a.m.) for further orders."

Feng Shan and Li Lien-ying both told me independently that the Council prepared to withdraw, Prince Ch'un almost in hysterics with rage and disappointment. It does not appear from what they said that he and his three colleagues, Chang Chih-tung, Yü Lang 毓朗 and Shih Hsü 世續 had any part nor lot in the subsequent event; personally, I should imagine Prince Ch'un was privy to the plot, and his guilty complicity would have been a motive for his intended decapitation of Yüan a couple of months later (only prevented by the totally unjustified intervention of Sir John Jordan, the British Minister, under orders from His Majesty's government to say that Yüan's death would be regarded by Great Britain, then (*quantum mutatus*)[36] a great power, as a *casus belli*.)[37]

Yüan Shih-k'ai and T'ieh Liang asked Her Majesty to grant to them a special private audience to submit their humble views on a matter of state. The Empress graciously acceded and they knelt before her. Yüan kotowed thrice and T'ieh followed his example. "Your Majesty is full of years, riches and honours. You should pass your remaining years in the profound seclusion of Yi Ho Yüan and not be troubled by multitudinous state affairs (*Cheng Shih Ts'ung Ts'o* 政事叢脞). I ask Your Majesty, and T'ieh Liang (who nodded assent) joins me in the prayer, to issue one more decree announcing your irrevocable abdication and appointing us as Grand Imperial Preceptors, *T'ai Shih* 太師, who will advise the new emperor on all governmental business as joint Regents."

The Old Buddha's wrath kindled even as thunder – *Ta Fa Lei T'ing* 大發雷霆; she shouted in her rage and fury: "You traitor, nay you two traitors. After all I have done for you, is this the way you repay my benevolence? I dismiss you both from your offices and shall order that you be handed for trial to the Minister of Justice. Though you die a thousand deaths, your retribution will be too light (*Ch'ien Ssu Wan Ssu Pu Tsu Pi Ku* 千死萬死不足蔽辜). The cup of your treason and iniquity is full to the brim. Leave the presence and await my orders."

Feng Shan (courtesy name Yü-men 禹門) who was in the side hall and T'ieh Liang who was kneeling before the Throne agree in saying that Yüan thereupon drew out a six-chambered revolver and fired three shots at the Empress. Both claimed that he wished to frighten her into acquiescence, whereas the eunuch Ts'ui says that he fired point blank, *à bout portant*, at her, hitting her (like Jacques Clément at Saint Cloud in

---

36 How it has changed (Virgil, *Aeneid* II.274).

37 "Reason for war". Sir John Jordan developed a strong liking for Yüan Shi-kai after his appointment to preside over the Ministry of Foreign Affairs, and the two worked closely on railroad and currency reform. Following the deaths of Kuang Hsü and Tz'u Hsi, Yüan Shi-kai was tasked with overseeing the imperial funerals and made senior guardian to the child Emperor P'u Yi before promptly being dismissed from office in Jan. 1909. In a breach of etiquette Jordan repeatedly petitioned the Chinese government to have him reinstated and persuaded other foreign ministers to jointly issue a statement with him that if Yüan was removed from office "China's foreign relations would suffer severely". Yüan's personal safety was vouched for by the Chinese government, but they remained firm on the matter of his dismissal.

August 1589, Henri III) *au bas ventre*.[38] She did not collapse on the instant but shouted: "Treason! arrest Yüan and decapitate him. Unnatural villain, why have I spared him so long?"

The court apothecaries, the women of the bedchamber, the eunuchs, hearing the shots, all came rushing in. Li Lien-ying, beside himself with grief and remorse, prostrated himself (kotowing) on the floor and wailing: "Old Ancestress! Live for us all."

The haemorrhage was terrible to witness and the physicians seemed utterly helpless. She tried to rise but sank back muttering: "So this is the end. Where is Junglu? What treason! Is this indeed my latest hour? Taoist Yogi, you deceived me in saying I had ten years to live. Buddha's curse on you traitors. Bury me according to my rank as Empress Dowager. Carry out my will. Behead Yüan and T'ieh, I can no more." (Compare the dying voice of Queen Catherine of Aragon: "As the daughter of a king inter me . . . can no more.") Thus saying, she expired amidst the wailing of the eunuchs and of the household who called upon her spirit not to leave the tenement of the body.

The dead body of the Old Buddha, whose pen had indeed been mightier than a thousand swords, was taken by eunuchs to her bedchamber and placed upon the bed (*Shang Ch'uang* 上床) after ablution and the arraying in royal robes, new and never previously worn, in accord with custom both Manchu and Chinese. Her mouth remained obstinately open; her eyes were not closed; the face was puckered and ghastly. She was dead. Truly a great personality had "fallen in Israel". How would the population take the news, with horror or with relief? Surely the former. In fact, the whole of North China was literally stunned and bewildered with grief.

The tidings did not become known immediately, as the public were only informed in instalments: the official announcement of her "fatal illness" was promulgated by the *Gazette* at about 3 p.m. on the Sunday, the following day, Kuang Hsü's death being announced on Saturday evening when I received the latter decree still in the Empress' name. I had heard the news of her murder but faithful to my promise, in calm, calculated defiance of the truth, allowed in my writings both the emperor's demise and that of the Old Buddha to appear as due to natural causes (unwillingly so, as regards the Empress' death). In fact, H.M. Government, on hearing the true facts, enjoined me almost with menaces never to give out the truth to the world, their blind faith in the traitor Yüan Shih-k'ai depriving them of all sense of perspective or of inclination to brand their beloved protégé as an assassin. In the city, and in China generally, the facts became known as in a glass darkly and Yüan was cursed, as he deserved to be, as a villain, unparalleled in history, not even by Ts'ao Ts'ao[39] 曹操 himself. It is exact (but may sound improbable) to add that in 1911,

---

38   "In the abdomen". Jacques Clément (1567-89), a fanatic French Catholic, assassinated the more religiously tolerant French King Henri III at Saint Cloud.

39   Ts'ao Ts'ao (155-220 AD) was the King of Wei and a gifted military strategist. Most famously, he is the arch-villain of Lo Kuan-chung's classic 14th century novel *Romance of the Three Kingdoms*.

when Yüan came back to office,[40] he offered me £3,500 a year for my life, if I would revise *China under the Empress* in a sense eulogistic to himself.

It was about 9 a.m. when the Council met, reversed the Empress' decrees and placed Prince Ch'un's baby on the Throne. For the second time in his career, the luckless Prince P'u Lun was deprived of his rights. Tsai Feng 載灃, the Regent, remembered his brother's dying wish and, as I have mentioned, fully intended to order Yüan's decapitation but for British interference.

All the joys of the flesh; all the sorrows that wear out the soul; the vision of greatness, the pomp of power: what is it all but a dream and a delusion? 'Tis indeed a lonely light that beats upon the proudest of thrones: this is the end of everyman's desire. To me it was a thunder clap in a clear sky: would that I had died in her stead!

"Call none happy," says Sophocles in *Oedipus the King*, "until the end of his life." After over thirty-four years, my anger and my sorrow for her dastardly murder are as poignant at this hour as on the day which brought to me those tidings of woe; when I was even as one who goes down into hell; or as one who mourneth for his mother. Since that hour, it has been my fate to witness the collapse, unwept and unsung, and the practical obliteration from the map, of a once Great Power: yet this tragedy moves me less, far less, than the murder of my benefactress and *mamie*, despite the abysmal differences of rank and public consideration and notwithstanding the barrier of race wrongly said to be the most invincible in human affairs. Yet it is by dreams, not by reason, that the world is, or was, governed: was it not ever so, at Athens, at Rome or Jerusalem, ay and in Ch'ang An 長安 or in Cambaluc the Mighty?[41]

> Sympathy is the foremost of links;
> Love is more than a kingdom, whether one lives or dies.

"*Tout comprendre, c'est tout pardonner*"[42] is as true now as when Voltaire wrote *Candide*; and I understood Tz'u Hsi, as she understood me.

Requiem aeternam dona[43] in her Buddhist heaven.

The Old Buddha's sacred remains were conveyed late that evening (November 15) into the Forbidden City, being placed for the short transit from the Lake in a seating posture on her state-chair borne, as usual, by eight attendants. They were taken to her inner palace, Yang Hsing Tien 養性殿, where she and I had spent so many golden hours in pervading

---

40 Yüan Shih-k'ai became Chief Councillor of the Ch'ing Dynasty in 1911 and was named the first President of the Republic of China following the dynasty's collapse the next year. He held the latter position until January 1916, when he named himself Emperor, sparking widespread revolt. Yüan abdicated the throne in March 1916 and died shortly thereafter.

41 Ch'ang An, later known as Hsian 西安 or "Western Peace", was the ancient capital of China from the 11th century BC until the 10th century AD, albeit with several interruptions. Cambaluc, which later evolved into Peking, was the capital of the Mongolian Yüan Dynasty (1271-1368).

42 To understand all is to forgive all.

43 "Grant rest eternal" from the Mass of the dead, *Roman Missal*.

untrammelled communion and where, on one occasion, she had, half jest-
ingly, chastised me for a flagrant breach of court etiquette. There, she was
again reverently enshrouded and wrapt in the imperial cerements before
encoffinment, her favourite bibelots being placed in enormous profusion
beside and around her, clad in all the glory of her robes of state. At dawn
of the following day the imperial coffin of catalpa wood was taken by
eight bearers to the main hall of her palace, the Huang Chi Tien 皇極殿,
Throne Hall of All Highest Supremacy (*Huang* 皇 here, as Emperor Ch'ien
Lung's 乾隆 translation in Manchu – *amba* – shows, referring to the Almighty, not to the Son of Heaven) and there placed in the lofty imposing
sarcophagus screened from view by elaborate curtains and itself envel-
oped in prayer coverlets with Tibetan and Sanskrit incantations. Masses
were chanted daily at dawn, noon and eve, for the repose of her soul; I
had the honour to attend the office specially chanted by His Holiness the
Dalai Lama a week or two later, and, as I listened to the melancholy heart-
wringing 'plain-chant' of those Tibetan choristers, I felt that they were
verily singing a farewell requiem to my buried happiness, to our affection
that shall not, and, can not, die; for it is as eternal as the K'un Lun range 崑
崙山 and as perennial as the springs of many-fountained Ida.

P.S. I feel bound to add that, at the time of the death of Kuang Hsü, I,
in common with most well-informed Manchus and Chinese (in those
days, it was *Man Han* 滿漢, now, it is *Han Man* 漢滿!),[44] understood that
poison had been the cause of death. It was not until Li Lien-ying and
Ts'ui independently recounted to me the exact facts, identical in essentials but slightly differing in detail, that I was undeceived; when I read
the former's diary in 1921, I obtained further confirmation.

My old friend, Mr. Yüeh Shih 樂十 (the tenth), one of the owners of
the old established Chinese drug store Tung Jen T'ang 同仁堂 outside
the Ch'ien Men 前門, told me after the Revolution of 1911 that palace
eunuchs (despite the abundant stock of poisons in the Forbidden City)
had purchased from his shop by the Empress Dowager's command four
ounces of *P'i Shuang* 砒霜 or arsenic crystals on the 12. X. 34 Kuang Hsü
(November 5, 1905) for the net price of Taels 16. Apparently the original
plan was to poison the emperor gradually by inserting small (not lethal)
doses in sponge cakes which His Majesty affected. But the British Legation physician had been instructed through Sir Edward Grey, the Foreign
Secretary, and Sir J. Jordan, the Minister, to ask permission to see Kuang
Hsü and to diagnose his malady. The Old Buddha could not very well
refuse but was aware of the fact that arsenic accumulates in the system;
hence her abandonment of the poisoning programmes for the simpler
and quicker method of strangulation (*Lei Ssu* 勒死).[45] It is said that this

---

44 Manchus and Chinese . . . Chinese and Manchus.
45 It seems almost certain that the popular explanation of Kuang Hsü's death, poisoning, was the
    correct one. In Nov. 2008 a five-year study on the emperor's remains revealed that at the time of
    his death the emperor had as much as 201mg of arsenic in his system, 2,000 times the normal level.
    The lethal dose of arsenic is generally between 70 and 200mg.

doctor (quite *ultra vires*)[46] asked leave to see Kuang Hsü's dead body, but the new Regent declined the request on the ostensible ground that decomposition had set in. Dr. Kuan 關 of the *Yuch'uanpu* 郵傳部, Ministry of Communications, a foreign trained physician, told me in the presence of His Excellency Liang Shih-yi 梁士貽, the "God of Wealth 財神", as he was called, that the emperor's face was distorted in the way Li and Ts'ui described and that his "penis" was in a state of erection which remained after death, as I presume was to be expected and is, I know, the case with hanged felons. The enormous "tool", nine and a half inches long, of the Victorian poisoner, Dr. Pritchard, is on exhibition at the Edinburgh College of Surgeons, a relic of unbridled lust.

---

46 Beyond his legal authority.

doctor (quite dibu tou)" asked leave to see Kuang Hsü's dead body, but the new Regent declined the request on the ostensible ground that decomposition had set in. De Ketan 閣 of the such men y 魏璟英. Ministry of communications, a foreign trained physician, told me in the presence of His Excellency Liang Shih... the period of Wealth 梁璟, as he was called, that the emperor's face was disturbed in the way, La and Kw described and that his "remains was in a state of repose which remained after death, 分裂... his... the ... ... the eye with hanged to lose. The enormous "foot", nine and a half inches long, of the Victorian poisoner, Dr. Pritchard, is on exhibition in the Edinburgh Col lege of surgeons, a relic of unbodied lust.

CHAPTER XVIII

THE DESECRATED MAUSOLEA

On or about July 15, 1928, the uncle of the Manchu prince Chêng 鄭親
王, Lo Shu-ho 樂叔和, who had been custodian, under the Machu House,
of the Eastern Tombs, came to tell me that he had been in Peking on
sick leave, had just received intelligence that Sun Tien-ying's 孫殿英
bandits soldatesque[1] under the command and of a certain colonel T'an
譚 had placed a cordon round the large enclosure of the Mausolea and
had violated the "jewelled citadels" (imperial grave chambers) of the
illustrious dead, stripping each tomb of its rich treasure of jade, gold,
tapestries, jewels, bronzes and porcelains and throwing out the imperial remains in "most admired disorder". He and Duke P'u T'ung 溥侗,
since deceased, brother of the late Prince P'u Lun 溥論, were leaving at
once for the Tung Ling 東陵: would I join them? Apparently the looters
had withdrawn with their spoil to Tsun Hua 遵化, no great distance
away, but Lo doubted their return: would I accompany them by car
which would enable us to travel the eighty odd miles before sundown,
travelling via Chi Hsien 薊縣 and Shih Men 石門? Lodging would be
provided at Ma Lan Yü 馬蘭峪, just outside the eastern entrance to the
once richly afforested, but now comparatively bare, enclosure. (I believe that since the Japanese occupation abundant tree planting has
been carried out.)

Reverence for the Great Dead and a curiosity which enters largely
into my complex (mayhap, repugnant) personality, alike forbade me to
say nay; although I half dreaded the sight that would surely greet my
world-wearied eyes and the poignant thought of diviner memories that
must needs there assail me, ay rise like a fountain for me night and
day. Had not the Old Buddha especially appointed me to be Chief Tea
Server to her sacred manes reposing in Bliss eternal, a mortal confront-
ing her immortal shade, our echoes still rolling from soul to soul? And
so I was fain to accept the tryst with Duke Lo Shu-ho at his residence in
the West City, where a car appertaining to the ex-Imperial Household
duly awaited us.

---

1   Soldierly.

In all there are ten mausolea, those of the wife of T'ai Tsung 太宗, T'ai Huang T'ai Hou 太皇太后, mother of Shun Chih 順治, known as Chao Tung Ling 昭東陵 (Hsiao Ling 孝陵) which had been left intact; Shun Chih's 順治 empress, the mother of K'ang Hsi 康熙 and later empress dowager, and the beloved Tung Fei 董妃, whose death was partially the cause of the emperor's abdication, were buried in an adjoining small mausoleum which had been stripped bare and its imperial occupants had disappeared without a trace; Shun Chih (which however contained no coffin, as the emperor's demise was, like Alexander I's, only official and the funeral pageant a make believe formality), K'ang Hsi, Ch'ien Lung 乾隆, the princely tomb of the latter's heir apparent, Hsien Feng 咸豐 and his two consorts who survived him, the "Eastern" Empress Dowager and the Old Buddha, T'ung Chih 同治 (Hui Ling 惠陵) and his empress A-lu-tê 阿祿德, canonised as Hsiao Chê I Huang Hou 孝哲毅皇后.

Of these Shun Chih's grave chamber contained an empty sarcophagus, K'ang Hsi's (Ching Ling 景陵) was flooded to a depth of six feet, water having percolated into the sarcophagus of catalpa wood (*Tzu Kung* 梓宮) supposed to be water-tight, so that the imperial remains and those of his three consorts were sodden and reduced to a sort of pulp which rendered it easy to detach an arm or a leg; Hsien Feng's had been blown open with dynamite and inside the tomb proper were three dead bodies of looting bandits who desperately fought over the division of the treasure: the emperor and his "*Chung* 中" or "*Cheng* 正" consort who had died before his accession were left lying in the coffin, both stripped of their funeral robes. Similarly T'ung Chih's grave had been blown open, but it was known that the empresses dowager had not deemed it worth while to waste treasures which could find appropriate use in the world of man for the comfort of the soul of so insignificant a monarch.

It remains to speak of Ch'ien Lung's, the Old Buddha's and the heir-apparent, Prince Jung's 榮 respective tombs. The first is known as Yü Ling 裕陵. We passed through the three courtyards and reached the *Pao Ch'eng*[2] 寶城 which had been blown open: the imperial coffin had been hacked into pieces and the bodies of Ch'ien Lung, his empress and nine consorts all buried in one enormous *cercueil*[3] including the favourite Mahomedan concubine Hsiang Fei 香妃, whose tragic death I have elsewhere narrated,[4] painted by the great Italian artist Castiglione (Lang Shih-ning 郎世寧) as a shepherdess and in many other guises, who had not been buried in Manchu robes but in her native Turkestan dress which for some reason had been left on the ground unremoved by the looters, were all lying on the pavement, skeletons bereft of even their inner garments, huddled together in most ungainly disorder. The great emperor, whose head had been hacked off, with the remnants of his queue lying near, was of much shorter height than I had imagined, perhaps not more than five feet four inches. As he died at the age of eighty-nine, he may

---

2   Jewelled citadels; imperial tombs.
3   Coffin.
4   See *Annals & Memoirs of the Court of Peking*, co-authored with J.O.P. Bland.

have shrunk in stature owing to advanced years. It was a ghastly spectacle far removed from the majesty of death, as we knelt before his remains and implored his pardon. Like Hamlet and his "alas! poor Yorick", in the grave-digger scene of the play, I took with all reverence Ch'ien Lung's skull in my hands and thought of Bossuet's funeral oration on Henrietta de France, queen of England, with its poignant moral for the great of the earth: "*Et nunc, reges, intelligite; erudimini qui judicatis terram.*"[5]

With the aid of Lo Shu-ho's retainers we made makeshift repairs for the broken coffin, placed it under cover, and replaced the skeletons, or rather their *disjecta membra*:[6] empress and concubines haphazard with the decapitated emperor in the centre; the grave chamber had been completely blown open and the great stone portal was in fragments, so that many days elapsed before the coffin could be put back on its pedestal; but it did not greatly matter, as the bandits had done their work thoroughly and left nothing to loot, except a number of seed pearls which they had overlooked. Amongst the articles removed from the tomb were many Sung pieces of jade, some of which became the property of a lady in the very highest place in Nanking.

Next we visited the T'ai Tzu Yüan Ch'in 太子園寢, the tomb of the heir-apparent, with its green-tiled roofs in contrast to the imperial yellow of the other mausolea which are called Ling Ch'in 陵寢. In this case the great stone door had not been interfered with but the roof had been partially blown open and we had to squirm in serpent-like fashion through the narrow, winding passage which led through the opened up cement to the ceiling of the grave-chamber, about twelve feet above the brick floor, by which the robbers had entered. The tall Banner attendant led the way, or rather crawled ahead of us, showing great agility in twisting himself through the gap in the ceiling and descending with the aid of a stool that the looters had used. We followed him not without difficulty and found that the small aperture in the roof in no way rendered the atmosphere supportable. The coffin had been opened at the top but was otherwise undisturbed: it seemed as if the bandits had respected that pathetic figure whose tragic grace I shall never forget. There lay before us a beautiful boy aged about fourteen, strangely life-like, of ivory complexion, with eyes wide open and looking, as it seemed, questioningly at the intruders: "Who art thou that cometh to break upon my rest?"

Min Hui T'ai Tzu 敏慧太子, Sage and Discerning, Prince Jung (Prince Jung was the great emperor's best beloved son; his personal name was Yung Lien 永璉, and the last character *Lien* was taboo during the Ch'ing 清 Dynasty and could not be written in documents of an official character or in the public examinations; he was specially canonized by his father, Ch'ien Lung, with the two – princes usually receive only one – honorific characters *Tuan Hui* 端慧 "upright and discerning" and was officially spoken and written of as Tuan Hui T'ai Tzu 端慧太子, the only case

---

5   Be wise now therefore, O ye Kings, be warned, ye that are judges of the earth (*Psalms* II.10).
6   Scattered parts or fragments.

under the Manchu Dynasty of a dead heir apparent being so named),[7] the gracious heir apparent, had been his father's idol: he seems to have been a most lovable and gentle child, worthy to succeed Ch'ien Lung, had fate willed: I thought of *Tu Marcellus eris*,[8] and the ruin of so many high hopes. His court robes had not been tampered with and a pathetic inscription in Ch'ien Lung's beautiful caligraphy "Sorrow blinding the eyes" *Sang Ming Chih Yu* 喪明之憂, in other words a father's grief for a son's death, was still attached to the front of the riding jacket. The atmosphere being unbearable, we made the best of our difficult way back to the light of day: it was an exceedingly hot afternoon and we still had to visit the Tung Ting Ling 東定陵, the Old Buddha's mausoleum.

The Empress Dowager, while meticulous about the construction of her tomb which, in fact, had at first failed to satisfy her and had to be rebuilt out of naval funds for geomantic reasons, had arrogated to herself no usurpatory features which properly only belonged to the Son of Heaven. We entered the spacious outer enclosure with its *Ch'ao Fang* 朝房, or side antechambers for waiting courtiers, Banner troops, and in the days of the dispossessed dynasty multitudinous functionaries in charge of the mausoleum under a custodian in chief, who was usually an imperial duke, walked through the main entrance at the head of a flight of steps which was not ordinarily opened to any but the emperor or empress, the side gates being normally used out of respect in order to avoid the "imperial way", noticed nothing particular in the first courtyard with the sacrificial kitchens, but on coming to the main hall of ritual in front of the towered terrace which overlooks the lofty grave tumulus, we were horrified to see huddled on the pavement in that blistering sun ("imperial Caesar, dead and turned to clay") an uncomely shape of tiny dimensions which was a human form, stark naked and ghastly in its lack of dignity and ungrateful negation of harmony. Shocked beyond words or the power of tongue or pen to describe, we hurried forward and saw what? the great despot dame who had ruled China for nearly fifty years, my gracious patroness that had showered on me such unparalleled favours which an Essex, a Potemkin, a Fersen, would not have disdained, was lying before us, her glorious raven hair shockingly dishevelled, half rust half ruined ebony, her face drawn and ghastly but with the familiar features as recognizable as when I had last seen her in her birthday robes twenty years ago; her mouth wide extended and set in a horrible grin, eyes partially open and glazed with a yellowish film, her breasts covered with thousands of hideous black spots, body distorted and transmuted to a leathery or parchment hue, the left side of the abdomen presenting a different colour from the rest of her body, probably due to the hemorrhage after Yüan's 袁 fatal shot, her once beautiful pudenda which I had

---

7   **Backhouse:** After death Tuan Hui was his canonical appellation. In life Min Hui 敏慧 was his father's "pet" name for him. His grave is known as Tuan Hui T'ai Tzu Yüan Ch'in 端慧太子園寢.

8   "You will be Marcellus" (Virgil, *Aeneid* VI.883). This section refers to a meeting in the underworld between Aeneas and the unborn Marcellus, future nephew and heir apparent of Augustus, who would die in his twentieth year.

formerly (to her pleasuring and mine own) so playfully fondled, while she said to me "*T'o Ni T'a* 托你塔, expose your pagoda", praising it, all unworthy, as "*K'uai Jan Ta Wu* 塊然大物, a thing on a big scale" (*T'a* 塔 is slang for the penis, as the pagoda is supposed in Buddhist lands to represent the phallic emblem; I could almost hear her falsetto accents as I knelt trying to offer a prayer to whatever gods there be), displayed before us in their full sacrilegious nudity, the pubic hair still abundant, signs of perhaps slight decomposition around the buttocks and thighs, her hands and feet just as I remembered them on our many *nuits d'amour*, delicate as ivory and made for the love of man. 'Twas a sight to haunt me to my dying day and in the darkness I shall not forget. P'u T'ung who was certainly not emotional but of distinctly pedestrian temperament, burst into floods of tears; while by common accord without sign nor suggestion of one to the other, we knelt in that sun-scorched quadrangle, kotowing again and again and beseeching the Old Buddha's gracious spirit in heaven, *Tsai T'ien Chih Ling* 在天之靈, to pardon us in that we had failed to sacrifice our lives, as in duty bound, rather than to allow her hallowed remains hearsed in death to suffer this unheard of outrage, this pollution without name. With difficulty (for everything had been looted) we obtained a strip of matting and covered up Her Majesty's secret parts from the gaze of the vulgar. The grave chamber had been stripped bare; all her favourite curios and bibelots had been rifled including the famous cabbage in jade (now appertaining to Sung Mei-ling 宋美齡)[9] which she particularly affected. "This is the end of every man's desire." Alas! that I had lived to see this day: *sunt lacrimae rerum mentem et mortalia tangunt.*[10]

NOTE

To complete this sad narration which even to name my memory quakes and fears, I have to add that the remains of T'ung Chih 同治, were found to be in a badly broken up condition, the skull being detached and the bones of the trunk so brittle that it was scarcely feasible to lift his body without collapse of the whole, while arms and legs were missing. I presume that the bandits, finding nothing of value in the grave chamber except the robes, had wrecked their vengeance on his corpse by spitefully hacking at it, although I saw no recent marks made by a sharp instrument. In view of the advanced syphilis of which he died, it may be that the nature of the disease would partially account for the brittleness of the bones. The bodies of the Eastern Empress, Tz'u Hsi's 慈禧 colleague in the Regency, and T'ung Chih's 同治 wife, resembled mummies of the XX

---

9   Sung Mei-ling (also Soong May-ling; 1898-2003) was the wife of the Chinese President at the time of this book's writing, Generalissimo Chiang Kai-shek. The jade cabbage in question is now one of the most prized artifacts on display at the Palace Museum in Taipei, where the couple and its government fled after being defeated in the Chinese Civil War in 1949.

10   They are the tears of mortal things and mortal matters affect the heart (Virgil, *Aeneid* I.462).

Dynasty[11] in the Cairo Museum, being absolutely black and desiccated. Since the former lady died from poison, while A-lu-tê's 阿祿德 death was from hanging (as the Empress herself stated), I thought that perhaps the explanation of the discolouration may be respectively found in the action of the drug and from the effects of strangulation which normally induces tumefaction and blackening of the features.

The emperor Hsien Feng's 咸豐 remains disclosed a microcephalous, small limbed type, whose bony structure was brittle, but less so than his son's. Being ignorant of anatomical matters, I can only record what I saw from a layman's point of view which is scientifically worth very little.

CHAPTER XIX

A RETROSPECT OF DIVINER HOURS

THERE they are, my fifty men and women, naming me the long day's task done. I have sought, while breasting the blows of circumstance and grappling with my evil star, to present an intelligible picture of an enigmatic (albeit not so to me) personality as also of her chiefest satellite, Li Lien-ying 李蓮英. The Empress Tz'u Hsi 慈禧 is the nexus on which the history of those eventful years depends: she is scarcely absent from the scene and even in the first chapter (which apparently is desultory gossip) about catamites her impress is visible, albeit at that time she had never heard of my existence, except in connection with my co-operation in saving Sun Wen's 孫文 life in October 1896,[1] not at all a proceeding which could be expected to encounter her favour and as to which she frequently rallied me good-humouredly in later years. I came to win approval from her in 1902 by a simple act of common, if politic, honesty in returning to her the bibelots and ceramics of her love which would otherwise have been surely looted by "Devils" in the shape of foreign soldiery, ay and civilians, missionaries and merchants, even the British envoy himself and his satellites.

I saw at the time of our first meeting that I attracted her by a certain quality that we (foolishly perhaps) term magnetism and that in any case Her Majesty possessed in a superlative degree. She plied me during that first audience of May 1902 with questions that seemed to connote a certain sexual interest; but it was over two years later and after Junglu's 榮祿 death, he, who, I presume, had ministered to her lusts, before she actually sent for me to prepare for a more intimate union; although I had met her several times in a purely platonic (but yet containing the "promise of spring" in the shape of future loves) between May 1902 and August 1904.

I think that an unprejudiced reader, if any reader of this work there be, will form the conclusion that I gained, all unworthy, Her Majesty's

---

[1] Sun Wen (better known as Sun Yat-sen; 1866-1925), anti-Manchu revolutionary involved in a failed 1895 coup attempt. In 1896 Sun, as a fugitive, was detained at the Chinese Legation in London, where Chinese leaders planned to have him executed. After tense diplomatic negotiations, Sun was released and quickly became an international celebrity. In 1912, he was appointed interim President of the Chinese Republic, and would later found the Kuomintang 國民黨 political party. He is now considered the "Father of Modern China". No known evidence connects Sun to Backhouse.

affections in erotic superabundance. The sexual apparatus of a European (not, of course, that mine differed greatly in content or shape from the thousand or more *rigidae* – tools in erection – of her long years of intimate acquaintance) seemed to appeal to her unchaste mind; my bizarre affinities amused her; my homosexuality, amoral, totally uncurbed by ordinary standards, and its concomitant manoeuvres, *masochismus, sadismus, pedicatio, fellatio, irrumatio,* anal titillation and osculation, labial evolutions (as of a Bacchanal or Menade)[2] which some might not, ay, could not, savour; all these things appealed to her temperament, as they assuredly did to Li Lien-ying, himself a would-be protagonist in such of my amorous "business" as (alas! in the scanty degree available to a eunuch's restriction) was feasible to him.

She attracted me without inspiring more than a deep devotion, but that love from my side was wanting is due to my own temperament to which the feminine element offers small appeal. I have sought to indicate her greatness even on occasions when dignity might have been dragged in the dust; as when she fondled the genitals of the princes of her clan or inspected the capacious anal cavities of pathic patricians and mimes. She possessed unique personal fascination, a keen sense of humour and throughout her fifty years regency was wonderfully favoured by Fortune, that fickle jade, to whom Juvenal refers in the fine peroration at the close of his famous tenth satira: "We mortals are to blame, because we make of Fortune our goddess." She had undoubtedly been beautiful in a challenging appeal that few could withstand and when first I met her, her face (without excelling beauty but with eyes that radiated fascination) which owed nothing to cosmetics belied her 67 years. In wit and ready *réplique*[3] she seemed to me to compare with Cleopatra; may I not quote Amyot's graceful translation of Plutarque:

> "*Sa beauté seule n'était point si incomparable qu'il n'y en eust pu bien avoir d'aussi belles comme elle, ni telle qu'elle ravît incontinent ceux qui la regardoient; mais sa conversation, à la hanter, étoit si aimable qu'il étoit impossible d'en éviter la prise, et avec sa beauté, la bonne grace qu'elle avoit à deviser, la douceur et la gentillesse de son naturel, qui assaisonnoit tout ce qu'elle disoit ou faisoit, étoit un aiguillon qui poignoit au vif et il y avoit outre cela grand plaisir au son de sa voix seulement et à, sa prononciation, parce que sa langue étoit comme un instrument de musique à plusieurs jeux et registres.*"[4] (Even so *le timbre de sa voix*[5] in Marie Antoinette charmed Horace Walpole.)

---

2   The male and female participants in a Bacchanalian orgy.

3   Reply.

4   Her beauty alone was neither so unique that there could not have been others as pretty as she, nor such as to forthwith dazzle those who would look at her; but her conversation, haunting her, was so delightful that it was impossible not to be absorbed by it. And with her beauty, her graceful way of conversing, the gentleness and kindness of her natural manners, which adorned everything that she said or did, was a spur cutting one to the quick. And besides, the sound of her voice alone was highly pleasant; as well as was her pronunciation, because her tongue was like a musical instrument playing several scales and ranges.

5   The resonance in the voice.

Plutarque goes on to speak of the Lagide's extraordinary "flair" such as Ch'ien Lung 乾隆 possessed for languages, Egyptian, Greek, Latin, Arabic, Hebrew, Median, Parthian and Syrian, which was alien to Tz'u Hsi who only managed to learn a few words of English. But the Old Buddha, like Cleopatra, was literary and certainly well read, though her language was often of set purpose extremely vulgar but not devoid of a certain flavour of *belles-lettres*,[6] as, e.g., when she evoked the Jade Emperor to descend from heaven and by a consummate stratagem ensured the suicide of the demented eunuch in the Western Hills.

I do not seek to justify her cold-blooded murder of those who had won access to her couch, nor yet her dynastic crimes (for she resembled the magnificent, perverted nature of Lady Macbeth in Shakspere's august creation) which might be justified on the score of expediency, albeit the latter word savours of subterfuge and shall be a dangerous palliation for offences that nothing can condone and I desire not "to blazon evil deeds nor consecrate a crime". Her murder of the Chen Fei 珍妃 or Pearl Concubine is intelligible, in view of the defiant foolish girl's ill-timed provocation; equally so is her revenge on her colleague for murdering her beloved favorite An Tê-hai 安德海; but for the barbarous poisoning of T'ung Chih's 同治 young widow there is no forgiveness,[7] any more than for the strangling of Kuang Hsü 光緒, for whom even Junglu by the Yellow Springs of *l'autre monde*,[8] if accurately reported by the medium, recommended mercy. It is to her credit that she did not dissemble this her contempt for human life – in fact, except as regards her carnal relations with Junglu which even to me she never admitted, she was always frank and sought not to gloze over her manifold errors and crimes.

Had she lived to the age of eighty or more years as she so confidently expected, I am conceited enough to believe that she would not have felt surfeit of my association: my conversation, without any claim to great originality or coruscating wit, undoubtedly, amused and gratified her. My reader who honours the preceding poor pages with his perusal will notice that flattery is by no means absent in my intercourse with Her Majesty, but on the other hand she often showed herself superior to lavish compliments and with her remarkable sense of humour often uttered sonorous platitudes with her tongue in her cheek, as if laughing at herself against her will.

That she enjoyed my sexual attentions I doubt not: the myriad forms of lust appealed to her exotic imagination, as when she demanded from me copulation from behind and found an ecstatic pleasure in that rapturous communion which is "caviar to the general". My libidinous dispositions found favour in her sight and she loved to pursue a sort of anal connexion with myself by means of her unusually long and erect clitoris,

---

6   Great literature.

7   This contradicts Backhouse's previous claim (see postscript to "The Mantle of Cagliostro") where he explicitly states that strangulation and not poisoning was the cause of A-lu-tê's death.

8   The other world.

when she was not inserting her long-nailed index finger in my proctal cavity. It may be that other foreign devils would have hesitated to allow such liberties even from Tz'u Hsi, but, even if they had revelled in her manifold vagaries, they lacked the mental vivacity which enabled me (Lord Buddha be praised) to minister to her alert unsleeping brain by *l'esprit d'à-propos*[9] wherewith I am (or was once) happily endowed. I have signally failed in my conscientious effort, if I have not conveyed to the reader some portion of the grace' and charm of that radiant nature, so full of the *joie de vivre* and of libidinous abundance such as a woman of thirty might have envied, without being able to rival.

On sait le mot profond de Pascal: "Le nez de Cléopâtre, s'il avait été plus court, toute la face de la terre avait été changée."[10] The face which inspired in Julius Caesar a love (exceeding even his passion for his brigadier, Mamurra) *jusqu'à la folie* was never spoiled by *un nez à la Cyrano de Bergerac*[11] in Rostand's play. So with regard to Tz'u Hsi, her acts of violence toward individuals did not deprive her of (nay, in a way they strangely increased) the undying devotion of her court and induced a readiness to find excuse for her misdeeds which, like the Ptolameian queen's nose, if indeed over-large, certainly were a blot on the spotless blazon of her fame. Although comparisons are vain things, in her defence, as in duty bound, I make bold to affirm that, as regards contempt for human life, the Old Buddha did not hold a candle in blood lust to the detestable Lü Hou 呂后; Empress Lü who usurped power at the beginning of the Han Dynasty after Emperor Liu Pang's 劉邦 death, nor to the great personality, mayhap, in some respects surpassing even Tz'u Hsi, that was Wu Tse-t'ien 武則天 of the T'ang 唐 regime, who sounded all the depths and shoals of honour.

My readers will recall the *bon mot*[12] of Augustus Caesar, that cold, calculating youth of delicate constitution, a stammerer, a coward, cruel and devoid of human feeling, that cunning fox, whose patient ambition enabled him against appalling odds to overcome Antony on whose side was ranged the whole of the Roman Empire except a ruined Italy! After the death of Antony, he (Octavian) remarked: "If my *mentula* (penis) had only been one inch longer when in erection, *la guerre civile n'aurait jamais éclaté.*"[13] Even so, perhaps, *magnis componere parva,*[14] my advanced sexuality (long ago become a memory like a stone whose gap is beautiful (!) with moss) may have confirmed me in the Old Buddha's erotic favours; whereas had there been another "Devil" of equal talent but endowed with a still longer and even more militant tool, he might have superseded me in the imperial couch. Who shall say? At any rate, she was

9   A ready wit.
10   "We know the profound words of Pascal: 'Cleopatra's nose, had it been shorter, would have changed the whole face of the earth.' " This is a slight misquotation of the original: "*Le nez de Cléopâtre: s'il eût été plus court, toute la face de la terre aurait changé.*"
11   To distraction . . . a nose like Cyrano de Bergerac.
12   Right word; witticism.
13   The civil war would have never broken out.
14   Comparing great with small.

faithful and true to me in the absence of "mettle more attractive";[15] and what more can one expect of a woman, *donna mobile*,[16] especially of an Empress who had roamed, in many a fair disguise, from one "penis" to another!

The Old Buddha was Asiatic but also queen; she was outside the ordinary standards of harmony and of the golden mean; yet she was in no sense what Propertiüs calls *Meretrix regina*, or *la reine courtisane*.[17] In the end she was punished by that Nemesis which the Greeks exalted above Zeus himself, the Anangke or Necessity which drives us onward as with rods, Lord above lords and god behind the gods. Her marvellous good luck failed her at the last and she, perhaps after all, fortunately for her temperament, *ging mit dem Tode ab*;[18] while *son regard n'était point terni et la débauche n'avait point fatigué les ardeurs de sa chair luxurieuse*.[19] So may we not say of her that she was *felix in opportunitate mortis*,[20] and the epigram that the Taoist Yogi, Hsing (Jen) Hsiang, applied to my own future "*Fortuna Infortuna, Fortuna*", as regards the final substantive at least, is apposite to the great despot that was the Old Buddha?

Whatever her incomparable charm, she could not have succeeded without unrivalled state-craft and the consummate flair which enabled her to catch the passing breeze and to turn it to her purposes. She was essentially truthful and her nature hated dissembling and pretence which was alien to her temperament. The self-confidence that she so abundantly possessed (as I have sought to show in my chapter on the conspiracy of the president of the Board of Communications, Ts'en Ch'un-hsüan 岑春煊) communicated itself to others; *grandement joyeuse, elle communiquait cette gaieté qui fait oublier les dangers et qui double les forces*.[21] She was Asiatic to the finger tips in her wonderful unchangeable humour and her admirable condescension such as few European monarchs (perhaps Napoléon when he chose) have equalled; although it was characteristic of Mark Antony who, however, was Asiatic in his love of pomp and style, a sort of Indian Bacchus gentle and beneficent, a lover of *masques* and oriental fêtes, surrounded by women dressed as Bacchanals to the lascivious playing *des syrinx et des flûtes*.[22] Even so did the Old Buddha love to masquerade as the Goddess of Mercy, Avalokitesvara 菩薩, who hearkeneth to prayer, as one of her best known photographs presents her, sitting on the sacred barge, Tz'u Hang 慈航, with the faithful Li Lien-ying portraying Deva and court ladies in appropriate costumes depicting the hierarchy of heaven.

She loved hieratic pomp and *la volupté splendide* of a Cléopâtre, *les splendeurs, les parfums, la poésie*[23] of the Orient with its treasures, its

---

15 **Backhouse:** *Hamlet.*
16 "Fickle woman", an allusion to Giuseppi Verdi's aria "La donna è mobile" in *Rigoletto*.
17 "Whore queen" (*Elegies* III.XI.39) or "courtesan queen".
18 Departed with death.
19 Her eyes had not faded and debauchery had not exhausted the passion of her lustful flesh.
20 Happy in the occasion of death (Tacitus, *Agricola* 45).
21 Greatly cheerful, she was able to communicate that joy which makes one forget about danger and greatly enhances one's strength.
22 Syringes and flutes.
23 The magnificent pleasures of the flesh of a Cleopatra, the grandeur, the fragrances, the poetry.

strange desires, its idealism unknown to our sordid, material Europe. When the end came, as far as her mortal existence was concerned, albeit the deified imperial tablet had to await her sepulture before entry in the Ancestral Temple, things in Cambaluc were far other than when Cléopâtre died. The Romans hated and feared the Ptolemeian queen; they trembled until the crowning glory of Actium, as both Horace and Propertius admit. And so, after her resolution *à se donner la mort*,[24] for she died royally (*d'une manière, dit Charmian, digne de la fille de tant de rois*),[25] clad in her queenly robes, nay in the attire of a goddess, reposing inanimate on the bed of solid gold, there were grandiose rejoicings in the eternal city: "*Nunc est bibendum! C'est maintenant qu'il faut boire!*"[26] But in Peking at that sad hour the heavens and the earth were darkened in eclipse, as on a certain day in Golgotha when the veil of the temple was rent in twain from the top to the bottom, and an old suspicion-ridden man in his imperial villa of Câpres of the Blue Grotto,[27] is said to have trembled before some sinister portent appearing in the south Italian sky simultaneously with the Judaean execution and to have called in his augurs and soothsayers to expound to him the meaning of those omens of death. Men said (*mutatis mutandis*)[28] with Wordsworth, writing at the hour of that best-beloved statesman Charles James Fox's dissolution: "For he must go who is their stay: their glory disappear." And it was a woman of tiny stature (of the same height as the English despot Queen Victoria), in her seventy-fourth year, whom the adoring Manchus (patricians or proletariat) believed (as it were) to be immortal, even as Le Roi Soleil (as recorded by Saint-Simon) in his mortal hour remarked to his attendant gentlemen: "*Alors, messieurs, vous m'avez donc cru immortel! Adieu, messieurs, je compte que vous vous souviendrez quelquefois de moi.*"[29] Happy then, I, if I may fain hope that some portion of the grace and charm of her nature may haply have entered into my portrait of China's Semiramis or rather perhaps *la Lagide du Nil*.[30]

Is not perverse sexuality, especially such as mine, a form of insanity with lucid intervals, though differing from what the Hellenes describe as a "malady of the senses and of the soul, not unlike *le mal sacré par la violence des accès et par la profondeur de la mélancolie*"?[31] In certain respects the Old Buddha was a disciple of Sade, although in others she was tender-hearted and pitiful. My own particular form of mentality or insanity if so it be, has never taken on itself that aspect of cruelty, except in the predilection for reciprocal flagellations (*éducation à l'anglaise*, as they said

24 "To commit suicide". Should be written "*de se donner la mort*".
25 "In a way, said Charmian, fitting for a princess descended of so many royal kings", a paraphrase of Shakspere (*Antony and Cleopatra* V.II.325-6).
26 Now is the time for drinking.
27 Emperor Tiberius (42 BC-32 AD), living in Capri at the time of Jesus Christ's crucifixion in 30 AD.
28 The necessary changes having been made.
29 So, gentlemen, you have believed me to be immortal! Farewell, gentlemen, I expect that you will sometimes recall me.
30 "The Legend of the Nile", Cleopatra. Semiramis was a legendary Assyrian queen, renowned for beauty and cunning.
31 The pain hallowed by an outburst of violence and the depths of melancholy.

in Paname),[32] e.g. in the case of Henri III and *les mignons*,[33] when there was no religious element involved. *Le Très Révérend Père*[34] Adolphe Tanquerey of Issy, in his great work *La Vie Spirituelle, un traité de Théologie mystique et ascétique*,[35] recommends in his chapter on Mortification that in order to subdue our bodies, we should submit ourselves to many severe strokes of *la discipline* from another person on the bared person (presumably the posterior), "when this last can be performed without attracting public notice". "Let us lacerate our flesh and draw much blood, and we shall be happy as the day is long." This is indeed admirable spiritual fervour, but my love of the exotic practice of flagellation is purely sensual and devoid of any wish to "temper the importunities of the flesh"; in fact is quite the contrary of the good father's admonition. It has no connexion with the ecstatic lacerations of the medieval cloister or the religious pilgrimages with reciprocal whippings so popular in the 13th or 14th centuries. Aubrey Beardsley drew a fine cartoon of one man chastising from salacious motives another's buttocks, but it was suppressed and (I fear) destroyed.[36]

Certainly I am in good company, if we may believe Jean-Jacques Rousseau's *Confessions*. It is interesting to find that the generality of eunuchs, *Yen* 閹, *castrati*, *Shu* 豎 as they are sometimes styled, also *Ssu* 寺, templars in view of their enforced celibacy as of the cloister, undoubtedly shared my penchant and were faithful adepts of Masoch and Sade, more perhaps of the latter than the former. I have shown that several young Manchu nobles savoured this *goût étrange*.[37]

As to the chief eunuch, Li Lien-ying, I found him kind-hearted, a loyal friend, generous to a fault, good-natured toward his staff, though he occasionally caused the *discipline* to be with severity applied to recalcitrant younger eunuchs' posteriors, a man of his word with whom (to use a vulgar expression) one could go tiger-hunting in perfect confidence that he would stand by one to the end. I think that I may be considered a good judge, knowing him so well. That he loved money I do not deny, equally that he exacted and attained enormous fees and perquisites. Yet in some ways he was absurdly quixotic and dispensed with what he was entitled to receive. In comparison with notorious eunuchs of history, Liu Chin 劉瑾 or Wei Chung-hsien 魏忠賢 who are elsewhere named in this narration, he was like a nenuphar in the surrounding slime. He was a most witty and original talker, redolent with *traits d'esprit*,[38] possessing the keenest sense of subtle humour. His single-minded devotion to his great mistress, his companion through all the eventful years, merits our sincere respect: I loved to hear him bandying

---

32 English education, as they said in Paris.
33 The favourites.
34 The Great Reverend Father.
35 *The Spiritual Life, a trait of mystical and ascetical Theology.*
36 Aubrey Beardsley (1872-98), a controversial artist and writer aligned with the *Yellow Book* periodical. Backhouse claimed association with the artist and evidence does exist linking Backhouse to the literary editor and publisher of the *Yellow Book*.
37 Bizarre taste.
38 Flashes of wit.

words with Tz'u Hsi on a footing of equality. It was really and truly a friendship which obliterated social distinctions, *Mo Ni Chih Chiao* 莫逆之交. That it was a mercenary affection may be emphatically denied by those who saw him, as I did; a pathetic figure trudging with painful steps in the wake of the Old Buddha's sarcophagus on that chill November day of 1909, which the Yogi had three years previously foretold to Her Majesty in the magic crystal at the Taoist temple which the long, long procession[39] passed on its way to the Eastern Mausolea. He had fallen from his high estate, was bereft of power, he whose might but yesterday had stood against the world, while now none was so poor to do him reverence. He never regarded me as a foreigner, most kindly ministered to my abnormal tastes, and remained my close friend during the two or more years of his widowed life after Her Majesty's demise, dying just as the Revolution was beginning. It was the day of small things after so many dreams of greatness and the panoply of power: he and I used to sit after 1908 in his sunny drawing room which was full of souvenirs of Her Majesty's bounty, solid gold Buddhas, Goddesses of Mercy, jade bowls and sceptres galore, paintings, tapestries, ceramics, bronzes, discoursing old times, not without *pleurs dans les yeux et larmes dans la voix*.[40]

I think that Lien-ying surpassed even myself in a sentimentality which at the moment was assuredly sincere; certainly he desired to please and seemed ever to have *le mot juste*,[41] sending his visitors away in full content. I understand that his fortune as invested in pawn shops, real estate, amounted to some Taels 40,000,000 (at that time say six million pounds sterling), not indeed an exceptionally large sum in comparison with the wealth ill-gotten by several famous (or infamous) eunuchs of the past.

About three weeks after the Old Buddha's assassination, early in December 1908, Lien-ying came to my house, looking twenty years older, with eyes marred by the mists of pain, and we both shed burning tears together as we spoke of our great bereavement. He had brought with him a case containing his journals from the year V of Kuang Hsü (1879), when he first entered the palace, meticulously written right up to Tz'u Hsi's death, when, like the Blessed Sage, he *Chüeh Pi* 絕筆, "laid down his pen". He asked me to take charge of the diary which consisted of thirty to thirty-five ordinary large account books as used by tradesmen in China, *Chang Pen* 賬本, on coarse paper.

"My position is very uncertain since the Old Ancestress became a guest of Heaven," said he, "and the New Regent has no love toward me. I hope he will have the traitor Yüan Shih-k'ai 袁世凱 decapitated, for my own life will be in danger while he lives: only I and Ts'ui Tsung Kuan 崔總管 know for certain that he killed the Old Buddha. Please oblige me in preserving the papers, but do not read them for (say) ten years after my

---

39 **Backhouse:** "The long, long procession", Tennyson.
40 Cries in the eyes and tears in the voice.
41 The right word.

death, because I have written frankly my own thoughts and there might be passages you would find fault with. Believe me, I have been your loyal friend ever since I met you in the 28th year, 1902! After my death, you may consider the papers your property; for my heirs these journals will be of little meaning, *Tui Niu T'an Ch'in* 對牛彈琴, like playing a fiddle to a cow, as they know nothing of all that I have seen."

I was vividly reminded by the last sentence of a famous letter of Mme. de Maintenon from her *retraite*[42] at Saint-Cyr after Le Roi Soleil's death on September 1, 1715;[43] it is dated September 15 of that year and after thanking her correspondent for her *compliments de condoléance* ("*vous avez bien de la bonté, Madame, d'avoir pensé à moi dans le grand événement qui vient de se passer*"): "*J'ai vu mourir le Roi comme un Saint et un Héros . . . Je voudrais de tout mon coeur, Mme., que votre état fût aussi heureux que le mien; je suis dans la plus aimable retraite que je puisse désirer . . . quant à la société, on ne peut l'avoir avec des personnes que n'ont point de connaissance de tout ce que j'ai vu*" (what she had seen was the history of Europe for thirty-five years!) . . . "*Et je serai, Mme., toute ma vie avec tout le respect que je vous dois . . . etc.*"[44]

Naturally, I could not refuse so earnest a request, though I own that my invincible curiosity was likely to give to me *la quart d'heure de Rabelais*,[45] for naturally I was all agog to peruse the journals which were to be forbidden fruit for many years! I may mention here that after Li's death in the first part of 1911 I naturally attended the funeral ceremonies and in accord with custom *Ch'u Fen Tzu*[46] 出分子 in memory of the *cher disparu*.[47] The sums of money and the presents of funeral scrolls and curtains are all obligatory, varying, as to the former, very greatly in amount. It seemed to me that, as I retained the great eunuch's diaries, it would be fitting to make a pecuniary gift of Taels 2,000 to his heir, truly a case of bringing coal to Newcastle or sending a hog to Liao Tung 遼東 that home of pigs.

I was faithful to my pledge and only inspected the manuscript in 1921 when I took it with me to London, where it still is (if not bombed by the eagles of "mighty Gross-Deutschland").[48] Li, without being a literate, writes artlessly and with decided humour. Here and there he evolves (like some great writers) *Leng Tzu* 冷字, cold (i.e. wrongly written) characters such as 扣 for 叩; 瘐 for 庾, *Shou*, thin, for *Yü*, which means "to die in prison". In one passage he mentions an enemy of the Old Buddha as

---

42 Retirement.

43 Françoise d'Aubigné (1635-1719), Madame de Maintenon, was the second wife of Louis XIV.

44 Condolences (you are very kind, Madame, for thinking of me in the important event that just happened): I saw the king die as a saint and a hero . . . I hope with all my heart, Madame, that your state has been as happy as ours; I am in the most agreeable retirement that I could want . . . as for companionship, I can't keep company with those who don't understand what I've seen . . . And I will be, Madame, for my whole life, with all the respect I owe you . . . etc.

45 "The quarter-hour of Rabelais". The phrase, meaning the time of uneasiness at a restaurant before the arrival of the bill, is a reference to a story by French writer François Rabelais (d. 1553).

46 Collective contribution; making a donation.

47 Dearly departed.

48 According to Backhouse biographer Hugh Trevor-Roper, no record has ever been found confirming the existence of this diary in London or elsewhere aside from Backhouse's personal correspondences, which alternatively list the diary's whereabouts as being in London and Peking.

having died of starvation (*Shou Ssu* 瘦死) when he means *Yü* 庾 died in gaol: as if an English writer should say "die of poison" instead of die in prison! But these are minor blemishes which only offend the nice taste of scholars. As may be supposed, much of the manuscript is unprintable, as is an infinity of veiled allusion to the Old Buddha's erotic adventures. I estimate that there are, in all, about 1½ million characters, so that, at best, only a careful selection can ever see the light of day in translation. Whether the whole unexpurgated manuscript in the original could ever be published in China, I do not know, but doubt if it would arouse great interest today, since so much water has flowed beneath the bridges since the days of Tz'u Hsi.

The diary has the ring of truth: it is largely composed in a matter of fact style, bereft, perhaps wisely, of flowers of fancy. Devotion to his adored mistress is visible in every line and one of the best features of his painstaking chronicle is that he quotes the Old Buddha's frequent sayings word for word. Names are largely disguised, especially in the later years; but Tz'u Hsi's *amants de passage*[49] are demonstrated in detail. There is a great deal concerning Junglu but only one passage seems to reveal the truth: it is dated April 1903 (Kuang Hsü 29) and written at Paotingfu 保定府 when the Old Buddha learnt of her favorite's passing. It runs as follows: "*Jung Hsiang O Hao Chih Tz'u* 槃相惡耗至此, *O O O* (Li always uses the "triple elevation" before the Old Buddha's holy name) *Lao Fo Pu Yen* 老佛不言, *Chih Nien Chiu Ch'ing* 只念舊情, *T'ung K'u Pu I* 痛 哭不已. *Wo Shen Nan Shou* 我甚難受: *Shih Tz'u Wei Jen* 失此偉人, *Fu Yu Ho Yen* 復有何言? *T'ung Tsai* 痛哉, *T'ung Tsai* 痛哉! The news of Grand Secretary Jung reached here: the Old Buddha remained dumb. She could only recall old love and wept bitterly without surcease. I felt very melancholy: we have lost this great man: what is there to say? Alack and again alas!" The words "old love" would suggest carnal affinity, even as when Marie Antoinette (according to a letter discovered in Sweden among Axel Fersen's archives) speaks of her *adoré* as *le plus aiment et le plus aimé des hommes!*[50]

Although Li Lien-ying's diary during the Boxer *émeute*[51] of 1900 is faithfully kept from day to day, except the period covering the journey of the migrating and stricken court ("The son of Heaven has left the capital, his head covered with dust, *T'ien Tzu Meng Ch'en Tsai Wai* 天子蒙塵在外", a quotation from *Tso Chuan* 左傳) in the discomfort of that panic-ridden flight when, I imagine, he was pre-occupied in listening to the Old Buddha's loud voiced dissatisfaction toward a novel situation of which she was the main cause, *fons et origo mali*, as the seer of Mantua (*il Mantovano*) says,[52] and had little inclination to put pen to paper or to narrate his grievances.

---

49 Passing lovers.

50 "Lover . . . the most loving and most beloved of men". Correctly written "*Aimant*".

51 Uprising.

52 "The fountain and origin of the evil". The seer of Mantua refers to Virgil (70-19 BC), a poet from the Mantua region believed by many to have been a magician and a prophet. Virgil, however, never made the attributed remark, which is of unknown origin.

His journal of the period of the siege of the Legations, while very full, really adds little to that of Ching Shan 景善 of which malevolent critics, not to mention men ignorant of Chinese but jealous of rivals, like that arch-liar Dr. G. E. Morrison, have doubted the authenticity; on no ground except that it was published by their *bête noire*,[53] me; were it not that "festering in his shroud", Morrison is now howling in the deathless flames of Hell, equally, I suppose, would he now suggest that Lien-ying's voluminous records of one and a half million ideographs had been "written up" by the present writer *dans ses moments perdus*.[54] "What fools these mortals be!" as Shakspere says; and as it did not need a Shakspere to discover.[55]

Lien-ying, while loyal to the Old Buddha, does not deny (in fact definitely states) that she could have stopped the anti-foreign movement with a word; it is exact that Her Majesty told to me on many occasions the same story, but there is no doubt but that she genuinely believed that the foreign devils had demanded her abdication and consequently issued in a moment of wild anger the fateful decree of Kuang Hsü 26, VI, 24 (June 20, 1900) declaring war on the Powers. Hence her action was intelligible, albeit unworthy of her great common sense. Perhaps the most interesting portion of Lien-ying's narrative is the description of the "hum-drum" life at the Saint-Germain[56] of the Court's exile and the indication of gradual recovery in the Old Buddha's depressed spirits after her gigantic loss of face, which, however, she turned to good account by typically frank admissions of her past errors and thus gaining the sympathy of her subjects in North China (if not in the South) *vis-à-vis* the predatory Powers.

When Lien-ying called at my house in December 1908, we were both of us clad in the garb of mourning, wearing the traditional white sheepskin robe reversed, red-eyed from incessant weeping, with dishevelled hair, unkempt, unshaven, sorry spectacles of distracted and heart-gnawing grief.

There are many allusions to myself, usually complimentary, but he always writes of me as *Chiao Hou'rh* 焦猴兒, the "monkey" *Chiao* 焦, because in the *Po Chia Hsing* 百家姓 or *Recueil de noms de famille*,[57] to which I have referred, my surname *Pa* 巴 is in the *verset* "*Wu Chiao Pa Kung* 烏焦巴弓", so that *Chiao* is my next-door-neighbor. He also names me as *Chü T'un* 巨臀, "Large arse", and occasionally *Ta Yen'rh* 大眼兒, "Big arse-hole", a pretty tribute to my amorous eccentricity! He quotes the Old

---

53 Nemesis.

54 In his spare time.

55 It is clear that Backhouse had no love for his former employer, *The Times* correspondent Dr. G.E. Morrison (1862-1920), the first man to publicly doubt the authenticity of Ching Shan's diary as presented in *China under the Empress Dowager*. Regardless of whether Morrison's reasons for doubting the diary's authenticity were personal, it was later proven to be a forgery by the prominent sinologist J.J.L. Duyvendak and others. It is unclear who was responsible for the fabrication, though many suspect Backhouse.

56 Saint-Germain is the royal French palace west of Paris, used here to refer to the western capital, Hsian 西安.

57 *Hundred Family Surnames*, a classic text recounting the most common names in China.

Buddha as extolling my "wit and charm" (sic), and also as saying: "Ten males could not satisfy his lusts, *Shih Nan Kung Pu Tsu T'a Ti Yin Kan* 十男供不足他的淫感!!"

He describes my eunuch affections and pays an undeserved tribute to my orgasm as being "colossal", although in fact Prince Kung, dear Chan Pao-ch'en, not to say my cherished Kuei Hua, Cassia Flower, had no cause to envy my exuberant salacity which they (all three of them) equalled. He says quite truly that his aphrodisiac drug acted most potently in my person and that I became "hard as iron or steel", *Ying Ju Kang T'ieh* 硬如鋼鐵 after quaffing it, "to the Old Buddha's joy". He narrates all the events that I have tried to describe, albeit in less detail and without the pathetic aspect which did not appeal to his matter-of-fact disposition. Of the "Lovers' Doom" he records few particulars, but the last sentence: "*Sui An Jan Erh Kuei* 雖安然而歸, *Wei Hu Tai Tsai* 危乎殆哉, *T'ien Hu T'ien Hu* 天乎天乎! Although we did return, what appalling danger! O God! O God!" indicates more emotion than he would perhaps admit. His account of the crystal gazing *séance* mentions the various visions evoked from the past, but regarding the prophecies of future events he writes guardedly, merely saying that several "dangerous" warnings were given by the Yogi who alarmed the Old Buddha. Of his relative, the mad eunuch, he writes very fully but rather minimizes the danger which I undoubtedly ran, while praising both the Old Buddha and myself for our *sang-froid*, *T'ai Jan Tzu Jo* 泰然自若.

Of Tz'u Hsi's death and the emperor's murder, his narrative corresponds exactly with mine, seeing that it was he who gave to me the main facts! But he does not name Yüan and T'ieh directly, obviously from motives of self-preservation: the former he calls "Round Twenty Common", the first ideograph being of the same sound 圓 and 袁, 廿 (or 念) *Nien* being short for 世, and *Fan* 凡, "common", minus the dot, *Tien'rh* 點兒, is abbreviated for K'ai 凱; the latter becomes *Shih Ken* 失艮, *T'ieh* 鐵, iron, being often written (incorrectly) as 鉄, and 艮 *Liang* is shorn by Li of its first stroke (sometimes called *Ts'ê* 側 or *Tien'rh* 點兒).

Coming from him, the "compliment" that he pays to me as the most libidinous man he has ever known, "whose plethoric carnality is even as the sea which can never be filled up", is, I suppose, praise of one expert to another and not without value. It reminds me of Cicero's quotation of the elder Cato's adage in *Traité de la Divination*, II.24, "*Si augur augurem . . .*",[58] which was *un trait lancé contre les augures lesquels, disait-il, ne pouvaient pas se rencontrer sans rire;*[59] in other words two of the same profession know the tricks of the trade too well to be impressed by each others' performances. Perhaps Lien-ying is right: anyhow, I am paying the penalty today for past lascivious exercises; and God knows I deserve my fate, the fate, in Othello's classic phrase, of "one who loved" (or lusted) "not wisely, but too well".[60]

---

58   If an augur . . . an augur.

59   A cutting remark made about the augurs who, he said, could not meet without laughing.

60   "Of one that lov'd not wisely but too well" (V.II.344).

After narrating in his journal the deaths of the *Liang Kung* 兩宮, "Two Palaces", as the Old Buddha and the emperor were always styled, Lien-ying terminates with a sort of *apologia pro sua vita*.[61] He says that none will compare him with the chief eunuchs of bygone dynasties, because the Manchu regime has consistently excluded *Yen Jen* 閹人 (*castrati*) from political power; his duty has simply been to serve the Old Buddha with single-heartedness and loyalty. Whether he is right in his anticipation of the verdict of history, so far as Clio, the Muse, will concern herself with him at all, having many other preoccupations for her unerring pen, I do not know, but the point of view is interesting, since he had persuaded himself into imagining that through all those eventful years political intrigues were alien to his nature and that he was merely the faithful and confidential attendant of Tz'u Hsi, something akin to François I's famous *bouffon*,[62] or Henri III's favorite *fou*[63] Chicot, or even to Victoria's adored John Brown! He contrasts his tender-heartedness with the blood-lust of a Liu Chin 劉瑾 or a Wei Chung-hsien 魏忠賢, to say nothing of notorious eunuchs of remoter times, such as he of the Ch'in 秦 Dynasty who marked out for distinction (and actually put to death) those of the courtiers who ventured to contradict his *obiter dictum*[64] that the picture of a stag represented a horse, *Chih Lu Wei Ma* 指鹿爲馬.

Regarding the Pearl Consort, Chen Fei 珍妃, I asked Lien-ying whether he could not have made (out of his "tender-heartedness") a greater effort to intercede with Tz'u Hsi for the wretched girl's life; his reply was that he could not move Her Majesty to mercy in the storm and stress of that hour; if Junglu had been with the Old Buddha on that fateful morning, he might (said Li) have succeeded in *Wan Hui T'ien Ming* 挽回天命, recalling the judgement of Heaven,[65] because Chen Fei had designated him as the Old Buddha's confessed paramour and if he was prepared to overlook the insult to himself, the Empress might have pardoned the *lèse-majesté*[66] as the utterance of a demented woman.

The last words that I heard the once all-powerful chief eunuch utter shortly ere his death in 1911 were a quotation from Po Chü-i 白居易 (Lo-t'ien 樂天) who concludes his majestic poem *Ch'ang Hen Ko* 長恨歌, "the Ode of Eternal Grief", thus: "天長地久有時盡, 此恨綿々無絕期, Heaven and earth shall one day pass away, but this our grief (for the Old Buddha) shall abide with us forever. *T'ien Ch'ang Ti Chiu Yu Shih Chin; Tz'u Hen Mien Mien Wu Chüeh Ch'i.*" There we may leave him; where better could we leave him? for after all (in the words of the seer of Mantua, the lord of language, moulder of the chosen coin of fancy shining forth in many a golden phrase with all the charm of all the muses oft adorning one lonely word), there are tears for great fortunes and human things touch

---

61 "Defence of his own life", the title of an 1800 poem by Samuel Taylor Coleridge.
62 Jester.
63 Fool.
64 Remark.
65 More commonly translated as "Mandate of Heaven".
66 Affront to the dignity of a Monarch.

the heart! (*Sunt lacrimae rerum mentem et mortalia tangunt*)[67] for life is made up of imperishable loyalties for lost causes and for the *Peripeteia*[68] of a hero, be he the great Emathian Conqueror[69] or Julius Caesar, Napoléon or the Old Buddha, whose story you and I know.

Ying Hsiung Mo Lu Ch'ien Ku T'ung T'an 英雄末路千古同歎, "The hero's last state has through the ages inspired a tributary sigh."

Ave atque vale.[70]

---

67 They are the tears of mortal things and mortal matters affect the heart (Virgil, *Aeneid* I.462).
68 Reversal of fortune (Aristotle, *Poetics*).
69 **Backhouse:** Milton, *Sonnets*, The Great Emathian Conqueror (Alexander the Great).
70 Hail and farewell (Catullus, 101).

APPENDIX

POSTSCRIPT
BY REINHARD HOEPPLI

SIR Edmund Trelawny Backhouse then in his seventy-first year wrote in the first half of 1943 two works "The Dead Past" and "Décadence Mandchoue", extraordinary in more than one sense, both entirely unsuitable for ordinary publication. The author who had been a resident of Peking for many years lived at the outbreak of the Pacific War very retired in the British Embassy Compound. The war imposed on him a few restrictions but fundamentally did not change his quiet life. On account of his age and failing health he was exempted from going with other allied nationals to the Civilian Internment Camp at Weihsien. In early summer 1943, he entered the French St. Michael's Hospital where he remained up to his death on January 8th, 1944.

The editor who had never met Sir Edmund before the war had been from 1930 to 1941 a staffmember of the Peiping Union Medical College. During the Pacific War he was, as Honorary Swiss Consul, in charge of American, British and Netherlands interests in Peiping and in this quality became acquainted with Sir Edmund. He visited him very frequently – for many months nearly daily – until his death.

The reader of "The Dead Past" and "Décadence Mandchoue" will learn in the first of the author's unhappy childhood and of his years in Europe, in the second of his life in China until the death of the Empress Dowager. The reader will form his own opinion but nevertheless may welcome some additional information about the author and his work based on the editor's personal experience and observations.

THE AUTHOR

According to Burke's "Peerage, Baronetage and Knightage" (96th edition 1938) and to "WHO'S WHO" (edition 1937), Sir Edmund was born on October 20, 1873; the same year was originally given in his last passport but evidently at his own request charged to 1872. He told the editor that the last mentioned year was the correct one but never properly explained why Burke's "Peerage", "'WHO'S WHO" and the first entry in his passport gave 1873.

Comparatively few, especially among foreigners knew him personally, although his name was familiar as that of co-author (with J. O. P. Bland) of "China under the Empress Dowager" (1910) and "Annals and Memoirs of the Court of Peking" (1913). It was also known that he had (together with Hillier and Barton) published an excellent Anglo-Chinese Dictionary. He had the reputation of a "récluse" who particularly disliked the contact with foreigners; even queer habits in this respect were reported. He was said to turn around when, walking on the city wall, he saw a foreigner coming towards him and to cover his face with a handkerchief when passing a foreigner in a rickshaw. These reports even though they may be exaggerated indicate not only his dislike of foreigners but also an eccentric mind.

When one lives apart from others, especially when one shows strange habits, as a rule rumours, mainly of an unfavorable kind, develop.

Sir Edmund had the reputation of being homosexual; another, sinister rumour spoke of a murder committed in his own house on one of his Chinese staff. It was whispered that he had at one time translated documents for the Soviet Embassy in Peking and that after the raid on that Embassy in 1927 these activities had been found out by the Japanese who later in their turn had forced him to translate for them.

A particularly ugly rumour which, if it represented the truth, would deprive him of his character as a gentleman, had it that after the death of the Empress Dowager, Sir Edmund, in connection with some palace eunuchs who had stolen a very valuable jacket of the late Empress adorned with beautiful pearls, tried to cheat a staffmember of a foreign bank who had paid in advance an agreed price but in consequence of a cleverly staged theatrical coup never obtained the object, while Sir Edmund or his family eventually had to refund the irritated prospective buyer.

It may be added here that when the editor's rickshawman, a Manchu, after the outbreak of the Pacific War, saw for the first time Sir Edmund, he mentioned spontaneously that there was a rumour that this old man in bygone days had been a lover of the Empress Dowager. This statement was made long before "Décadence Mandchoue" was written.

Those various rumours – whether false or true – have been mentioned only, because they indicate the highly complex personality of the author.

The impression the editor got when meeting Sir Edmund first was that of a distinguished looking old scholarly gentleman dressed in a shabby black, somewhat formal, suit who had a definite charm and spoke and behaved with exquisite slightly old-style politeness. His long white beard gave him a venerable aspect, his walking was slow and somewhat unsteady, so that one feared he might fall down. His hands were well-shaped and white, slightly feminine; they moved nervously and often showed tremor. His eyes were remarkable for the very different expressions they were able to show in rapid succession, as the editor could observe in the course of many visits. They might at one moment have the quiet look of an old scholar, quite in line with beard, dress and refined politeness; suddenly they became the eyes of a monk in religious ecstasy, to charge a change again into the eyes of an old salacious profligate with a very clever cunning look which gave the face a certain resemblance to that of Aretino on Titian's painting in the Pitti Palace in Florence. It was his eyes which betrayed that fact that the first and dominant impression of an old scholar represented only a part of his personality. Gradually after somewhat closer contact one obtained an entirely different aspect, that of a person who notwithstanding age and ailments, still harboured a strong sexuality and after some external inhibitions had been overcome, revealed with lascivious pleasure the erotic part of his personality. In such moments, he presented occasionally the very picture of an old satyr enjoying happy memories.

By preference he was wearing a long Chinese gown of dark colour which made him timeless in the sense that he might have looked in place in a Roman house at the time of the late emperors, in a Renaissance setting and in the studyroom of one of the Jesuit fathers at the time or K'ang Hsi. When sitting on the verandah of his residence in the British Embassy Compound, he used to wear a black Chinese cap with a large piece of Rose-quartz fastened to its front part in the old Chinese fashion. During the hot summer months, he was wearing a light yellow Chinese gown of grass-cloth.

He was a gourmet who occasionally indulged in small luxuries such as strawberries and asparagus out of season which he could hardly afford in view of his very limited funds. He was also fond of good wine, especially red Bordeaux and Burgundy. As far as the editor could ascertain, he had never indulged in opium-smoking but took daily much caffein in crystals and during the last year of his life, sleeping-powders and pills in large quantities.

His conversation was always interesting dealing as rule with a great variety of topics, but giving preference to historic matters, literature and erotic subjects. He was a bibliophile who had given a very large collection of Chinese and Manchu books and manuscripts to the Bodleian Library in Oxford.

His memory was prodigious, his gift for languages extraordinary. It was therefore somewhat surprising to find occasionally an exaggerated sensitiveness in man whose knowledge of languages was so great that he could afford to make a mistake. He, whose Chinese including calligraphy was very good, but who unavoidably sometimes made small mistakes when writing Chinese characters, took it more or less as a personal insult if the editor's Chinese secretary corrected them. His ability to converse with great facility in different languages, together with a certain pride and perhaps wish to show it, induced him to introduce words of some other language, especially French, into his English conversation. It was very fascinating to hear him speak of the past, he brought back scenes of bygone days with many details and when on winter afternoons, sitting in half-darkness in his arm chair, he spoke of people dead since long, they seemed as if by magic to return to life and to reveal some of their secrets, charming, scandalous and even horrible as they may have been.

There can be no doubt that nature had given Sir Edmund not only a prodigious memory but also an extraordinary power of imagination. This last made his stories particularly vivid and fascinating, but obviously represented to a certain extent a danger to their truthfulness.

What had Sir Edmund been doing during all these years in Peking where he had first arrived in 1898? This simple question is not quite as simple to answer. For some time he was a Professor in the University of Peking, later he seemed to have been connected in a semi-official character with the British Embassy. There were several indications that he belonged to the British Intelligence Service.

For example, his knowledge of persons who had to all appearances nothing to do with him, was often very great. When once his conversation with the editor turned to a famous Peking murder case, which apparently had not been solved, Sir Edmund not only explained it in detail as a case of mistaken identity, but gave the names of the culprits, their subsequent fate and death, the source of his information and also the reason why at that time the prosecution had to be stopped.

Anybody with a lot of highly dangerous knowledge is likely to feel not safe. Sir Edmund sometimes seemed to be subject to some fear and this may also explain to a certain extent his highly unusual attitude towards England and the allies on one side and towards Germany and Japan on the other. In addition there can be no question that he harboured a strong and lasting resentment against the British and the country of his birth. The original manuscripts of "Décadence Mandchoue" and "The Dead Past" give numerous examples which at the editor' s request were later omitted or changed when the manuscripts were typed.

Some explanation may be found in Sir Edmund's family milieu in Cornwall which contrasted markedly with his tastes and interests. His mother was a Salusbury-Trelawny a member of a very old Cornwall family which traced its history back to Edward the Confessor. On the paternal side there was a link with Germany dating from the eighteenth century. Sir Edmund's family was related with that of Charles James Fox, the famous statesman whom he greatly admired and counted among its members a number of officers in the Army and Navy. Two of his own brothers were distinguished admirals while another brother had held a position in the Army.

It is rather likely that Sir Edmund while still a boy showed already qualities which were alien to his family and possibly a good deal of the illtreatment (sic) by his parents of which he so bitterly complains in "Tangled Skein"[1] may have been due to an antagonism perhaps subconscious between the very uncongenial personalities of parents and son.

---

1   A chapter from his second autobiographical work, *The Dead Past*.

Also to his brothers he must have seemed strange at an early time. "Did you dream this, Edme" as he quotes himself, was the retort of one of his brothers to whom he had spoken.

It is probable that Sir Edmund felt somewhat a stranger in his family and among the members of the British aristocracy of his time who in turn most likely sensed and resented it, without appreciating Sir Edmund's unusual qualities. His wish to leave the uncongenial British atmosphere was very likely one of the reasons why he went to China where he found just the milieu he was looking for and which corresponded to his interests and tastes. His admitted dislike of British society seems in China to have gradually developed to dislike of foreigners in general as mentioned before.

The editor has during the Pacific War never heard from any Englishman, especially not one of high education and good social standing, such unkind remarks on Great Britain, the British Government and the British character in general as made by Sir Edmund. On the other side, there was nobody in the Peking British community who spoke so highly of Germany and Japan. It may be of interest to add that while Sir Edmund himself did not hesitate to blame the British, he did not like to hear other people attacking them, he was even very sensitive about this point. There can be no doubt that he was very fond of Germany, especially the cultural past of that country with which he was connected by ancestral links. In Japanese he appreciated their politeness and admired their courage in war. He seemed to enjoy Japanese victories just as if he was a Japanese and recorded with sadistic pleasure the various defeats of the allies, especially of the British, during the first period of the war. It has to remain an open question whether this peculiar attitude represented his real feelings or was possibly the result of a constant hidden fear of a real or imaginary danger from the Japanese authorities. Concerning France and the French he always, from the beginning to the end, manifested a liking, dwelling with delight in many conversations on interesting periods in French history and on French cultural achievements; the last Valois,[2] as might be expected, was among his favorites. Likewise for Russians he had only good words, but it has to be pointed out that when speaking of Russia he had the old imperial Russia in mind.

Sir Edmund who was never married, became Catholic in summer 1942, and subsequently signed by preference "Paul" Backhouse. He had evidently since long contemplated to enter "Holy Church" as he called it and the general political situation probably precipitated his step. He felt alone, somewhat lost and looked for a shelter. The beautiful ceremonies impressed and attracted him, just as they have attracted many others. In addition it is very likely that he hoped that by accepting the Catholic faith he would be provided by the church not only with money which he always needed but eventually also with some peaceful abode, secluded and sheltered such as a monastery with an old garden where he could

---

2   King Henri III of France (1551-89), who is believed to have been homosexual and, as Backhouse often mentions, an indulger in flagellation.

sit and contemplate, removed from the world and safe. He expressed this wish on several occasions and mentioned "Monreale" near Palermo with its beautiful old garden and its exquisite architecture as a model for his dream of a peaceful place of retirement before the end.

He was deceived in this respect. Not only did the Church not provide funds but also his dream of a sheltered peaceful life in a monastery-garden could not be realized and for good reasons. The Catholic Church enjoyed certain privileges during the Japanese occupation but was always closely watched and had to be very careful in all relations with "enemy" nationals. "Monseigneur always says: the Lord will provide", Sir Edmund once complained, speaking of visits by the Bishop of Peking whom he had evidently approached with a request for funds. The Lord did not provide and therefore the much criticised British Government had after all to continue to help him with relief payments.

Sir Edmund's Father Confessor was Irish and not highly cultured "better suited to convert coolies than people like myself" to use one of Sir Edmund's judgments about this priest who like many of his compatriots hated Great Britain. It is very likely that he and Sir Edmund met on common ground in their criticism of England and their love for Germany. His Father Confessor brought Sir Edmund many of the well known small religious pictures on cards so dear to the lower classes in Catholic countries who place them usually in religious books. Sir Edmund kept them on his table for months while at the same time he wrote some of the most immoral chapters of "Décadence Mandchoue".

During the last months of his life, he seemed to have lost to a certain degree his admiration for Catholicism and especially a good deal of his former respect for the priests. "They come pestering me all the time with their impertinent indiscreet questions, I wished they would leave me alone", he remarked on several occasions. Anyhow he ended his life in peace with his church receiving the sacraments of which he once remarked "if they don't help, they will at least do no harm".

To draw conclusion from such remarks that he was with regard to the Catholic Church a hypocrite pure and simple, would do him unjustice (sic). He certainly had a sincere liking for the Catholic religion but his nature was such that he might mock and be devoted, even be a believer to a certain extent and all that at the same time; some element of superstition may likewise have played a rôle.

It would have been easy for Sir Edmund as far as his earthly possessions were concerned to give up everything and to enter a monastery because he had hardly anything left. He who in his youth had been evidently quite wealthy died, as far as his possessions in China were concerned, practically a beggar. The same scholar who had presented the Bodleian Library in Oxford with about 30,000 books and manuscripts died with only such few personal belongings as some worn Chinese and foreign clothes – a fur coat was the only article of some value – an old Victorian travelling clock and a small collection of books, all, with one or two exceptions, cheap editions and practically valueless. He had hardly any linen, no watch, no cufflinks and apart from the piece of rose-quartz fastened on his Chinese cap and mentioned before, no jewelry of any kind. A red leather case containing the document of his succession to the baronetcy was somewhat incongruent with the other items.

Most important of the things he once possessed was his library, the loss of which he often deplored. A gold watch, several valuable manuscripts, such as an autograph letter by Marie Antoinette, were other items he mentioned on various occasions. How could he lose all this and evidently much more? His answer always was "thanks to unfaithful servants and treacherous friends". But why did he never try to recover at least some of his property, especially as he obviously knew those who had robbed him?

What seemed to have happened was that apparently in 1939 while the Japanese conducted an anti-British and anti-American propaganda in Peking which however to all of the editor's knowledge never led to looting, let alone attacks on the life of ordinary civilians, Sir Edmund for unknown reasons was suddenly seized by such a fear that he left his house in the West City and only with a few of his belongings took refuge in a German boarding-house within the precincts of the Ex-Austrian Legation Compound in the Legation Quarter. This alone represents a somewhat strange act but much more strange is that subsequently he to all evidence never again entered his former house leaving and abandoning everything – and all this happened about two years before the outbreak of the Pacific War!

According to statements in his autobiography he had sent already many years before his end some of his belongings for safekeeping to Lloyds Bank in London. Among them should be found the diary of Li Lien-ying the famous chief eunuch of the Empress Dowager. This diary contains according to Sir Edmund references to his visits to the Forbidden City and therefore might substantiate and verify one of the most interesting parts of "Décdence Mandchoue": the author's intimate relations with Tz'u Hsi.

Little need be said of his outward life from the beginning of the Pacific War to his death. At the outbreak, he lived in a single room, very modestly furnished in a house of the British Embassy Compound, some of these houses having been rented by British nationals. He had one servant whom he treated with great consideration but who in return often played the rôle of the master. Easy to understand that notwithstanding Sir Edmund's age, rumours developed, especially as opium-smoking and heavy drinking did not cause the dismissal of Pien, the "attendant", as Sir Edmund always called him. It should however be stated that with all his shortcomings, Pien knew well Sir Edmund's little pecularities (sic) and wishes and tried in general his best – provided he was sober – to serve him well. He was, notwithstanding the occasional rough treatment of his master, quite attached to him, although he had not been very long in his service. On the occasion's of Sir Edmund's death and funeral he showed a great grief which was certainly genuine.

Sir Edmund on account of high blood pressure, dizziness, prostatic hyperplasia with urinary troubles, entered the French St. Michael's Hospital on April 6, 1943 and remained there to his end, occupying a small room on the groundfloor (sic) of the east wing. This hospital, being under the administration of Catholic sisters, with priests visiting patients nearly every day, formed in some way a kind of substitute to the monastery which Sir Edmund had hoped would give him shelter.

In fall 1943, the editor as well as others noticed a certain change in his behavior, he became irritable, his usual exquisite politeness left him occasionally, he was often gloomy and spoke of his approaching end. On the occasion of his last birthday after having received some wine from the editor, he returned his card with "mille remerciements de votre très généreux cadeau. Vous êtes bien bon pour moie. C'est anjourd'hui mon dernier anniversaire."[3] Christmas 1943, he became suddenly unconscious, fell and after having regained consciousness, showed asymmetry of mouth and difficulty in speaking. These symptoms improved but were followed by others such bluish and black patches on his legs indicating disorders of his circulation. Two days before the end, the temperature rose suddenly and on January 8th, 1944 at seven o'clock in the morning Sir Edmund died without pain and having been conscious nearly to the end. The medical certificate gave "Softening of the Brain" as the cause of death.

After a service in St. Joseph's Church – the Tung T'ang – he was buried on January 10th, 1944 in the Catholic cemetery of Chala outside P'ing Tze Men, near the burial places of some of the famous Jesuit fathers of K'ang Hsi's time.

A few hours after his death, a young Chinese called at the Swiss Consul's Office and inquired whether the contents of Sir Edmund's last will and testament were known, as Sir Edmund whom he had met for the first time a few weeks before in the French Hospital, had promised that he would leave him by his testament a beautiful large diamond.

It is hardly necessary to add that no such diamond nor any other diamond existed and nothing was mentioned of such a legacy in the testament. The latter left practically everything to his family in England besides three modest legacies to three of his servants, the last one "Pien" being one of them.

Sir Edmund's personality is in the editor's opinion to some extent typical of certain highly gifted homosexuals whom he has met in the past end shows the abnormal sexual instinct merely as one of several characteristics. There exists as a rule a great rather feminine sensitiveness. Partly by force of circumstances, partly also by natural inclination there is often found a lack of directness and a tendency for mystification which in the worst cases may produce insincerity and direct lies.

---

3   Many thanks for your very generous gift. You are much too kind to me. Today is my last birthday.

Politeness, often exaggerated, is partly an expression of the personality but is primarily used and doubtless often deliberately to keep others at a distance. Sir Edmund's somewhat old-style but exquisite politeness has been mentioned before. It even extended to ordinary communications concerning small unimportant matters and hardly a letter or a brief note was received by the editor which did not begin with "Much revered", "My dear and deeply revered", or "My dear and deeply honoured".

A tendency to indulge in eccentric habits is likewise often found. Whereas on the one side dignity and social standards are carefully maintained and people of the higher classes are often treated haughtily, there is at the same time a tendency to become rapidly intimate with members of the lower classes – well understood not necessarily always in order to indulge in sexual practices. Servants, especially males, are usually treated well and with consideration by such homosexuals, Sir Edmund showed this attitude very pronounced. The world of imagination, even if not based on such extraordinary natural gifts as in Sir Edmund, is often cherished and cultivated, partly perhaps because in the sexual sphere indulgence is not always easy and therefore has to be supplemented by wishful dreams which subconsciously are also applied to other realms. Sir Edmund's creative imaginative power was astonishing, he used it very frequently and, as the story of the bequeathed large diamond, sometimes merely for its own sake, "l'art pour l'art" because nothing could be gained. – Fear is another characteristic, and this was very definite in Sir Edmund, although in his case one may assume that he had possibly stronger reasons than mere blackmail for homosexual practices.

Powerful gifts of the intellect are often, as experience shows, coupled with particularly strong sexual instincts in "normal" individuals; Sir Edmund is a good example that this rule also applies to homosexuals.

Last but not least should be mentioned a certain kindness and goodheartedness, not seldom observed in them. It may in the first moment seem a paradox that a person who has a number of characteristics which are not particularly attractive, should be fundamentally good-hearted, nevertheless this is true as the editor could observe on various occasions. This good-heartedness in the case of Sir Edmund was the chief secret of his charm. It was immediately felt by most people of the lower classes but also by his equals in society and perhaps subconsciously induced them to overlook certain weaknesses which they would not have forgiven in others.

A person of Sir Edmund's complex type, living an extraordinary life in a highly complex environment will be judged differently according to the viewpoint of the critic. The editor refraining from any judgement wishes only to state that he regards himself fortunate to have come in contact with Sir Edmund who having moved for many years in a vanished world brilliant in art and literature and at an extraordinary oriental court could in his conversation bring all back so colourful and vivid that persons who belong to history whom he had once met, seemed alive and spoke through him.

Although his imagination may occasionally have interfered with his memory, his conversation had such fascination that he who had known personally Verlaine, Mallarmé, Beardsley, Pater and Wilde not to speak of Tz'u Hsi and her court, could by a few remarks give their peculiar atmosphere and characteristics. Of Mallarmé, he once remarked that he had just a little the touch of the "bourgeois", a remark possibly gives the truth and represents an observation the young, rich English nobleman was liable to make when meeting the school-teacher Mallarmé.

Sir Edmund with all his shortcomings was most extraordinary and perhaps never revealed his personality completely. The editor after many months of nearly daily contact with him fully realized it more than when he saw him for the last time, in his coffin. REQUIESCAT IN PACE![4]

THE WORK

Most of Sir Edmund's literary work in the past consisted of translations of official documents for the London Foreign Office and the British Embassy in Peking of no interest to the general public and remaining in consequence more or less unknown except to a few. Besides he wrote many articles on different subjects for the *London Times*, the *Westminster Gazette*, the *Pall Mall Gazette* and the *Atlantic Monthly* apart from articles for journals in China. He had also prepared a wealth of material for a Chinese-English Dictionary which however was never published.

It has been mentioned before that he was the co-author of an excellent Anglo-Chinese Dictionary and of two other publications "China under the Empress Dowager" and "Annals and Memoirs of the Court of Peking". Those two works are not publications on history in a strict scholarly sense and were not intended to be. However, even if this is admitted, there remains the somewhat unpleasant fact that "China under the Empress Dowager" is in the main based on a diary (supposed to have been that of Ching Shan, a high government official) which according to recent research of Prof. J. J. L. Duyvendak of the University of Leyden must be regarded in its presented form as a forgery; Sir Edmund claims to have found and translated it. It must be admitted that a diary of Ching Shan may have existed and that it may have been used. The diary as published in "China under the Empress Dowager" is however according to Duyvendak certainly a forgery and it is only natural to suspect Sir Edmund as either having committed the forgery or having translated the text as an authentic document while knowing that it was a forgery. On rare occasions, because Sir Edmund being very sensitive by nature was particularly sensitive on this point, the editor tried to

---

4   May he rest in peace.

induce him to give an explanation. The result was that he always declared that he had found the diary as he translated it and had acted in good faith. Asked whether in the light of recent research he still regarded the diary as genuine, he answered evasively in terms such as "*I did not falsify it*" and did not commit himself. In the editor's opinion – but this is merely a personal impression – Sir Edmund did not himself commit the forgery; whether he suspected or even knew that the diary was not genuine was impossible to judge on the basis of Sir Edmund's conversation. Should he have been an accomplice, his somewhat redeeming virtue would have been that he acted in the interest of two persons he admired and cherished, the Grand Councillor Jung Lu and the Empress Dowager Tz'u Hsi.

"China under the Empress Dowager" when compared with "Décadence Mandchoue" contains besides the diary another questionable part, the report on the death of Kuang Hsü and Tz'u Hsi. The end of both is stated to have been due to natural causes and is described quite in detail. Just an account of these details, the average reader will not suspect that the actual facts – according to "Décadence Mandchoue" – were entirely different. There have been since long strange rumours about the coincidence of these deaths and some suspicion of foul play had been voiced. The reader of "Décadence Mandchoue" will find this suspicion fully justified as both Kuang Hsü and Tz'u Hsi according to this work were murdered. The emperor is said to have been strangled not poisoned. When the editor mentioned the old rumour that Kuang Hsü had died after having eaten poisoned tarts, Sir Edmund declared that such an attempt had been made but had failed. A scholar with access to the Archives of the British Foreign Office will have no difficulty to verify Sir Edmund's statement in "Décadence Mandchoue" as he personally told the editor that he at that time had fully informed the British Government. There remains the question of why he intentionally distorted facts. The answer is simple: Sir Edmund for various reasons wished to continue his life in China; publication of the true facts concerning the death of Kuang Hsü and Tz'u Hsi would have made his further life in China impossible, and "Pékin vaut bien une messe".[5]

"Annals and Memoirs of the Court of Peking" has no bearing on Sir Edmund's two last works with which we are concerned and therefore need not be discussed.

The editor realizes that he is responsible for the existence of "The Dead Past" and "Décadence Mandchoue". Both represent essentially collections of the various stories which Sir Edmund told him on his frequent visits during the first year of the Pacific War. Whatever the historic value of these stories may be, it seemed regrettable that they should be lost and in order to preserve them and to have at the same time a good pretext to provide him with additional funds from his private means the editor suggested to Sir Edmund to write the most interesting of his

5 Derived from the French expression "Paris vaut bien une messe", literally "Paris is worth a mass", a phrase attributed to Henri IV, which means "one important advantage is worth a small sacrifice".

experiences and to sell the manuscripts to him as would a professional writer.

Sir Edmund had a great facility in writing, sending the editor in rapid succession sheets covered with the thin, highly nervous products of his penmanship, rather difficult to read. There was in consequence the additional advantage that he could fill many hours of his long days by an occupation which cost him little effort and at the same time gave him a certain pleasure by enjoying once more in memory the unusual and remarkable scenes of his past life. There can be no doubt that he was really benefitted by this occupation, his temporary improvement being so obvious that various visitors remarked upon it.

He wrote "Décadence Mandchoue" between December 1942 and May 1943 to be followed by "The Dead Past" which he had completed at the end of June. Considering that he had no possibility to consult books and had no literary help whatever, solely and entirely relying on his memory one had to admit that the creation of the two works especially in the comparatively short period of slightly over 6 months represents a rather remarkable achievement at the age of seventy.

"The Dead Past" contains besides *Tangled Skein* – in principle a mere autobiography – separate essays on Verlaine, Mallarmé, Beardsley and Pater which furnish considerable further autobiographical material. The most sensational one is the essay on Verlaine who according to Sir Edmund was for one term his teacher in French at St. George's School in Ascot. The appreciation of Beardsley's work by emphasizing the essentials of his art proves that Sir Edmund who not very frequently spoke of purely pictorial problems, had a fine feeling for the beauty of line and the essentials of a drawing. The editor regards the essay on Pater as the best one, as it is evidently based on a longer and deeper connection between author and subject than is the case in the other essays.

"Décadence Mandchoue" consists of a collection of twenty chapters dealing with happenings at the Manchu court or with persons directly or indirectly connected with it. The Empress Dowager stands in the center of interest; the author took part in most of the related scenes, but a few are based on reports of eye witnesses. The whole gives excellently the atmosphere of a decadent court society just before its end. From a historic point of view, the most important chapter is that dealing with the death of the emperor and the empress dowager, already referred to.

The most fantastic part of the whole work is that describing the author's intimate relations with Tz'u Hsi. Who, among those who read Segalen's *René Leys*, will in this connection not remember the French author's book; but even René Leys is supposed not to be based entirely on imagination. Should the existence of intimate relations between Sir Edmund and the Empress Dowager be proved, we have the grotesque fact that a man who in general had only homosexual interests became for several years not only a sort of lover of an old Manchu woman – admitted she was the all-powerful Empress Dowager – but that stimulated and fortified by Li Lien-ying's "love philters" he performed to the physical satisfaction of a woman who certainly had experience and knew how to choose.

The explanation, in the editor's opinion, rests in the pleasure the Empress Dowager found in the company of a clever, witty, amusing foreigner, always respectful and discreet who as far as the purely physical side of the question is concerned, perhaps just on account of his perverted sexual instincts was able by clever devices to provide enjoyment even for an old oversexed woman like Tz'u Hsi. Sir Edmund told the editor on several occasions that it was chiefly his conversation which made him to be treated as a "favori" and it is most likely that this statement gives the truth.

With regard to "The Dead Past" and "Décadence Mandchoue", the fundamental question presents itself immediately. How far do the two works give the truth; do they to some extent possess historic value or are they simply products of the author's fertile imagination?

Sir Edmund's status as a scholar is uncertain, chiefly on account of the publication of the forged diary of Ching Shan. But even being fully aware of this, there is no doubt for the editor that Sir Edmund in writing "The Dead Past" and "Décadence Mandchoue" firmly believed he was stating the truth.

Evidently realizing the extraordinary character of his work, he, on various occasions in the text, again and again pledges his word that he gave the truth and nothing but the truth. How far he subconsciously deceived himself, eventual future investigations may show.

Sir Edmund's memory, extraordinary as it was, was imperfect like every other faculty of man. Whether old age had weakened it, or had allowed his equally extraordinary imagination occasionally to get the better of it, is impossible to decide. It is certain in any case that in some instances which could be checked, his memory was at fault.

As an example may be quoted in "Décadence Mandchoue" (The Mantle of Cagliostro) the reference to the event – supposed to be historic – when Cagliostro in a dark room showed Marie Antoinette in a crystal the guillotine and her own body with the head severed. This scene is not historic but evidently confused with one in Dumas' novel *Joseph Balsamo*. There Cagliostro shows to Marie Antoinette in a grotto at the country house of the Baron de Taverney in a globe shaped carafe filled with water her own body under the guillotine and her head falling into the basket. Just as Sir Edmund mentions in his story, Dumas makes the Dauphine cry out before she faints.

There is the possibility, not to say likelihood that Sir Edmund's memory led him still to a confusion of other scenes which he knew from books with those he had himself witnessed. This particular kind of confusion has to be considered especially, as Sir Edmund was a great reader. An example is in all probability also the description of his conversations with members of the former Russian Imperial Family. There is no reason to doubt that he had been presented to the Czar, the Empress Dowager and the Grand Duchess Sergius. It is however not very likely that these high-placed persons opened their heart about unhappy events in their family and sinister forebodings to a young foreign visitor whom they met for the first time, even if this foreigner had been introduced by the British Ambassador. It is more likely that in this case Sir Edmund, either based on his knowledge of members of the Imperial Family made them say words which they might have said to others more intimate with them, or that, deceived by his memory, he reported as having witnessed conversations of which he had read long ago perhaps in some memoirs.

It is more or less obvious that events as described by Sir Edmund could not have occurred in exactly the some way as related by the author, even if given with all details. In "Décadence Mandchoue" (the Mantle of Cagliostro), the Empress Dowager in a very lengthy "séance" sees in the crystal all important events of her past life. It is extremely unlikely that the old despot would have tolerated – not to say enjoyed – the recollection of past events well known to her and to a high degree unpleasant, when she was eager to see the future. It is still less probable that she spoke in a loud voice and somewhat explained her former actions before the rather mixed assembly.

In "Decadence Mandchoue" (The Lovers Doom), Sir Edmund in the first description of the remnants of the unfortunate couple killed by lightning and subsequently burned in the conflageration spoke of a small heap of white ashes. After the editor had pointed out that remnants of persons burned in the fire of a building as a rule have a very different aspect, he readily changed his former description and presented it more in line with the usual picture seen on such occasions.

In the absence of proof to the contrary a reader of "The Dead Past" and "Décadence Mandchoue" may hold the opinion that both works are entirely products of an extraordinary, rather morbid, imagination. Assuming for a moment that future research would demonstrate the correctness of this opinion, "The Dead Past" would lose most of its value but "Décadence Mandchoue", even as a work of imagination, would keep the merit of giving extraordinarily well the general atmosphere of Tz'u Hsi's court especially as far as the erotic side is concerned. In a certain sense, the author's achievement would be still more extraordinary if all the colourful vivid and in their way fascinating stories had been created by the author's imagination, especially if one remembers his age and the absence of any literary or other help.

The Empress Dowager shows a considerable resemblance to Catherine II of Russia, the "Semiramis of the North" with the difference that in Peking death and not banishment to Siberia waited for the unfortunate "favori" who had done his duty. Also apart from her enormously developed sexuality Tz'u Hsi is most remarkable especially on account of her courage and rapid decisions in cases of personal danger. Her well known ambition and enjoyment of power becomes frequently evident just as a certain kindness when her personal interests were not involved, otherwise the life of her fellow human beings meant nothing whatever to her and she pronounced horrible death sentences between topics of ordinary harmless conversation. It is easy to understand that most of her subjects who had to deal with her lived in constant fear, as even a small accident might mean the loss of life. As usual at the former courts of oriental despots she had a few devoted friends also among the servants and with all his shortcomings Li Lien-ying shows the redeeming virtue of perfect loyalty and sincere attachment to his mistress.

In the editor's opinion, "The Dead Past" and "Décadence Mandchoue" are not purely imaginary but are fundamentally based on facts. How far these facts have been distorted by a confused memory and to what extent purely imaginary happenings have been added can only be judged by a future critical examination which will have to make use of all available documents. Concerning "The Dead Past", it should be possible to verify whether Verlaine was actually for a brief period teacher in St. George's School in Ascot. His life has been thoroughly checked, but even so, there remains evidently still some "lacunae", unrecorded periods, especially concerning his visits of England.

It seems incredible but is not impossible that Sir Edmund who was charmed and fascinated by Verlaine's personality and work and who spoke frequently of him, had reached a stage when misled by his imagination he believed he had had at school Verlaine as a teacher of French. It would have been pointless, had he deliberately invented this story and had intentionally told a lie. Should future research show that Verlaine had never been a teacher in Ascot, we have the curious fact, well known however to alienists, that a person not only sincerely believes in some event which never took place but, is even able to give about it a wealth of intimate details.

The editor is obliged to M. R. de Margerie, Counsellor of the French Embassy in Peking for informing him of a somewhat similar case concerning Chateaubriand who in general may be regarded as an author who honestly tried to present the truth. Joseph Bédier in his *Etudes Critiques* could nevertheless show that Chateaubriand in his *Memoires d'outre-tombe* relates in all sincerity as witnessed, events at which he could not have been present. Sir Edmund therefore with regard to this, point finds himself in good company.

The reason why the editor with regard to Verlaine's teaching in St. George's School in Ascot feels slightly suspicious, is that Sir Edmund when he first told of his personal relations with Verlaine, also mentioned that he had met Rimbaud at Mallarmé's residence in the Rue de Rome on the occasion of his visit to Paris in company of his teacher. Sir Edmund, one has to keep in mind, was at that time a schoolboy who might have noticed some special external pecularities (sic) of Rimbaud but who could obviously not grasp his genius and had fundamentally hardly any reason to remember details of an unknown stranger whom he had accidentally once met. He gives nevertheless a rather detailed description of his face remembering even the colour of the eyes and mentioning a slight limp.

The editor by a number of questions was able more or less to ascertain that this meeting could not have taken place. Sir Edmund apparently realizing this left in the manuscript the description of the nearly impossible meeting but some days later added a few lines about a cobbler "Rimbot" a friend of Verlaine whom he had also met. In his conversation, he admitted that he had possibly confused this cobbler with the famous Rimbaud, in some other recollections which he had told the editor without however including them in his essay on Verlaine.

It will be easily understood that on such an occasion, the editor with all respect due to Sir Edmund somewhat wondered to what degree his stories could be regarded as representing facts considering the extreme facility by which the author introduced on the spur of the moment conveniently new persons and altered the situation after his former statements had become untenable.

With regard to "Décadence Mandchoue", it will be possible, provided permission is given to use certain documents in the Archives of the British Foreign Office, to check Sir Edmund's report on the death of Kuang Hsü and the Empress Dowager. The author's intimate relations with Tz'u Hsi can in all probability likewise be examined. Sir Edmund mentions a letter by Sir Edward Grey referring to his relations with one, not to be named. A copy of this letter and other documents concerning this point may be found and may allow a final judgment as to the correctness of Sir Edmund's statements.

Apart from their possible historic value, "The Dead Past" and "Décadence Mandchoue" are valuable also as material for research in sexual perversions. In this connection it may be pointed out that Sir Edmund was not only essentially homosexual but that he was apparently also very fond of sensations provoked by flagellation active and passive to judge from "Décadence Mandchoue". He on several occasions referred in this respect to the "Mignons" of Henry III of France for whom he had a special liking.

The two works furthermore represent a wealth of material for a psychological study of the author's highly complex personality. It is obvious that an ordinary publication of both "The Dead Past" and "Décadence Mandchoue" is impossible. Should in some future an opportunity offer, the editor has the intention to have both works privately printed in a very small edition and to have them distributed to some leading libraries of several countries for the eventual benefit of research.

For the time being, the editor has prepared four typewritten copies of each manuscript to be given after his death to the Library of the British Museum in London, the Bodleian Library in Oxford, the Bibliothèque Nationale in Paris and the Harvard College Library, Cambridge, Massachusetts, U. S. A., each library to receive one copy of both works. The original manuscripts and the first typewritten copy of each work with corrections by the author's hand are to be given to the Bodleian Library in Oxford. By this arrangement, the editor hopes to serve those scholars for whom the two works may be of value and to prevent their use by unauthorized persons.

R. HOEPPLI

Peking, February 1946.

SPECIMENS OF THE
ORIGINAL MANUSCRIPTS

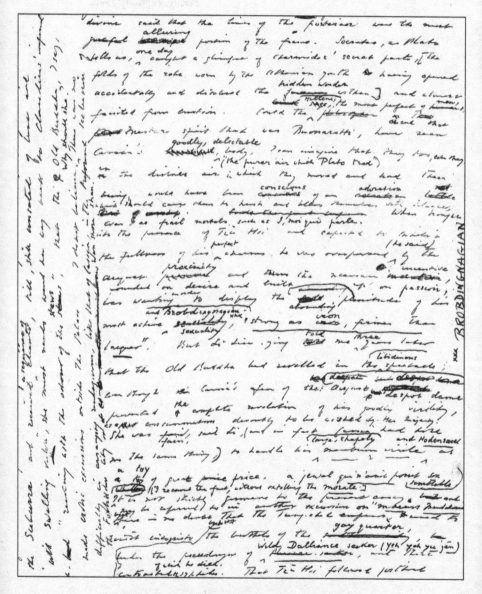

Original manuscript handwritten by Edmund Backhouse

2 8
tadly." (So said Napoleon: "Une ~~soulève~~ rien organisée n'empâte jamais rien.").

"I forgot to tell you," went on Li, "that my brother wished to be remembered. He says that you interceded for him when a British officer had him flogged, in order to make him disclose the whereabouts of his supposed treasure."

"Yes, Your Honour, it was much against my wish: I was acting as interpreter under orders from the British Commander in Chief who was, in fact, anxious to know whether you were in Peking and used this pretext to perform a domiciliary search. The Captain, a man named Begger, was supercilious and arrogant; he ~~was a typical product of the British Army,~~ one of those Britons swift of foot like Achilles, as their ~~recent displays in battle had shown to an~~ and always knew better than the man on the spot. I might as well have argued with a wolf: the man was incapable of pity,

Second draft typewritten and edited by Reinhard Hoeppli with notes by the author

is that of my parents' home in Hsi La 錫拉 Lane (near the Tung An Men 東安門); the picture in the crystal is exact and recalls to me the well-remembered day when I, a girl of sixteen, received the imperial mandate of His Majesty Hsien Feng 咸豐 to enter the palace as a concubine of the lowest rank, Kung Feng Wen Tsung Hsien Huang Ti Ts'e Ming Pei Wei Kung Wei 恭奉文宗顯皇帝冊命備位宮闈."

The vision is blotted out, but Tz'u Hsi trembles with wonder and expectation. More than before she engages in prayer, and I am fain to confess that, carried away by the wonders of her description, I too proffer a petition to High Heaven for, even from the selfish aspect, on the Old Buddha's happiness mine greatly depended, but my devotion was really and truly selfless. Li and Ts'ui exchanged to one another the words: "Pien Hsi Fa'rh 變戲法兒, it is conjuring". But I doubt if the saint heard the ill-timed interruption. He is wrestling in prayer and a stranger to the environment, seeming to

Final typewritten manuscript

The author in the early nineteen-forties

The author on his deathbed